Complete Las Vegas Shooting Search Warrants

Unsealed Stephen Paddock Court Documents

Documents show that FBI agents knew the gunman behind the deadliest mass shooting in modern U.S. history left behind stockpiles of guns, ammunition and explosives when they sought warrants to search his properties and online accounts.

Details about Stephen Paddock's motive in the Las Vegas shooting remained a mystery.

AO 93 (Rev. 11/13) Search and Seizure Warrant

UNITED STATES DISTRICT COURT
for the
District of Nevada

In the Matter of the Search of)
(Briefly describe the property to be searched)
or identify the person by name and address))
) Case No. 2:17-mj- 972-NJK
AMAZON ACCOUNT LINKED TO)
CENTRA! PARK1@LIVE.COM THAT IS STORED AT A)
PREMISES CONTROLLED BY AMAZON, INC.)

SEARCH AND SEIZURE WARRANT

To: Any authorized law enforcement officer

An application by a federal law enforcement officer or an attorney for the government requests the search of the following person or property located in the _____ District of _____ Nevada
(identify the person or describe the property to be searched and give its location):

SEE ATTACHMENT A

I find that the affidavit(s), or any recorded testimony, establish probable cause to search and seize the person or property described above, and that such search will reveal *(identify the person or describe the property to be seized)*:

SEE ATTACHMENTS B and C

YOU ARE COMMANDED to execute this warrant on or before October 20, 2017 *(not to exceed 14 days)*
☒ in the daytime 6:00 a.m. to 10:00 p.m.   ☐ at any time in the day or night because good cause has been established.

Unless delayed notice is authorized below, you must give a copy of the warrant and a receipt for the property taken to the person from whom, or from whose premises, the property was taken, or leave the copy and receipt at the place where the property was taken.

The officer executing this warrant, or an officer present during the execution of the warrant, must prepare an inventory as required by law and promptly return this warrant and inventory to ___Nancy J. Koppe___
(United States Magistrate Judge)

☐ Pursuant to 18 U.S.C. § 3103a(b), I find that immediate notification may have an adverse result listed in 18 U.S.C. § 2705 (except for delay of trial), and authorize the officer executing this warrant to delay notice to the person who, or whose property, will be searched or seized *(check the appropriate box)*
☐ for _____ days *(not to exceed 30)*   ☐ until, the facts justifying, the later specific date of _____.

Date and time issued: 10/6/2017 9:00 pm

_____
Judge's signature

City and state: Las Vegas, Nevada   Nancy J. Koppe US Magistrate Judge
                                              Printed name and title

ATTACHMENT "A"

ONLINE ACCOUNT TO BE SEARCHED

1. This warrant applies to information related to the Amazon.com account associated with centralpark1@live.com (the "Target Amazon Account") from its inception to present, which is stored at premises owned, maintained, controlled, or operated by Amazon.com, Inc., headquartered at 300 Deschutes Way SW, Suite 304, Tumwater, WA 98501.

ATTACHMENT "B"
Particular Things to be Seized

I. **Information to be disclosed by the Service Provider**

To the extent that the information described in Attachment A is within the possession, custody, or control of Amazon.com, including any Emails, records, files, logs, or information that have been deleted but are still available to Service Provider, or have been preserved pursuant to a request made under 18 U.S.C. § 2703(f), Service Provider is required to disclose the following information to the government for each account or identifier listed in Attachment A from account inception to present:

    a. All names, addresses, email addresses, shipping addresses, and billing information associated with the Target Amazon Account;
    b. Date of account creation;
    c. All purchase history;
    d. Service usage information;
    e. All Internet Protocol Address logs and information;
    f. All messages and/or communications exchanged with Amazon.com representative;
    g. Any and all information, files, and data in possession of Amazon.com and/or any other entities controlled or operation by Amazon.com, Inc. related to the Target Amazon Account.

II. **Information to be seized by the United States**

After reviewing all information described in Section I, the United States will seize evidence of violations of Title 18, United States Code Sections 32(a) (Destruction/Damage of Aircraft or Aircraft Facilities); 37(a)(2) (Violence at International Airport); and 922(a)(3); 5 (Unlawful Interstate Transport/Delivery of Firearms by Non Federal Firearms Licensee) (the "Subject Offenses") that occur in the form of the following, from account inception to present:

    a. Communications, transactions and records that may establish ownership and control (or the degree thereof) of the Target Account, including address books, contact or buddy lists, bills, invoices, receipts, registration records, bills, correspondence, notes, records, memoranda, telephone/address books, photographs, video recordings, audio recordings, lists of names, records of

payment for access to newsgroups or other online subscription services, and attachments to said communications, transactions and records.

b. Communications, transactions and records to/from persons who may be co-conspirators of the Subject Offenses, or which may identify co-conspirators.

c. Communications, transactions and records which may show motivation to commit the Subject Offenses.

d. Communications, transactions and records that relate to the Subject Offenses.

e. Information related to wire transfers and/or the movement, possession, or storage of currency and valuable items.

ATTACHMENT "C"

PROTOCOL FOR SEARCHING THE ELECTRONIC DATA SEIZED PURSUANT TO THIS SEARCH WARRANT

1. In executing this warrant, the government must make reasonable efforts to use methods and procedures that will locate and expose in the electronic data produced in response to this search warrant ("the Search Warrant Data") those categories of data, files, documents, or other electronically stored information that are identified with particularity in the warrant, while minimizing exposure or examination of irrelevant, privileged, or confidential files to the extent reasonably practicable.

2. When the Search Warrant Data is received, the government will make a duplicate copy of the Search Warrant Data ("the Search Warrant Data Copy"). The original version of the Search Warrant Data will be sealed and preserved for purposes of: later judicial review or order to return or dispose of the Search Warrant Data; production to the defense in any criminal case if authorized by statute, rule, or the Constitution; for purposes of showing the chain of custody of the Search Warrant Data and the Search Warrant Data Copy; or for any other lawful purpose. The original of the Search Warrant Data will not be searched or examined except to ensure that it has been fully and completely replicated in the Search Warrant Data Copy.

3. The investigating agents will then search the entirety of the Search Warrant Data Copy using any and all methods and procedures deemed appropriate by the United States designed to identify the information listed as Information to be Seized in Attachment B, Section II. The United States may copy, extract or otherwise segregate information or data listed as Information to be Seized in Attachment B, Section II. Information or data so copied, extracted or otherwise segregated will no longer be subject to any handling restrictions that might be set out in this protocol beyond those required by binding law. To the extent evidence of crimes not within the scope of this warrant appear in plain view during this review, a supplemental or "piggyback" warrant will be applied for in order to further search that document, data, or other item.

4. Once the Search Warrant Data Copy has been thoroughly and completely examined for any document, data, or other items identified in Attachment B, Section II as Information to be Seized, the Search Warrant Data Copy will be sealed and not subject to any further search or examination unless authorized by another search warrant or other appropriate court order. The Search Warrant Data Copy will be held and preserved for the same purposes identified above in Paragraph 2.

5. The search procedures utilized for this review are at the sole discretion of the investigating and prosecuting authorities, and may include the following techniques (the following is a non-exclusive list, as other search procedures may be used):

a. examination of all of the data contained in the Search Warrant Data to view the data and determine whether that data falls within the items to be seized as set forth herein;

b. searching for and attempting to recover from the Search Warrant Data any deleted, hidden, or encrypted data to determine whether that data falls within the list of items to be seized as set forth herein (any data that is encrypted and unreadable will not be returned unless law enforcement personnel have determined that the data is not (1) an instrumentality of the offenses, (2) a fruit of the criminal activity, (3) contraband, (4) otherwise unlawfully possessed, or (5) evidence of the offenses specified above);

c. surveying various file directories and the individual files they contain;

d. opening files in order to determine their contents;

e. using hash values to narrow the scope of what may be found. Hash values are under- inclusive, but are still a helpful tool;

f. scanning storage areas;

g. performing keyword searches through all electronic storage areas to determine whether occurrences of language contained in such storage areas exist that are likely to appear in the evidence described in Attachment A; and/or

h. performing any other data analysis technique that may be necessary to locate and retrieve the evidence described in Attachment B, Section II.

Return and Review Procedures

6. Rule 41 of the Federal Rules of Criminal Procedure provides, in relevant part:

(e) Issuing the Warrant.

(2) Contents of the Warrant.

(A) Warrant to Search for and Seize a Person or Property. Except for a tracking-device warrant, the warrant must identify the person or property to be searched, identify any person or property to be seized, and designate the magistrate judge to whom it must be returned. The warrant must command the officer to:

(i) execute the warrant within a specified time no longer than 14 days;

(B) Warrant Seeking Electronically Stored Information. A warrant under Rule 41(e)(2)(A) may authorize the seizure of electronic storage media or the seizure or copying of electronically stored information. Unless otherwise specified, the warrant authorizes a later review of the media or information consistent with the warrant. The time for executing the warrant in Rule 41(e)(2)(A) and (f)(1)(A) refers to the seizure or on-site copying of the media or information, and not to any later off-site copying or review.

(f) Executing and Returning the Warrant.

(1) Warrant to Search for and Seize a Person or Property.

(B) Inventory. An officer present during the execution of the warrant must prepare and verify an inventory of any property seized. . . . In a case involving the seizure of electronic storage media or the seizure or copying of electronically stored information, the inventory may be limited to describing the physical storage media that were seized or copied. The officer may retain a copy of the electronically stored information that was seized or copied.

7. Pursuant to this Rule, the government understands and will act in accordance with the following:

a. Pursuant to Rule 41(e)(2)(A)(iii), within fourteen (14) days of the execution of the warrant, an agent is required to file an inventory return with the Court, that is, to file an itemized list of the property seized. Execution of the warrant begins when the United States serves the warrant on the named custodian; execution is complete when the custodian provides all Search Warrant Data to the United States. Within fourteen (14) days of completion of the execution of the warrant, the inventory will be filed.

b. Pursuant to Rule 41(e)(2)(B), Rule 41(e)(2)(A) governs the time within which the electronically stored information must be seized after the issuance of the warrant and copied after the execution of the warrant, not the "later review of the media or information" seized, or the later off-site digital copying of that media.

c. Under Rule 41(f)(1)(B), the inventory return that is to be filed with the court may be limited to a description of the "physical storage media" into which the Search Warrant Data that was seized was placed, not an itemization of the information or data stored on the "physical storage media" into which the Search Warrant Data was placed;

d. Under Rule 41(f)(1)(B), the government may retain a copy of that information for purposes of the investigation. The government proposes that the original storage media on which the Search Warrant Data was placed plus a full image copy of the seized Search Warrant Data be retained by the government.

e. If the person from whom any Search Warrant Data was seized requests the return of any information in the Search Warrant Data that is not set forth in Attachment B, Section II, that information will be copied onto appropriate media and returned to the person from whom the information was seized.

SEALED

Office of the United States Attorney
District of Nevada
501 Las Vegas Boulevard, Suite 1100
Las Vegas, Nevada 89101
(702) 388-6336

STEVEN W. MYHRE
Acting United States Attorney
District of Nevada
CRISTINA D. SILVA
PATRICK BURNS
Assistant United States Attorneys
501 Las Vegas Blvd. South, Ste. 1100
Las Vegas, Nevada 89101
Telephone: (702) 388-6336
Fax (702) 388-6698
john.p.burns@usdoj.gov

Attorney for the United States of America

UNITED STATES DISTRICT COURT
DISTRICT OF NEVADA
-oOo-

IN THE MATTER OF THE SEARCH OF INFORMATION RELATED TO THE AMAZON ACCOUNT LINKED TO CENTRALPARK1@LIVE.COM THAT IS STORED AT A PREMISES CONTROLLED BY AMAZON, INC.	Magistrate No. 17-mj-972-NJK **AFFIDAVIT IN SUPPORT OF AN APPLICATION FOR A SEARCH WARRANT** (Under Seal)

STATE OF NEVADA)
) ss:
COUNTY OF CLARK)

AFFIDAVIT IN SUPPORT OF AN
APPLICATION FOR A SEARCH WARRANT

I, Ryan S. Burke, Special Agent, Federal Bureau of Investigation (FBI), having been duly sworn, hereby depose and say:

INTRODUCTION AND AGENT BACKGROUND

1. Your Affiant makes this affidavit in support of an application for a search warrant for information related to the Amazon account associated with email account centralpark1@live.com ("Target Amazon Account"). The Target Amazon Account is

associated with STEPHEN PADDOCK and the information is stored at a premises owned, maintained, controlled, or operated by Amazon.com, Inc. ("Amazon"), an American electronic commerce and cloud computing company based in Tumwater, Washington. More generally, Amazon is a website that allows account holders to browse for and purchase a variety of goods. Separately, Amazon offers and provides internet-based cloud services to various individuals/entities. The information to be searched is described in the following paragraphs and in Attachment "A" (attached hereto and incorporated herein by reference). This affidavit is made in support of an application for a search warrant under 18 U.S.C. §§ 2703(a), 2703(b)(1)(A), and 2703(c)(1)(A) to require Amazon to disclose to the government records and other information in its possession, pertaining to the subscriber or customer associated with the Target Amazon Account.

2. I am an "investigative or law enforcement officer of the United States" within the meaning of Title 18, United States Code, Section 2510(7), that is, an officer of the United States who is empowered by law to conduct investigations of, and to make arrests for, offenses enumerated in Title 18, United States Code, Section 2516.

3. I have been employed as a Special Agent of the FBI for approximately five years, which began at the FBI Academy in October 2012. Upon completion of the academy, I was transferred to the Las Vegas Division's white collar crime squad and then the human trafficking squad. Since October 2015, I have been assigned to the Las Vegas Division's violent crime/gang squad. Additionally, I have been a certified member of the FBI's Cellular Analysis Survey Team since August 2015 due to my expertise in the field of historical cell site analysis.

4. During my tenure with the FBI, I have conducted surveillance, analyzed telephone records, interviewed witnesses, supervised activities of sources, executed search warrants, executed arrest warrants, and participated in court-authorized interceptions of wire and electronic communications. These investigative activities have been conducted in conjunction with a variety of investigations, to include those involving robbery, drug trafficking, kidnapping, murder, criminal enterprises, and more. In addition to my practical experiences, I received five months of extensive law enforcement training at the FBI Academy.

5. The facts in this affidavit are derived from your Affiant's personal observations, his training and experience, and information obtained from other agents, detectives, and witnesses. This affidavit is intended to show merely that there is sufficient probable cause for the requested warrant and does not set forth all of the Affiant's knowledge about this matter.

6. Based on your Affiant's training and experience and the facts as set forth in this affidavit, there is probable cause to believe that violations of:

    a. Destruction/Damage of Aircraft or Aircraft Facilities - 18 U.S.C.A. § 32(a);

    b. Violence at International Airport - 18 U.S.C. § 37(a)(2); and

    c. Unlawful Interstate Transport/Delivery of Firearms by Non Federal Firearms Licensee – 18 USC 922(a)(3) and (5).

(hereafter, "Subject Offenses") have been committed by STEPHEN PADDOCK and others yet unknown. There is also probable cause to search the information described in Attachment "A" for evidence of these crimes and information which might reveal the

identities of others involved in these crimes, as described in Attachment "B" (attached hereto and incorporated herein by reference).

PROBABLE CAUSE

7. On the evening of Sunday, October 1, 2017, Route 91 Harvest, a music festival, was in progress at 3901 South Las Vegas Boulevard, Las Vegas, Nevada. At approximately 10:08 p.m., the Las Vegas Metropolitan Police Department (LVMPD) received calls reporting shots had been fired at the concert and multiple victims were struck. LVMPD determined the shots were coming from Rooms 134 and 135 on the 32nd floor of the Mandalay Bay Resort and Casino, located due west of the festival rounds at 3950 South Las Vegas Boulevard, Las Vegas, Nevada. These rooms are an elevated position which overlooks the concert venue. Witness statements and video footage captured during the attack indicates that the weapons being used were firing in a fully-automatic fashion.

8. LVMPD officers ultimately made entry into the room and located an individual later identified as STEPHEN PADDOCK. Paddock was deceased from an apparent self-inflicted gunshot wound.

9. Paddock's Nevada driver's license was located in the Mandalay Bay hotel room with Paddock, and both hotel rooms were registered in his name. A player's club card in name of Marilou Danley was located in Paddock's room, and the card returned to the address located on Babbling Brook Street in Mesquite, Nevada. FBI Agents located Danley, who was traveling outside the United States at the time of the shooting. It was ultimately determined that Danley resided with Paddock at the Babbling Brook address.

10. On October 2, 2017, search warrants were executed on Paddock's Mandalay Bay hotel rooms, Paddock's vehicle at Mandalay Bay, and two Nevada residences owned by Paddock: 1372 Babbling Brook Court in Mesquite, and 1735 Del Webb Parkway in Reno, Nevada. Officers and Agents found over 20 firearms, hundreds of rounds of ammunition, and hundreds of spent shell casings in the Mandalay Bay hotel rooms, in close proximity to Paddock's body. Over a thousand rounds of rifle ammunition and 100 pounds of explosive material were found in Paddock's vehicle. Additional explosive material, approximately 18 firearms, and over 1,000 rounds of ammunition were located at the Mesquite residence. A large quantity of ammunition and multiple firearms were recovered from the Reno residence.

11. As of this date, 58 people have been identified to have been killed in Paddock's attack and another 557 were reportedly injured. Additionally, investigators discovered that STEPHEN PADDOCK also utilized a firearm to shoot large fuel tanks on Las Vegas McCarran International Airport property. Multiple bullet holes were found on the tank, which investigators believe was an attempt by STEPHEN PADDOCK to cause the tanks to explode.

12. In an effort to determine whether or not STEPHEN PADDOCK was assisted and/or conspired with unknown individuals, investigators have attempted to identify all of STEPHEN PADDOCK's communication facilities. Based on a review of his financial accounts, email address centralpark1@live.com ("Email Account") was determined to belong to STEPHEN PADDOCK. On October 3, 2017, investigators requested an emergency disclosure of records from Microsoft related to the Email Account so it could be searched for any evidence of additional co-conspirators. Within

the Email Account, investigators identified the Target Amazon Account as one that required further investigation.

13. Numerous emails sent from Amazon to the Email Account were discovered in the Email Account which were addressed by Amazon to "Stephen" and listed STEPHEN PADDOCK's residence in Mesquite, Nevada as the shipping destination. For these reasons in conjunction with the Target Amazon Account being associated with the Email Account, investigators strongly believe the Target Amazon Account was controlled and operated by STEPHEN PADDOCK.

14. On September 7, 2017, the Email Account received an email relating to the Target Amazon Account's purchase of an EOTech 512.A65 Tactical Holographic firearm accessory. Within the email, which was addressed to STEPHEN PADDOCK, Amazon confirmed the firearm accessory would be delivered to STEPHEN PADDOCK's residence. Investigators believe this piece of equipment was utilized in the attack carried out by STEPHEN PADDOCK.

15. Your Affiant believes the requested search warrant will yield significant information from Amazon such as STEPHEN PADDOCK's search history, purchase history, IP addresses, shipping addresses, payment information, and more, which may constitute evidence of his planning of the attack and potentially identify other participants in the attack. Ultimately, your Affiant strongly believes the requested information will lead investigators to determine the full scope of STEPHEN PADDOCK's plan and/or conspiracy.

INFORMATION TO BE SEARCHED AND THINGS TO BE SEIZED

16. Your Affiant anticipates executing this warrant under the Electronic Communications Privacy Act, in particular 18 U.S.C. §§ 2703(a), 2703(b)(1)(A) and 2703(c)(1)(A), by using the warrant to require Amazon to disclose to the government copies of the records and other information (including the content of communications) particularly described in Section I of Attachment "B." Upon receipt of the information described in Section I of Attachment "B," government-authorized persons will review that information to locate the items described in Section II of Attachment "B."

CONCLUSION

17. Based on the forgoing, I request that the Court issue the proposed search warrant. This Court has jurisdiction to issue the requested warrant because it is "a court of competent jurisdiction" as defined by 18 U.S.C. § 2711. 18 U.S.C. §§ 2703(a), (b)(1)(A) & (c)(1)(A). Specifically, the Court is "a district court of the United States . . . that – has jurisdiction over the offense being investigated." 18 U.S.C. § 2711(3)(A)(i). Pursuant to 18 U.S.C. § 2703(g), the presence of a law enforcement officer is not required for the service or execution of this warrant.

REQUEST FOR SEALING

18. I further request that the Court order that all papers in support of this application, including the affidavit and search warrant, be sealed until further order of the Court. These documents discuss an ongoing criminal investigation that is neither public nor known to all of the targets of the investigation. Accordingly, there is good

///

cause to seal these documents because their premature disclosure may seriously jeopardize that investigation.

Respectfully Submitted,

_____
Ryan S. Burke, Special Agent
Federal Bureau of Investigation

SWORN TO AND SUBSCRIBED
before me this 6th day of October 2017.

_____
UNITED STATES MAGISTRATE JUDGE

ATTACHMENT "A"

ONLINE ACCOUNT TO BE SEARCHED

1. This warrant applies to information related to the Amazon.com account associated with centralpark1@live.com (the "Target Amazon Account") from its inception to present, which is stored at premises owned, maintained, controlled, or operated by Amazon.com, Inc., headquartered at 300 Deschutes Way SW, Suite 304, Tumwater, WA 98501.

ATTACHMENT "B"
Particular Things to be Seized

I. **Information to be disclosed by the Service Provider**

To the extent that the information described in Attachment A is within the possession, custody, or control of Amazon.com, including any Emails, records, files, logs, or information that have been deleted but are still available to Service Provider, or have been preserved pursuant to a request made under 18 U.S.C. § 2703(f), Service Provider is required to disclose the following information to the government for each account or identifier listed in Attachment A from account inception to present:

    a. All names, addresses, email addresses, shipping addresses, and billing information associated with the Target Amazon Account;
    b. Date of account creation;
    c. All purchase history;
    d. Service usage information;
    e. All Internet Protocol Address logs and information;
    f. All messages and/or communications exchanged with Amazon.com representative;
    g. Any and all information, files, and data in possession of Amazon.com and/or any other entities controlled or operation by Amazon.com, Inc. related to the Target Amazon Account.

II. **Information to be seized by the United States**

After reviewing all information described in Section I, the United States will seize evidence of violations of Title 18, United States Code Sections 32(a) (Destruction/Damage of Aircraft or Aircraft Facilities); 37(a)(2) (Violence at International Airport); and 922(a)(3); 5 (Unlawful Interstate Transport/Delivery of Firearms by Non Federal Firearms Licensee) (the "Subject Offenses") that occur in the form of the following, from account inception to present:

    a. Communications, transactions and records that may establish ownership and control (or the degree thereof) of the Target Account, including address books, contact or buddy lists, bills, invoices, receipts, registration records, bills, correspondence, notes, records, memoranda, telephone/address books, photographs, video recordings, audio recordings, lists of names, records of

payment for access to newsgroups or other online subscription services, and attachments to said communications, transactions and records.

b. Communications, transactions and records to/from persons who may be co-conspirators of the Subject Offenses, or which may identify co-conspirators.

c. Communications, transactions and records which may show motivation to commit the Subject Offenses.

d. Communications, transactions and records that relate to the Subject Offenses.

e. Information related to wire transfers and/or the movement, possession, or storage of currency and valuable items.

ATTACHMENT "C"

PROTOCOL FOR SEARCHING THE ELECTRONIC DATA SEIZED PURSUANT TO THIS SEARCH WARRANT

1. In executing this warrant, the government must make reasonable efforts to use methods and procedures that will locate and expose in the electronic data produced in response to this search warrant ("the Search Warrant Data") those categories of data, files, documents, or other electronically stored information that are identified with particularity in the warrant, while minimizing exposure or examination of irrelevant, privileged, or confidential files to the extent reasonably practicable.

2. When the Search Warrant Data is received, the government will make a duplicate copy of the Search Warrant Data ("the Search Warrant Data Copy"). The original version of the Search Warrant Data will be sealed and preserved for purposes of: later judicial review or order to return or dispose of the Search Warrant Data; production to the defense in any criminal case if authorized by statute, rule, or the Constitution; for purposes of showing the chain of custody of the Search Warrant Data and the Search Warrant Data Copy; or for any other lawful purpose. The original of the Search Warrant Data will not be searched or examined except to ensure that it has been fully and completely replicated in the Search Warrant Data Copy.

3. The investigating agents will then search the entirety of the Search Warrant Data Copy using any and all methods and procedures deemed appropriate by the United States designed to identify the information listed as Information to be Seized in Attachment B, Section II. The United States may copy, extract or otherwise segregate information or data listed as Information to be Seized in Attachment B, Section II. Information or data so copied, extracted or otherwise segregated will no longer be subject to any handling restrictions that might be set out in this protocol beyond those required by binding law. To the extent evidence of crimes not within the scope of this warrant appear in plain view during this review, a supplemental or "piggyback" warrant will be applied for in order to further search that document, data, or other item.

4. Once the Search Warrant Data Copy has been thoroughly and completely examined for any document, data, or other items identified in Attachment B, Section II as Information to be Seized, the Search Warrant Data Copy will be sealed and not subject to any further search or examination unless authorized by another search warrant or other appropriate court order. The Search Warrant Data Copy will be held and preserved for the same purposes identified above in Paragraph 2.

5. The search procedures utilized for this review are at the sole discretion of the investigating and prosecuting authorities, and may include the following techniques (the following is a non-exclusive list, as other search procedures may be used):

a. examination of all of the data contained in the Search Warrant Data to view the data and determine whether that data falls within the items to be seized as set forth herein;

b. searching for and attempting to recover from the Search Warrant Data any deleted, hidden, or encrypted data to determine whether that data falls within the list of items to be seized as set forth herein (any data that is encrypted and unreadable will not be returned unless law enforcement personnel have determined that the data is not (1) an instrumentality of the offenses, (2) a fruit of the criminal activity, (3) contraband, (4) otherwise unlawfully possessed, or (5) evidence of the offenses specified above);

c. surveying various file directories and the individual files they contain;

d. opening files in order to determine their contents;

e. using hash values to narrow the scope of what may be found. Hash values are under- inclusive, but are still a helpful tool;

f. scanning storage areas;

g. performing keyword searches through all electronic storage areas to determine whether occurrences of language contained in such storage areas exist that are likely to appear in the evidence described in Attachment A; and/or

h. performing any other data analysis technique that may be necessary to locate and retrieve the evidence described in Attachment B, Section II.

Return and Review Procedures

6. Rule 41 of the Federal Rules of Criminal Procedure provides, in relevant part:

(e) Issuing the Warrant.

(2) Contents of the Warrant.

(A) Warrant to Search for and Seize a Person or Property. Except for a tracking-device warrant, the warrant must identify the person or property to be searched, identify any person or property to be seized, and designate the magistrate judge to whom it must be returned. The warrant must command the officer to:

(i) execute the warrant within a specified time no longer than 14 days;

(B) Warrant Seeking Electronically Stored Information. A warrant under Rule 41(e)(2)(A) may authorize the seizure of electronic storage media or the seizure or copying of electronically stored information. Unless otherwise specified, the warrant authorizes a later review of the media or information consistent with the warrant. The time for executing the warrant in Rule 41(e)(2)(A) and (f)(1)(A) refers to the seizure or on-site copying of the media or information, and not to any later off-site copying or review.

(f) Executing and Returning the Warrant.

(1) Warrant to Search for and Seize a Person or Property.

(B) Inventory. An officer present during the execution of the warrant must prepare and verify an inventory of any property seized. . . . In a case involving the seizure of electronic storage media or the seizure or copying of electronically stored information, the inventory may be limited to describing the physical storage media that were seized or copied. The officer may retain a copy of the electronically stored information that was seized or copied.

    7.   Pursuant to this Rule, the government understands and will act in accordance with the following:

    a.   Pursuant to Rule 41(e)(2)(A)(iii), within fourteen (14) days of the execution of the warrant, an agent is required to file an inventory return with the Court, that is, to file an itemized list of the property seized. Execution of the warrant begins when the United States serves the warrant on the named custodian; execution is complete when the custodian provides all Search Warrant Data to the United States. Within fourteen (14) days of completion of the execution of the warrant, the inventory will be filed.

    b.   Pursuant to Rule 41(e)(2)(B), Rule 41(e)(2)(A) governs the time within which the electronically stored information must be seized after the issuance of the warrant and copied after the execution of the warrant, not the "later review of the media or information" seized, or the later off-site digital copying of that media.

    c.   Under Rule 41(f)(1)(B), the inventory return that is to be filed with the court may be limited to a description of the "physical storage media" into which the Search Warrant Data that was seized was placed, not an itemization of the information or data stored on the "physical storage media" into which the Search Warrant Data was placed;

d. Under Rule 41(f)(1)(B), the government may retain a copy of that information for purposes of the investigation. The government proposes that the original storage media on which the Search Warrant Data was placed plus a full image copy of the seized Search Warrant Data be retained by the government.

e. If the person from whom any Search Warrant Data was seized requests the return of any information in the Search Warrant Data that is not set forth in Attachment B, Section II, that information will be copied onto appropriate media and returned to the person from whom the information was seized.

AO 93 (Rev. 11/13) Search and Seizure Warrant

UNITED STATES DISTRICT COURT
for the
District of Nevada

In the Matter of the Search of)
(Briefly describe the property to be searched)
or identify the person by name and address))
) Case No. 2:17-mj- 971-NJK
ACCOUNT(S) ASSOCIATED WITH THE CELLULAR)
DEVICE BEARING IMEI 990006880858377 STORED)
AT A PREMISES CONTROLLED BY GOOGLE)

SEARCH AND SEIZURE WARRANT

To: Any authorized law enforcement officer

An application by a federal law enforcement officer or an attorney for the government requests the search of the following person or property located in the _____ District of ___Nevada___
(identify the person or describe the property to be searched and give its location):

SEE ATTACHMENT A

I find that the affidavit(s), or any recorded testimony, establish probable cause to search and seize the person or property described above, and that such search will reveal *(identify the person or describe the property to be seized):*

SEE ATTACHMENTS B and C

YOU ARE COMMANDED to execute this warrant on or before ___October 20, 2017___ *(not to exceed 14 days)*
☒ in the daytime 6:00 a.m. to 10:00 p.m. ☐ at any time in the day or night because good cause has been established.

Unless delayed notice is authorized below, you must give a copy of the warrant and a receipt for the property taken to the person from whom, or from whose premises, the property was taken, or leave the copy and receipt at the place where the property was taken.

The officer executing this warrant, or an officer present during the execution of the warrant, must prepare an inventory as required by law and promptly return this warrant and inventory to ___Nancy J. Koppe___.
(United States Magistrate Judge)

☐ Pursuant to 18 U.S.C. § 3103a(b), I find that immediate notification may have an adverse result listed in 18 U.S.C. § 2705 (except for delay of trial), and authorize the officer executing this warrant to delay notice to the person who, or whose property, will be searched or seized *(check the appropriate box)*
☐ for ___ days *(not to exceed 30)* ☐ until, the facts justifying, the later specific date of _____.

Date and time issued: 10/6/2017 8:45 pm

Judge's signature

City and state: Las Vegas, Nevada ___Nancy J. Koppe, US Magistrate Judge___
Printed name and title

ATTACHMENT "A"

ONLINE ACCOUNT TO BE SEARCHED

1. This warrant applies to information related to the Google account associated with the cellular device bearing IMEI 990006880858377 (the "Target Account") from its inception to present, which is stored at premises owned, maintained, controlled, or operated by Google, Inc., headquartered at 1600 Amphitheatre Way, Mountain View, California, 94043.

ATTACHMENT "B"
Particular Things to be Seized

I. **Information to be disclosed by the Service Provider**

To the extent that the information described in Attachment A is within the possession, custody, or control of Google, including any Emails, records, files, logs, or information that have been deleted but are still available to Service Provider, or have been preserved pursuant to a request made under 18 U.S.C. § 2703(f), Service Provider is required to disclose the following information to the government for each account or identifier listed in Attachment A from account inception to present:

a. The contents of all messages and emails associated with the account, including copies of messages and emails sent to and from the account, draft messages/emails, the source and destination addresses associated with each message/email, the date and time at which each message/email was sent, and the size and length of each message/email;

b. All records or other information regarding the identification of the account, to include full name, physical address, telephone numbers and other identifiers, records of session times and durations, the date on which the account was created, the length of service, the types of service utilized, the IP address used to register the account, log-in IP addresses associated with session times and dates, account status, alternative email addresses provided during registration, methods of connecting, log files, and means and source of payment (including any credit or bank account number);

c. All records or other information stored in the Online Accounts, including address books, contact and buddy lists, calendar data, pictures, applications, documents, and other files;

d. All records pertaining to communications between Service Provider and any person regarding the account, including contacts with support services and records of actions taken.

e. All data and contents related to the following Google Services associated with the Target Account: Android; Gmail; Google Calendar; Google Docs; Google Drive; Google Talk; Multilogin; Web History; YouTube; and all other applications.

f. All information and content associated with any third-party application associated with the Target Account and the dates when the applications were installed;

g. Based on an analysis of cookies assigned to computers and devices that accessed the Target Account, identify all other Google accounts that have been accessed from any computers and devices that have logged into the Target Account.

II. **Information to be seized by the United States**

After reviewing all information described in Section I, the United States will seize evidence of violations of Title 18, United States Code Sections 32(a) (Destruction/Damage of Aircraft or Aircraft Facilities); 37(a)(2) (Violence at International Airport); and 922(a)(3); 5 (Unlawful Interstate Transport/Delivery of Firearms by Non Federal Firearms Licensee) (the "Subject Offenses") that occur in the form of the following, from account inception to present:

a. Communications, transactions and records that may establish ownership and control (or the degree thereof) of the Target Account, including address books, contact or buddy lists, bills, invoices, receipts, registration records, bills, correspondence, notes, records, memoranda, telephone/address books, photographs, video recordings, audio recordings, lists of names, records of payment for access to newsgroups or other online subscription services, and attachments to said communications, transactions and records.

b. Communications, transactions and records to/from persons who may be co-conspirators of the Subject Offenses, or which may identify co-conspirators.

c. Communications, transactions and records which may show motivation to commit the Subject Offenses.

d. Communications, transactions and records that relate to the Subject Offenses.

e. The terms "communications," "transactions", "records," "documents," "programs," or "materials" include all information recorded in any form, visual or aural, and by any means, whether in handmade form (including, but not limited to, writings, drawings, paintings), photographic form (including, but not limited to, pictures or videos), or electrical, electronic or magnetic form, as well as digital data files. These terms also include any applications (i.e. software programs). These terms expressly include, among other things, Emails, instant messages, chat logs, correspondence attached as to Emails (or drafts), calendar entries, buddy lists.

ATTACHMENT "C"

PROTOCOL FOR SEARCHING THE ELECTRONIC DATA SEIZED PURSUANT TO THIS SEARCH WARRANT

1. In executing this warrant, the government must make reasonable efforts to use methods and procedures that will locate and expose in the electronic data produced in response to this search warrant ("the Search Warrant Data") those categories of data, files, documents, or other electronically stored information that are identified with particularity in the warrant, while minimizing exposure or examination of irrelevant, privileged, or confidential files to the extent reasonably practicable.

2. When the Search Warrant Data is received, the government will make a duplicate copy of the Search Warrant Data ("the Search Warrant Data Copy"). The original version of the Search Warrant Data will be sealed and preserved for purposes of: later judicial review or order to return or dispose of the Search Warrant Data; production to the defense in any criminal case if authorized by statute, rule, or the Constitution; for purposes of showing the chain of custody of the Search Warrant Data and the Search Warrant Data Copy; or for any other lawful purpose. The original of the Search Warrant Data will not be searched or examined except to ensure that it has been fully and completely replicated in the Search Warrant Data Copy.

3. The investigating agents will then search the entirety of the Search Warrant Data Copy using any and all methods and procedures deemed appropriate by the United States designed to identify the information listed as Information to be Seized in Attachment B, Section II. The United States may copy, extract or otherwise segregate information or data listed as Information to be Seized in Attachment B, Section II. Information or data so copied, extracted or otherwise segregated will no longer be subject to any handling restrictions that might be set out in this protocol beyond those required by binding law. To the extent evidence of crimes not within the scope of this warrant appear in plain view during this review, a supplemental or "piggyback" warrant will be applied for in order to further search that document, data, or other item.

4. Once the Search Warrant Data Copy has been thoroughly and completely examined for any document, data, or other items identified in Attachment B, Section II as Information to be Seized, the Search Warrant Data Copy will be sealed and not subject to any further search or examination unless authorized by another search warrant or other appropriate court order. The Search Warrant Data Copy will be held and preserved for the same purposes identified above in Paragraph 2.

5. The search procedures utilized for this review are at the sole discretion of the investigating and prosecuting authorities, and may include the following techniques (the following is a non-exclusive list, as other search procedures may be used):

a. examination of all of the data contained in the Search Warrant Data to view the data and determine whether that data falls within the items to be seized as set forth herein;

b. searching for and attempting to recover from the Search Warrant Data any deleted, hidden, or encrypted data to determine whether that data falls within the list of items to be seized as set forth herein (any data that is encrypted and unreadable will not be returned unless law enforcement personnel have determined that the data is not (1) an instrumentality of the offenses, (2) a fruit of the criminal activity, (3) contraband, (4) otherwise unlawfully possessed, or (5) evidence of the offenses specified above);

c. surveying various file directories and the individual files they contain;

d. opening files in order to determine their contents;

e. using hash values to narrow the scope of what may be found. Hash values are under- inclusive, but are still a helpful tool;

f. scanning storage areas;

g. performing keyword searches through all electronic storage areas to determine whether occurrences of language contained in such storage areas exist that are likely to appear in the evidence described in Attachment A; and/or

h. performing any other data analysis technique that may be necessary to locate and retrieve the evidence described in Attachment B, Section II.

Return and Review Procedures

6. Rule 41 of the Federal Rules of Criminal Procedure provides, in relevant part:

(e) Issuing the Warrant.

(2) Contents of the Warrant.

(A) Warrant to Search for and Seize a Person or Property. Except for a tracking-device warrant, the warrant must identify the person or property to be searched, identify any person or property to be seized, and designate the magistrate judge to whom it must be returned. The warrant must command the officer to:

(i) execute the warrant within a specified time no longer than 14 days;

(B) Warrant Seeking Electronically Stored Information. A warrant under Rule 41(e)(2)(A) may authorize the seizure of electronic storage media or the seizure or copying of electronically stored information. Unless otherwise specified, the warrant authorizes a later review of the media or information consistent with the warrant. The time for executing the warrant in Rule 41(e)(2)(A) and (f)(1)(A) refers to the seizure or on-site copying of the media or information, and not to any later off-site copying or review.

(f) Executing and Returning the Warrant.

(1) Warrant to Search for and Seize a Person or Property.

(B) Inventory. An officer present during the execution of the warrant must prepare and verify an inventory of any property seized. . . . In a case involving the seizure of electronic storage media or the seizure or copying of electronically stored information, the inventory may be limited to describing the physical storage media that were seized or copied. The officer may retain a copy of the electronically stored information that was seized or copied.

7. Pursuant to this Rule, the government understands and will act in accordance with the following:

a. Pursuant to Rule 41(e)(2)(A)(iii), within fourteen (14) days of the execution of the warrant, an agent is required to file an inventory return with the Court, that is, to file an itemized list of the property seized. Execution of the warrant begins when the United States serves the warrant on the named custodian; execution is complete when the custodian provides all Search Warrant Data to the United States. Within fourteen (14) days of completion of the execution of the warrant, the inventory will be filed.

b. Pursuant to Rule 41(e)(2)(B), Rule 41(e)(2)(A) governs the time within which the electronically stored information must be seized after the issuance of the warrant and copied after the execution of the warrant, not the "later review of the media or information" seized, or the later off-site digital copying of that media.

c. Under Rule 41(f)(1)(B), the inventory return that is to be filed with the court may be limited to a description of the "physical storage media" into which the Search Warrant Data that was seized was placed, not an itemization of the information or data stored on the "physical storage media" into which the Search Warrant Data was placed;

d. Under Rule 41(f)(1)(B), the government may retain a copy of that information for purposes of the investigation. The government proposes that the original storage media on which the Search Warrant Data was placed plus a full image copy of the seized Search Warrant Data be retained by the government.

e. If the person from whom any Search Warrant Data was seized requests the return of any information in the Search Warrant Data that is not set forth in Attachment B, Section II, that information will be copied onto appropriate media and returned to the person from whom the information was seized.

STEVEN W. MYHRE
Acting United States Attorney
District of Nevada
CRISTINA D. SILVA
PATRICK BURNS
Assistant United States Attorneys
501 Las Vegas Blvd. South, Ste. 1100
Las Vegas, Nevada 89101
Telephone: (702) 388-6336
Fax (702) 388-6698
john.p.burns@usdoj.gov

Attorney for the United States of America

UNITED STATES DISTRICT COURT
DISTRICT OF NEVADA
-oOo-

IN THE MATTER OF THE SEARCH OF INFORMATION RELATED TO THE ACCOUNT(S) ASSOCIATED WITH THE CELLULAR DEVICE BEARING IMEI 990006880858377 THAT IS STORED AT A PREMISES CONTROLLED BY GOOGLE.	Magistrate No. 17-mj-971-NJK **AFFIDAVIT IN SUPPORT OF AN APPLICATION FOR A SEARCH WARRANT** (Under Seal)

STATE OF NEVADA   )
) ss:
COUNTY OF CLARK   )

AFFIDAVIT IN SUPPORT OF AN APPLICATION FOR A SEARCH WARRANT

I, Ryan S. Burke, Special Agent, Federal Bureau of Investigation (FBI), having been duly sworn, hereby depose and say:

INTRODUCTION AND AGENT BACKGROUND

1. Your Affiant makes this affidavit in support of an application for a search warrant for information related to the Google account(s) associated with the cellular device bearing IMEI 990006880858377 ["Target Account(s)"], which are associated with

STEPHEN PADDOCK. This information is stored at a premises owned, maintained, controlled, or operated by Google, Inc. ("Google"), an American multinational technology based in Mountain View, California that specializes in Internet-related services and products. Those services include, but are not limited to, online advertising technologies, a search engine, email services, cloud computing, and many other services. The information to be searched is described in the following paragraphs and in Attachment "A" (attached hereto and incorporated herein by reference). This affidavit is made in support of an application for a search warrant under 18 U.S.C. §§ 2703(a), 2703(b)(1)(A), and 2703(c)(1)(A) to require Google to disclose to the government records and other information in its possession, pertaining to the subscriber or customer associated with the Target Account.

2. I am an "investigative or law enforcement officer of the United States" within the meaning of Title 18, United States Code, Section 2510(7), that is, an officer of the United States who is empowered by law to conduct investigations of, and to make arrests for, offenses enumerated in Title 18, United States Code, Section 2516.

3. I have been employed as a Special Agent of the FBI for approximately five years, which began at the FBI Academy in October 2012. Upon completion of the academy, I was transferred to the Las Vegas Division's white collar crime squad and then the human trafficking squad. Since October 2015, I have been assigned to the Las Vegas Division's violent crime/gang squad. Additionally, I have been a certified member of the FBI's Cellular Analysis Survey Team since August 2015 due to my expertise in the field of historical cell site analysis.

4. During my tenure with the FBI, I have conducted surveillance, analyzed telephone records, interviewed witnesses, supervised activities of sources, executed search warrants, executed arrest warrants, and participated in court-authorized interceptions of wire and electronic communications. These investigative activities have been conducted in conjunction with a variety of investigations, to include those involving robbery, drug trafficking, kidnapping, murder, criminal enterprises, and more. In addition to my practical experiences, I received five months of extensive law enforcement training at the FBI Academy.

5. The facts in this affidavit are derived from your Affiant's personal observations, his training and experience, and information obtained from other agents, detectives, and witnesses. This affidavit is intended to show merely that there is sufficient probable cause for the requested warrant and does not set forth all of the Affiant's knowledge about this matter.

6. Based on your Affiant's training and experience and the facts as set forth in this affidavit, there is probable cause to believe that violations of:

   a. Destruction/Damage of Aircraft or Aircraft Facilities - 18 U.S.C.A. § 32(a);

   b. Violence at International Airport - 18 U.S.C. § 37(a)(2); and

   c. Unlawful Interstate Transport/Delivery of Firearms by Non Federal Firearms Licensee – 18 U.S.C. §§ 922(a)(3) and (5);

(hereafter, "Subject Offenses") have been committed by STEPHEN PADDOCK and others yet unknown. There is also probable cause to search the information described in Attachment "A" for evidence of these crimes and information which might reveal the

identities of others involved in these crimes, as described in Attachment "B" (attached hereto and incorporated herein by reference).

PROBABLE CAUSE

7. On the evening of Sunday, October 1, 2017, Route 91 Harvest, a music festival, was in progress at 3901 South Las Vegas Boulevard, Las Vegas, Nevada. At approximately 10:08 p.m., the Las Vegas Metropolitan Police Department (LVMPD) received calls reporting shots had been fired at the concert and multiple victims were struck. LVMPD determined the shots were coming from Rooms 134 and 135 on the 32nd floor of the Mandalay Bay Resort and Casino, located due west of the festival rounds at 3950 South Las Vegas Boulevard, Las Vegas, Nevada. These rooms are an elevated position which overlooks the concert venue. Witness statements and video footage captured during the attack indicates that the weapons being used were firing in a fully-automatic fashion.

8. LVMPD officers ultimately made entry into the room and located an individual later identified as Stephen Paddock. Paddock was deceased from an apparent self-inflicted gunshot wound.

9. Paddock's Nevada driver's license was located in the Mandalay Bay hotel room with Paddock, and both hotel rooms were registered in his name. A player's club card in name of Marilou Danley was located in Paddock's room, and the card returned to the address located on Babbling Brook Street in Mesquite, Nevada. FBI Agents located Danley, who was traveling outside the United States at the time of the shooting. It was ultimately determined that Danley resided with Paddock at the Babbling Brook address.

10. On October 2, 2017, search warrants were executed on Paddock's Mandalay Bay hotel rooms, Paddock's vehicle at Mandalay Bay, and two Nevada residences owed by Paddock: 1372 Babbling Brook Court in Mesquite, and 1735 Del Webb Parkway in Reno, Nevada. Officers and Agents found over 20 firearms, hundreds of rounds of ammunition, and hundreds of spent shell casings in the Mandalay Bay hotel rooms, in close proximity to Paddock's body. Over a thousand rounds of rifle ammunition and 100 pounds of explosive material was found in Paddock's vehicle. Additional explosive material, approximately 18 firearms, and over 1,000 rounds of ammunition was located at the Mesquite residence. A large quantity of ammunition and multiple firearms were recovered from the Reno residence.

11. As of this date, 58 people have been identified to have been killed in Paddock's attack and another 557 were reportedly injured. Additionally, investigators discovered that STEPHEN PADDOCK also utilized a firearm to shoot large fuel tanks on Las Vegas McCarran International Airport property. Multiple bullet holes were found on the tank, which investigators believe was an attempt by STEPHEN PADDOCK to cause the tanks to explode.

12. During the execution of the search warrant at the Mandalay Bay hotel room where the attack occurred, three cellular phones were seized. All of the phones are believed to have belonged to STEPHEN PADDOCK. Two of those phones were unlocked and able to be forensically examined. Neither phone contained significant information that allowed investigators to determine the full scope of STEPHEN PADDOCK's planning and preparation for the attack. The other phone, however, a ZTE Model Z837VL bearing IMEI 990006880858377, was locked and investigators do not believe it

can be forensically examined. Investigators believe the only way to gain access to the content of the locked ZTE phone will be through the authorization to demand information associated with the Target Account from Google, the company which owns the operating system software installed on the phone.

13. Your Affiant knows through training and experience that criminals typically make effort to secure and keep hidden information that may incriminate themselves or others. Due to the fact that two of the cellular phones were unlocked and the cellular phone associated with the Target Account was locked, your Affiant believes if there were any information related to a potential conspiracy it would be found within the Target Account.

14. Your Affiant believes the requested search warrant will yield significant information from Google such as STEPHEN PADDOCK's contact list, email message content, IP address usage, photographs, third-party applications, and more, which may constitute evidence of his planning of the attack and potentially identify other participants in the attack. Ultimately, your Affiant strongly believes the requested information will lead investigators to determine the full scope of STEPHEN PADDOCK's plan.

RELEVANT TECHNICAL TERMS

15. The following non-exhaustive list of definitions applies to this Affidavit and the Attachments to this Affidavit:

    a. The "Internet" is a worldwide network of computer systems operated by governmental entities, corporations, and universities. In order to access the Internet, an individual computer user must subscribe to an access provider, which operates a host computer system with direct access to the Internet. The World Wide Web is a functionality of the Internet which allows users of the Internet to share information.

  b. "Internet Service Providers" are companies that provide access to the Internet. ISPs can also provide other services for their customers including website hosting, email service, remote storage, and co-location of computers and other communications equipment. ISPs offer different ways to access the Internet including telephone-based (dial-up), broadband-based access via a digital subscriber line (DSL) or cable television, dedicated circuits, or satellite-based subscription. ISPs typically charge a fee based upon the type of connection and volume of data (bandwidth). Many ISPs assign each subscriber an account name, such as a user name, an email address, and an email mailbox, and the subscriber typically creates a password for his/her account.

  c. "ISP Records" are records maintained by ISPs pertaining to their subscribers (regardless of whether those subscribers are individuals or entities). These records may include account application information, subscriber and billing information, account access information (often in the form of log files), emails, information concerning content uploaded and/or stored on the ISP's servers, and other information, which may be stored both in computer data format and in written or printed record format. ISPs reserve and/or maintain computer disk storage space on their computer system for their subscribers' use. This service by ISPs allows for both temporary and long-term storage of electronic communications and many other types of electronic data and files.

  d. "Online service providers" (also referred to here as "service providers") are companies that provide online services such as email, chat or instant messaging, word processing applications, spreadsheet applications, presentation applications similar to PowerPoint, online calendar, photo storage and remote storage services. Sometimes they also can provide web hosting, remote storage, and co-location of computers and other communications equipment. Typically, each service provider assigns each subscriber an account name, such as a user name or screen name and the subscriber typically creates a password for his/her account.

  e. "Computer," as used herein, is defined as "an electronic, magnetic, optical, electrochemical, or other high speed data processing device performing logical or storage functions, and includes any data storage facility or communications facility directly related to or operating in conjunction with such device."

  f. A "server" is a centralized computer that provides services for other computers connected to it via a network. The other computers attached to a server are sometimes called "clients." For example, in a large company, it is common for individual employees to have client computers at their desktops. When the employees access their email, or access files stored on the network itself, those files are pulled electronically from the server, where they are stored, and are sent to the client's computer via the network. Notably, servers can be physically stored in any location: it is not uncommon for a network's server to be located hundreds (and even thousands) of miles away from the client computers.

  g. "Internet Protocol address," or "IP address," refers to a unique number used by a computer to access the Internet. IP addresses can be dynamic, meaning that the Internet Service Provider (ISP) assigns a different unique number to a computer every time it accesses the Internet. IP addresses might also be static, that

is, an ISP assigns a user's computer a particular IP address which is used each time the computer accesses the Internet.

  h. The term "domain" refers to a word used as a name for computers, networks, services, etc. A domain name typically represents a website, a server computer that hosts that website, or even some computer (or other digital device) connected to the internet. Essentially, when a website (or a server computer that hosts that website) is connected to the internet, it is assigned an IP address. Because IP addresses are difficult for people to remember, domain names are instead used because they are easier to remember than IP addresses. Domain names are formed by the rules and procedures of the Domain Name System (DNS). A common top level domain under these rules is ".com" for commercial organizations, ".gov" for the United States government, and ".org" for organizations. For example, www.usdoj.gov is the domain name that identifies a server used by the U.S. Department of Justice, and which uses IP address of 149.101.46.71.

  i. "Web hosting services" maintain server computers connected to the Internet. Their customers use those computers to operate websites on the Internet. Customers of web hosting companies place files, software code, databases, and other data on servers. To do this, customers typically connect from their own computers to the server computers across the Internet.

  j. The term "WhoIs" lookup refers to a search of a publicly available online database that lists information provided when a domain is registered or when an IP address is assigned.

  k. The terms "communications," "records," "documents," "programs," or "materials" include all information recorded in any form, visual or aural, and by any

means, whether in handmade form (including, but not limited to, writings, drawings, paintings), photographic form (including, but not limited to, pictures or videos), or electrical, electronic or magnetic form, as well as digital data files. These terms also include any applications (i.e. software programs). These terms expressly include, among other things, emails, instant messages, chat logs, correspondence attached as to emails (or drafts), calendar entries, buddy lists.

l. "Chat" is usually a real time electronic communication between two or more individuals. Unlike email, which is frequently sent, then read and responded to minutes, hours, or even days later, chats frequently involve an immediate conversation between individuals, similar to a face-to-face conversation. Nearly all chat programs are capable of saving the chat transcript, to enable users to preserve a record of the conversation. By default, some chat programs have this capability enabled, while others do not. Many popular web-based email providers, like Google and Google, provide chat functionality as part of the online services they provide to account holders.

m. "Apps or Applications" are third-party programs that may be installed through the Android operating system, which is owned by Google, for use on a cellular device.

FACTS ABOUT GOOGLE

16. In my training, my experience and this investigation, I have learned that Google owns and operates Android OS, which is an operating system found on many cellular devices to include the device associated with the Target Account. Through this operating system, users can install applications with a variety of functionalities, such as

various social media websites, mapping software, banking portals, etc. Records of the applications installed on a specific device are maintained by Google.

17. In my training and experience, evidence of which applications were utilized by a specific device can be useful in identifying additional communication facilities, content of communications, financial account information, information related to whom the user associates with, and more. Oftentimes, an individual utilizing a Google account has the option to store certain information located on the device to a cloud, which Google also retains. All of this information can help investigators locate evidence of various criminal activity associated with the user.

INFORMATION TO BE SEARCHED AND THINGS TO BE SEIZED

18. Your Affiant anticipates executing this warrant under the Electronic Communications Privacy Act, in particular 18 U.S.C. §§ 2703(a), 2703(b)(1)(A) and 2703(c)(1)(A), by using the warrant to require Google to disclose to the government copies of the records and other information (including the content of communications) particularly described in Section I of Attachment "B." Upon receipt of the information described in Section I of Attachment "B," government-authorized persons will review that information to locate the items described in Section II of Attachment "B."

CONCLUSION

19. Based on the forgoing, I request that the Court issue the proposed search warrant. This Court has jurisdiction to issue the requested warrant because it is "a court of competent jurisdiction" as defined by 18 U.S.C. § 2711. 18 U.S.C. §§ 2703(a), (b)(1)(A) & (c)(1)(A). Specifically, the Court is "a district court of the United States . . . that – has jurisdiction over the offense being investigated." 18 U.S.C. § 2711(3)(A)(i). Pursuant to

18 U.S.C. § 2703(g), the presence of a law enforcement officer is not required for the service or execution of this warrant.

REQUEST FOR SEALING

20. I further request that the Court order that all papers in support of this application, including the affidavit and search warrant, be sealed until further order of the Court. These documents discuss an ongoing criminal investigation that is neither public nor known to all of the targets of the investigation. Accordingly, there is good cause to seal these documents because their premature disclosure may seriously jeopardize that investigation.

Respectfully Submitted,

Ryan S. Burke, Special Agent
Federal Bureau of Investigation

SWORN TO AND SUBSCRIBED
before me this __ day of October 2017.

UNITED STATES MAGISTRATE JUDGE

ATTACHMENT "A"

ONLINE ACCOUNT TO BE SEARCHED

1. This warrant applies to information related to the Google account associated with the cellular device bearing IMEI 990006880858377 (the "Target Account") from its inception to present, which is stored at premises owned, maintained, controlled, or operated by Google, Inc., headquartered at 1600 Amphitheatre Way, Mountain View, California, 94043.

ATTACHMENT "B"
Particular Things to be Seized

I. **Information to be disclosed by the Service Provider**

To the extent that the information described in Attachment A is within the possession, custody, or control of Google, including any Emails, records, files, logs, or information that have been deleted but are still available to Service Provider, or have been preserved pursuant to a request made under 18 U.S.C. § 2703(f), Service Provider is required to disclose the following information to the government for each account or identifier listed in Attachment A from account inception to present:

a. The contents of all messages and emails associated with the account, including copies of messages and emails sent to and from the account, draft messages/emails, the source and destination addresses associated with each message/email, the date and time at which each message/email was sent, and the size and length of each message/email;

b. All records or other information regarding the identification of the account, to include full name, physical address, telephone numbers and other identifiers, records of session times and durations, the date on which the account was created, the length of service, the types of service utilized, the IP address used to register the account, log-in IP addresses associated with session times and dates, account status, alternative email addresses provided during registration, methods of connecting, log files, and means and source of payment (including any credit or bank account number);

c. All records or other information stored in the Online Accounts, including address books, contact and buddy lists, calendar data, pictures, applications, documents, and other files;

d. All records pertaining to communications between Service Provider and any person regarding the account, including contacts with support services and records of actions taken.

e. All data and contents related to the following Google Services associated with the Target Account: Android; Gmail; Google Calendar; Google Docs; Google Drive; Google Talk; Multilogin; Web History; YouTube; and all other applications.

f. All information and content associated with any third-party application associated with the Target Account and the dates when the applications were installed;

g. Based on an analysis of cookies assigned to computers and devices that accessed the Target Account, identify all other Google accounts that have been accessed from any computers and devices that have logged into the Target Account.

II. **Information to be seized by the United States**

After reviewing all information described in Section I, the United States will seize evidence of violations of Title 18, United States Code Sections 32(a) (Destruction/Damage of Aircraft or Aircraft Facilities); 37(a)(2) (Violence at International Airport); and 922(a)(3); 5 (Unlawful Interstate Transport/Delivery of Firearms by Non Federal Firearms Licensee) (the "Subject Offenses") that occur in the form of the following, from account inception to present:

a. Communications, transactions and records that may establish ownership and control (or the degree thereof) of the Target Account, including address books, contact or buddy lists, bills, invoices, receipts, registration records, bills, correspondence, notes, records, memoranda, telephone/address books, photographs, video recordings, audio recordings, lists of names, records of payment for access to newsgroups or other online subscription services, and attachments to said communications, transactions and records.

b. Communications, transactions and records to/from persons who may be co-conspirators of the Subject Offenses, or which may identify co-conspirators.

c. Communications, transactions and records which may show motivation to commit the Subject Offenses.

d. Communications, transactions and records that relate to the Subject Offenses.

e. The terms "communications," "transactions", "records," "documents," "programs," or "materials" include all information recorded in any form, visual or aural, and by any means, whether in handmade form (including, but not limited to, writings, drawings, paintings), photographic form (including, but not limited to, pictures or videos), or electrical, electronic or magnetic form, as well as digital data files. These terms also include any applications (i.e. software programs). These terms expressly include, among other things, Emails, instant messages, chat logs, correspondence attached as to Emails (or drafts), calendar entries, buddy lists.

ATTACHMENT "C"

PROTOCOL FOR SEARCHING THE ELECTRONIC DATA SEIZED PURSUANT TO THIS SEARCH WARRANT

1. In executing this warrant, the government must make reasonable efforts to use methods and procedures that will locate and expose in the electronic data produced in response to this search warrant ("the Search Warrant Data") those categories of data, files, documents, or other electronically stored information that are identified with particularity in the warrant, while minimizing exposure or examination of irrelevant, privileged, or confidential files to the extent reasonably practicable.

2. When the Search Warrant Data is received, the government will make a duplicate copy of the Search Warrant Data ("the Search Warrant Data Copy"). The original version of the Search Warrant Data will be sealed and preserved for purposes of: later judicial review or order to return or dispose of the Search Warrant Data; production to the defense in any criminal case if authorized by statute, rule, or the Constitution; for purposes of showing the chain of custody of the Search Warrant Data and the Search Warrant Data Copy; or for any other lawful purpose. The original of the Search Warrant Data will not be searched or examined except to ensure that it has been fully and completely replicated in the Search Warrant Data Copy.

3. The investigating agents will then search the entirety of the Search Warrant Data Copy using any and all methods and procedures deemed appropriate by the United States designed to identify the information listed as Information to be Seized in Attachment B, Section II. The United States may copy, extract or otherwise segregate information or data listed as Information to be Seized in Attachment B, Section II. Information or data so copied, extracted or otherwise segregated will no longer be subject to any handling restrictions that might be set out in this protocol beyond those required by binding law. To the extent evidence of crimes not within the scope of this warrant appear in plain view during this review, a supplemental or "piggyback" warrant will be applied for in order to further search that document, data, or other item.

4. Once the Search Warrant Data Copy has been thoroughly and completely examined for any document, data, or other items identified in Attachment B, Section II as Information to be Seized, the Search Warrant Data Copy will be sealed and not subject to any further search or examination unless authorized by another search warrant or other appropriate court order. The Search Warrant Data Copy will be held and preserved for the same purposes identified above in Paragraph 2.

5. The search procedures utilized for this review are at the sole discretion of the investigating and prosecuting authorities, and may include the following techniques (the following is a non-exclusive list, as other search procedures may be used):

a. examination of all of the data contained in the Search Warrant Data to view the data and determine whether that data falls within the items to be seized as set forth herein;

b. searching for and attempting to recover from the Search Warrant Data any deleted, hidden, or encrypted data to determine whether that data falls within the list of items to be seized as set forth herein (any data that is encrypted and unreadable will not be returned unless law enforcement personnel have determined that the data is not (1) an instrumentality of the offenses, (2) a fruit of the criminal activity, (3) contraband, (4) otherwise unlawfully possessed, or (5) evidence of the offenses specified above);

c. surveying various file directories and the individual files they contain;

d. opening files in order to determine their contents;

e. using hash values to narrow the scope of what may be found. Hash values are under- inclusive, but are still a helpful tool;

f. scanning storage areas;

g. performing keyword searches through all electronic storage areas to determine whether occurrences of language contained in such storage areas exist that are likely to appear in the evidence described in Attachment A; and/or

h. performing any other data analysis technique that may be necessary to locate and retrieve the evidence described in Attachment B, Section II.

Return and Review Procedures

6. Rule 41 of the Federal Rules of Criminal Procedure provides, in relevant part:

(e) Issuing the Warrant.

(2) Contents of the Warrant.

(A) Warrant to Search for and Seize a Person or Property. Except for a tracking-device warrant, the warrant must identify the person or property to be searched, identify any person or property to be seized, and designate the magistrate judge to whom it must be returned. The warrant must command the officer to:

(i) execute the warrant within a specified time no longer than 14 days;

(B) Warrant Seeking Electronically Stored Information. A warrant under Rule 41(e)(2)(A) may authorize the seizure of electronic storage media or the seizure or copying of electronically stored information. Unless otherwise specified, the warrant authorizes a later review of the media or information consistent with the warrant. The time for executing the warrant in Rule 41(e)(2)(A) and (f)(1)(A) refers to the seizure or on-site copying of the media or information, and not to any later off-site copying or review.

(f) Executing and Returning the Warrant.

(1) Warrant to Search for and Seize a Person or Property.

(B) Inventory. An officer present during the execution of the warrant must prepare and verify an inventory of any property seized. . . . In a case involving the seizure of electronic storage media or the seizure or copying of electronically stored information, the inventory may be limited to describing the physical storage media that were seized or copied. The officer may retain a copy of the electronically stored information that was seized or copied.

7. Pursuant to this Rule, the government understands and will act in accordance with the following:

a. Pursuant to Rule 41(e)(2)(A)(iii), within fourteen (14) days of the execution of the warrant, an agent is required to file an inventory return with the Court, that is, to file an itemized list of the property seized. Execution of the warrant begins when the United States serves the warrant on the named custodian; execution is complete when the custodian provides all Search Warrant Data to the United States. Within fourteen (14) days of completion of the execution of the warrant, the inventory will be filed.

b. Pursuant to Rule 41(e)(2)(B), Rule 41(e)(2)(A) governs the time within which the electronically stored information must be seized after the issuance of the warrant and copied after the execution of the warrant, not the "later review of the media or information" seized, or the later off-site digital copying of that media.

c. Under Rule 41(f)(1)(B), the inventory return that is to be filed with the court may be limited to a description of the "physical storage media" into which the Search Warrant Data that was seized was placed, not an itemization of the information or data stored on the "physical storage media" into which the Search Warrant Data was placed;

d. Under Rule 41(f)(1)(B), the government may retain a copy of that information for purposes of the investigation. The government proposes that the original storage media on which the Search Warrant Data was placed plus a full image copy of the seized Search Warrant Data be retained by the government.

e. If the person from whom any Search Warrant Data was seized requests the return of any information in the Search Warrant Data that is not set forth in Attachment B, Section II, that information will be copied onto appropriate media and returned to the person from whom the information was seized.

STEVEN W. MYHRE
Acting United States Attorney
District of Nevada
CRISTINA D. SILVA
PATRICK BURNS
Assistant United States Attorneys
501 Las Vegas Blvd. South, Ste. 1100
Las Vegas, Nevada 89101
Telephone: (702) 388-6336
Fax (702) 388-6698
john.p.burns@usdoj.gov

Attorney for the United States of America

FILED
2017 OCT 13 PM 12: 36
U.S. MAGISTRATE JUDGE
BY_____

UNITED STATES DISTRICT COURT
DISTRICT OF NEVADA
-oOo-

IN THE MATTER OF THE SEARCH OF INFORMATION ASSOCIATED WITH EMAIL ACCOUNT CENTRALPARK1@LIVE.COM THAT IS STORED AT A PREMISES CONTROLLED BY MICROSOFT. **A1**	Magistrate No. AFFIDAVIT IN SUPPORT OF AN APPLICATION FOR SEARCH WARRANTS (Under Seal)
IN THE MATTER OF THE SEARCH OF INFORMATION ASSOCIATED WITH EMAIL ACCOUNT MARILOUROSES@LIVE.COM THAT IS STORED AT A PREMISES CONTROLLED BY MICROSOFT. **A2**	Magistrate No. 2:17-mj-01010-NJK AFFIDAVIT IN SUPPORT OF AN APPLICATION FOR SEARCH WARRANTS (Under Seal)

STATE OF NEVADA   )
) ss:
COUNTY OF CLARK)

///

///

AFFIDAVIT IN SUPPORT OF AN APPLICATION FOR SEARCH WARRANTS

I, Zachary C. Mckinney, Special Agent, Federal Bureau of Investigation (FBI), having been duly sworn, hereby depose and say:

INTRODUCTION AND AGENT BACKGROUND

1. Your Affiant makes this affidavit in support of an application for search warrants for information associated with email accounts centralpark1@live.com ("Target Account 1") and marilouroses@live.com ("Target Account 2"). Target Account 1 is an account associated with STEPHEN PADDOCK. Target Account 2 is an account associated with MARILOU DANLEY. The information associated with both accounts is stored at a premises owned, maintained, controlled, or operated by Microsoft Corporation ("Microsoft"), an American multinational technology company based in Redmond, Washington that specializes in Internet-related services and products along with the development and manufacturing of computer-related items. Those online services include, but are not limited to, email services, cloud computing, and many other services. The information to be searched is described in the following paragraphs and in Attachment "A" (attached hereto and incorporated herein by reference). This affidavit is made in support of an application for search warrants under 18 U.S.C. §§ 2703(a), 2703(b)(1)(A), and 2703(c)(1)(A) to require Microsoft to disclose to the government records and other information in its possession, pertaining to the subscriber or customer associated with the Target Accounts.

2. I am a Special Agent with the Federal Bureau of Investigation, currently assigned to Las Vegas, Nevada. I have been employed as a Special Agent of the FBI since

March of 2017. Over the course of my employment with the FBI, I have conducted surveillance, analyzed telephone records, interviewed witnesses, supervised activities of sources, executed search warrants, and executed arrest warrants. These investigative activities have been conducted in conjunction with a variety of investigations, to include those involving robbery, drug trafficking, human trafficking, criminal enterprises, and more. In addition to my practical experiences, I received five months of extensive law enforcement training at the FBI Academy. Previous to the FBI, I was employed as a human intelligence gatherer with the United States Army. I was trained extensively in interrogation, interview, and source handling techniques and best practices. I also received an MBA in International Business and worked with ExxonMobil as a financial manager.

3. I make this affidavit in support of an application for a search warrant for information associated with the Microsoft accounts associated with centralpark1@live.com" and "marilouroses@live.com," which is stored at a premises owned, maintained, controlled, or operated by Microsoft Corporation, headquartered at One Microsoft Way, Redmond, WA 98052-6399, hereinafter referred to as "premises," and further described in Attachments A-1 and A-2 hereto.

    a. Destruction/Damage of Aircraft or Aircraft Facilities - 18 U.S.C.A. § 32(a);

    b. Violence at International Airport - 18 U.S.C. § 37(a)(2); and

    c. Unlawful Interstate Transport/Delivery of Firearms by Non Federal Firearms Licensee – 18 U.S.C. §§ 922(a)(3) and (5);

    d. Aiding and Abetting – 18 U.S.C. § 2.

(hereafter, "Subject Offenses") have been committed by STEPHEN PADDOCK, MARILOU DANLEY, and others yet unknown. There is also probable cause to search the information described in Attachment "A" for evidence of these crimes and information which might reveal the identities of others involved in these crimes, as described in Attachment "B" (attached hereto and incorporated herein by reference).

PROBABLE CAUSE

4. On the evening of Sunday, October 1, 2017, Route 91 Harvest, a music festival, was in progress at 3901 South Las Vegas Boulevard, Las Vegas, Nevada. At approximately 10:08 p.m., the Las Vegas Metropolitan Police Department (LVMPD) received calls reporting shots had been fired at the concert and multiple victims were struck. LVMPD determined the shots were coming from Rooms 134 and 135 on the 32nd floor of the Mandalay Bay Resort and Casino, located due west of the festival rounds at 3950 South Las Vegas Boulevard, Las Vegas, Nevada. These rooms are an elevated position which overlooks the concert venue. Witness statements and video footage captured during the attack indicates that the weapons being used were firing in a fully-automatic fashion.

5. LVMPD officers ultimately made entry into the room and located an individual later identified as Stephen Paddock. Paddock was deceased from an apparent self-inflicted gunshot wound.

6. Paddock's Nevada driver's license was located in the Mandalay Bay hotel room with Paddock, and both hotel rooms were registered in his name. A player's club card in name of Marilou Danley was located in Paddock's room, and the card returned to the address located on Babbling Brook Street in Mesquite, Nevada. FBI Agents

located Danley, who was traveling outside the United States at the time of the shooting. It was ultimately determined that Danley resided with Paddock at the Babbling Brook address.

7. On October 2, 2017, search warrants were executed on Paddock's Mandalay Bay hotel rooms, Paddock's vehicle at Mandalay Bay, and two Nevada residences owed by Paddock: 1372 Babbling Brook Court in Mesquite, and 1735 Del Webb Parkway in Reno, Nevada. Officers and Agents found over 20 firearms, hundreds of rounds of ammunition, and hundreds of spent shell casings in the Mandalay Bay hotel rooms, in close proximity to Paddock's body. Over a thousand rounds of rifle ammunition and 100 pounds of explosive material was found in Paddock's vehicle. Additional explosive material, approximately 18 firearms, and over 1,000 rounds of ammunition was located at the Mesquite residence. A large quantity of ammunition and multiple firearms were recovered from the Reno residence.

8. As of this date, 58 people have been identified to have been killed in Paddock's attack and another 557 were reportedly injured. Additionally, investigators discovered that STEPHEN PADDOCK also utilized a firearm to shoot large fuel tanks on Las Vegas McCarran International Airport property. Multiple bullet holes were found on the tank, which investigators believe was an attempt by STEPHEN PADDOCK to cause the tanks to explode.

9. In an effort to determine whether or not STEPHEN PADDOCK was assisted and/or conspired with unknown individuals, investigators have attempted to identify all of STEPHEN PADDOCK's associated. It was quickly determined that a casino player's card in the name of MARILOU DANLEY was located in the room at the

time of the attack. She has been identified thus far as the most likely person who aided or abetted STEPHEN PADDOCK based on her informing law enforcement that her fingerprints would likely be found on the ammunition used during the attack. Subsequently, investigators worked to identify the communication facilities utilized by STEPHEN PADDOCK and MARILOU DANLEY.

10. Based on a review of STEPHEN PADDOCK's financial accounts, Target Account 1 was determined to belong to STEPHEN PADDOCK. On October 3, 2017, investigators requested an emergency disclosure of records from Microsoft related to Target Account 1 so it could be immediately searched for any evidence of additional co-conspirators. Unfortunately, the information was only requested for a six-month timeframe. Within the account, investigators identified Target Account 2 as one that belonged to MARILOU DANLEY, which was clear based on the communications between the two email accounts. In an interview, DANLEY stated that PADDOCK had access to one of her email accounts, which investigators believe to be Target Account 2.

11. On September 25, 2017, an email was exchanged between the Target Accounts which discussed a wire transfer of funds which was to be sent by STEPHEN PADDOCK to MARILOU DANLEY. It is unclear what the purpose of the wire transfer was, but MARILOU DANLEY is known to have been in the Philippines at the time.

12. Additionally, on July 6, 2017, Target Account 1 sent an email to centralpark4804@gmail.com which read, "try an ar before u buy. we have huge selection. located in the las vegas area." Later that day, an email was received back from centralpark4804@gmail.com to Target Account 1 that read, "we have a wide variety of optics and ammunition to try." And lastly, Target Account 1 later sent an email to

centralpark4804@gmail.com that read, "for a thrill try out bumpfire ar's with a 100 round magazine." Investigators believe these communications may have been related to the eventual attack that occurred at the Mandalay Bay in Las Vegas.

13. Your Affiant believes the requested search warrants will yield significant information from Microsoft such as STEPHEN PADDOCK's and MARILOU DANLEY's contact lists, email messages content, IP address usage, photographs, third-party applications associated with the account, and more, which may constitute evidence of the planning of the attack and potentially identify other participants in the attack. Ultimately, your Affiant strongly believes the requested information will lead investigators to determine the full scope of STEPHEN PADDOCK's plan and MARILOU DANLEY's possible involvement.

14. Investigators have previously sought and obtained a search warrant to examine the contents of both Target Accounts 1 and 2. After execution of that warrant, however, it became apparent and was confirmed with Microsoft that Microsoft was refusing to provide data related to/contained in the OneDrive online storage files for either account. Microsoft indicated to investigators that it did not believe such information was encompassed by the items to be produced that were specified in the original warrant. Investigators believe therefore that there is additional evidence Microsoft currently possesses that relates to the OneDrive online storage service, as well as potentially in a suite of other online services that Microsoft offers, including Office 365, Windows Live Mail, Windows Live Writer, Windows Photo Gallery, Windows Live Messenger, Microsoft Family Safety, and Microsoft Outlook Hotmail Connector. Thus,

your Affiant seeks more specific authorization to seize and search the OneDrive and other service data specified in Attachment B of the instant warrant application.

RELEVANT TECHNICAL TERMS

15. The following non-exhaustive list of definitions applies to this Affidavit and the Attachments to this Affidavit:

    a. The "Internet" is a worldwide network of computer systems operated by governmental entities, corporations, and universities. In order to access the Internet, an individual computer user must subscribe to an access provider, which operates a host computer system with direct access to the Internet. The World Wide Web is a functionality of the Internet which allows users of the Internet to share information.

    b. "Internet Service Providers" are companies that provide access to the Internet. ISPs can also provide other services for their customers including website hosting, email service, remote storage, and co-location of computers and other communications equipment. ISPs offer different ways to access the Internet including telephone-based (dial-up), broadband-based access via a digital subscriber line (DSL) or cable television, dedicated circuits, or satellite-based subscription. ISPs typically charge a fee based upon the type of connection and volume of data (bandwidth). Many ISPs assign each subscriber an account name, such as a user name, an email address, and an email mailbox, and the subscriber typically creates a password for his/her account.

    c. "ISP Records" are records maintained by ISPs pertaining to their subscribers (regardless of whether those subscribers are individuals or entities). These records may include account application information, subscriber and billing information, account access information (often in the form of log files), emails, information concerning

content uploaded and/or stored on the ISP's servers, and other information, which may be stored both in computer data format and in written or printed record format. ISPs reserve and/or maintain computer disk storage space on their computer system for their subscribers' use. This service by ISPs allows for both temporary and long-term storage of electronic communications and many other types of electronic data and files.

    d.   "Online service providers" (also referred to here as "service providers") are companies that provide online services such as email, chat or instant messaging, word processing applications, spreadsheet applications, presentation applications similar to PowerPoint, online calendar, photo storage and remote storage services. Sometimes they also can provide web hosting, remote storage, and co-location of computers and other communications equipment. Typically, each service provider assigns each subscriber an account name, such as a user name or screen name and the subscriber typically creates a password for his/her account.

    e.   "Computer," as used herein, is defined as "an electronic, magnetic, optical, electrochemical, or other high speed data processing device performing logical or storage functions, and includes any data storage facility or communications facility directly related to or operating in conjunction with such device."

    f.   A "server" is a centralized computer that provides services for other computers connected to it via a network. The other computers attached to a server are sometimes called "clients." For example, in a large company, it is common for individual employees to have client computers at their desktops. When the employees access their email, or access files stored on the network itself, those files are pulled electronically from the server, where they are stored, and are sent to the client's computer via the

network. Notably, servers can be physically stored in any location: it is not uncommon for a network's server to be located hundreds (and even thousands) of miles away from the client computers.

g. "Internet Protocol address," or "IP address," refers to a unique number used by a computer to access the Internet. IP addresses can be dynamic, meaning that the Internet Service Provider (ISP) assigns a different unique number to a computer every time it accesses the Internet. IP addresses might also be static, that is, an ISP assigns a user's computer a particular IP address which is used each time the computer accesses the Internet.

h. The term "domain" refers to a word used as a name for computers, networks, services, etc. A domain name typically represents a website, a server computer that hosts that website, or even some computer (or other digital device) connected to the internet. Essentially, when a website (or a server computer that hosts that website) is connected to the internet, it is assigned an IP address. Because IP addresses are difficult for people to remember, domain names are instead used because they are easier to remember than IP addresses. Domain names are formed by the rules and procedures of the Domain Name System (DNS). A common top level domain under these rules is ".com" for commercial organizations, ".gov" for the United States government, and ".org" for organizations. For example, www.usdoj.gov is the domain name that identifies a server used by the U.S. Department of Justice, and which uses IP address of 149.101.46.71.

i. "Web hosting services" maintain server computers connected to the Internet. Their customers use those computers to operate websites on the Internet. Customers of web hosting companies place files, software code, databases, and other data

on servers. To do this, customers typically connect from their own computers to the server computers across the Internet.

j. The term "WhoIs" lookup refers to a search of a publicly available online database that lists information provided when a domain is registered or when an IP address is assigned.

k. The terms "communications," "records," "documents," "programs," or "materials" include all information recorded in any form, visual or aural, and by any means, whether in handmade form (including, but not limited to, writings, drawings, paintings), photographic form (including, but not limited to, pictures or videos), or electrical, electronic or magnetic form, as well as digital data files. These terms also include any applications (i.e. software programs). These terms expressly include, among other things, emails, instant messages, chat logs, correspondence attached as to emails (or drafts), calendar entries, buddy lists.

l. "Chat" is usually a real time electronic communication between two or more individuals. Unlike email, which is frequently sent, then read and responded to minutes, hours, or even days later, chats frequently involve an immediate conversation between individuals, similar to a face-to-face conversation. Nearly all chat programs are capable of saving the chat transcript, to enable users to preserve a record of the conversation. By default, some chat programs have this capability enabled, while others do not. Many popular web-based email providers, like Microsoft and Microsoft, provide chat functionality as part of the online services they provide to account holders.

///

///

FACTS ABOUT EMAIL PROVIDERS

16. In my training, my experience and this investigation, I have learned that Microsoft (the Service Provider) is a company that provides free web-based Internet email access to the general public, and that stored electronic communications, including opened and unopened email for Microsoft subscribers may be located on the computers of Microsoft. I have also learned that Microsoft Inc. provides various on-line service messaging services to the general public. Instant Messaging ("IM") is a form of real-time direct text-based communication between two or more people using shared clients. The text is conveyed via devices connected over a network such as the Internet. In addition to text, Microsoft's software allows users with the most current updated versions to utilize its webcam service. This option enables users from distances all over the world to view others who have installed a webcam on their end. Thus, the Service Provider's servers will contain a wide variety of the subscriber's files, including emails, address books, contact or buddy lists, calendar data, pictures, chat logs, and other files.

17. To use these services, subscribers register for online accounts like the Target Accounts. During the registration process, service providers such as the ones here ask subscribers to provide basic personal information. This information can include the subscriber's full name, physical address, telephone numbers and other identifiers, alternative email addresses, and, for paying subscribers, means and source of payment (including any credit card or bank account number). Based on my training and my experience, I know that subscribers may insert false information to conceal their identity; even if this proves to be the case, however, I know that this information often provide clues to their identity, location or illicit activities.

18. In general, when a subscriber receives an email, it is typically stored in the subscriber's "mail box" on that service provider's servers until the subscriber deletes the Email. If the subscriber does not delete the message, the message (and any attachments) can remain on that service provider's servers indefinitely.

19. Similarly, when the subscriber sends an email, it is initiated at the subscriber's computer, transferred via the Internet to the service provider's servers, and then transmitted to its end destination. That service provider often saves a copy of the email sent. Unless the sender of the email specifically deletes the Email from the provider's server, the email can remain on the system indefinitely.

20. A sent or received email typically includes the content of the message, source and destination addresses, the date and time at which the email was sent, and the size and length of the email. If an email user writes a draft message but does not send it, that message may also be saved by that service provider, but may not include all of these categories of data.

21. Just as a computer on a desk can be used to store a wide variety of files, so can online accounts, such as the accounts subject to this application. First, subscribers can store many types of files as attachments to emails in online accounts. Second, because service providers provide the services listed above (e.g. word processing, spreadsheets, pictures), subscribers who use these services usually store documents on servers maintained and/or owned by service providers. Thus, these online accounts often contain documents such as pictures, audio or video recordings, logs, spreadsheets, applications and other files.

22. Reviewing files stored in online accounts raises many of the same difficulties as with reviewing files stored on a local computer. For example, based on my training, my experience and this investigation, I know that subscribers of these online services can conceal their activities by altering files before they upload them to the online service. Subscribers can change file names to more innocuous sounding names (e.g. renaming "FraudRecords.doc" to "ChristmasList.doc"), they can change file extensions to make one kind of file appear like a different type of file (e.g. changing the spreadsheet "StolenCreditProfiles.xls" to "FamilyPhoto.jpg" to appear to be a picture file, where the file extension ".xls" denotes an Excel spreadsheet file and ".jpg" a JPEG format image file), or they can change the times and dates a file was last accessed or modified by changing a computer's system time/date and then uploading that file to the Online Accounts. Thus, to detect any files that the subscriber may have concealed, agents will need to review all of the files in the Target Accounts; they will, however, only seize the items that the Court authorizes to be seized. Similarly, subscribers can conceal their activities by encrypting files. Thus, these files may need to be decrypted to detect whether it constitutes an Item to be Seized.

23. I also believe that people engaged in crimes such as the one described herein often use online accounts because they give people engaged in these crimes a way to easily communicate with other co-conspirators. Moreover, online accounts are easily concealed from law enforcement. Unlike physical documents, electronic documents can be stored in a physical place far away, where they are less likely to be discovered.

24. Service providers typically retain certain transactional information about the creation and use of each account on their systems. This information can include the

date on which the account was created, the length of service, records of log-in (i.e., session) times and durations, the types of service utilized, the status of the account (including whether the account is inactive or closed), the methods used to connect to the account (such as logging into the account via websites controlled by the Service Provider), and other log files that reflect usage of the account. In addition, service providers often have records of the Internet Protocol address ("IP address") used to register the account and the IP addresses associated with particular logins to the account. Because every device that connects to the Internet must use an IP address, IP address information can help to identify which computers or other devices were used to access the online account.

25. In some cases, subscribers will communicate directly with a service provider about issues relating to the account, such as technical problems, billing inquiries, or complaints from or about other users. Service providers typically retain records about such communications, including records of contacts between the user and the provider's support services, as well records of any actions taken by the provider or user as a result of the communications.

26. In my training and experience, evidence of who was using an online account may be found in address books, contact or buddy lists, emails in the account, and pictures and files, whether stored as attachments or in the suite of the service provider's online applications. Therefore, the computers of the Service Providers are likely to contain stored electronic communications (including retrieved and un-retrieved email for their subscribers) and information concerning subscribers and their use of the provider's

services, such as account access information, email transaction information, documents, pictures, and account application information.

27. Microsoft maintains and offers its users the use of OneDrive. OneDrive is a file-hosting service operated by Microsoft as part of its suite of online services. It allows users to store files as well as other personal data like Windows settings or BitLocker recovery keys in the cloud. Files can be synced to a PC and accessed from a web browser or a mobile device, as well as shared publicly or with specific people. OneDrive offers 5 gigabytes of storage space free of charge; additional storage can be added either separately or through subscriptions to other Microsoft services including Office 365 and Groove Music.

28. Microsoft offers additional services that may be accessed in relation to and share associated information with a user's email account, including: Office 365, Windows Live Mail, Windows Live Writer, Windows Photo Gallery, Windows Live Messenger, Microsoft Family Safety, and Microsoft Outlook Hotmail Connector.

INFORMATION TO BE SEARCHED AND THINGS TO BE SEIZED

29. Your Affiant anticipates executing these warrants under the Electronic Communications Privacy Act, in particular 18 U.S.C. §§ 2703(a), 2703(b)(1)(A) and 2703(c)(1)(A), by using the warrant to require Microsoft to disclose to the government copies of the records and other information (including the content of communications) particularly described in Section I of Attachment "B." Upon receipt of the information described in Section I of Attachment "B," government-authorized persons will review that information to locate the items described in Section II of Attachment "B."

CONCLUSION

30. Based on the forgoing, I request that the Court issue the proposed search warrant. This Court has jurisdiction to issue the requested warrant because it is "a court of competent jurisdiction" as defined by 18 U.S.C. § 2711. 18 U.S.C. §§ 2703(a), (b)(1)(A) & (c)(1)(A). Specifically, the Court is "a district court of the United States . . . that – has jurisdiction over the offense being investigated." 18 U.S.C. § 2711(3)(A)(i). Pursuant to 18 U.S.C. § 2703(g), the presence of a law enforcement officer is not required for the service or execution of this warrant.

REQUEST FOR SEALING

31. I further request that the Court order that all papers in support of this application, including the affidavit and search warrant, be sealed until further order of the Court. These documents discuss an ongoing criminal investigation that is neither public nor known to all of the targets of the investigation. Accordingly, there is good cause to seal these documents because their premature disclosure may seriously jeopardize that investigation.

Respectfully Submitted,

/s/

Zachary C. McKinney, Special Agent
Federal Bureau of Investigation

SWORN TO AND SUBSCRIBED
before me this 13 day of October 2017.

_____
NANCY J. KOPPE
UNITED STATES MAGISTRATE JUDGE

I hereby attest and certify on 10/13/17 that the foregoing document is a full true and correct copy of the original on file in my office, and in my legal custody.

NANCY J. KOPPE
U.S. MAGISTRATE JUDGE
DISTRICT OF NEVADA

By _____ Deputy Clerk

ATTACHMENT "A-1"

ONLINE ACCOUNT TO BE SEARCHED

This warrant applies to information associated with the Microsoft email account centralpark1@live.com (the "Target Account 1") from inception to present, which is stored at premises owned, maintained, controlled, or operated by Microsoft Corporation, headquartered at 1 Microsoft Way, Redmond, Washington, 98052.

ATTACHMENT "A-2"

ONLINE ACCOUNT TO BE SEARCHED

This warrant applies to information associated with the Microsoft email account marilouroses@live.com (the "Target Account 2") from inception to present, which is stored at premises owned, maintained, controlled, or operated by Microsoft Corporation, headquartered at 1 Microsoft Way, Redmond, Washington, 98052.

ATTACHMENT "B"
Particular Things to be Seized

I. **Information to be disclosed by the Service Provider**

To the extent that the information described in Attachments A1 and A2 is within the possession, custody, or control of Microsoft, including any Emails, records, files, logs, or information that have been deleted but are still available to Service Provider, or have been preserved pursuant to a request made under 18 U.S.C. § 2703(f), Service Provider is required to disclose the following information to the government for each account or identifier listed in Attachments A-1 and A-2 from account inception to present:

a. The contents of all communications, transactions, records, documents, programs, or materials stored in or associated with any OneDrive accounts associated with or assigned to Target Accounts 1 and 2.

b. The contents of all communications, transactions, records, documents, programs, or materials stored in or associated with any Office 360 accounts associated with or assigned to Target Accounts 1 and 2.

c. The contents of all communications, transactions, records, documents, programs, or materials stored in or associated with any Microsoft Family Safety accounts or services associated with or assigned to Target Accounts 1 and 2.

d. The contents of all communications, transactions, records, documents, programs, or materials stored in or associated with any Windows Live Writer accounts or services associated with or assigned to Target Accounts 1 and 2.

e. The contents of all communications, transactions, records, documents, programs, or materials stored in or associated with any Windows Live Mail accounts or services associated with or assigned to Target Accounts 1 and 2.

f. The contents of all communications, transactions, records, documents, programs, or materials stored in or associated with any Windows Photo Gallery accounts or services associated with or assigned to Target Accounts 1 and 2.

g. The contents of all communications, transactions, records, documents, programs, or materials stored in or associated with any Windows Live Messenger accounts or services associated with or assigned to Target Accounts 1 and 2.

II. Information to be seized by the United States

After reviewing all information described in Section I, the United States will seize evidence of violations of Title 18, United States Code Sections 32(a) (Destruction/Damage of Aircraft or Aircraft Facilities); 37(a)(2) (Violence at International Airport); and 922(a)(3); and 5 (Unlawful Interstate Transport/Delivery of Firearms by Non Federal Firearms Licensee); and 2 (Aiding and Abetting) (the "Subject Offenses") that occur in the form of the following, from account inception to present:

a. Communications, transactions and records that may establish ownership and control (or the degree thereof) of the Target Account, including address books, contact or buddy lists, bills, invoices, receipts, registration records, bills, correspondence, notes, records, memoranda, telephone/address books, photographs, video recordings, audio recordings, lists of names, records of payment for access to newsgroups or other online subscription services, and attachments to said communications, transactions and records.

b. Communications, transactions and records to/from persons who may be co-conspirators of the Subject Offenses, or which may identify co-conspirators.

c. Communications, transactions and records which may show motivation to commit the Subject Offenses.

d. Communications, transactions and records that relate to the Subject Offenses.

e. The terms "communications," "transactions", "records," "documents," "programs," or "materials" include all information recorded in any form, visual or aural, and by any means, whether in handmade form (including, but not limited to, writings, drawings, paintings), photographic form (including, but not limited to, pictures or videos), or electrical, electronic or magnetic form, as well as digital data files. These terms also include any applications (i.e. software programs). These terms expressly include, among other things, Emails, instant messages, chat logs, correspondence attached as to Emails (or drafts), calendar entries, buddy lists.

ATTACHMENT "C"

PROTOCOL FOR SEARCHING THE ELECTRONIC DATA SEIZED PURSUANT TO THIS SEARCH WARRANT

1. In executing this warrant, the government must make reasonable efforts to use methods and procedures that will locate and expose in the electronic data produced in response to this search warrant ("the Search Warrant Data") those categories of data, files, documents, or other electronically stored information that are identified with particularity in the warrant, while minimizing exposure or examination of irrelevant, privileged, or confidential files to the extent reasonably practicable.

2. When the Search Warrant Data is received, the government will make a duplicate copy of the Search Warrant Data ("the Search Warrant Data Copy"). The original version of the Search Warrant Data will be sealed and preserved for purposes of: later judicial review or order to return or dispose of the Search Warrant Data; production to the defense in any criminal case if authorized by statute, rule, or the Constitution; for purposes of showing the chain of custody of the Search Warrant Data and the Search Warrant Data Copy; or for any other lawful purpose. The original of the Search Warrant Data will not be searched or examined except to ensure that it has been fully and completely replicated in the Search Warrant Data Copy.

3. The investigating agents will then search the entirety of the Search Warrant Data Copy using any and all methods and procedures deemed appropriate by the United States designed to identify the information listed as Information to be Seized in Attachment B, Section II. The United States may copy, extract or otherwise segregate information or data listed as Information to be Seized in Attachment B, Section II. Information or data so copied, extracted or otherwise segregated will no longer be subject to any handling restrictions that might be set out in this protocol beyond those required by binding law. To the extent evidence of crimes not within the scope of this warrant appear in plain view during this review, a supplemental or "piggyback" warrant will be applied for in order to further search that document, data, or other item.

4. Once the Search Warrant Data Copy has been thoroughly and completely examined for any document, data, or other items identified in Attachment B, Section II as Information to be Seized, the Search Warrant Data Copy will be sealed and not subject to any further search or examination unless authorized by another search warrant or other appropriate court order. The Search Warrant Data Copy will be held and preserved for the same purposes identified above in Paragraph 2.

5. The search procedures utilized for this review are at the sole discretion of the investigating and prosecuting authorities, and may include the following techniques (the following is a non-exclusive list, as other search procedures may be used):

   a. examination of all of the data contained in the Search Warrant Data to view the data and determine whether that data falls within the items to be seized as set forth herein;

   b. searching for and attempting to recover from the Search Warrant Data any deleted, hidden, or encrypted data to determine whether that data falls within the list of items to be seized as set forth herein (any data that is encrypted and unreadable will not be returned unless law enforcement personnel have determined that the data is not (1) an instrumentality of the offenses, (2) a fruit of the criminal activity, (3) contraband, (4) otherwise unlawfully possessed, or (5) evidence of the offenses specified above);

   c. surveying various file directories and the individual files they contain;

   d. opening files in order to determine their contents;

   e. using hash values to narrow the scope of what may be found. Hash values are under- inclusive, but are still a helpful tool;

   f. scanning storage areas;

   g. performing keyword searches through all electronic storage areas to determine whether occurrences of language contained in such storage areas exist that are likely to appear in the evidence described in Attachment A1 and A2; and/or

   h. performing any other data analysis technique that may be necessary to locate and retrieve the evidence described in Attachment B, Section II.

Return and Review Procedures

6. Rule 41 of the Federal Rules of Criminal Procedure provides, in relevant part:

(e) Issuing the Warrant.

(2) Contents of the Warrant.

(A) Warrant to Search for and Seize a Person or Property. Except for a tracking-device warrant, the warrant must identify the person or property to be searched, identify any person or property to be seized, and designate the magistrate judge to whom it must be returned. The warrant must command the officer to:

(i) execute the warrant within a specified time no longer than 14 days;

(B) Warrant Seeking Electronically Stored Information. A warrant under Rule 41(e)(2)(A) may authorize the seizure of electronic storage media or the seizure or copying of electronically stored information. Unless otherwise specified, the warrant authorizes a later review of the media or information consistent with the warrant. The time for executing the warrant in Rule 41(e)(2)(A) and (f)(1)(A) refers to the seizure or on-site copying of the media or information, and not to any later off-site copying or review.

(f) Executing and Returning the Warrant.

(1) Warrant to Search for and Seize a Person or Property.

(B) Inventory. An officer present during the execution of the warrant must prepare and verify an inventory of any property seized. . . . In a case involving the seizure of electronic storage media or the seizure or copying of electronically stored information, the inventory may be limited to describing the physical storage media that were seized or copied. The officer may retain a copy of the electronically stored information that was seized or copied.

7. Pursuant to this Rule, the government understands and will act in accordance with the following:

a. Pursuant to Rule 41(e)(2)(A)(iii), within fourteen (14) days of the execution of the warrant, an agent is required to file an inventory return with the Court, that is, to file an itemized list of the property seized. Execution of the warrant begins when the United States serves the warrant on the named custodian; execution is complete when the custodian provides all Search Warrant Data to the United States. Within fourteen (14) days of completion of the execution of the warrant, the inventory will be filed.

b. Pursuant to Rule 41(e)(2)(B), Rule 41(e)(2)(A) governs the time within which the electronically stored information must be seized after the issuance of the warrant and copied after the execution of the warrant, not the "later review of the media or information" seized, or the later off-site digital copying of that media.

c. Under Rule 41(f)(1)(B), the inventory return that is to be filed with the court may be limited to a description of the "physical storage media" into which the Search Warrant Data that was seized was placed, not an itemization of the information or data stored on the "physical storage media" into which the Search Warrant Data was placed;

d. Under Rule 41(f)(1)(B), the government may retain a copy of that information for purposes of the investigation. The government proposes that the original storage media on which the Search Warrant Data was placed plus a full image copy of the seized Search Warrant Data be retained by the government.

e. If the person from whom any Search Warrant Data was seized requests the return of any information in the Search Warrant Data that is not set forth in Attachment B, Section II, that information will be copied onto appropriate media and returned to the person from whom the information was seized.

STEVEN W. MYHRE
Acting United States Attorney
District of Nevada
CRISTINA D. SILVA
PATRICK BURNS
Assistant United States Attorneys
501 Las Vegas Blvd. South, Ste. 1100
Las Vegas, Nevada 89101
Telephone: (702) 388-6336
Fax (702) 388-6698
john.p.burns@usdoj.gov

Attorney for the United States of America

UNITED STATES DISTRICT COURT
DISTRICT OF NEVADA
-oOo-

IN THE MATTER OF THE SEARCH OF INFORMATION ASSOCIATED WITH EMAIL ACCOUNT CENTRALPARK1@LIVE.COM THAT IS STORED AT A PREMISES CONTROLLED BY MICROSOFT. A1	Magistrate No. 2:17-mj-01009-NJK AFFIDAVIT IN SUPPORT OF AN APPLICATION FOR SEARCH WARRANTS (Under Seal)
IN THE MATTER OF THE SEARCH OF INFORMATION ASSOCIATED WITH EMAIL ACCOUNT MARILOUROSES@LIVE.COM THAT IS STORED AT A PREMISES CONTROLLED BY MICROSOFT. A2	Magistrate No. AFFIDAVIT IN SUPPORT OF AN APPLICATION FOR SEARCH WARRANTS (Under Seal)

STATE OF NEVADA   )
) ss:
COUNTY OF CLARK   )

///

///

AFFIDAVIT IN SUPPORT OF AN APPLICATION FOR SEARCH WARRANTS

I, Zachary C. Mckinney, Special Agent, Federal Bureau of Investigation (FBI), having been duly sworn, hereby depose and say:

INTRODUCTION AND AGENT BACKGROUND

1. Your Affiant makes this affidavit in support of an application for search warrants for information associated with email accounts centralpark1@live.com ("Target Account 1") and marilouroses@live.com ("Target Account 2"). Target Account 1 is an account associated with STEPHEN PADDOCK. Target Account 2 is an account associated with MARILOU DANLEY. The information associated with both accounts is stored at a premises owned, maintained, controlled, or operated by Microsoft Corporation ("Microsoft"), an American multinational technology company based in Redmond, Washington that specializes in Internet-related services and products along with the development and manufacturing of computer-related items. Those online services include, but are not limited to, email services, cloud computing, and many other services. The information to be searched is described in the following paragraphs and in Attachment "A" (attached hereto and incorporated herein by reference). This affidavit is made in support of an application for search warrants under 18 U.S.C. §§ 2703(a), 2703(b)(1)(A), and 2703(c)(1)(A) to require Microsoft to disclose to the government records and other information in its possession, pertaining to the subscriber or customer associated with the Target Accounts.

2. I am a Special Agent with the Federal Bureau of Investigation, currently assigned to Las Vegas, Nevada. I have been employed as a Special Agent of the FBI since

March of 2017. Over the course of my employment with the FBI, I have conducted surveillance, analyzed telephone records, interviewed witnesses, supervised activities of sources, executed search warrants, and executed arrest warrants. These investigative activities have been conducted in conjunction with a variety of investigations, to include those involving robbery, drug trafficking, human trafficking, criminal enterprises, and more. In addition to my practical experiences, I received five months of extensive law enforcement training at the FBI Academy. Previous to the FBI, I was employed as a human intelligence gatherer with the United States Army. I was trained extensively in interrogation, interview, and source handling techniques and best practices. I also received an MBA in International Business and worked with ExxonMobil as a financial manager.

3. I make this affidavit in support of an application for a search warrant for information associated with the Microsoft accounts associated with centralpark1@live.com" and "marilouroses@live.com," which is stored at a premises owned, maintained, controlled, or operated by Microsoft Corporation, headquartered at One Microsoft Way, Redmond, WA 98052-6399, hereinafter referred to as "premises," and further described in Attachments A-1 and A-2 hereto.

    a. Destruction/Damage of Aircraft or Aircraft Facilities - 18 U.S.C.A. § 32(a);

    b. Violence at International Airport - 18 U.S.C. § 37(a)(2); and

    c. Unlawful Interstate Transport/Delivery of Firearms by Non Federal Firearms Licensee – 18 U.S.C. §§ 922(a)(3) and (5);

    d. Aiding and Abetting – 18 U.S.C. § 2.

(hereafter, "Subject Offenses") have been committed by STEPHEN PADDOCK, MARILOU DANLEY, and others yet unknown. There is also probable cause to search the information described in Attachment "A" for evidence of these crimes and information which might reveal the identities of others involved in these crimes, as described in Attachment "B" (attached hereto and incorporated herein by reference).

PROBABLE CAUSE

4. On the evening of Sunday, October 1, 2017, Route 91 Harvest, a music festival, was in progress at 3901 South Las Vegas Boulevard, Las Vegas, Nevada. At approximately 10:08 p.m., the Las Vegas Metropolitan Police Department (LVMPD) received calls reporting shots had been fired at the concert and multiple victims were struck. LVMPD determined the shots were coming from Rooms 134 and 135 on the 32nd floor of the Mandalay Bay Resort and Casino, located due west of the festival rounds at 3950 South Las Vegas Boulevard, Las Vegas, Nevada. These rooms are an elevated position which overlooks the concert venue. Witness statements and video footage captured during the attack indicates that the weapons being used were firing in a fully-automatic fashion.

5. LVMPD officers ultimately made entry into the room and located an individual later identified as Stephen Paddock. Paddock was deceased from an apparent self-inflicted gunshot wound.

6. Paddock's Nevada driver's license was located in the Mandalay Bay hotel room with Paddock, and both hotel rooms were registered in his name. A player's club card in name of Marilou Danley was located in Paddock's room, and the card returned to the address located on Babbling Brook Street in Mesquite, Nevada. FBI Agents

located Danley, who was traveling outside the United States at the time of the shooting. It was ultimately determined that Danley resided with Paddock at the Babbling Brook address.

7. On October 2, 2017, search warrants were executed on Paddock's Mandalay Bay hotel rooms, Paddock's vehicle at Mandalay Bay, and two Nevada residences owed by Paddock: 1372 Babbling Brook Court in Mesquite, and 1735 Del Webb Parkway in Reno, Nevada. Officers and Agents found over 20 firearms, hundreds of rounds of ammunition, and hundreds of spent shell casings in the Mandalay Bay hotel rooms, in close proximity to Paddock's body. Over a thousand rounds of rifle ammunition and 100 pounds of explosive material was found in Paddock's vehicle. Additional explosive material, approximately 18 firearms, and over 1,000 rounds of ammunition was located at the Mesquite residence. A large quantity of ammunition and multiple firearms were recovered from the Reno residence.

8. As of this date, 58 people have been identified to have been killed in Paddock's attack and another 557 were reportedly injured. Additionally, investigators discovered that STEPHEN PADDOCK also utilized a firearm to shoot large fuel tanks on Las Vegas McCarran International Airport property. Multiple bullet holes were found on the tank, which investigators believe was an attempt by STEPHEN PADDOCK to cause the tanks to explode.

9. In an effort to determine whether or not STEPHEN PADDOCK was assisted and/or conspired with unknown individuals, investigators have attempted to identify all of STEPHEN PADDOCK's associated. It was quickly determined that a casino player's card in the name of MARILOU DANLEY was located in the room at the

time of the attack. She has been identified thus far as the most likely person who aided or abetted STEPHEN PADDOCK based on her informing law enforcement that her fingerprints would likely be found on the ammunition used during the attack. Subsequently, investigators worked to identify the communication facilities utilized by STEPHEN PADDOCK and MARILOU DANLEY.

10. Based on a review of STEPHEN PADDOCK's financial accounts, Target Account 1 was determined to belong to STEPHEN PADDOCK. On October 3, 2017, investigators requested an emergency disclosure of records from Microsoft related to Target Account 1 so it could be immediately searched for any evidence of additional co-conspirators. Unfortunately, the information was only requested for a six-month timeframe. Within the account, investigators identified Target Account 2 as one that belonged to MARILOU DANLEY, which was clear based on the communications between the two email accounts. In an interview, DANLEY stated that PADDOCK had access to one of her email accounts, which investigators believe to be Target Account 2.

11. On September 25, 2017, an email was exchanged between the Target Accounts which discussed a wire transfer of funds which was to be sent by STEPHEN PADDOCK to MARILOU DANLEY. It is unclear what the purpose of the wire transfer was, but MARILOU DANLEY is known to have been in the Philippines at the time.

12. Additionally, on July 6, 2017, Target Account 1 sent an email to centralpark4804@gmail.com which read, "try an ar before u buy. we have huge selection. located in the las vegas area." Later that day, an email was received back from centralpark4804@gmail.com to Target Account 1 that read, "we have a wide variety of optics and ammunition to try." And lastly, Target Account 1 later sent an email to

centralpark4804@gmail.com that read, "for a thrill try out bumpfire ar's with a 100 round magazine." Investigators believe these communications may have been related to the eventual attack that occurred at the Mandalay Bay in Las Vegas.

13. Your Affiant believes the requested search warrants will yield significant information from Microsoft such as STEPHEN PADDOCK's and MARILOU DANLEY's contact lists, email messages content, IP address usage, photographs, third-party applications associated with the account, and more, which may constitute evidence of the planning of the attack and potentially identify other participants in the attack. Ultimately, your Affiant strongly believes the requested information will lead investigators to determine the full scope of STEPHEN PADDOCK's plan and MARILOU DANLEY's possible involvement.

14. Investigators have previously sought and obtained a search warrant to examine the contents of both Target Accounts 1 and 2. After execution of that warrant, however, it became apparent and was confirmed with Microsoft that Microsoft was refusing to provide data related to/contained in the OneDrive online storage files for either account. Microsoft indicated to investigators that it did not believe such information was encompassed by the items to be produced that were specified in the original warrant. Investigators believe therefore that there is additional evidence Microsoft currently possesses that relates to the OneDrive online storage service, as well as potentially in a suite of other online services that Microsoft offers, including Office 365, Windows Live Mail, Windows Live Writer, Windows Photo Gallery, Windows Live Messenger, Microsoft Family Safety, and Microsoft Outlook Hotmail Connector. Thus,

your Affiant seeks more specific authorization to seize and search the OneDrive and other service data specified in Attachment B of the instant warrant application.

RELEVANT TECHNICAL TERMS

15. The following non-exhaustive list of definitions applies to this Affidavit and the Attachments to this Affidavit:

　　a.　The "Internet" is a worldwide network of computer systems operated by governmental entities, corporations, and universities. In order to access the Internet, an individual computer user must subscribe to an access provider, which operates a host computer system with direct access to the Internet. The World Wide Web is a functionality of the Internet which allows users of the Internet to share information.

　　b.　"Internet Service Providers" are companies that provide access to the Internet. ISPs can also provide other services for their customers including website hosting, email service, remote storage, and co-location of computers and other communications equipment. ISPs offer different ways to access the Internet including telephone-based (dial-up), broadband-based access via a digital subscriber line (DSL) or cable television, dedicated circuits, or satellite-based subscription. ISPs typically charge a fee based upon the type of connection and volume of data (bandwidth). Many ISPs assign each subscriber an account name, such as a user name, an email address, and an email mailbox, and the subscriber typically creates a password for his/her account.

　　c.　"ISP Records" are records maintained by ISPs pertaining to their subscribers (regardless of whether those subscribers are individuals or entities). These records may include account application information, subscriber and billing information, account access information (often in the form of log files), emails, information concerning

content uploaded and/or stored on the ISP's servers, and other information, which may be stored both in computer data format and in written or printed record format. ISPs reserve and/or maintain computer disk storage space on their computer system for their subscribers' use. This service by ISPs allows for both temporary and long-term storage of electronic communications and many other types of electronic data and files.

  d. "Online service providers" (also referred to here as "service providers") are companies that provide online services such as email, chat or instant messaging, word processing applications, spreadsheet applications, presentation applications similar to PowerPoint, online calendar, photo storage and remote storage services. Sometimes they also can provide web hosting, remote storage, and co-location of computers and other communications equipment. Typically, each service provider assigns each subscriber an account name, such as a user name or screen name and the subscriber typically creates a password for his/her account.

  e. "Computer," as used herein, is defined as "an electronic, magnetic, optical, electrochemical, or other high speed data processing device performing logical or storage functions, and includes any data storage facility or communications facility directly related to or operating in conjunction with such device."

  f. A "server" is a centralized computer that provides services for other computers connected to it via a network. The other computers attached to a server are sometimes called "clients." For example, in a large company, it is common for individual employees to have client computers at their desktops. When the employees access their email, or access files stored on the network itself, those files are pulled electronically from the server, where they are stored, and are sent to the client's computer via the

network. Notably, servers can be physically stored in any location: it is not uncommon for a network's server to be located hundreds (and even thousands) of miles away from the client computers.

g. "Internet Protocol address," or "IP address," refers to a unique number used by a computer to access the Internet. IP addresses can be dynamic, meaning that the Internet Service Provider (ISP) assigns a different unique number to a computer every time it accesses the Internet. IP addresses might also be static, that is, an ISP assigns a user's computer a particular IP address which is used each time the computer accesses the Internet.

h. The term "domain" refers to a word used as a name for computers, networks, services, etc. A domain name typically represents a website, a server computer that hosts that website, or even some computer (or other digital device) connected to the internet. Essentially, when a website (or a server computer that hosts that website) is connected to the internet, it is assigned an IP address. Because IP addresses are difficult for people to remember, domain names are instead used because they are easier to remember than IP addresses. Domain names are formed by the rules and procedures of the Domain Name System (DNS). A common top level domain under these rules is ".com" for commercial organizations, ".gov" for the United States government, and ".org" for organizations. For example, www.usdoj.gov is the domain name that identifies a server used by the U.S. Department of Justice, and which uses IP address of 149.101.46.71.

i. "Web hosting services" maintain server computers connected to the Internet. Their customers use those computers to operate websites on the Internet. Customers of web hosting companies place files, software code, databases, and other data

on servers. To do this, customers typically connect from their own computers to the server computers across the Internet.

  j. The term "WhoIs" lookup refers to a search of a publicly available online database that lists information provided when a domain is registered or when an IP address is assigned.

  k. The terms "communications," "records," "documents," "programs," or "materials" include all information recorded in any form, visual or aural, and by any means, whether in handmade form (including, but not limited to, writings, drawings, paintings), photographic form (including, but not limited to, pictures or videos), or electrical, electronic or magnetic form, as well as digital data files. These terms also include any applications (i.e. software programs). These terms expressly include, among other things, emails, instant messages, chat logs, correspondence attached as to emails (or drafts), calendar entries, buddy lists.

  l. "Chat" is usually a real time electronic communication between two or more individuals. Unlike email, which is frequently sent, then read and responded to minutes, hours, or even days later, chats frequently involve an immediate conversation between individuals, similar to a face-to-face conversation. Nearly all chat programs are capable of saving the chat transcript, to enable users to preserve a record of the conversation. By default, some chat programs have this capability enabled, while others do not. Many popular web-based email providers, like Microsoft and Microsoft, provide chat functionality as part of the online services they provide to account holders.

///

///

FACTS ABOUT EMAIL PROVIDERS

16. In my training, my experience and this investigation, I have learned that Microsoft (the Service Provider) is a company that provides free web-based Internet email access to the general public, and that stored electronic communications, including opened and unopened email for Microsoft subscribers may be located on the computers of Microsoft. I have also learned that Microsoft Inc. provides various on-line service messaging services to the general public. Instant Messaging ("IM") is a form of real-time direct text-based communication between two or more people using shared clients. The text is conveyed via devices connected over a network such as the Internet. In addition to text, Microsoft's software allows users with the most current updated versions to utilize its webcam service. This option enables users from distances all over the world to view others who have installed a webcam on their end. Thus, the Service Provider's servers will contain a wide variety of the subscriber's files, including emails, address books, contact or buddy lists, calendar data, pictures, chat logs, and other files.

17. To use these services, subscribers register for online accounts like the Target Accounts. During the registration process, service providers such as the ones here ask subscribers to provide basic personal information. This information can include the subscriber's full name, physical address, telephone numbers and other identifiers, alternative email addresses, and, for paying subscribers, means and source of payment (including any credit card or bank account number). Based on my training and my experience, I know that subscribers may insert false information to conceal their identity; even if this proves to be the case, however, I know that this information often provide clues to their identity, location or illicit activities.

18. In general, when a subscriber receives an email, it is typically stored in the subscriber's "mail box" on that service provider's servers until the subscriber deletes the Email. If the subscriber does not delete the message, the message (and any attachments) can remain on that service provider's servers indefinitely.

19. Similarly, when the subscriber sends an email, it is initiated at the subscriber's computer, transferred via the Internet to the service provider's servers, and then transmitted to its end destination. That service provider often saves a copy of the email sent. Unless the sender of the email specifically deletes the Email from the provider's server, the email can remain on the system indefinitely.

20. A sent or received email typically includes the content of the message, source and destination addresses, the date and time at which the email was sent, and the size and length of the email. If an email user writes a draft message but does not send it, that message may also be saved by that service provider, but may not include all of these categories of data.

21. Just as a computer on a desk can be used to store a wide variety of files, so can online accounts, such as the accounts subject to this application. First, subscribers can store many types of files as attachments to emails in online accounts. Second, because service providers provide the services listed above (e.g. word processing, spreadsheets, pictures), subscribers who use these services usually store documents on servers maintained and/or owned by service providers. Thus, these online accounts often contain documents such as pictures, audio or video recordings, logs, spreadsheets, applications and other files.

22. Reviewing files stored in online accounts raises many of the same difficulties as with reviewing files stored on a local computer. For example, based on my training, my experience and this investigation, I know that subscribers of these online services can conceal their activities by altering files before they upload them to the online service. Subscribers can change file names to more innocuous sounding names (e.g. renaming "FraudRecords.doc" to "ChristmasList.doc"), they can change file extensions to make one kind of file appear like a different type of file (e.g. changing the spreadsheet "StolenCreditProfiles.xls" to "FamilyPhoto.jpg" to appear to be a picture file, where the file extension ".xls" denotes an Excel spreadsheet file and ".jpg" a JPEG format image file), or they can change the times and dates a file was last accessed or modified by changing a computer's system time/date and then uploading that file to the Online Accounts. Thus, to detect any files that the subscriber may have concealed, agents will need to review all of the files in the Target Accounts; they will, however, only seize the items that the Court authorizes to be seized. Similarly, subscribers can conceal their activities by encrypting files. Thus, these files may need to be decrypted to detect whether it constitutes an Item to be Seized.

23. I also believe that people engaged in crimes such as the one described herein often use online accounts because they give people engaged in these crimes a way to easily communicate with other co-conspirators. Moreover, online accounts are easily concealed from law enforcement. Unlike physical documents, electronic documents can be stored in a physical place far away, where they are less likely to be discovered.

24. Service providers typically retain certain transactional information about the creation and use of each account on their systems. This information can include the

date on which the account was created, the length of service, records of log-in (i.e., session) times and durations, the types of service utilized, the status of the account (including whether the account is inactive or closed), the methods used to connect to the account (such as logging into the account via websites controlled by the Service Provider), and other log files that reflect usage of the account. In addition, service providers often have records of the Internet Protocol address ("IP address") used to register the account and the IP addresses associated with particular logins to the account. Because every device that connects to the Internet must use an IP address, IP address information can help to identify which computers or other devices were used to access the online account.

25. In some cases, subscribers will communicate directly with a service provider about issues relating to the account, such as technical problems, billing inquiries, or complaints from or about other users. Service providers typically retain records about such communications, including records of contacts between the user and the provider's support services, as well records of any actions taken by the provider or user as a result of the communications.

26. In my training and experience, evidence of who was using an online account may be found in address books, contact or buddy lists, emails in the account, and pictures and files, whether stored as attachments or in the suite of the service provider's online applications. Therefore, the computers of the Service Providers are likely to contain stored electronic communications (including retrieved and un-retrieved email for their subscribers) and information concerning subscribers and their use of the provider's

services, such as account access information, email transaction information, documents, pictures, and account application information.

27. Microsoft maintains and offers its users the use of OneDrive. OneDrive is a file-hosting service operated by Microsoft as part of its suite of online services. It allows users to store files as well as other personal data like Windows settings or BitLocker recovery keys in the cloud. Files can be synced to a PC and accessed from a web browser or a mobile device, as well as shared publicly or with specific people. OneDrive offers 5 gigabytes of storage space free of charge; additional storage can be added either separately or through subscriptions to other Microsoft services including Office 365 and Groove Music.

28. Microsoft offers additional services that may be accessed in relation to and share associated information with a user's email account, including: Office 365, Windows Live Mail, Windows Live Writer, Windows Photo Gallery, Windows Live Messenger, Microsoft Family Safety, and Microsoft Outlook Hotmail Connector.

INFORMATION TO BE SEARCHED AND THINGS TO BE SEIZED

29. Your Affiant anticipates executing these warrants under the Electronic Communications Privacy Act, in particular 18 U.S.C. §§ 2703(a), 2703(b)(1)(A) and 2703(c)(1)(A), by using the warrant to require Microsoft to disclose to the government copies of the records and other information (including the content of communications) particularly described in Section I of Attachment "B." Upon receipt of the information described in Section I of Attachment "B," government-authorized persons will review that information to locate the items described in Section II of Attachment "B."

CONCLUSION

30. Based on the forgoing, I request that the Court issue the proposed search warrant. This Court has jurisdiction to issue the requested warrant because it is "a court of competent jurisdiction" as defined by 18 U.S.C. § 2711. 18 U.S.C. §§ 2703(a), (b)(1)(A) & (c)(1)(A). Specifically, the Court is "a district court of the United States . . . that – has jurisdiction over the offense being investigated." 18 U.S.C. § 2711(3)(A)(i). Pursuant to 18 U.S.C. § 2703(g), the presence of a law enforcement officer is not required for the service or execution of this warrant.

REQUEST FOR SEALING

31. I further request that the Court order that all papers in support of this application, including the affidavit and search warrant, be sealed until further order of the Court. These documents discuss an ongoing criminal investigation that is neither public nor known to all of the targets of the investigation. Accordingly, there is good cause to seal these documents because their premature disclosure may seriously jeopardize that investigation.

Respectfully Submitted,

/s/
_____
Zachary C. McKinney, Special Agent
Federal Bureau of Investigation

SWORN TO AND SUBSCRIBED
before me this 13th day of October 2017.

_____
NANCY J. KOPPE
UNITED STATES MAGISTRATE JUDGE

I hereby attest and certify on 10/13/17 that the foregoing document is a full true and correct copy of the original on file in my office, and in my legal custody.

NANCY J. KOPPE
U.S. MAGISTRATE JUDGE
DISTRICT OF NEVADA

By _____ Deputy Clerk

ATTACHMENT "A-1"

ONLINE ACCOUNT TO BE SEARCHED

This warrant applies to information associated with the Microsoft email account centralpark1@live.com (the "Target Account 1") from inception to present, which is stored at premises owned, maintained, controlled, or operated by Microsoft Corporation, headquartered at 1 Microsoft Way, Redmond, Washington, 98052.

ATTACHMENT "A-2"

ONLINE ACCOUNT TO BE SEARCHED

This warrant applies to information associated with the Microsoft email account marilouroses@live.com (the "Target Account 2") from inception to present, which is stored at premises owned, maintained, controlled, or operated by Microsoft Corporation, headquartered at 1 Microsoft Way, Redmond, Washington, 98052.

ATTACHMENT "B"
Particular Things to be Seized

I. **Information to be disclosed by the Service Provider**

To the extent that the information described in Attachments A1 and A2 is within the possession, custody, or control of Microsoft, including any Emails, records, files, logs, or information that have been deleted but are still available to Service Provider, or have been preserved pursuant to a request made under 18 U.S.C. § 2703(f), Service Provider is required to disclose the following information to the government for each account or identifier listed in Attachments A-1 and A-2 from account inception to present:

a. The contents of all communications, transactions, records, documents, programs, or materials stored in or associated with any OneDrive accounts associated with or assigned to Target Accounts 1 and 2.

b. The contents of all communications, transactions, records, documents, programs, or materials stored in or associated with any Office 360 accounts associated with or assigned to Target Accounts 1 and 2.

c. The contents of all communications, transactions, records, documents, programs, or materials stored in or associated with any Microsoft Family Safety accounts or services associated with or assigned to Target Accounts 1 and 2.

d. The contents of all communications, transactions, records, documents, programs, or materials stored in or associated with any Windows Live Writer accounts or services associated with or assigned to Target Accounts 1 and 2.

e. The contents of all communications, transactions, records, documents, programs, or materials stored in or associated with any Windows Live Mail accounts or services associated with or assigned to Target Accounts 1 and 2.

f. The contents of all communications, transactions, records, documents, programs, or materials stored in or associated with any Windows Photo Gallery accounts or services associated with or assigned to Target Accounts 1 and 2.

g. The contents of all communications, transactions, records, documents, programs, or materials stored in or associated with any Windows Live Messenger accounts or services associated with or assigned to Target Accounts 1 and 2.

II. **Information to be seized by the United States**

After reviewing all information described in Section I, the United States will seize evidence of violations of Title 18, United States Code Sections 32(a) (Destruction/Damage of Aircraft or Aircraft Facilities); 37(a)(2) (Violence at International Airport); and 922(a)(3); and 5 (Unlawful Interstate Transport/Delivery of Firearms by Non Federal Firearms Licensee); and 2 (Aiding and Abetting) (the "Subject Offenses") that occur in the form of the following, from account inception to present:

a. Communications, transactions and records that may establish ownership and control (or the degree thereof) of the Target Account, including address books, contact or buddy lists, bills, invoices, receipts, registration records, bills, correspondence, notes, records, memoranda, telephone/address books, photographs, video recordings, audio recordings, lists of names, records of payment for access to newsgroups or other online subscription services, and attachments to said communications, transactions and records.

b. Communications, transactions and records to/from persons who may be co-conspirators of the Subject Offenses, or which may identify co-conspirators.

c. Communications, transactions and records which may show motivation to commit the Subject Offenses.

d. Communications, transactions and records that relate to the Subject Offenses.

e. The terms "communications," "transactions", "records," "documents," "programs," or "materials" include all information recorded in any form, visual or aural, and by any means, whether in handmade form (including, but not limited to, writings, drawings, paintings), photographic form (including, but not limited to, pictures or videos), or electrical, electronic or magnetic form, as well as digital data files. These terms also include any applications (i.e. software programs). These terms expressly include, among other things, Emails, instant messages, chat logs, correspondence attached as to Emails (or drafts), calendar entries, buddy lists.

ATTACHMENT "C"

PROTOCOL FOR SEARCHING THE ELECTRONIC DATA SEIZED PURSUANT TO THIS SEARCH WARRANT

1. In executing this warrant, the government must make reasonable efforts to use methods and procedures that will locate and expose in the electronic data produced in response to this search warrant ("the Search Warrant Data") those categories of data, files, documents, or other electronically stored information that are identified with particularity in the warrant, while minimizing exposure or examination of irrelevant, privileged, or confidential files to the extent reasonably practicable.

2. When the Search Warrant Data is received, the government will make a duplicate copy of the Search Warrant Data ("the Search Warrant Data Copy"). The original version of the Search Warrant Data will be sealed and preserved for purposes of: later judicial review or order to return or dispose of the Search Warrant Data; production to the defense in any criminal case if authorized by statute, rule, or the Constitution; for purposes of showing the chain of custody of the Search Warrant Data and the Search Warrant Data Copy; or for any other lawful purpose. The original of the Search Warrant Data will not be searched or examined except to ensure that it has been fully and completely replicated in the Search Warrant Data Copy.

3. The investigating agents will then search the entirety of the Search Warrant Data Copy using any and all methods and procedures deemed appropriate by the United States designed to identify the information listed as Information to be Seized in Attachment B, Section II. The United States may copy, extract or otherwise segregate information or data listed as Information to be Seized in Attachment B, Section II. Information or data so copied, extracted or otherwise segregated will no longer be subject to any handling restrictions that might be set out in this protocol beyond those required by binding law. To the extent evidence of crimes not within the scope of this warrant appear in plain view during this review, a supplemental or "piggyback" warrant will be applied for in order to further search that document, data, or other item.

4. Once the Search Warrant Data Copy has been thoroughly and completely examined for any document, data, or other items identified in Attachment B, Section II as Information to be Seized, the Search Warrant Data Copy will be sealed and not subject to any further search or examination unless authorized by another search warrant or other appropriate court order. The Search Warrant Data Copy will be held and preserved for the same purposes identified above in Paragraph 2.

5. The search procedures utilized for this review are at the sole discretion of the investigating and prosecuting authorities, and may include the following techniques (the following is a non-exclusive list, as other search procedures may be used):

    a. examination of all of the data contained in the Search Warrant Data to view the data and determine whether that data falls within the items to be seized as set forth herein;

    b. searching for and attempting to recover from the Search Warrant Data any deleted, hidden, or encrypted data to determine whether that data falls within the list of items to be seized as set forth herein (any data that is encrypted and unreadable will not be returned unless law enforcement personnel have determined that the data is not (1) an instrumentality of the offenses, (2) a fruit of the criminal activity, (3) contraband, (4) otherwise unlawfully possessed, or (5) evidence of the offenses specified above);

    c. surveying various file directories and the individual files they contain;

    d. opening files in order to determine their contents;

    e. using hash values to narrow the scope of what may be found. Hash values are under-inclusive, but are still a helpful tool;

    f. scanning storage areas;

    g. performing keyword searches through all electronic storage areas to determine whether occurrences of language contained in such storage areas exist that are likely to appear in the evidence described in Attachment A1 and A2; and/or

    h. performing any other data analysis technique that may be necessary to locate and retrieve the evidence described in Attachment B, Section II.

Return and Review Procedures

6. Rule 41 of the Federal Rules of Criminal Procedure provides, in relevant part:

(e) Issuing the Warrant.

(2) Contents of the Warrant.

(A) Warrant to Search for and Seize a Person or Property. Except for a tracking-device warrant, the warrant must identify the person or property to be searched, identify any person or property to be seized, and designate the magistrate judge to whom it must be returned. The warrant must command the officer to:

(i) execute the warrant within a specified time no longer than 14 days;

(B) Warrant Seeking Electronically Stored Information. A warrant under Rule 41(e)(2)(A) may authorize the seizure of electronic storage media or the seizure or copying of electronically stored information. Unless otherwise specified, the warrant authorizes a later review of the media or information consistent with the warrant. The time for executing the warrant in Rule 41(e)(2)(A) and (f)(1)(A) refers to the seizure or on-site copying of the media or information, and not to any later off-site copying or review.

(f) Executing and Returning the Warrant.

(1) Warrant to Search for and Seize a Person or Property.

(B) Inventory. An officer present during the execution of the warrant must prepare and verify an inventory of any property seized. . . . In a case involving the seizure of electronic storage media or the seizure or copying of electronically stored information, the inventory may be limited to describing the physical storage media that were seized or copied. The officer may retain a copy of the electronically stored information that was seized or copied.

7. Pursuant to this Rule, the government understands and will act in accordance with the following:

a. Pursuant to Rule 41(e)(2)(A)(iii), within fourteen (14) days of the execution of the warrant, an agent is required to file an inventory return with the Court, that is, to file an itemized list of the property seized. Execution of the warrant begins when the United States serves the warrant on the named custodian; execution is complete when the custodian provides all Search Warrant Data to the United States. Within fourteen (14) days of completion of the execution of the warrant, the inventory will be filed.

b. Pursuant to Rule 41(e)(2)(B), Rule 41(e)(2)(A) governs the time within which the electronically stored information must be seized after the issuance of the warrant and copied after the execution of the warrant, not the "later review of the media or information" seized, or the later off-site digital copying of that media.

c. Under Rule 41(f)(1)(B), the inventory return that is to be filed with the court may be limited to a description of the "physical storage media" into which the Search Warrant Data that was seized was placed, not an itemization of the information or data stored on the "physical storage media" into which the Search Warrant Data was placed;

d. Under Rule 41(f)(1)(B), the government may retain a copy of that information for purposes of the investigation. The government proposes that the original storage media on which the Search Warrant Data was placed plus a full image copy of the seized Search Warrant Data be retained by the government.

e. If the person from whom any Search Warrant Data was seized requests the return of any information in the Search Warrant Data that is not set forth in Attachment B, Section II, that information will be copied onto appropriate media and returned to the person from whom the information was seized.

AO 93 (Rev. 11/13) Search and Seizure Warrant

UNITED STATES DISTRICT COURT
for the
District of Nevada

2017 OCT 13 PM 12: 30
U.S. MAGISTRATE JUDGE
BY_____

In the Matter of the Search of)
(Briefly describe the property to be searched)
or identify the person by name and address)) Case No. 2:17-mj-01009-NJK
)
EMAIL ACCOUNT CENTRALPARK1@LIVE.COM THAT)
IS STORED AT A PREMISES CONTROLLED BY)
MICROSOFT. A1)

SEARCH AND SEIZURE WARRANT

To: Any authorized law enforcement officer

An application by a federal law enforcement officer or an attorney for the government requests the search of the following person or property located in the _____ District of _____Nevada_____
(identify the person or describe the property to be searched and give its location):

SEE ATTACHMENT A1

I find that the affidavit(s), or any recorded testimony, establish probable cause to search and seize the person or property described above, and that such search will reveal *(identify the person or describe the property to be seized):*

SEE ATTACHMENTS B and C

YOU ARE COMMANDED to execute this warrant on or before October 27, 2017 *(not to exceed 14 days)*
☑ in the daytime 6:00 a.m. to 10:00 p.m.   ☐ at any time in the day or night because good cause has been established.

Unless delayed notice is authorized below, you must give a copy of the warrant and a receipt for the property taken to the person from whom, or from whose premises, the property was taken, or leave the copy and receipt at the place where the property was taken.

The officer executing this warrant, or an officer present during the execution of the warrant, must prepare an inventory as required by law and promptly return this warrant and inventory to _____NANCY J. KOPPE_____.
(United States Magistrate Judge)

☐ Pursuant to 18 U.S.C. § 3103a(b), I find that immediate notification may have an adverse result listed in 18 U.S.C. § 2705 (except for delay of trial), and authorize the officer executing this warrant to delay notice to the person who, or whose property, will be searched or seized *(check the appropriate box)*
☐ for ____ days *(not to exceed 30)* ☐ until, the facts justifying, the later specific date of _____.

Date and time issued: 10/13/17 12:30 p.m.

City and state: Las Vegas, Nevada

NANCY J. KOPPE
Judge's signature

UNITED STATES MAGISTRATE JUDGE
Printed name and title

ATTACHMENT "A-1"

ONLINE ACCOUNT TO BE SEARCHED

This warrant applies to information associated with the Microsoft email account centralpark1@live.com (the "Target Account 1") from inception to present, which is stored at premises owned, maintained, controlled, or operated by Microsoft Corporation, headquartered at 1 Microsoft Way, Redmond, Washington, 98052.

ATTACHMENT "B"
Particular Things to be Seized

I. **Information to be disclosed by the Service Provider**

To the extent that the information described in Attachments A1 and A2 is within the possession, custody, or control of Microsoft, including any Emails, records, files, logs, or information that have been deleted but are still available to Service Provider, or have been preserved pursuant to a request made under 18 U.S.C. § 2703(f), Service Provider is required to disclose the following information to the government for each account or identifier listed in Attachments A-1 and A-2 from account inception to present:

a. The contents of all communications, transactions, records, documents, programs, or materials stored in or associated with any OneDrive accounts associated with or assigned to Target Accounts 1 and 2.

b. The contents of all communications, transactions, records, documents, programs, or materials stored in or associated with any Office 360 accounts associated with or assigned to Target Accounts 1 and 2.

c. The contents of all communications, transactions, records, documents, programs, or materials stored in or associated with any Microsoft Family Safety accounts or services associated with or assigned to Target Accounts 1 and 2.

d. The contents of all communications, transactions, records, documents, programs, or materials stored in or associated with any Windows Live Writer accounts or services associated with or assigned to Target Accounts 1 and 2.

e. The contents of all communications, transactions, records, documents, programs, or materials stored in or associated with any Windows Live Mail accounts or services associated with or assigned to Target Accounts 1 and 2.

f. The contents of all communications, transactions, records, documents, programs, or materials stored in or associated with any Windows Photo Gallery accounts or services associated with or assigned to Target Accounts 1 and 2.

g. The contents of all communications, transactions, records, documents, programs, or materials stored in or associated with any Windows Live Messenger accounts or services associated with or assigned to Target Accounts 1 and 2.

II. **Information to be seized by the United States**

After reviewing all information described in Section I, the United States will seize evidence of violations of Title 18, United States Code Sections 32(a) (Destruction/Damage of Aircraft or Aircraft Facilities); 37(a)(2) (Violence at International Airport); and 922(a)(3); and 5 (Unlawful Interstate Transport/Delivery of Firearms by Non Federal Firearms Licensee); and 2 (Aiding and Abetting) (the "Subject Offenses") that occur in the form of the following, from account inception to present:

a. Communications, transactions and records that may establish ownership and control (or the degree thereof) of the Target Account, including address books, contact or buddy lists, bills, invoices, receipts, registration records, bills, correspondence, notes, records, memoranda, telephone/address books, photographs, video recordings, audio recordings, lists of names, records of payment for access to newsgroups or other online subscription services, and attachments to said communications, transactions and records.

b. Communications, transactions and records to/from persons who may be co-conspirators of the Subject Offenses, or which may identify co-conspirators.

c. Communications, transactions and records which may show motivation to commit the Subject Offenses.

d. Communications, transactions and records that relate to the Subject Offenses.

e. The terms "communications," "transactions", "records," "documents," "programs," or "materials" include all information recorded in any form, visual or aural, and by any means, whether in handmade form (including, but not limited to, writings, drawings, paintings), photographic form (including, but not limited to, pictures or videos), or electrical, electronic or magnetic form, as well as digital data files. These terms also include any applications (i.e. software programs). These terms expressly include, among other things, Emails, instant messages, chat logs, correspondence attached as to Emails (or drafts), calendar entries, buddy lists.

STEVEN W. MYHRE
Acting United States Attorney
District of Nevada
CRISTINA D. SILVA
PATRICK BURNS
Assistant United States Attorneys
501 Las Vegas Blvd. South, Ste. 1100
Las Vegas, Nevada 89101
Telephone: (702) 388-6336
Fax (702) 388-6698
john.p.burns@usdoj.gov

Attorney for the United States of America

UNITED STATES DISTRICT COURT
DISTRICT OF NEVADA
-oOo-

IN THE MATTER OF THE SEARCH OF INFORMATION ASSOCIATED WITH EMAIL ACCOUNTS CENTRALPARK1@LIVE.COM THAT IS STORED AT A PREMISES CONTROLLED BY MICROSOFT. A1	Magistrate No. 17-mj-968-NJK **AFFIDAVIT IN SUPPORT OF AN APPLICATION FOR SEARCH WARRANTS** (Under Seal)
IN THE MATTER OF THE SEARCH OF INFORMATION ASSOCIATED WITH EMAIL ACCOUNTS MARILOUROSES@LIVE.COM THAT IS STORED AT A PREMISES CONTROLLED BY MICROSOFT. A2	Magistrate No. **AFFIDAVIT IN SUPPORT OF AN APPLICATION FOR SEARCH WARRANTS** (Under Seal)

STATE OF NEVADA   )
) ss:
COUNTY OF CLARK   )

AFFIDAVIT IN SUPPORT OF AN APPLICATION FOR SEARCH WARRANTS

I, Ryan S. Burke, Special Agent, Federal Bureau of Investigation (FBI), having been duly sworn, hereby depose and say:

INTRODUCTION AND AGENT BACKGROUND

1. Your Affiant makes this affidavit in support of an application for search warrants for information associated with email accounts centralpark1@live.com ("Target Account 1") and marilouroses@live.com ("Target Account 2"). Target Account 1 is an account associated with STEPHEN PADDOCK. Target Account 2 is an account associated with MARILOU DANLEY. The information associated with both accounts is stored at a premises owned, maintained, controlled, or operated by Microsoft Corporation ("Microsoft"), an American multinational technology company based in Redmond, Washington that specializes in Internet-related services and products along with the development and manufacturing of computer-related items. Those online services include, but are not limited to, email services, cloud computing, and many other services. The information to be searched is described in the following paragraphs and in Attachment "A" (attached hereto and incorporated herein by reference). This affidavit is made in support of an application for search warrants under 18 U.S.C. §§ 2703(a), 2703(b)(1)(A), and 2703(c)(1)(A) to require Microsoft to disclose to the government records and other information in its possession, pertaining to the subscriber or customer associated with the Target Accounts.

2. I am an "investigative or law enforcement officer of the United States" within the meaning of Title 18, United States Code, Section 2510(7), that is, an officer of

the United States who is empowered by law to conduct investigations of, and to make arrests for, offenses enumerated in Title 18, United States Code, Section 2516.

3. I have been employed as a Special Agent of the FBI for approximately five years, which began at the FBI Academy in October 2012. Upon completion of the academy, I was transferred to the Las Vegas Division's white collar crime squad and then the human trafficking squad. Since October 2015, I have been assigned to the Las Vegas Division's violent crime/gang squad. Additionally, I have been a certified member of the FBI's Cellular Analysis Survey Team since August 2015 due to my expertise in the field of historical cell site analysis.

4. During my tenure with the FBI, I have conducted surveillance, analyzed telephone records, interviewed witnesses, supervised activities of sources, executed search warrants, executed arrest warrants, and participated in court-authorized interceptions of wire and electronic communications. These investigative activities have been conducted in conjunction with a variety of investigations, to include those involving robbery, drug trafficking, kidnapping, murder, criminal enterprises, and more. In addition to my practical experiences, I received five months of extensive law enforcement training at the FBI Academy.

5. The facts in this affidavit are derived from your Affiant's personal observations, his training and experience, and information obtained from other agents, detectives, and witnesses. This affidavit is intended to show merely that there is sufficient probable cause for the requested warrants and does not set forth all of the Affiant's knowledge about this matter.

6. Based on your Affiant's training and experience and the facts as set forth in this affidavit, there is probable cause to believe that violations of:

    a. Destruction/Damage of Aircraft or Aircraft Facilities - 18 U.S.C.A. § 32(a);

    b. Violence at International Airport - 18 U.S.C. § 37(a)(2); and

    c. Unlawful Interstate Transport/Delivery of Firearms by Non Federal Firearms Licensee – 18 U.S.C. §§ 922(a)(3) and (5);

    d. Aiding and Abetting – 18 U.S.C. § 2.

(hereafter, "Subject Offenses") have been committed by STEPHEN PADDOCK, MARILOU DANLEY, and others yet unknown. There is also probable cause to search the information described in Attachment "A" for evidence of these crimes and information which might reveal the identities of others involved in these crimes, as described in Attachment "B" (attached hereto and incorporated herein by reference).

PROBABLE CAUSE

7. On the evening of Sunday, October 1, 2017, Route 91 Harvest, a music festival, was in progress at 3901 South Las Vegas Boulevard, Las Vegas, Nevada. At approximately 10:08 p.m., the Las Vegas Metropolitan Police Department (LVMPD) received calls reporting shots had been fired at the concert and multiple victims were struck. LVMPD determined the shots were coming from Rooms 134 and 135 on the 32nd floor of the Mandalay Bay Resort and Casino, located due west of the festival rounds at 3950 South Las Vegas Boulevard, Las Vegas, Nevada. These rooms are an elevated position which overlooks the concert venue. Witness statements and video footage captured during the attack indicates that the weapons being used were firing in a fully-automatic fashion.

8. LVMPD officers ultimately made entry into the room and located an individual later identified as Stephen Paddock. Paddock was deceased from an apparent self-inflicted gunshot wound.

9. Paddock's Nevada driver's license was located in the Mandalay Bay hotel room with Paddock, and both hotel rooms were registered in his name. A player's club card in name of Marilou Danley was located in Paddock's room, and the card returned to the address located on Babbling Brook Street in Mesquite, Nevada. FBI Agents located Danley, who was traveling outside the United States at the time of the shooting. It was ultimately determined that Danley resided with Paddock at the Babbling Brook address.

10. On October 2, 2017, search warrants were executed on Paddock's Mandalay Bay hotel rooms, Paddock's vehicle at Mandalay Bay, and two Nevada residences owed by Paddock: 1372 Babbling Brook Court in Mesquite, and 1735 Del Webb Parkway in Reno, Nevada. Officers and Agents found over 20 firearms, hundreds of rounds of ammunition, and hundreds of spent shell casings in the Mandalay Bay hotel rooms, in close proximity to Paddock's body. Over a thousand rounds of rifle ammunition and 100 pounds of explosive material was found in Paddock's vehicle. Additional explosive material, approximately 18 firearms, and over 1,000 rounds of ammunition was located at the Mesquite residence. A large quantity of ammunition and multiple firearms were recovered from the Reno residence.

11. As of this date, 58 people have been identified to have been killed in Paddock's attack and another 557 were reportedly injured. Additionally, investigators discovered that STEPHEN PADDOCK also utilized a firearm to shoot large fuel tanks

on Las Vegas McCarran International Airport property. Multiple bullet holes were found on the tank, which investigators believe was an attempt by STEPHEN PADDOCK to cause the tanks to explode.

12. In an effort to determine whether or not STEPHEN PADDOCK was assisted and/or conspired with unknown individuals, investigators have attempted to identify all of STEPHEN PADDOCK's associated. It was quickly determined that a casino player's card in the name of MARILOU DANLEY was located in the room at the time of the attack. She has been identified thus far as the most likely person who aided or abetted STEPHEN PADDOCK based on her informing law enforcement that her fingerprints would likely be found on the ammunition used during the attack. Subsequently, investigators worked to identify the communication facilities utilized by STEPHEN PADDOCK and MARILOU DANLEY.

13. Based on a review of STEPHEN PADDOCK's financial accounts, Target Account 1 was determined to belong to STEPHEN PADDOCK. On October 3, 2017, investigators requested an emergency disclosure of records from Microsoft related to Target Account 1 so it could be immediately searched for any evidence of additional co-conspirators. Unfortunately, the information was only requested for a six month timeframe. Within the account, investigators identified Target Account 2 as one that belonged to MARILOU DANLEY, which was clear based on the communications between the two email accounts.

14. On September 25, 2017, an email was exchanged between the Target Accounts which discussed a wire transfer of funds which was to be sent by STEPHEN

PADDOCK to MARILOU DANLEY. It is unclear what the purpose of the wire transfer was, but MARILOU DANLEY is known to have been in the Philippines at the time.

15. Additionally, on July 6, 2017, Target Account 1 sent an email to centralpark4804@gmail.com which read, "try an ar before u buy. we have huge selection. located in the las vegas area." Later that day, an email was received back from centralpark4804@gmail.com to Target Account 1 that read, "we have a wide variety of optics and ammunition to try." And lastly, Target Account 1 later sent an email to centralpark4804@gmail.com that read, "for a thrill try out bumpfire ar's with a 100 round magazine." Investigators believe these communications may have been related to the eventual attack that occurred at the Mandalay Bay in Las Vegas.

16. Your Affiant believes the requested search warrants will yield significant information from Microsoft such as STEPHEN PADDOCK's and MARILOU DANLEY's contact lists, email messages content, IP address usage, photographs, third-party applications associated with the account, and more, which may constitute evidence of the planning of the attack and potentially identify other participants in the attack. Ultimately, your Affiant strongly believes the requested information will lead investigators to determine the full scope of STEPHEN PADDOCK's plan and MARILOU DANLEY's possible involvement.

RELEVANT TECHNICAL TERMS

17. The following non-exhaustive list of definitions applies to this Affidavit and the Attachments to this Affidavit:

a. The "Internet" is a worldwide network of computer systems operated by governmental entities, corporations, and universities. In order to access the Internet, an individual computer user must subscribe to an access provider, which operates a host computer system with direct access to the Internet. The World Wide Web is a functionality of the Internet which allows users of the Internet to share information.

   b. "Internet Service Providers" are companies that provide access to the Internet. ISPs can also provide other services for their customers including website hosting, email service, remote storage, and co-location of computers and other communications equipment. ISPs offer different ways to access the Internet including telephone-based (dial-up), broadband-based access via a digital subscriber line (DSL) or cable television, dedicated circuits, or satellite-based subscription. ISPs typically charge a fee based upon the type of connection and volume of data (bandwidth). Many ISPs assign each subscriber an account name, such as a user name, an email address, and an email mailbox, and the subscriber typically creates a password for his/her account.

   c. "ISP Records" are records maintained by ISPs pertaining to their subscribers (regardless of whether those subscribers are individuals or entities). These records may include account application information, subscriber and billing information, account access information (often in the form of log files), emails, information concerning content uploaded and/or stored on the ISP's servers, and other information, which may be stored both in computer data format and in written or printed record format. ISPs reserve and/or maintain computer disk storage space on their computer system for their subscribers' use. This service by ISPs allows for both temporary and long-term storage of electronic communications and many other types of electronic data and files.

   d. "Online service providers" (also referred to here as "service providers") are companies that provide online services such as email, chat or instant messaging, word processing applications, spreadsheet applications, presentation applications similar to PowerPoint, online calendar, photo storage and remote storage services. Sometimes they also can provide web hosting, remote storage, and co-location of computers and other communications equipment. Typically, each service provider assigns each subscriber an account name, such as a user name or screen name and the subscriber typically creates a password for his/her account.

e. "Computer," as used herein, is defined as "an electronic, magnetic, optical, electrochemical, or other high speed data processing device performing logical or storage functions, and includes any data storage facility or communications facility directly related to or operating in conjunction with such device."

f. A "server" is a centralized computer that provides services for other computers connected to it via a network. The other computers attached to a server are sometimes called "clients." For example, in a large company, it is common for individual employees to have client computers at their desktops. When the employees access their email, or access files stored on the network itself, those files are pulled electronically from the server, where they are stored, and are sent to the client's computer via the network. Notably, servers can be physically stored in any location: it is not uncommon for a network's server to be located hundreds (and even thousands) of miles away from the client computers.

g. "Internet Protocol address," or "IP address," refers to a unique number used by a computer to access the Internet. IP addresses can be dynamic, meaning that the Internet Service Provider (ISP) assigns a different unique number to a computer every time it accesses the Internet. IP addresses might also be static, that

is, an ISP assigns a user's computer a particular IP address which is used each time the computer accesses the Internet.

      h.   The term "domain" refers to a word used as a name for computers, networks, services, etc. A domain name typically represents a website, a server computer that hosts that website, or even some computer (or other digital device) connected to the internet. Essentially, when a website (or a server computer that hosts that website) is connected to the internet, it is assigned an IP address. Because IP addresses are difficult for people to remember, domain names are instead used because they are easier to remember than IP addresses. Domain names are formed by the rules and procedures of the Domain Name System (DNS). A common top level domain under these rules is ".com" for commercial organizations, ".gov" for the United States government, and ".org" for organizations. For example, www.usdoj.gov is the domain name that identifies a server used by the U.S. Department of Justice, and which uses IP address of 149.101.46.71.

      i.   "Web hosting services" maintain server computers connected to the Internet. Their customers use those computers to operate websites on the Internet. Customers of web hosting companies place files, software code, databases, and other data on servers. To do this, customers typically connect from their own computers to the server computers across the Internet.

      j.   The term "WhoIs" lookup refers to a search of a publicly available online database that lists information provided when a domain is registered or when an IP address is assigned.

      k.   The terms "communications," "records," "documents," "programs," or "materials" include all information recorded in any form, visual or aural, and by any

means, whether in handmade form (including, but not limited to, writings, drawings, paintings), photographic form (including, but not limited to, pictures or videos), or electrical, electronic or magnetic form, as well as digital data files. These terms also include any applications (i.e. software programs). These terms expressly include, among other things, emails, instant messages, chat logs, correspondence attached as to emails (or drafts), calendar entries, buddy lists.

l. "Chat" is usually a real time electronic communication between two or more individuals. Unlike email, which is frequently sent, then read and responded to minutes, hours, or even days later, chats frequently involve an immediate conversation between individuals, similar to a face-to-face conversation. Nearly all chat programs are capable of saving the chat transcript, to enable users to preserve a record of the conversation. By default, some chat programs have this capability enabled, while others do not. Many popular web-based email providers, like Microsoft and Microsoft, provide chat functionality as part of the online services they provide to account holders.

FACTS ABOUT EMAIL PROVIDERS

18. In my training, my experience and this investigation, I have learned that Microsoft (the Service Provider) is a company that provides free web-based Internet email access to the general public, and that stored electronic communications, including opened and unopened email for Microsoft subscribers may be located on the computers of Microsoft. I have also learned that Microsoft Inc. provides various on-line service messaging services to the general public. Instant Messaging ("IM") is a form of real-time direct text-based communication between two or more people using shared clients. The text is conveyed via devices connected over a network such as the Internet. In addition

to text, Microsoft's software allows users with the most current updated versions to utilize its webcam service. This option enables users from distances all over the world to view others who have installed a webcam on their end. Thus, the Service Provider's servers will contain a wide variety of the subscriber's files, including emails, address books, contact or buddy lists, calendar data, pictures, chat logs, and other files.

19. To use these services, subscribers register for online accounts like the Target Accounts. During the registration process, service providers such as the ones here ask subscribers to provide basic personal information. This information can include the subscriber's full name, physical address, telephone numbers and other identifiers, alternative email addresses, and, for paying subscribers, means and source of payment (including any credit card or bank account number). Based on my training and my experience, I know that subscribers may insert false information to conceal their identity; even if this proves to be the case, however, I know that this information often provide clues to their identity, location or illicit activities.

20. In general, when a subscriber receives an email, it is typically stored in the subscriber's "mail box" on that service provider's servers until the subscriber deletes the Email. If the subscriber does not delete the message, the message (and any attachments) can remain on that service provider's servers indefinitely.

21. Similarly, when the subscriber sends an email, it is initiated at the subscriber's computer, transferred via the Internet to the service provider's servers, and then transmitted to its end destination. That service provider often saves a copy of the email sent. Unless the sender of the email specifically deletes the Email from the provider's server, the email can remain on the system indefinitely.

22. A sent or received email typically includes the content of the message, source and destination addresses, the date and time at which the email was sent, and the size and length of the email. If an email user writes a draft message but does not send it, that message may also be saved by that service provider, but may not include all of these categories of data.

23. Just as a computer on a desk can be used to store a wide variety of files, so can online accounts, such as the accounts subject to this application. First, subscribers can store many types of files as attachments to emails in online accounts. Second, because service providers provide the services listed above (e.g. word processing, spreadsheets, pictures), subscribers who use these services usually store documents on servers maintained and/or owned by service providers. Thus, these online accounts often contain documents such as pictures, audio or video recordings, logs, spreadsheets, applications and other files.

24. Reviewing files stored in online accounts raises many of the same difficulties as with reviewing files stored on a local computer. For example, based on my training, my experience and this investigation, I know that subscribers of these online services can conceal their activities by altering files before they upload them to the online service. Subscribers can change file names to more innocuous sounding names (e.g. renaming "FraudRecords.doc" to "ChristmasList.doc"), they can change file extensions to make one kind of file appear like a different type of file (e.g. changing the spreadsheet "StolenCreditProfiles.xls" to "FamilyPhoto.jpg" to appear to be a picture file, where the file extension ".xls" denotes an Excel spreadsheet file and ".jpg" a JPEG format image file), or they can change the times and dates a file was last accessed or modified by

changing a computer's system time/date and then uploading that file to the Online Accounts. Thus, to detect any files that the subscriber may have concealed, agents will need to review all of the files in the Target Accounts; they will, however, only seize the items that the Court authorizes to be seized. Similarly, subscribers can conceal their activities by encrypting files. Thus, these files may need to be decrypted to detect whether it constitutes an Item to be Seized.

25. I also believe that people engaged in crimes such as the one described herein often use online accounts because they give people engaged in these crimes a way to easily communicate with other co-conspirators. Moreover, online accounts are easily concealed from law enforcement. Unlike physical documents, electronic documents can be stored in a physical place far away, where they are less likely to be discovered.

26. Service providers typically retain certain transactional information about the creation and use of each account on their systems. This information can include the date on which the account was created, the length of service, records of log-in (i.e., session) times and durations, the types of service utilized, the status of the account (including whether the account is inactive or closed), the methods used to connect to the account (such as logging into the account via websites controlled by the Service Provider), and other log files that reflect usage of the account. In addition, service providers often have records of the Internet Protocol address ("IP address") used to register the account and the IP addresses associated with particular logins to the account. Because every device that connects to the Internet must use an IP address, IP address information can help to identify which computers or other devices were used to access the online account.

27. In some cases, subscribers will communicate directly with a service provider about issues relating to the account, such as technical problems, billing inquiries, or complaints from or about other users. Service providers typically retain records about such communications, including records of contacts between the user and the provider's support services, as well records of any actions taken by the provider or user as a result of the communications.

28. In my training and experience, evidence of who was using an online account may be found in address books, contact or buddy lists, emails in the account, and pictures and files, whether stored as attachments or in the suite of the service provider's online applications. Therefore, the computers of the Service Providers are likely to contain stored electronic communications (including retrieved and un-retrieved email for their subscribers) and information concerning subscribers and their use of the provider's services, such as account access information, email transaction information, documents, pictures, and account application information.

INFORMATION TO BE SEARCHED AND THINGS TO BE SEIZED

29. Your Affiant anticipates executing these warrants under the Electronic Communications Privacy Act, in particular 18 U.S.C. §§ 2703(a), 2703(b)(1)(A) and 2703(c)(1)(A), by using the warrant to require Microsoft to disclose to the government copies of the records and other information (including the content of communications) particularly described in Section I of Attachment "B." Upon receipt of the information described in Section I of Attachment "B," government-authorized persons will review that information to locate the items described in Section II of Attachment "B."

CONCLUSION

30. Based on the forgoing, I request that the Court issue the proposed search warrant. This Court has jurisdiction to issue the requested warrant because it is "a court of competent jurisdiction" as defined by 18 U.S.C. § 2711. 18 U.S.C. §§ 2703(a), (b)(1)(A) & (c)(1)(A). Specifically, the Court is "a district court of the United States . . . that – has jurisdiction over the offense being investigated." 18 U.S.C. § 2711(3)(A)(i). Pursuant to 18 U.S.C. § 2703(g), the presence of a law enforcement officer is not required for the service or execution of this warrant.

REQUEST FOR SEALING

31. I further request that the Court order that all papers in support of this application, including the affidavit and search warrant, be sealed until further order of the Court. These documents discuss an ongoing criminal investigation that is neither public nor known to all of the targets of the investigation. Accordingly, there is good cause to seal these documents because their premature disclosure may seriously jeopardize that investigation.

Respectfully Submitted,

Ryan S. Burke, Special Agent
Federal Bureau of Investigation

SWORN TO AND SUBSCRIBED
before me this 6th day of October 2017.

UNITED STATES MAGISTRATE JUDGE

ATTACHMENT "A1"

ONLINE ACCOUNT TO BE SEARCHED

1. This warrant applies to information associated with the Microsoft email account centralpark1@live.com (the "Target Accounts") from their inception to present, which is stored at premises owned, maintained, controlled, or operated by Microsoft Corporation, headquartered at 1 Microsoft Way, Redmond, Washington, 98052.

ATTACHMENT "A2"

ONLINE ACCOUNT TO BE SEARCHED

1. This warrant applies to information associated with the Microsoft email account marilouroses@live.com (the "Target Accounts") from their inception to present, which is stored at premises owned, maintained, controlled, or operated by Microsoft Corporation, headquartered at 1 Microsoft Way, Redmond, Washington, 98052.

ATTACHMENT "B"
Particular Things to be Seized

I. **Information to be disclosed by the Service Provider**

To the extent that the information described in Attachment A1 and A2 is within the possession, custody, or control of Microsoft, including any Emails, records, files, logs, or information that have been deleted but are still available to Service Provider, or have been preserved pursuant to a request made under 18 U.S.C. § 2703(f), Service Provider is required to disclose the following information to the government for each account or identifier listed in Attachment A1 and A2 from account inception to present:

   a. The contents of all emails associated with the account, including copies of emails sent to and from the account, draft emails, the source and destination addresses associated with each email, the date and time at which each email was sent, and the size and length of each email;

   b. All records or other information regarding the identification of the account, to include full name, physical address, telephone numbers and other identifiers, records of session times and durations, the date on which the account was created, the length of service, the types of service utilized, the IP address used to register the account, log-in IP addresses associated with session times and dates, account status, alternative email addresses provided during registration, methods of connecting, log files, and means and source of payment (including any credit or bank account number);

   c. All records or other information stored in the Online Accounts, including address books, contact and buddy lists, calendar data, pictures, applications, documents, and other files;

   d. All records pertaining to communications between Service Provider and any person regarding the account, including contacts with support services and records of actions taken.

   e. All third-party application data and content associated with the Target Account through any Android operating system and/or any Microsoft-related facility.

II. **Information to be seized by the United States**

After reviewing all information described in Section I, the United States will seize evidence of violations of Title 18, United States Code Sections 32(a) (Destruction/Damage of Aircraft or Aircraft Facilities); 37(a)(2) (Violence at International Airport); and 922(a)(3); and 5 (Unlawful Interstate Transport/Delivery of Firearms by Non Federal Firearms Licensee); and 2 (Aiding and Abetting) (the "Subject Offenses") that occur in the form of the following, from account inception to present:

a. Communications, transactions and records that may establish ownership and control (or the degree thereof) of the Target Account, including address books, contact or buddy lists, bills, invoices, receipts, registration records, bills, correspondence, notes, records, memoranda, telephone/address books, photographs, video recordings, audio recordings, lists of names, records of payment for access to newsgroups or other online subscription services, and attachments to said communications, transactions and records.

b. Communications, transactions and records to/from persons who may be co-conspirators of the Subject Offenses, or which may identify co-conspirators.

c. Communications, transactions and records which may show motivation to commit the Subject Offenses.

d. Communications, transactions and records that relate to the Subject Offenses.

e. The terms "communications," "transactions", "records," "documents," "programs," or "materials" include all information recorded in any form, visual or aural, and by any means, whether in handmade form (including, but not limited to, writings, drawings, paintings), photographic form (including, but not limited to, pictures or videos), or electrical, electronic or magnetic form, as well as digital data files. These terms also include any applications (i.e. software programs). These terms expressly include, among other things, Emails, instant messages, chat logs, correspondence attached as to Emails (or drafts), calendar entries, buddy lists.

ATTACHMENT "C"

PROTOCOL FOR SEARCHING THE ELECTRONIC DATA SEIZED PURSUANT TO THIS SEARCH WARRANT

1. In executing this warrant, the government must make reasonable efforts to use methods and procedures that will locate and expose in the electronic data produced in response to this search warrant ("the Search Warrant Data") those categories of data, files, documents, or other electronically stored information that are identified with particularity in the warrant, while minimizing exposure or examination of irrelevant, privileged, or confidential files to the extent reasonably practicable.

2. When the Search Warrant Data is received, the government will make a duplicate copy of the Search Warrant Data ("the Search Warrant Data Copy"). The original version of the Search Warrant Data will be sealed and preserved for purposes of: later judicial review or order to return or dispose of the Search Warrant Data; production to the defense in any criminal case if authorized by statute, rule, or the Constitution; for purposes of showing the chain of custody of the Search Warrant Data and the Search Warrant Data Copy; or for any other lawful purpose. The original of the Search Warrant Data will not be searched or examined except to ensure that it has been fully and completely replicated in the Search Warrant Data Copy.

3. The investigating agents will then search the entirety of the Search Warrant Data Copy using any and all methods and procedures deemed appropriate by the United States designed to identify the information listed as Information to be Seized in Attachment B, Section II. The United States may copy, extract or otherwise segregate information or data listed as Information to be Seized in Attachment B, Section II. Information or data so copied, extracted or otherwise segregated will no longer be subject to any handling restrictions that might be set out in this protocol beyond those required by binding law. To the extent evidence of crimes not within the scope of this warrant appear in plain view during this review, a supplemental or "piggyback" warrant will be applied for in order to further search that document, data, or other item.

4. Once the Search Warrant Data Copy has been thoroughly and completely examined for any document, data, or other items identified in Attachment B, Section II as Information to be Seized, the Search Warrant Data Copy will be sealed and not subject to any further search or examination unless authorized by another search warrant or other appropriate court order. The Search Warrant Data Copy will be held and preserved for the same purposes identified above in Paragraph 2.

5. The search procedures utilized for this review are at the sole discretion of the investigating and prosecuting authorities, and may include the following techniques (the following is a non-exclusive list, as other search procedures may be used):

a. examination of all of the data contained in the Search Warrant Data to view the data and determine whether that data falls within the items to be seized as set forth herein;

b. searching for and attempting to recover from the Search Warrant Data any deleted, hidden, or encrypted data to determine whether that data falls within the list of items to be seized as set forth herein (any data that is encrypted and unreadable will not be returned unless law enforcement personnel have determined that the data is not (1) an instrumentality of the offenses, (2) a fruit of the criminal activity, (3) contraband, (4) otherwise unlawfully possessed, or (5) evidence of the offenses specified above);

c. surveying various file directories and the individual files they contain;

d. opening files in order to determine their contents;

e. using hash values to narrow the scope of what may be found. Hash values are under- inclusive, but are still a helpful tool;

f. scanning storage areas;

g. performing keyword searches through all electronic storage areas to determine whether occurrences of language contained in such storage areas exist that are likely to appear in the evidence described in Attachment A1 and A2; and/or

h. performing any other data analysis technique that may be necessary to locate and retrieve the evidence described in Attachment B, Section II.

Return and Review Procedures

6. Rule 41 of the Federal Rules of Criminal Procedure provides, in relevant part:

(e) Issuing the Warrant.

(2) Contents of the Warrant.

(A) Warrant to Search for and Seize a Person or Property. Except for a tracking-device warrant, the warrant must identify the person or property to be searched, identify any person or property to be seized, and designate the magistrate judge to whom it must be returned. The warrant must command the officer to:

(i) execute the warrant within a specified time no longer than 14 days;

(B) Warrant Seeking Electronically Stored Information. A warrant under Rule 41(e)(2)(A) may authorize the seizure of electronic storage media or the seizure or copying of electronically stored information. Unless otherwise specified, the warrant authorizes a later review of the media or information consistent with the warrant. The time for executing the warrant in Rule 41(e)(2)(A) and (f)(1)(A) refers to the seizure or on-site copying of the media or information, and not to any later off-site copying or review.

(f) Executing and Returning the Warrant.

(1) Warrant to Search for and Seize a Person or Property.

(B) Inventory. An officer present during the execution of the warrant must prepare and verify an inventory of any property seized. . . . In a case involving the seizure of electronic storage media or the seizure or copying of electronically stored information, the inventory may be limited to describing the physical storage media that were seized or copied. The officer may retain a copy of the electronically stored information that was seized or copied.

7. Pursuant to this Rule, the government understands and will act in accordance with the following:

a. Pursuant to Rule 41(e)(2)(A)(iii), within fourteen (14) days of the execution of the warrant, an agent is required to file an inventory return with the Court, that is, to file an itemized list of the property seized. Execution of the warrant begins when the United States serves the warrant on the named custodian; execution is complete when the custodian provides all Search Warrant Data to the United States. Within fourteen (14) days of completion of the execution of the warrant, the inventory will be filed.

b. Pursuant to Rule 41(e)(2)(B), Rule 41(e)(2)(A) governs the time within which the electronically stored information must be seized after the issuance of the warrant and copied after the execution of the warrant, not the "later review of the media or information" seized, or the later off-site digital copying of that media.

c. Under Rule 41(f)(1)(B), the inventory return that is to be filed with the court may be limited to a description of the "physical storage media" into which the Search Warrant Data that was seized was placed, not an itemization of the information or data stored on the "physical storage media" into which the Search Warrant Data was placed;

d. Under Rule 41(f)(1)(B), the government may retain a copy of that information for purposes of the investigation. The government proposes that the original storage media on which the Search Warrant Data was placed plus a full image copy of the seized Search Warrant Data be retained by the government.

e. If the person from whom any Search Warrant Data was seized requests the return of any information in the Search Warrant Data that is not set forth in Attachment B, Section II, that information will be copied onto appropriate media and returned to the person from whom the information was seized.

AO 93 (Rev. 11/13) Search and Seizure Warrant   10-3-17

UNITED STATES DISTRICT COURT
for the
District of Nevada

I hereby attest and certify on _____
that the foregoing document is a full true and correct
copy of the original on file in my office, and in my legal
custody.

CAM FERENBACH
U.S. MAGISTRATE JUDGE
DISTRICT OF NEVADA

By _____ ☒ Deputy / Secretary

In the Matter of the Search of)
(Briefly describe the property to be searched)
or identify the person by name and address))   Case No.   2:17-mj-00960-VCF
)
Mariloudanleyy A3   )
)
)

SEARCH AND SEIZURE WARRANT

To: Any authorized law enforcement officer

An application by a federal law enforcement officer or an attorney for the government requests the search
of the following person or property located in the _____ District of _____Nevada_____
(identify the person or describe the property to be searched and give its location):

SEE ATTACHMENT A3

I find that the affidavit(s), or any recorded testimony, establish probable cause to search and seize the person or property
described above, and that such search will reveal *(identify the person or describe the property to be seized):*

SEE ATTACHMENTS B and C

☒ **YOU ARE COMMANDED** to execute this warrant on or before ___10-12-17___ *(not to exceed 14 days)*
☒ in the daytime 6:00 a.m. to 10:00 p.m.   ☐ at any time in the day or night because good cause has been established.

Unless delayed notice is authorized below, you must give a copy of the warrant and a receipt for the property taken to the
person from whom, or from whose premises, the property was taken, or leave the copy and receipt at the place where the
property was taken.

The officer executing this warrant, or an officer present during the execution of the warrant, must prepare an inventory
as required by law and promptly return this warrant and inventory to _____CAM FERENBACH_____
                                                                    (United States Magistrate Judge)

☐ Pursuant to 18 U.S.C. § 3103a(b), I find that immediate notification may have an adverse result listed in 18 U.S.C.
§ 2705 (except for delay of trial), and authorize the officer executing this warrant to delay notice to the person who, or whose
property, will be searched or seized *(check the appropriate box)*
 ☐ for ____ days *(not to exceed 30)*   ☐ until, the facts justifying, the later specific date of _____

Date and time issued: 10-3-17 4:04p   CAM FERENBACH
                                               Judge's Signature
                                               CAM FERENBACH
                                               U.S. MAGISTRATE JUDGE

City and state: Las Vegas, Nevada   *Printed name and title*

Attachment "A3"

Property to Be Searched

This warrant applies to information associated with the Instagram user IDs **mariloudanleyy**, that is stored at premises owned, maintained, controlled, or operated by Facebook, a company headquartered in Menlo Park, California for the time period beginning September 1, 2016 to present.

ATTACHMENT "B"

Particular Things to be Seized

I. **Information to be disclosed by Facebook**

To the extent that the information described in Attachment A is within the possession, custody, or control of Instagram LLC ("Instagram"), including any messages, records, files, logs, or information that have been deleted but are still available to Instagram, or have been preserved pursuant to a request made under 18 U.S.C. § 2703(f) on October 3, 2017. Facebook is required to disclose the following information to the government for each user IDs listed in Attachment A for the period of September 1, 2016 to present:

(a) All contact and personal identifying information, including: full name, user identification number, birth date, gender, contact e-mail addresses, Instagram passwords, Instagram security questions and answers, physical address (including city, state, and zip code), telephone numbers, screen names, websites, and other personal identifiers;

(b) All activity logs for the account and all other documents showing the user's posts and other Instagram activities;

(c) All photos and videos uploaded by that user ID and all photos and videos uploaded by any user that have that user tagged in them;

(d) All profile information; status updates; links to videos, photographs, bios, articles, and other items; Wall postings; friend lists, including the friends' Instagram user identification numbers; future and past event postings; comments; and tags;

(e) All other records of communications and messages made or received by the user, chat history, and pending "Friend" requests;

(f) All user content created, uploaded, or shared by the account, including any comments made by the account on photographs or other content;

(g) All IP logs, including all records of the IP addresses that logged into the account;

(h) All records of the account's usage of the "Like" feature, including all Instagram posts and content that the user has "liked";

(i) All location data associated with the account, including geotags;

(j) All data and information that has been deleted by the user;

(k) All past and present lists of friends created by the account;

(l) All records of Instagram searches performed by the account;

(m) The types of service utilized by the user;

(n) The length of service (including start date) and the means and source of any payments associated with the service (including any credit card or bank account number);

(o) All privacy settings and other account settings, including privacy settings for individual Instagram posts and activities, and all records showing which Instagram users have been blocked by the account;

(p) All records pertaining to communications between Instagram and any person regarding the user or the user's Instagram account, including contacts with support services and records of actions taken.

(q) All information regarding the particular device or devices used to login to or access the account, including all device identifier information or cookie information, including all information about the particular device or devices used to access the account and the date and time of those accesses;

II. Information to be seized by the government

All information described above in Section I that constitutes fruits, evidence, and instrumentalities of violations of:

Violation of National Firearms Act – Registration of Firearms, Title 26, United States Code, Section 5841.

involving STEPHEN PADDOCK and others yet unidentified, including, for each user ID identified on Attachment "A," information pertaining to the following matters:

(a) Evidence showing the possession, use, purchase, or sale of firearms, firearms accessories, ammunition, or explosives by Paddock, including through conspiring and cooperating to possess, use, purchase, or sell prohibited firearms, firearms accessories, ammunition, or explosives.

(b) Evidence indicating how and when the Instagram account was accessed or used, to determine the chronological and geographic context of account access, use, and events relating to the crime under investigation and to the Facebook account owner;

(c) Evidence indicating the Instagram account owner's state of mind as it relates to the crime under investigation;

(d) The identity of the person(s) who created or used the user ID, including records that help reveal the whereabouts of such person(s).

(e) The identity of the person(s) who communicated with the user ID about matters relating to the illegal possession, purchase, use, or sale of firearms, firearms accessories, ammunition, or explosives, including records that help reveal their whereabouts.

The Warrant expressly incorporates the Affidavit submitted in support of the Warrant, and separately sealed, as though set forth fully herein.

ATTACHMENT C

PROTOCOL FOR SEARCHING THE ELECTRONIC DATA SEIZED

PURSUANT TO THIS SEARCH WARRANT

1. In executing this warrant, the government must make reasonable efforts to use methods and procedures that will locate and expose in the electronic data produced in response to this search warrant ("the Search Warrant Data") those categories of data, files, documents, or other electronically stored information that are identified with particularity in the warrant, while minimizing exposure or examination of irrelevant, privileged, or confidential files to the extent reasonably practicable.

2. When the Search Warrant Data is received, the government will make a duplicate copy of the Search Warrant Data ("the Search Warrant Data Copy"). The original version of the Search Warrant Data will be sealed and preserved for purposes of: later judicial review or order to return or dispose of the Search Warrant Data; production to the defense in any criminal case if authorized by statute, rule, or the Constitution; for purposes of showing the chain of custody of the Search Warrant Data and the Search Warrant Data Copy; or for any other lawful purpose. The original of the Search Warrant Data will not be searched or examined except to ensure that it has been fully and completely replicated in the Search Warrant Data Copy.

3. The investigating agents will then search the entirety of the Search Warrant Data Copy using any and all methods and procedures deemed appropriate by the United States designed to identify the information listed as Information to be Seized in Attachment B, Section II. The United States may copy, extract or otherwise segregate information or data listed as Information to be Seized in Attachment B, Section II. Information or data so copied, extracted or otherwise segregated will no longer be subject to any handling restrictions that might be set out in this protocol beyond those required by binding law. To the extent evidence of crimes not within the scope of this warrant appear in plain view during this review, a supplemental or "piggyback" warrant will be applied for in order to further search that document, data, or other item.

4. The Government will have ninety (90) days from receipt of the data disclosed under Attachment B, Section I to complete its examination of the Search Warrant Data Copy. Once the Search Warrant Data Copy has been thoroughly and completely examined for any document, data, or other items identified in Attachment B, Section II as Information to be Seized, the Search Warrant Data Copy will be sealed and not subject to any further search or examination unless authorized by another search warrant or other appropriate court order. The Search Warrant Data Copy will be held and preserved for the same purposes identified above in Paragraph 2.

5. The search procedures utilized for this review are at the sole discretion of the investigating and prosecuting authorities, and may include the following techniques (the following is a non-exclusive list, as other search procedures may be used):

a. examination of all of the data contained in the Search Warrant Data to view the data and determine whether that data falls within the items to be seized as set forth herein;

b. searching for and attempting to recover from the Search Warrant Data any deleted, hidden, or encrypted data to determine whether that data falls within the list of items to be seized as set forth herein (any data that is encrypted and unreadable will not be returned unless law enforcement personnel have determined that the data is not (1) an instrumentality of the offenses, (2) a fruit of the criminal activity, (3) contraband, (4) otherwise unlawfully possessed, or (5) evidence of the offenses specified above);

c. surveying various file directories and the individual files they contain;

d. opening files in order to determine their contents;

e. using hash values to narrow the scope of what may be found. Hash values are under-inclusive, but are still a helpful tool;

f. scanning storage areas;

g. performing keyword searches through all electronic storage areas to determine whether occurrences of language contained in such storage areas exist that are likely to appear in the evidence described in Attachment A; and/or

h. performing any other data analysis technique that may be necessary to locate and retrieve the evidence described in Attachment B, Section II.

Return and Review Procedures

6. Rule 41 of the Federal Rules of Criminal Procedure provides, in relevant part:

(e) Issuing the Warrant.

(2) Contents of the Warrant.

(A) Warrant to Search for and Seize a Person or Property. Except for a tracking-device warrant, the warrant must identify the person or property to be searched, identify any person or property to be seized, and designate the magistrate judge to whom it must be returned. The warrant must command the officer to:

(i) execute the warrant within a specified time no longer than 14 days;

(B) Warrant Seeking Electronically Stored Information. A warrant under Rule 41(e)(2)(A) may authorize the seizure of electronic storage media or the seizure or copying of electronically stored information. Unless otherwise specified, the warrant authorizes a later review of the media or information consistent with the warrant. The time for executing the warrant in Rule 41(e)(2)(A) and

(f)(1)(A) refers to the seizure or on-site copying of the media or information, and not to any later off-site copying or review.

(f) Executing and Returning the Warrant.

(1) Warrant to Search for and Seize a Person or Property.

(B) Inventory. An officer present during the execution of the warrant must prepare and verify an inventory of any property seized. . . . In a case involving the seizure of electronic storage media or the seizure or copying of electronically stored information, the inventory may be limited to describing the physical storage media that were seized or copied. The officer may retain a copy of the electronically stored information that was seized or copied.

7. Pursuant to this Rule, the government understands and will act in accordance with the following:

a. Pursuant to Rule 41(e)(2)(A)(iii), within fourteen (14) days of the execution of the warrant, an agent is required to file an inventory return with the Court, that is, to file an itemized list of the property seized. Execution of the warrant begins when the United States serves the warrant on the named custodian; execution is complete when the custodian provides all Search Warrant Data to the United States. Within fourteen (14) days of completion of the execution of the warrant, the inventory will be filed.

b. Pursuant to Rule 41(e)(2)(B), Rule 41(e)(2)(A) governs the time within which the electronically stored information must be seized after the issuance of the warrant and copied after the execution of the warrant, not the "later review of the media or information" seized, or the later off-site digital copying of that media.

c. Under Rule 41(f)(1)(B), the inventory return that is to be filed with the court may be limited to a description of the "physical storage media" into which the Search Warrant Data that was seized was placed, not an itemization of the information or data stored on the "physical storage media" into which the Search Warrant Data was placed;

d. Under Rule 41(f)(1)(B), the government may retain a copy of that information for purposes of the investigation. The government proposes that the original storage media on which the Search Warrant Data was placed plus a full image copy of the seized Search Warrant Data be retained by the government.

e. If the person from whom any Search Warrant Data was seized requests the return of any information in the Search Warrant Data that is not set forth in Attachment B, Section II, that information will be copied onto appropriate media and returned to the person from whom the information was seized.

AO 106 (Rev. 04/10) Application for a Search Warrant

UNITED STATES DISTRICT COURT
for the
District of Nevada

I hereby attest and certify on 10-3-17 that the foregoing document is a full true and correct copy of the original on file in my office, and in my legal custody.

CAM FERENBACH
U.S. MAGISTRATE JUDGE
DISTRICT OF NEVADA

By _____ Deputy Secretary

In the Matter of the Search of
(Briefly describe the property to be searched or identify the person by name and address)

INSTAGRAM ACCOUNTS STORED AT PREMISES CONTROLLED BY FACEBOOK CORPORATION: Mariloudanleypaddock A 4

Case No. 2:17-mj-0096

APPLICATION FOR A SEARCH WARRANT

I, a federal law enforcement officer or an attorney for the government, request a search warrant and state under penalty of perjury that I have reason to believe that on the following person or property *(identify the person or describe the property to be searched and give its location)*:

INSTAGRAM ACCOUNTS STORED AT PREMISES CONTROLLED BY FACEBOOK CORPORATION: Mariloudanleypaddock A4

located in the ____DEA____ District of _____, there is now concealed *(identify the person or describe the property to be seized)*:

INSTAGRAM ACCOUNTS STORED AT PREMISES CONTROLLED BY FACEBOOK CORPORATION: Mariloudanleypaddock A4

The basis for the search under Fed. R. Crim. P. 41(c) is *(check one or more)*:

- ☑ evidence of a crime;
- ☑ contraband, fruits of crime, or other items illegally possessed;
- ☑ property designed for use, intended for use, or used in committing a crime;
- ☑ a person to be arrested or a person who is unlawfully restrained.

The search is related to a violation of:

Code Section	Offense Description
Title 26, United States Code, Section 5841.	Violation of National Firearms Act

FILED 2017 OCT -3 PM 3:55 U.S. MAGISTRATE JUDGE BY _____

The application is based on these facts:
I believe there is probable cause to believe that in the subject accounts listed in Attachments "A1", "A2", "A3", "A4", "A5" there is proof that constitutes evidence of the commission of criminal offense(s); contraband, the fruits of crime and things otherwise criminally possessed and been used as the means of committing criminal offense(s)

- ☐ Continued on the attached sheet.
- ☐ Delayed notice of _____ days (give exact ending date if more than 30 days: _____) is requested under 18 U.S.C. § 3103a, the basis of which is set forth on the attached sheet.

/s/
Applicant's signature

_____
Printed name and title

Sworn to before me and signed in my presence.

Date: 10-3-17

City and state: Las Vegas, Nevada

CAM FERENBACH
Judge's signature
CAM FERENBACH
U.S. MAGISTRATE JUDGE
Printed name and title

AO 93 (Rev. 11/13) Search and Seizure Warrant

UNITED STATES DISTRICT COURT
for the
District of Nevada

I hereby attest and certify on 10-3-17 that the foregoing document is a full true and correct copy of the original on file in my office, and in my legal custody.

CAM FERENBACH
U.S. MAGISTRATE JUDGE
DISTRICT OF NEVADA

By _____ Deputy Secretary

In the Matter of the Search of)
(Briefly describe the property to be searched)
or identify the person by name and address)) Case No. 2:17-mj-00961-VCF
Mariloudanleypaddock A4)
)
)

SEARCH AND SEIZURE WARRANT

To: Any authorized law enforcement officer

An application by a federal law enforcement officer or an attorney for the government requests the search of the following person or property located in the _____ District of _____ Nevada
(identify the person or describe the property to be searched and give its location):

SEE ATTACHMENT A4

I find that the affidavit(s), or any recorded testimony, establish probable cause to search and seize the person or property described above, and that such search will reveal *(identify the person or describe the property to be seized)*:

SEE ATTACHMENTS B and C

YOU ARE COMMANDED to execute this warrant on or before ___10-12-17___ *(not to exceed 14 days)*
☒ in the daytime 6:00 a.m. to 10:00 p.m.   ☐ at any time in the day or night because good cause has been established.

Unless delayed notice is authorized below, you must give a copy of the warrant and a receipt for the property taken to the person from whom, or from whose premises, the property was taken, or leave the copy and receipt at the place where the property was taken.

The officer executing this warrant, or an officer present during the execution of the warrant, must prepare an inventory as required by law and promptly return this warrant and inventory to ___CAM FERENBACH___
(United States Magistrate Judge)

☐ Pursuant to 18 U.S.C. § 3103a(b), I find that immediate notification may have an adverse result listed in 18 U.S.C. § 2705 (except for delay of trial), and authorize the officer executing this warrant to delay notice to the person who, or whose property, will be searched or seized *(check the appropriate box)*
☐ for _____ days *(not to exceed 30)* ☐ until, the facts justifying, the later specific date of _____

Date and time issued: __10-3-17 4:08pm__   CAM FERENBACH
                                              Judge's signature

City and state: Las Vegas, Nevada   CAM FERENBACH
                                          U.S. MAGISTRATE JUDGE
                                          Printed name and title

Attachment "A4"

Property to Be Searched

This warrant applies to information associated with the Instagram user IDs **mariloudanleypaddock**, that is stored at premises owned, maintained, controlled, or operated by Facebook, a company headquartered in Menlo Park, California for the time period beginning September 1, 2016 to present.

ATTACHMENT "B"

Particular Things to be Seized

I. **Information to be disclosed by Facebook**

To the extent that the information described in Attachment A is within the possession, custody, or control of Instagram LLC ("Instagram"), including any messages, records, files, logs, or information that have been deleted but are still available to Instagram, or have been preserved pursuant to a request made under 18 U.S.C. § 2703(f) on October 3, 2017. Facebook is required to disclose the following information to the government for each user IDs listed in Attachment A for the period of September 1, 2016 to present:

(a) All contact and personal identifying information, including: full name, user identification number, birth date, gender, contact e-mail addresses, Instagram passwords, Instagram security questions and answers, physical address (including city, state, and zip code), telephone numbers, screen names, websites, and other personal identifiers;

(b) All activity logs for the account and all other documents showing the user's posts and other Instagram activities;

(c) All photos and videos uploaded by that user ID and all photos and videos uploaded by any user that have that user tagged in them;

(d) All profile information; status updates; links to videos, photographs, bios, articles, and other items; Wall postings; friend lists, including the friends' Instagram user identification numbers; future and past event postings; comments; and tags;

(e) All other records of communications and messages made or received by the user, chat history, and pending "Friend" requests;

(f) All user content created, uploaded, or shared by the account, including any comments made by the account on photographs or other content;

(g) All IP logs, including all records of the IP addresses that logged into the account;

(h) All records of the account's usage of the "Like" feature, including all Instagram posts and content that the user has "liked";

(i) All location data associated with the account, including geotags;

(j) All data and information that has been deleted by the user;

(k) All past and present lists of friends created by the account;

(l) All records of Instagram searches performed by the account;

(m) The types of service utilized by the user;

(n) The length of service (including start date) and the means and source of any payments associated with the service (including any credit card or bank account number);

(o) All privacy settings and other account settings, including privacy settings for individual Instagram posts and activities, and all records showing which Instagram users have been blocked by the account;

(p) All records pertaining to communications between Instagram and any person regarding the user or the user's Instagram account, including contacts with support services and records of actions taken.

(q) All information regarding the particular device or devices used to login to or access the account, including all device identifier information or cookie information, including all information about the particular device or devices used to access the account and the date and time of those accesses;

II. Information to be seized by the government

All information described above in Section I that constitutes fruits, evidence, and instrumentalities of violations of:

Violation of National Firearms Act – Registration of Firearms, Title 26, United States Code, Section 5841.

involving STEPHEN PADDOCK and others yet unidentified, including, for each user ID identified on Attachment "A," information pertaining to the following matters:

(a) Evidence showing the possession, use, purchase, or sale of firearms, firearms accessories, ammunition, or explosives by Paddock, including through conspiring and cooperating to possess, use, purchase, or sell prohibited firearms, firearms accessories, ammunition, or explosives.

(b) Evidence indicating how and when the Instagram account was accessed or used, to determine the chronological and geographic context of account access, use, and events relating to the crime under investigation and to the Facebook account owner;

(c) Evidence indicating the Instagram account owner's state of mind as it relates to the crime under investigation;

(d) The identity of the person(s) who created or used the user ID, including records that help reveal the whereabouts of such person(s).

(e) The identity of the person(s) who communicated with the user ID about matters relating to the illegal possession, purchase, use, or sale of firearms, firearms accessories, ammunition, or explosives, including records that help reveal their whereabouts.

The Warrant expressly incorporates the Affidavit submitted in support of the Warrant, and separately sealed, as though set forth fully herein.

ATTACHMENT C

PROTOCOL FOR SEARCHING THE ELECTRONIC DATA SEIZED

PURSUANT TO THIS SEARCH WARRANT

1. In executing this warrant, the government must make reasonable efforts to use methods and procedures that will locate and expose in the electronic data produced in response to this search warrant ("the Search Warrant Data") those categories of data, files, documents, or other electronically stored information that are identified with particularity in the warrant, while minimizing exposure or examination of irrelevant, privileged, or confidential files to the extent reasonably practicable.

2. When the Search Warrant Data is received, the government will make a duplicate copy of the Search Warrant Data ("the Search Warrant Data Copy"). The original version of the Search Warrant Data will be sealed and preserved for purposes of: later judicial review or order to return or dispose of the Search Warrant Data; production to the defense in any criminal case if authorized by statute, rule, or the Constitution; for purposes of showing the chain of custody of the Search Warrant Data and the Search Warrant Data Copy; or for any other lawful purpose. The original of the Search Warrant Data will not be searched or examined except to ensure that it has been fully and completely replicated in the Search Warrant Data Copy.

3. The investigating agents will then search the entirety of the Search Warrant Data Copy using any and all methods and procedures deemed appropriate by the United States designed to identify the information listed as Information to be Seized in Attachment B, Section II. The United States may copy, extract or otherwise segregate information or data listed as Information to be Seized in Attachment B, Section II. Information or data so copied, extracted or otherwise segregated will no longer be subject to any handling restrictions that might be set out in this protocol beyond those required by binding law. To the extent evidence of crimes not within the scope of this warrant appear in plain view during this review, a supplemental or "piggyback" warrant will be applied for in order to further search that document, data, or other item.

4. The Government will have ninety (90) days from receipt of the data disclosed under Attachment B, Section I to complete its examination of the Search Warrant Data Copy. Once the Search Warrant Data Copy has been thoroughly and completely examined for any document, data, or other items identified in Attachment B, Section II as Information to be Seized, the Search Warrant Data Copy will be sealed and not subject to any further search or examination unless authorized by another search warrant or other appropriate court order. The Search Warrant Data Copy will be held and preserved for the same purposes identified above in Paragraph 2.

5. The search procedures utilized for this review are at the sole discretion of the investigating and prosecuting authorities, and may include the following techniques (the following is a non-exclusive list, as other search procedures may be used):

a. examination of all of the data contained in the Search Warrant Data to view the data and determine whether that data falls within the items to be seized as set forth herein;

b. searching for and attempting to recover from the Search Warrant Data any deleted, hidden, or encrypted data to determine whether that data falls within the list of items to be seized as set forth herein (any data that is encrypted and unreadable will not be returned unless law enforcement personnel have determined that the data is not (1) an instrumentality of the offenses, (2) a fruit of the criminal activity, (3) contraband, (4) otherwise unlawfully possessed, or (5) evidence of the offenses specified above);

c. surveying various file directories and the individual files they contain;

d. opening files in order to determine their contents;

e. using hash values to narrow the scope of what may be found. Hash values are under-inclusive, but are still a helpful tool;

f. scanning storage areas;

g. performing keyword searches through all electronic storage areas to determine whether occurrences of language contained in such storage areas exist that are likely to appear in the evidence described in Attachment A; and/or

h. performing any other data analysis technique that may be necessary to locate and retrieve the evidence described in Attachment B, Section II.

Return and Review Procedures

6. Rule 41 of the Federal Rules of Criminal Procedure provides, in relevant part:

(e) Issuing the Warrant.

(2) Contents of the Warrant.

(A) Warrant to Search for and Seize a Person or Property. Except for a tracking-device warrant, the warrant must identify the person or property to be searched, identify any person or property to be seized, and designate the magistrate judge to whom it must be returned. The warrant must command the officer to:

(i) execute the warrant within a specified time no longer than 14 days;

(B) Warrant Seeking Electronically Stored Information. A warrant under Rule 41(e)(2)(A) may authorize the seizure of electronic storage media or the seizure or copying of electronically stored information. Unless otherwise specified, the warrant authorizes a later review of the media or information consistent with the warrant. The time for executing the warrant in Rule 41(e)(2)(A) and

(f)(1)(A) refers to the seizure or on-site copying of the media or information, and not to any later off-site copying or review.

(f) Executing and Returning the Warrant.

(1) Warrant to Search for and Seize a Person or Property.

(B) Inventory. An officer present during the execution of the warrant must prepare and verify an inventory of any property seized. . . . In a case involving the seizure of electronic storage media or the seizure or copying of electronically stored information, the inventory may be limited to describing the physical storage media that were seized or copied. The officer may retain a copy of the electronically stored information that was seized or copied.

7. Pursuant to this Rule, the government understands and will act in accordance with the following:

a. Pursuant to Rule 41(e)(2)(A)(iii), within fourteen (14) days of the execution of the warrant, an agent is required to file an inventory return with the Court, that is, to file an itemized list of the property seized. Execution of the warrant begins when the United States serves the warrant on the named custodian; execution is complete when the custodian provides all Search Warrant Data to the United States. Within fourteen (14) days of completion of the execution of the warrant, the inventory will be filed.

b. Pursuant to Rule 41(e)(2)(B), Rule 41(e)(2)(A) governs the time within which the electronically stored information must be seized after the issuance of the warrant and copied after the execution of the warrant, not the "later review of the media or information" seized, or the later off-site digital copying of that media.

c. Under Rule 41(f)(1)(B), the inventory return that is to be filed with the court may be limited to a description of the "physical storage media" into which the Search Warrant Data that was seized was placed, not an itemization of the information or data stored on the "physical storage media" into which the Search Warrant Data was placed;

d. Under Rule 41(f)(1)(B), the government may retain a copy of that information for purposes of the investigation. The government proposes that the original storage media on which the Search Warrant Data was placed plus a full image copy of the seized Search Warrant Data be retained by the government.

e. If the person from whom any Search Warrant Data was seized requests the return of any information in the Search Warrant Data that is not set forth in Attachment B, Section II, that information will be copied onto appropriate media and returned to the person from whom the information was seized.

AO 106 (Rev. 04/10) Application for a Search Warrant

10-3-17

UNITED STATES DISTRICT COURT
for the
District of Nevada

I hereby attest and certify on _____
that the foregoing document is a full true and correct
copy of the original on file in my office, and in my legal
custody.

CAM FERENBACH
U.S. MAGISTRATE JUDGE
DISTRICT OF NEVADA

By _____ Deputy
                              Secretary

In the Matter of the Search of
*(Briefly describe the property to be searched
or identify the person by name and address)*

INSTAGRAM ACCOUNTS STORED AT
PREMISES CONTROLLED BY FACEBOOK
CORPORATION: marilou.danley A5

Case No. 2:17-mj-00962-VCF

APPLICATION FOR A SEARCH WARRANT

I, a federal law enforcement officer or an attorney for the government, request a search warrant and state under penalty of perjury that I have reason to believe that on the following person or property *(identify the person or describe the property to be searched and give its location)*:

INSTAGRAM ACCOUNTS STORED AT PREMISES CONTROLLED BY FACEBOOK CORPORATION: marilou.danley A5

located in the _____DEA_____ District of _____, there is now concealed *(identify the person or describe the property to be seized)*:

INSTAGRAM ACCOUNTS STORED AT PREMISES CONTROLLED BY FACEBOOK CORPORATION: marilou.danley A5

The basis for the search under Fed. R. Crim. P. 41(c) is *(check one or more)*:
- ☑ evidence of a crime;
- ☑ contraband, fruits of crime, or other items illegally possessed;
- ☑ property designed for use, intended for use, or used in committing a crime;
- ☑ a person to be arrested or a person who is unlawfully restrained.

The search is related to a violation of:

Code Section	Offense Description
Title 26, United States Code, Section 5841.	Violation of National Firearms Act

The application is based on these facts:
I believe there is probable cause to believe that in the subject accounts listed in Attachments "A1", "A2", "A3", "A4", "A5" there is proof that constitutes evidence of the commission of criminal offense(s); contraband, the fruits of crime and things otherwise criminally possessed and been used as the means of committing criminal offense(s)

- ☐ Continued on the attached sheet.
- ☐ Delayed notice of _____ days (give exact ending date if more than 30 days: _____) is requested under 18 U.S.C. § 3103a, the basis of which is set forth on the attached sheet.

/S/
Applicant's signature

Printed name and title

Sworn to before me and signed in my presence.

Date: 10-3-17

City and state: Las Vegas, Nevada

CAM FERENBACH
Judge's signature

CAM FERENBACH
U.S. MAGISTRATE JUDGE
Printed name and title

AO 93 (Rev. 11/13) Search and Seizure Warrant

UNITED STATES DISTRICT COURT
for the
District of Nevada

I hereby attest and certify on 10-3-17 that the foregoing document is a full, true and correct copy of the original on file in my office, and in my legal custody.

CAM FERENBACH
U.S. MAGISTRATE JUDGE
DISTRICT OF NEVADA

By _____ Deputy Secretary

In the Matter of the Search of)
(Briefly describe the property to be searched)
or identify the person by name and address)) Case No. 2:17-mj-00962-VCF
marilou.danley A5)
)
)

SEARCH AND SEIZURE WARRANT

To: Any authorized law enforcement officer

An application by a federal law enforcement officer or an attorney for the government requests the search of the following person or property located in the _____ District of _____ Nevada _____
(identify the person or describe the property to be searched and give its location):

SEE ATTACHMENT A5

I find that the affidavit(s), or any recorded testimony, establish probable cause to search and seize the person or property described above, and that such search will reveal *(identify the person or describe the property to be seized):*

SEE ATTACHMENTS B and C

YOU ARE COMMANDED to execute this warrant on or before 10-12-17 *(not to exceed 14 days)*
☒ in the daytime 6:00 a.m. to 10:00 p.m. ☐ at any time in the day or night because good cause has been established.

Unless delayed notice is authorized below, you must give a copy of the warrant and a receipt for the property taken to the person from whom, or from whose premises, the property was taken, or leave the copy and receipt at the place where the property was taken.

The officer executing this warrant, or an officer present during the execution of the warrant, must prepare an inventory as required by law and promptly return this warrant and inventory to CAM FERENBACH
(United States Magistrate Judge)

☐ Pursuant to 18 U.S.C. § 3103a(b), I find that immediate notification may have an adverse result listed in 18 U.S.C. § 2705 (except for delay of trial), and authorize the officer executing this warrant to delay notice to the person who, or whose property, will be searched or seized *(check the appropriate box)*
☐ for _____ days *(not to exceed 30)* ☐ until, the facts justifying, the later specific date of _____

Date and time issued: 10-3-17 4:05pm   CAM FERENBACH
                                        Judge's signature
                                        CAM FERENBACH
City and state: Las Vegas, Nevada   U.S. MAGISTRATE JUDGE
                                        Printed name and title

Attachment "A5"

Property to Be Searched

This warrant applies to information associated with the Instagram user IDs and **marilou.danley** that is stored at premises owned, maintained, controlled, or operated by Facebook, a company headquartered in Menlo Park, California for the time period beginning September 1, 2016 to present.

ATTACHMENT "B"

Particular Things to be Seized

I. Information to be disclosed by Facebook

To the extent that the information described in Attachment A is within the possession, custody, or control of Instagram LLC ("Instagram"), including any messages, records, files, logs, or information that have been deleted but are still available to Instagram, or have been preserved pursuant to a request made under 18 U.S.C. § 2703(f) on October 3, 2017. Facebook is required to disclose the following information to the government for each user IDs listed in Attachment A for the period of September 1, 2016 to present:

(a) All contact and personal identifying information, including: full name, user identification number, birth date, gender, contact e-mail addresses, Instagram passwords, Instagram security questions and answers, physical address (including city, state, and zip code), telephone numbers, screen names, websites, and other personal identifiers;

(b) All activity logs for the account and all other documents showing the user's posts and other Instagram activities;

(c) All photos and videos uploaded by that user ID and all photos and videos uploaded by any user that have that user tagged in them;

(d) All profile information; status updates; links to videos, photographs, bios, articles, and other items; Wall postings; friend lists, including the friends' Instagram user identification numbers; future and past event postings; comments; and tags;

(e) All other records of communications and messages made or received by the user, chat history, and pending "Friend" requests;

II. Information to be seized by the government

All information described above in Section I that constitutes fruits, evidence, and instrumentalities of violations of:

> Violation of National Firearms Act – Registration of Firearms, Title 26, United States Code, Section 5841.

involving STEPHEN PADDOCK and others yet unidentified, including, for each user ID identified on Attachment "A," information pertaining to the following matters:

(a) Evidence showing the possession, use, purchase, or sale of firearms, firearms accessories, ammunition, or explosives by Paddock, including through conspiring and cooperating to possess, use, purchase, or sell prohibited firearms, firearms accessories, ammunition, or explosives.

(b) Evidence indicating how and when the Instagram account was accessed or used, to determine the chronological and geographic context of account access, use, and events relating to the crime under investigation and to the Facebook account owner;

(c) Evidence indicating the Instagram account owner's state of mind as it relates to the crime under investigation;

(d) The identity of the person(s) who created or used the user ID, including records that help reveal the whereabouts of such person(s).

(e) The identity of the person(s) who communicated with the user ID about matters relating to the illegal possession, purchase, use, or sale of firearms, firearms accessories, ammunition, or explosives, including records that help reveal their whereabouts.

The Warrant expressly incorporates the Affidavit submitted in support of the Warrant, and separately sealed, as though set forth fully herein.

(f) All user content created, uploaded, or shared by the account, including any comments made by the account on photographs or other content;

(g) All IP logs, including all records of the IP addresses that logged into the account;

(h) All records of the account's usage of the "Like" feature, including all Instagram posts and content that the user has "liked";

(i) All location data associated with the account, including geotags;

(j) All data and information that has been deleted by the user;

(k) All past and present lists of friends created by the account;

(l) All records of Instagram searches performed by the account;

(m) The types of service utilized by the user;

(n) The length of service (including start date) and the means and source of any payments associated with the service (including any credit card or bank account number);

(o) All privacy settings and other account settings, including privacy settings for individual Instagram posts and activities, and all records showing which Instagram users have been blocked by the account;

(p) All records pertaining to communications between Instagram and any person regarding the user or the user's Instagram account, including contacts with support services and records of actions taken.

(q) All information regarding the particular device or devices used to login to or access the account, including all device identifier information or cookie information, including all information about the particular device or devices used to access the account and the date and time of those accesses;

ATTACHMENT C

PROTOCOL FOR SEARCHING THE ELECTRONIC DATA SEIZED

PURSUANT TO THIS SEARCH WARRANT

1. In executing this warrant, the government must make reasonable efforts to use methods and procedures that will locate and expose in the electronic data produced in response to this search warrant ("the Search Warrant Data") those categories of data, files, documents, or other electronically stored information that are identified with particularity in the warrant, while minimizing exposure or examination of irrelevant, privileged, or confidential files to the extent reasonably practicable.

2. When the Search Warrant Data is received, the government will make a duplicate copy of the Search Warrant Data ("the Search Warrant Data Copy"). The original version of the Search Warrant Data will be sealed and preserved for purposes of: later judicial review or order to return or dispose of the Search Warrant Data; production to the defense in any criminal case if authorized by statute, rule, or the Constitution; for purposes of showing the chain of custody of the Search Warrant Data and the Search Warrant Data Copy; or for any other lawful purpose. The original of the Search Warrant Data will not be searched or examined except to ensure that it has been fully and completely replicated in the Search Warrant Data Copy.

3. The investigating agents will then search the entirety of the Search Warrant Data Copy using any and all methods and procedures deemed appropriate by the United States designed to identify the information listed as Information to be Seized in Attachment B, Section II. The United States may copy, extract or otherwise segregate information or data listed as Information to be Seized in Attachment B, Section II. Information or data so copied, extracted or otherwise segregated will no longer be subject to any handling restrictions that might be set out in this protocol beyond those required by binding law. To the extent evidence of crimes not within the scope of this warrant appear in plain view during this review, a supplemental or "piggyback" warrant will be applied for in order to further search that document, data, or other item.

4. The Government will have ninety (90) days from receipt of the data disclosed under Attachment B, Section I to complete its examination of the Search Warrant Data Copy. Once the Search Warrant Data Copy has been thoroughly and completely examined for any document, data, or other items identified in Attachment B, Section II as Information to be Seized, the Search Warrant Data Copy will be sealed and not subject to any further search or examination unless authorized by another search warrant or other appropriate court order. The Search Warrant Data Copy will be held and preserved for the same purposes identified above in Paragraph 2.

5. The search procedures utilized for this review are at the sole discretion of the investigating and prosecuting authorities, and may include the following techniques (the following is a non-exclusive list, as other search procedures may be used):

a. examination of all of the data contained in the Search Warrant Data to view the data and determine whether that data falls within the items to be seized as set forth herein;

b. searching for and attempting to recover from the Search Warrant Data any deleted, hidden, or encrypted data to determine whether that data falls within the list of items to be seized as set forth herein (any data that is encrypted and unreadable will not be returned unless law enforcement personnel have determined that the data is not (1) an instrumentality of the offenses, (2) a fruit of the criminal activity, (3) contraband, (4) otherwise unlawfully possessed, or (5) evidence of the offenses specified above);

c. surveying various file directories and the individual files they contain;

d. opening files in order to determine their contents;

e. using hash values to narrow the scope of what may be found. Hash values are under-inclusive, but are still a helpful tool;

f. scanning storage areas;

g. performing keyword searches through all electronic storage areas to determine whether occurrences of language contained in such storage areas exist that are likely to appear in the evidence described in Attachment A; and/or

h. performing any other data analysis technique that may be necessary to locate and retrieve the evidence described in Attachment B, Section II.

Return and Review Procedures

6. Rule 41 of the Federal Rules of Criminal Procedure provides, in relevant part:

(e) Issuing the Warrant.

(2) Contents of the Warrant.

(A) Warrant to Search for and Seize a Person or Property. Except for a tracking-device warrant, the warrant must identify the person or property to be searched, identify any person or property to be seized, and designate the magistrate judge to whom it must be returned. The warrant must command the officer to:

(i) execute the warrant within a specified time no longer than 14 days;

(B) Warrant Seeking Electronically Stored Information. A warrant under Rule 41(e)(2)(A) may authorize the seizure of electronic storage media or the seizure or copying of electronically stored information. Unless otherwise specified, the warrant authorizes a later review of the media or information consistent with the warrant. The time for executing the warrant in Rule 41(e)(2)(A) and

(f)(1)(A) refers to the seizure or on-site copying of the media or information, and not to any later off-site copying or review.

(f) Executing and Returning the Warrant.

(1) Warrant to Search for and Seize a Person or Property.

(B) Inventory. An officer present during the execution of the warrant must prepare and verify an inventory of any property seized. . . . In a case involving the seizure of electronic storage media or the seizure or copying of electronically stored information, the inventory may be limited to describing the physical storage media that were seized or copied. The officer may retain a copy of the electronically stored information that was seized or copied.

7. Pursuant to this Rule, the government understands and will act in accordance with the following:

a. Pursuant to Rule 41(e)(2)(A)(iii), within fourteen (14) days of the execution of the warrant, an agent is required to file an inventory return with the Court, that is, to file an itemized list of the property seized. Execution of the warrant begins when the United States serves the warrant on the named custodian; execution is complete when the custodian provides all Search Warrant Data to the United States. Within fourteen (14) days of completion of the execution of the warrant, the inventory will be filed.

b. Pursuant to Rule 41(e)(2)(B), Rule 41(e)(2)(A) governs the time within which the electronically stored information must be seized after the issuance of the warrant and copied after the execution of the warrant, not the "later review of the media or information" seized, or the later off-site digital copying of that media.

c. Under Rule 41(f)(1)(B), the inventory return that is to be filed with the court may be limited to a description of the "physical storage media" into which the Search Warrant Data that was seized was placed, not an itemization of the information or data stored on the "physical storage media" into which the Search Warrant Data was placed;

d. Under Rule 41(f)(1)(B), the government may retain a copy of that information for purposes of the investigation. The government proposes that the original storage media on which the Search Warrant Data was placed plus a full image copy of the seized Search Warrant Data be retained by the government.

e. If the person from whom any Search Warrant Data was seized requests the return of any information in the Search Warrant Data that is not set forth in Attachment B, Section II, that information will be copied onto appropriate media and returned to the person from whom the information was seized.

AO 93 (Rev. 11/13) Search and Seizure Warrant

UNITED STATES DISTRICT COURT
for the
District of Nevada

In the Matter of the Search of)
(Briefly describe the property to be searched)
or identify the person by name and address))
        CENTRALPARK1@LIVE.COM - A1)
) Case No. 2:17-mj- 968 - NJK
)
)

SEARCH AND SEIZURE WARRANT

To: Any authorized law enforcement officer

An application by a federal law enforcement officer or an attorney for the government requests the search of the following person or property located in the _____ District of _____Nevada_____
(identify the person or describe the property to be searched and give its location):

SEE ATTACHMENT A1

I find that the affidavit(s), or any recorded testimony, establish probable cause to search and seize the person or property described above, and that such search will reveal *(identify the person or describe the property to be seized):*

SEE ATTACHMENTS B and C

YOU ARE COMMANDED to execute this warrant on or before October 20, 2017 *(not to exceed 14 days)*
☑ in the daytime 6:00 a.m. to 10:00 p.m.   ☐ at any time in the day or night because good cause has been established.

Unless delayed notice is authorized below, you must give a copy of the warrant and a receipt for the property taken to the person from whom, or from whose premises, the property was taken, or leave the copy and receipt at the place where the property was taken.

The officer executing this warrant, or an officer present during the execution of the warrant, must prepare an inventory as required by law and promptly return this warrant and inventory to __Nancy J. Koppe__.
                                                                                                        (United States Magistrate Judge)

☐ Pursuant to 18 U.S.C. § 3103a(b), I find that immediate notification may have an adverse result listed in 18 U.S.C. § 2705 (except for delay of trial), and authorize the officer executing this warrant to delay notice to the person who, or whose property, will be searched or seized *(check the appropriate box)*
☐ for _____ days *(not to exceed 30)*   ☐ until, the facts justifying, the later specific date of _____.

Date and time issued: 10/16/2017 4:05 pm   _____
                                                                                  Judge's signature

City and state: Las Vegas, Nevada   Nancy J. Koppe, US Magistrate Judge
                                                                                               Printed name and title

ATTACHMENT "A1"

ONLINE ACCOUNT TO BE SEARCHED

1. This warrant applies to information associated with the Microsoft email account centralpark1@live.com (the "Target Accounts") from their inception to present, which is stored at premises owned, maintained, controlled, or operated by Microsoft Corporation, headquartered at 1 Microsoft Way, Redmond, Washington, 98052.

ATTACHMENT "B"
Particular Things to be Seized

I. Information to be disclosed by the Service Provider

To the extent that the information described in Attachment A1 and A2 is within the possession, custody, or control of Microsoft, including any Emails, records, files, logs, or information that have been deleted but are still available to Service Provider, or have been preserved pursuant to a request made under 18 U.S.C. § 2703(f), Service Provider is required to disclose the following information to the government for each account or identifier listed in Attachment A1 and A2 from account inception to present:

a. The contents of all emails associated with the account, including copies of emails sent to and from the account, draft emails, the source and destination addresses associated with each email, the date and time at which each email was sent, and the size and length of each email;

b. All records or other information regarding the identification of the account, to include full name, physical address, telephone numbers and other identifiers, records of session times and durations, the date on which the account was created, the length of service, the types of service utilized, the IP address used to register the account, log-in IP addresses associated with session times and dates, account status, alternative email addresses provided during registration, methods of connecting, log files, and means and source of payment (including any credit or bank account number);

c. All records or other information stored in the Online Accounts, including address books, contact and buddy lists, calendar data, pictures, applications, documents, and other files;

d. All records pertaining to communications between Service Provider and any person regarding the account, including contacts with support services and records of actions taken.

e. All third-party application data and content associated with the Target Account through any Android operating system and/or any Microsoft-related facility.

II. Information to be seized by the United States

After reviewing all information described in Section I, the United States will seize evidence of violations of Title 18, United States Code Sections 32(a) (Destruction/Damage of Aircraft or Aircraft Facilities); 37(a)(2) (Violence at International Airport); and 922(a)(3); and 5 (Unlawful Interstate Transport/Delivery of Firearms by Non Federal Firearms Licensee); and 2 (Aiding and Abetting) (the "Subject Offenses") that occur in the form of the following, from account inception to present:

a. Communications, transactions and records that may establish ownership and control (or the degree thereof) of the Target Account, including address books, contact or buddy lists, bills, invoices, receipts, registration records, bills, correspondence, notes, records, memoranda, telephone/address books, photographs, video recordings, audio recordings, lists of names, records of payment for access to newsgroups or other online subscription services, and attachments to said communications, transactions and records.

b. Communications, transactions and records to/from persons who may be co-conspirators of the Subject Offenses, or which may identify co-conspirators.

c. Communications, transactions and records which may show motivation to commit the Subject Offenses.

d. Communications, transactions and records that relate to the Subject Offenses.

e. The terms "communications," "transactions", "records," "documents," "programs," or "materials" include all information recorded in any form, visual or aural, and by any means, whether in handmade form (including, but not limited to, writings, drawings, paintings), photographic form (including, but not limited to, pictures or videos), or electrical, electronic or magnetic form, as well as digital data files. These terms also include any applications (i.e. software programs). These terms expressly include, among other things, Emails, instant messages, chat logs, correspondence attached as to Emails (or drafts), calendar entries, buddy lists.

ATTACHMENT "C"

PROTOCOL FOR SEARCHING THE ELECTRONIC DATA SEIZED PURSUANT TO THIS SEARCH WARRANT

1. In executing this warrant, the government must make reasonable efforts to use methods and procedures that will locate and expose in the electronic data produced in response to this search warrant ("the Search Warrant Data") those categories of data, files, documents, or other electronically stored information that are identified with particularity in the warrant, while minimizing exposure or examination of irrelevant, privileged, or confidential files to the extent reasonably practicable.

2. When the Search Warrant Data is received, the government will make a duplicate copy of the Search Warrant Data ("the Search Warrant Data Copy"). The original version of the Search Warrant Data will be sealed and preserved for purposes of: later judicial review or order to return or dispose of the Search Warrant Data; production to the defense in any criminal case if authorized by statute, rule, or the Constitution; for purposes of showing the chain of custody of the Search Warrant Data and the Search Warrant Data Copy; or for any other lawful purpose. The original of the Search Warrant Data will not be searched or examined except to ensure that it has been fully and completely replicated in the Search Warrant Data Copy.

3. The investigating agents will then search the entirety of the Search Warrant Data Copy using any and all methods and procedures deemed appropriate by the United States designed to identify the information listed as Information to be Seized in Attachment B, Section II. The United States may copy, extract or otherwise segregate information or data listed as Information to be Seized in Attachment B, Section II. Information or data so copied, extracted or otherwise segregated will no longer be subject to any handling restrictions that might be set out in this protocol beyond those required by binding law. To the extent evidence of crimes not within the scope of this warrant appear in plain view during this review, a supplemental or "piggyback" warrant will be applied for in order to further search that document, data, or other item.

4. Once the Search Warrant Data Copy has been thoroughly and completely examined for any document, data, or other items identified in Attachment B, Section II as Information to be Seized, the Search Warrant Data Copy will be sealed and not subject to any further search or examination unless authorized by another search warrant or other appropriate court order. The Search Warrant Data Copy will be held and preserved for the same purposes identified above in Paragraph 2.

5. The search procedures utilized for this review are at the sole discretion of the investigating and prosecuting authorities, and may include the following techniques (the following is a non-exclusive list, as other search procedures may be used):

a. examination of all of the data contained in the Search Warrant Data to view the data and determine whether that data falls within the items to be seized as set forth herein;

b. searching for and attempting to recover from the Search Warrant Data any deleted, hidden, or encrypted data to determine whether that data falls within the list of items to be seized as set forth herein (any data that is encrypted and unreadable will not be returned unless law enforcement personnel have determined that the data is not (1) an instrumentality of the offenses, (2) a fruit of the criminal activity, (3) contraband, (4) otherwise unlawfully possessed, or (5) evidence of the offenses specified above);

c. surveying various file directories and the individual files they contain;

d. opening files in order to determine their contents;

e. using hash values to narrow the scope of what may be found. Hash values are under- inclusive, but are still a helpful tool;

f. scanning storage areas;

g. performing keyword searches through all electronic storage areas to determine whether occurrences of language contained in such storage areas exist that are likely to appear in the evidence described in Attachment A1 and A2; and/or

h. performing any other data analysis technique that may be necessary to locate and retrieve the evidence described in Attachment B, Section II.

Return and Review Procedures

6. Rule 41 of the Federal Rules of Criminal Procedure provides, in relevant part:

(e) Issuing the Warrant.

(2) Contents of the Warrant.

(A) Warrant to Search for and Seize a Person or Property. Except for a tracking-device warrant, the warrant must identify the person or property to be searched, identify any person or property to be seized, and designate the magistrate judge to whom it must be returned. The warrant must command the officer to:

(i) execute the warrant within a specified time no longer than 14 days;

(B) Warrant Seeking Electronically Stored Information. A warrant under Rule 41(e)(2)(A) may authorize the seizure of electronic storage media or the seizure or copying of electronically stored information. Unless otherwise specified, the warrant authorizes a later review of the media or information consistent with the warrant. The time for executing the warrant in Rule 41(e)(2)(A) and (f)(1)(A) refers to the seizure or on-site copying of the media or information, and not to any later off-site copying or review.

(f) Executing and Returning the Warrant.

(1) Warrant to Search for and Seize a Person or Property.

(B) Inventory. An officer present during the execution of the warrant must prepare and verify an inventory of any property seized. . . . In a case involving the seizure of electronic storage media or the seizure or copying of electronically stored information, the inventory may be limited to describing the physical storage media that were seized or copied. The officer may retain a copy of the electronically stored information that was seized or copied.

7. Pursuant to this Rule, the government understands and will act in accordance with the following:

a. Pursuant to Rule 41(e)(2)(A)(iii), within fourteen (14) days of the execution of the warrant, an agent is required to file an inventory return with the Court, that is, to file an itemized list of the property seized. Execution of the warrant begins when the United States serves the warrant on the named custodian; execution is complete when the custodian provides all Search Warrant Data to the United States. Within fourteen (14) days of completion of the execution of the warrant, the inventory will be filed.

b. Pursuant to Rule 41(e)(2)(B), Rule 41(e)(2)(A) governs the time within which the electronically stored information must be seized after the issuance of the warrant and copied after the execution of the warrant, not the "later review of the media or information" seized, or the later off-site digital copying of that media.

c. Under Rule 41(f)(1)(B), the inventory return that is to be filed with the court may be limited to a description of the "physical storage media" into which the Search Warrant Data that was seized was placed, not an itemization of the information or data stored on the "physical storage media" into which the Search Warrant Data was placed;

d. Under Rule 41(f)(1)(B), the government may retain a copy of that information for purposes of the investigation. The government proposes that the original storage media on which the Search Warrant Data was placed plus a full image copy of the seized Search Warrant Data be retained by the government.

e. If the person from whom any Search Warrant Data was seized requests the return of any information in the Search Warrant Data that is not set forth in Attachment B, Section II, that information will be copied onto appropriate media and returned to the person from whom the information was seized.

AO 93 (Rev. 11/13) Search and Seizure Warrant

UNITED STATES DISTRICT COURT
for the
District of Nevada

In the Matter of the Search of)
(Briefly describe the property to be searched)
or identify the person by name and address)) Case No. 2:17-mj- 970-NJK
EMAIL ACCOUNT CENTRALPARK4804@GMAIL.COM)
)
)

SEARCH AND SEIZURE WARRANT

To: Any authorized law enforcement officer

An application by a federal law enforcement officer or an attorney for the government requests the search of the following person or property located in the _____ District of _____ Nevada _____
(identify the person or describe the property to be searched and give its location):

SEE ATTACHMENT A

I find that the affidavit(s), or any recorded testimony, establish probable cause to search and seize the person or property described above, and that such search will reveal *(identify the person or describe the property to be seized):*

SEE ATTACHMENTS B and C

YOU ARE COMMANDED to execute this warrant on or before October 20, 2017 *(not to exceed 14 days)*
☒ in the daytime 6:00 a.m. to 10:00 p.m. ☐ at any time in the day or night because good cause has been established.

Unless delayed notice is authorized below, you must give a copy of the warrant and a receipt for the property taken to the person from whom, or from whose premises, the property was taken, or leave the copy and receipt at the place where the property was taken.

The officer executing this warrant, or an officer present during the execution of the warrant, must prepare an inventory as required by law and promptly return this warrant and inventory to ___Nancy J. Koppe___.
(United States Magistrate Judge)

☐ Pursuant to 18 U.S.C. § 3103a(b), I find that immediate notification may have an adverse result listed in 18 U.S.C. § 2705 (except for delay of trial), and authorize the officer executing this warrant to delay notice to the person who, or whose property, will be searched or seized *(check the appropriate box)*
☐ for _____ days *(not to exceed 30)* ☐ until, the facts justifying, the later specific date of _____.

Date and time issued: 10/6/2017 6:30 pm _____
Judge's signature

City and state: Las Vegas, Nevada Nancy J. Koppe, US Magistrate Judge
Printed name and title

ATTACHMENT "A"

ONLINE ACCOUNT TO BE SEARCHED

1. This warrant applies to information associated with the Google email account centralpark4804@gmail.com (the "Target Account") from its inception to present, which is stored at premises owned, maintained, controlled, or operated by Google, Inc., headquartered at 1600 Amphitheatre Way, Mountain View, California, 94043.

ATTACHMENT "B"
Particular Things to be Seized

I. **Information to be disclosed by the Service Provider**

To the extent that the information described in Attachment A is within the possession, custody, or control of Google, including any Emails, records, files, logs, or information that have been deleted but are still available to Service Provider, or have been preserved pursuant to a request made under 18 U.S.C. § 2703(f), Service Provider is required to disclose the following information to the government for each account or identifier listed in Attachment A from account inception to present:

a. The contents of all emails associated with the account, including copies of emails sent to and from the account, draft emails, the source and destination addresses associated with each email, the date and time at which each email was sent, and the size and length of each email;

b. All records or other information regarding the identification of the account, to include full name, physical address, telephone numbers and other identifiers, records of session times and durations, the date on which the account was created, the length of service, the types of service utilized, the IP address used to register the account, log-in IP addresses associated with session times and dates, account status, alternative email addresses provided during registration, methods of connecting, log files, and means and source of payment (including any credit or bank account number);

c. All records or other information stored in the Online Accounts, including address books, contact and buddy lists, calendar data, pictures, applications, documents, and other files;

d. All records pertaining to communications between Service Provider and any person regarding the account, including contacts with support services and records of actions taken.

e. All third-party application data and content associated with the Target Account through any Android operating system and/or any Google-related facility.

II. **Information to be seized by the United States**

After reviewing all information described in Section I, the United States will seize evidence of violations of Title 18, United States Code Sections 32(a) (Destruction/Damage of Aircraft or Aircraft Facilities); 37(a)(2) (Violence at International Airport); and 922(a)(3); 5 (Unlawful Interstate Transport/Delivery of Firearms by Non Federal Firearms Licensee) (the "Subject Offenses") that occur in the form of the following, from account inception to present:

a. Communications, transactions and records that may establish ownership and control (or the degree thereof) of the Target Account, including address books, contact or buddy lists, bills, invoices, receipts, registration records, bills, correspondence, notes, records, memoranda, telephone/address books, photographs, video recordings, audio recordings, lists of names, records of payment for access to newsgroups or other online subscription services, and attachments to said communications, transactions and records.

b. Communications, transactions and records to/from persons who may be co-conspirators of the Subject Offenses, or which may identify co-conspirators.

c. Communications, transactions and records which may show motivation to commit the Subject Offenses.

d. Communications, transactions and records that relate to the Subject Offenses.

e. The terms "communications," "transactions", "records," "documents," "programs," or "materials" include all information recorded in any form, visual or aural, and by any means, whether in handmade form (including, but not limited to, writings, drawings, paintings), photographic form (including, but not limited to, pictures or videos), or electrical, electronic or magnetic form, as well as digital data files. These terms also include any applications (i.e. software programs). These terms expressly include, among other things, Emails, instant messages, chat logs, correspondence attached as to Emails (or drafts), calendar entries, buddy lists.

ATTACHMENT "C"

PROTOCOL FOR SEARCHING THE ELECTRONIC DATA SEIZED PURSUANT TO THIS SEARCH WARRANT

1. In executing this warrant, the government must make reasonable efforts to use methods and procedures that will locate and expose in the electronic data produced in response to this search warrant ("the Search Warrant Data") those categories of data, files, documents, or other electronically stored information that are identified with particularity in the warrant, while minimizing exposure or examination of irrelevant, privileged, or confidential files to the extent reasonably practicable.

2. When the Search Warrant Data is received, the government will make a duplicate copy of the Search Warrant Data ("the Search Warrant Data Copy"). The original version of the Search Warrant Data will be sealed and preserved for purposes of: later judicial review or order to return or dispose of the Search Warrant Data; production to the defense in any criminal case if authorized by statute, rule, or the Constitution; for purposes of showing the chain of custody of the Search Warrant Data and the Search Warrant Data Copy; or for any other lawful purpose. The original of the Search Warrant Data will not be searched or examined except to ensure that it has been fully and completely replicated in the Search Warrant Data Copy.

3. The investigating agents will then search the entirety of the Search Warrant Data Copy using any and all methods and procedures deemed appropriate by the United States designed to identify the information listed as Information to be Seized in Attachment B, Section II. The United States may copy, extract or otherwise segregate information or data listed as Information to be Seized in Attachment B, Section II. Information or data so copied, extracted or otherwise segregated will no longer be subject to any handling restrictions that might be set out in this protocol beyond those required by binding law. To the extent evidence of crimes not within the scope of this warrant appear in plain view during this review, a supplemental or "piggyback" warrant will be applied for in order to further search that document, data, or other item.

4. Once the Search Warrant Data Copy has been thoroughly and completely examined for any document, data, or other items identified in Attachment B, Section II as Information to be Seized, the Search Warrant Data Copy will be sealed and not subject to any further search or examination unless authorized by another search warrant or other appropriate court order. The Search Warrant Data Copy will be held and preserved for the same purposes identified above in Paragraph 2.

5. The search procedures utilized for this review are at the sole discretion of the investigating and prosecuting authorities, and may include the following techniques (the following is a non-exclusive list, as other search procedures may be used):

a. examination of all of the data contained in the Search Warrant Data to view the data and determine whether that data falls within the items to be seized as set forth herein;

b. searching for and attempting to recover from the Search Warrant Data any deleted, hidden, or encrypted data to determine whether that data falls within the list of items to be seized as set forth herein (any data that is encrypted and unreadable will not be returned unless law enforcement personnel have determined that the data is not (1) an instrumentality of the offenses, (2) a fruit of the criminal activity, (3) contraband, (4) otherwise unlawfully possessed, or (5) evidence of the offenses specified above);

c. surveying various file directories and the individual files they contain;

d. opening files in order to determine their contents;

e. using hash values to narrow the scope of what may be found. Hash values are under-inclusive, but are still a helpful tool;

f. scanning storage areas;

g. performing keyword searches through all electronic storage areas to determine whether occurrences of language contained in such storage areas exist that are likely to appear in the evidence described in Attachment A; and/or

h. performing any other data analysis technique that may be necessary to locate and retrieve the evidence described in Attachment B, Section II.

Return and Review Procedures

6. Rule 41 of the Federal Rules of Criminal Procedure provides, in relevant part:

(e) Issuing the Warrant.

(2) Contents of the Warrant.

(A) Warrant to Search for and Seize a Person or Property. Except for a tracking-device warrant, the warrant must identify the person or property to be searched, identify any person or property to be seized, and designate the magistrate judge to whom it must be returned. The warrant must command the officer to:

(i) execute the warrant within a specified time no longer than 14 days;

(B) Warrant Seeking Electronically Stored Information. A warrant under Rule 41(e)(2)(A) may authorize the seizure of electronic storage media or the seizure or copying of electronically stored information. Unless otherwise specified, the warrant authorizes a later review of the media or information consistent with the warrant. The time for executing the warrant in Rule 41(e)(2)(A) and (f)(1)(A) refers to the seizure or on-site copying of the media or information, and not to any later off-site copying or review.

(f) Executing and Returning the Warrant.

(1) Warrant to Search for and Seize a Person or Property.

(B) Inventory. An officer present during the execution of the warrant must prepare and verify an inventory of any property seized. . . . In a case involving the seizure of electronic storage media or the seizure or copying of electronically stored information, the inventory may be limited to describing the physical storage media that were seized or copied. The officer may retain a copy of the electronically stored information that was seized or copied.

7. Pursuant to this Rule, the government understands and will act in accordance with the following:

a. Pursuant to Rule 41(e)(2)(A)(iii), within fourteen (14) days of the execution of the warrant, an agent is required to file an inventory return with the Court, that is, to file an itemized list of the property seized. Execution of the warrant begins when the United States serves the warrant on the named custodian; execution is complete when the custodian provides all Search Warrant Data to the United States. Within fourteen (14) days of completion of the execution of the warrant, the inventory will be filed.

b. Pursuant to Rule 41(e)(2)(B), Rule 41(e)(2)(A) governs the time within which the electronically stored information must be seized after the issuance of the warrant and copied after the execution of the warrant, not the "later review of the media or information" seized, or the later off-site digital copying of that media.

c. Under Rule 41(f)(1)(B), the inventory return that is to be filed with the court may be limited to a description of the "physical storage media" into which the Search Warrant Data that was seized was placed, not an itemization of the information or data stored on the "physical storage media" into which the Search Warrant Data was placed;

d.   Under Rule 41(f)(1)(B), the government may retain a copy of that information for purposes of the investigation. The government proposes that the original storage media on which the Search Warrant Data was placed plus a full image copy of the seized Search Warrant Data be retained by the government.

e.   If the person from whom any Search Warrant Data was seized requests the return of any information in the Search Warrant Data that is not set forth in Attachment B, Section II, that information will be copied onto appropriate media and returned to the person from whom the information was seized.

SEALED

Office of the United States Attorney
District of Nevada
501 Las Vegas Boulevard, Suite 1100
Las Vegas, Nevada 89101
(702) 388-6336

STEVEN W. MYHRE
Acting United States Attorney
District of Nevada
CRISTINA D. SILVA
PATRICK BURNS
Assistant United States Attorneys
501 Las Vegas Blvd. South, Ste. 1100
Las Vegas, Nevada 89101
Telephone: (702) 388-6336
Fax (702) 388-6698
john.p.burns@usdoj.gov

Attorney for the United States of America

UNITED STATES DISTRICT COURT
DISTRICT OF NEVADA
-oOo-

IN THE MATTER OF THE SEARCH OF INFORMATION ASSOCIATED WITH EMAIL ACCOUNT CENTRALPARK4804@GMAIL.COM THAT IS STORED AT A PREMISES CONTROLLED BY GOOGLE.	Magistrate No. 17-mj-970-NJK AFFIDAVIT IN SUPPORT OF AN APPLICATION FOR A SEARCH WARRANT (Under Seal)

STATE OF NEVADA   )
) ss:
COUNTY OF CLARK   )

AFFIDAVIT IN SUPPORT OF AN
APPLICATION FOR A SEARCH WARRANT

I, Ryan S. Burke, Special Agent, Federal Bureau of Investigation (FBI), having been duly sworn, hereby depose and say:

INTRODUCTION AND AGENT BACKGROUND

1. Your Affiant makes this affidavit in support of an application for a search warrant for information associated with email account centralpark4804@gmail.com ("Target Account"), an account associated with STEPHEN PADDOCK, that is stored at

a premises owned, maintained, controlled, or operated by Google, Inc. ("Google"), an American multinational technology based in Mountain View, California that specializes in Internet-related services and products. Those services include, but are not limited to, online advertising technologies, a search engine, email services, cloud computing, and many other services. The information to be searched is described in the following paragraphs and in Attachment "A" (attached hereto and incorporated herein by reference). This affidavit is made in support of an application for a search warrant under 18 U.S.C. §§ 2703(a), 2703(b)(1)(A), and 2703(c)(1)(A) to require Google to disclose to the government records and other information in its possession, pertaining to the subscriber or customer associated with the Target Account.

2. I am an "investigative or law enforcement officer of the United States" within the meaning of Title 18, United States Code, Section 2510(7), that is, an officer of the United States who is empowered by law to conduct investigations of, and to make arrests for, offenses enumerated in Title 18, United States Code, Section 2516.

3. I have been employed as a Special Agent of the FBI for approximately five years, which began at the FBI Academy in October 2012. Upon completion of the academy, I was transferred to the Las Vegas Division's white collar crime squad and then the human trafficking squad. Since October 2015, I have been assigned to the Las Vegas Division's violent crime/gang squad. Additionally, I have been a certified member of the FBI's Cellular Analysis Survey Team since August 2015 due to my expertise in the field of historical cell site analysis.

4. During my tenure with the FBI, I have conducted surveillance, analyzed telephone records, interviewed witnesses, supervised activities of sources, executed

search warrants, executed arrest warrants, and participated in court-authorized interceptions of wire and electronic communications. These investigative activities have been conducted in conjunction with a variety of investigations, to include those involving robbery, drug trafficking, kidnapping, murder, criminal enterprises, and more. In addition to my practical experiences, I received five months of extensive law enforcement training at the FBI Academy.

5. The facts in this affidavit are derived from your Affiant's personal observations, his training and experience, and information obtained from other agents, detectives, and witnesses. This affidavit is intended to show merely that there is sufficient probable cause for the requested warrant and does not set forth all of the Affiant's knowledge about this matter.

6. Based on your Affiant's training and experience and the facts as set forth in this affidavit, there is probable cause to believe that violations of:

    a. Destruction/Damage of Aircraft or Aircraft Facilities - 18 U.S.C.A. § 32(a);

    b. Violence at International Airport - 18 U.S.C. § 37(a)(2); and

    c. Unlawful Interstate Transport/Delivery of Firearms by Non Federal Firearms Licensee – 18 USC 922(a)(3) and (5).

(hereafter, "Subject Offenses") have been committed by STEPHEN PADDOCK and others yet unknown. There is also probable cause to search the information described in Attachment "A" for evidence of these crimes and information which might reveal the identities of others involved in these crimes, as described in Attachment "B" (attached hereto and incorporated herein by reference).

///

PROBABLE CAUSE

7. On the evening of Sunday, October 1, 2017, Route 91 Harvest, a music festival, was in progress at 3901 South Las Vegas Boulevard, Las Vegas, Nevada. At approximately 10:08 p.m., the Las Vegas Metropolitan Police Department (LVMPD) received calls reporting shots had been fired at the concert and multiple victims were struck. LVMPD determined the shots were coming from Rooms 134 and 135 on the 32nd floor of the Mandalay Bay Resort and Casino, located due west of the festival rounds at 3950 South Las Vegas Boulevard, Las Vegas, Nevada. These rooms are an elevated position which overlooks the concert venue. Witness statements and video footage captured during the attack indicates that the weapons being used were firing in a fully-automatic fashion.

8. LVMPD officers ultimately made entry into the room and located an individual later identified as Stephen Paddock. Paddock was deceased from an apparent self-inflicted gunshot wound.

9. Paddock's Nevada driver's license was located in the Mandalay Bay hotel room with Paddock, and both hotel rooms were registered in his name. A player's club card in name of Marilou Danley was located in Paddock's room, and the card returned to the address located on Babbling Brook Street in Mesquite, Nevada. FBI Agents located Danley, who was traveling outside the United States at the time of the shooting. It was ultimately determined that Danley resided with Paddock at the Babbling Brook address.

10. On October 2, 2017, search warrants were executed on Paddock's Mandalay Bay hotel rooms, Paddock's vehicle at Mandalay Bay, and two Nevada residences owed

by Paddock: 1372 Babbling Brook Court in Mesquite, and 1735 Del Webb Parkway in Reno, Nevada. Officers and Agents found over 20 firearms, hundreds of rounds of ammunition, and hundreds of spent shell casings in the Mandalay Bay hotel rooms, in close proximity to Paddock's body. Over a thousand rounds of rifle ammunition and 100 pounds of explosive material was found in Paddock's vehicle. Additional explosive material, approximately 18 firearms, and over 1,000 rounds of ammunition was located at the Mesquite residence. A large quantity of ammunition and multiple firearms were recovered from the Reno residence.

11. As of this date, 58 people have been identified to have been killed in Paddock's attack and another 557 were reportedly injured. Additionally, investigators discovered that STEPHEN PADDOCK also utilized a firearm to shoot large fuel tanks on Las Vegas McCarran International Airport property. Multiple bullet holes were found on the tank, which investigators believe was an attempt by STEPHEN PADDOCK to cause the tanks to explode.

12. In an effort to determine whether or not STEPHEN PADDOCK was assisted and/or conspired with unknown individuals, investigators have attempted to identify all of STEPHEN PADDOCK's communication facilities. Based on a review of his financial accounts, email address centralpark1@live.com ("Account 2") was determined to belong to STEPHEN PADDOCK. On October 3, 2017, investigators requested an emergency disclosure of records from Microsoft related to Account 2 so it could be searched for any evidence of additional co-conspirators. Within the account, investigators identified the Target Account as one that required further investigation.

13. On July 6, 2017, the Target Account sent an email to Account 2 that read, "try an ar before u buy. we have huge selection. located in the las vegas area." Later that day, Account 2 sent an email to the Target Account that read, "we have a wide variety of optics and ammunition to try." And lastly, Account 2 later sent an email to the Target Account that read, "for a thrill try out bumpfire ar's with a 100 round magazine."

14. Based on the similarity of both email account names, investigators believe the Target Account may also be controlled by STEPHEN PADDOCK. Additionally, STEPHEN PADDOCK was previously a manager of an apartment complex in the Reno, Nevada area called "Central Park," which investigators believe further substantiates his association to the Target Account. However, investigators have been unable to figure out why STEPHEN PADDOCK would be exchanging messages related to weapons that were utilized in the attack between two of his email accounts. Conversely, if the Target Account was not controlled by STEPHEN PADDOCK, investigators need to determine who was communicating with him about weapons that were used in the attack. Paddock acquired a substantial amount of firearms from out of state which appear to have been transported into the state of Nevada where he resides.

15. Your Affiant believes the requested search warrant will yield significant information from Google such as STEPHEN PADDOCK's contact list, email message content, IP address usage, photographs, third-party applications associated with the account, and more, which may constitute evidence of his planning of the attack and potentially identify other participants in the attack. Ultimately, your Affiant strongly believes the requested information will lead investigators to determine the full scope of STEPHEN PADDOCK's plan.

RELEVANT TECHNICAL TERMS

16. The following non-exhaustive list of definitions applies to this Affidavit and the Attachments to this Affidavit:

   a. The "Internet" is a worldwide network of computer systems operated by governmental entities, corporations, and universities. In order to access the Internet, an individual computer user must subscribe to an access provider, which operates a host computer system with direct access to the Internet. The World Wide Web is a functionality of the Internet which allows users of the Internet to share information.

   b. "Internet Service Providers" are companies that provide access to the Internet. ISPs can also provide other services for their customers including website hosting, email service, remote storage, and co-location of computers and other communications equipment. ISPs offer different ways to access the Internet including telephone-based (dial-up), broadband-based access via a digital subscriber line (DSL) or cable television, dedicated circuits, or satellite-based subscription. ISPs typically charge a fee based upon the type of connection and volume of data (bandwidth). Many ISPs assign each subscriber an account name, such as a user name, an email address, and an email mailbox, and the subscriber typically creates a password for his/her account.

   c. "ISP Records" are records maintained by ISPs pertaining to their subscribers (regardless of whether those subscribers are individuals or entities). These records may include account application information, subscriber and billing information, account access information (often in the form of log files), emails, information concerning content uploaded and/or stored on the ISP's servers, and other information, which may be stored both in computer data format and in written or printed record format. ISPs reserve and/or maintain computer disk storage space on their computer system for their subscribers' use. This service by ISPs allows for both temporary and long-term storage of electronic communications and many other types of electronic data and files.

   d. "Online service providers" (also referred to here as "service providers") are companies that provide online services such as email, chat or instant messaging, word processing applications, spreadsheet applications, presentation applications similar to PowerPoint, online calendar, photo storage and remote storage services. Sometimes they also can provide web hosting, remote storage, and co-location of computers and other communications equipment. Typically, each service provider assigns each subscriber an account name, such as a user name or screen name and the subscriber typically creates a password for his/her account.

   e. "Computer," as used herein, is defined as "an electronic, magnetic, optical, electrochemical, or other high speed data processing device performing logical or storage functions, and includes any data storage facility or communications facility directly related to or operating in conjunction with such device."

   f. A "server" is a centralized computer that provides services for other computers connected to it via a network. The other computers attached to a server are sometimes called "clients." For example, in a large company, it is common for individual employees to have client computers at their desktops. When the employees access their email, or access files stored on the network itself, those files are pulled electronically from the server, where they are stored, and are sent to the client's computer via the network. Notably, servers can be physically stored in any location: it is not uncommon for a network's server to be located hundreds (and even thousands) of miles away from the client computers.

g. "Internet Protocol address," or "IP address," refers to a unique number used by a computer to access the Internet. IP addresses can be dynamic, meaning that the Internet Service Provider (ISP) assigns a different unique number to a computer every time it accesses the Internet. IP addresses might also be static, that is, an ISP assigns a user's computer a particular IP address which is used each time the computer accesses the Internet.

h. The term "domain" refers to a word used as a name for computers, networks, services, etc. A domain name typically represents a website, a server computer that hosts that website, or even some computer (or other digital device) connected to the internet. Essentially, when a website (or a server computer that hosts that website) is connected to the internet, it is assigned an IP address. Because IP addresses are difficult for people to remember, domain names are instead used because they are easier to remember than IP addresses. Domain names are formed by the rules and procedures of the Domain Name System (DNS). A common top level domain under these rules is ".com" for commercial organizations, ".gov" for the United States government, and ".org" for organizations. For example, www.usdoj.gov is the domain name that identifies a server used by the U.S. Department of Justice, and which uses IP address of 149.101.46.71.

i. "Web hosting services" maintain server computers connected to the Internet. Their customers use those computers to operate websites on the Internet. Customers of web hosting companies place files, software code, databases, and other data

on servers. To do this, customers typically connect from their own computers to the server computers across the Internet.

   j. The term "WhoIs" lookup refers to a search of a publicly available online database that lists information provided when a domain is registered or when an IP address is assigned.

   k. The terms "communications," "records," "documents," "programs," or "materials" include all information recorded in any form, visual or aural, and by any means, whether in handmade form (including, but not limited to, writings, drawings, paintings), photographic form (including, but not limited to, pictures or videos), or electrical, electronic or magnetic form, as well as digital data files. These terms also include any applications (i.e. software programs). These terms expressly include, among other things, emails, instant messages, chat logs, correspondence attached as to emails (or drafts), calendar entries, buddy lists.

   l. "Chat" is usually a real time electronic communication between two or more individuals. Unlike email, which is frequently sent, then read and responded to minutes, hours, or even days later, chats frequently involve an immediate conversation between individuals, similar to a face-to-face conversation. Nearly all chat programs are capable of saving the chat transcript, to enable users to preserve a record of the conversation. By default, some chat programs have this capability enabled, while others do not. Many popular web-based email providers, like Google and Google, provide chat functionality as part of the online services they provide to account holders.

///

///

FACTS ABOUT EMAIL PROVIDERS

17. In my training, my experience and this investigation, I have learned that Google (the Service Provider) is a company that provides free web-based Internet email access to the general public, and that stored electronic communications, including opened and unopened email for Google subscribers may be located on the computers of Google. I have also learned that Google Inc. provides various on-line service messaging services to the general public. Instant Messaging ("IM") is a form of real-time direct text-based communication between two or more people using shared clients. The text is conveyed via devices connected over a network such as the Internet. In addition to text, Google's software allows users with the most current updated versions to utilize its webcam service. This option enables users from distances all over the world to view others who have installed a webcam on their end. Thus, the Service Provider's servers will contain a wide variety of the subscriber's files, including emails, address books, contact or buddy lists, calendar data, pictures, chat logs, and other files.

18. To use these services, subscribers register for online accounts like the Target Account. During the registration process, service providers such as the ones here ask subscribers to provide basic personal information. This information can include the subscriber's full name, physical address, telephone numbers and other identifiers, alternative email addresses, and, for paying subscribers, means and source of payment (including any credit card or bank account number). Based on my training and my experience, I know that subscribers may insert false information to conceal their identity; even if this proves to be the case, however, I know that this information often provide clues to their identity, location or illicit activities.

19. In general, when a subscriber receives an email, it is typically stored in the subscriber's "mail box" on that service provider's servers until the subscriber deletes the Email. If the subscriber does not delete the message, the message (and any attachments) can remain on that service provider's servers indefinitely.

20. Similarly, when the subscriber sends an email, it is initiated at the subscriber's computer, transferred via the Internet to the service provider's servers, and then transmitted to its end destination. That service provider often saves a copy of the email sent. Unless the sender of the email specifically deletes the Email from the provider's server, the email can remain on the system indefinitely.

21. A sent or received email typically includes the content of the message, source and destination addresses, the date and time at which the email was sent, and the size and length of the email. If an email user writes a draft message but does not send it, that message may also be saved by that service provider, but may not include all of these categories of data.

22. Just as a computer on a desk can be used to store a wide variety of files, so can online accounts, such as the accounts subject to this application. First, subscribers can store many types of files as attachments to emails in online accounts. Second, because service providers provide the services listed above (e.g. word processing, spreadsheets, pictures), subscribers who use these services usually store documents on servers maintained and/or owned by service providers. Thus, these online accounts often contain documents such as pictures, audio or video recordings, logs, spreadsheets, applications and other files.

23. Reviewing files stored in online accounts raises many of the same difficulties as with reviewing files stored on a local computer. For example, based on my training, my experience and this investigation, I know that subscribers of these online services can conceal their activities by altering files before they upload them to the online service. Subscribers can change file names to more innocuous sounding names (e.g. renaming "FraudRecords.doc" to "ChristmasList.doc"), they can change file extensions to make one kind of file appear like a different type of file (e.g. changing the spreadsheet "StolenCreditProfiles.xls" to "FamilyPhoto.jpg" to appear to be a picture file, where the file extension ".xls" denotes an Excel spreadsheet file and ".jpg" a JPEG format image file), or they can change the times and dates a file was last accessed or modified by changing a computer's system time/date and then uploading that file to the Online Accounts. Thus, to detect any files that the subscriber may have concealed, agents will need to review all of the files in the Target Account; they will, however, only seize the items that the Court authorizes to be seized. Similarly, subscribers can conceal their activities by encrypting files. Thus, these files may need to be decrypted to detect whether it constitutes an Item to be Seized.

24. I also believe that people engaged in crimes such as the one described herein often use online accounts because they give people engaged in these crimes a way to easily communicate with other co-conspirators. Moreover, online accounts are easily concealed from law enforcement. Unlike physical documents, electronic documents can be stored in a physical place far away, where they are less likely to be discovered.

25. Service providers typically retain certain transactional information about the creation and use of each account on their systems. This information can include the

13

date on which the account was created, the length of service, records of log-in (i.e., session) times and durations, the types of service utilized, the status of the account (including whether the account is inactive or closed), the methods used to connect to the account (such as logging into the account via websites controlled by the Service Provider), and other log files that reflect usage of the account. In addition, service providers often have records of the Internet Protocol address ("IP address") used to register the account and the IP addresses associated with particular logins to the account. Because every device that connects to the Internet must use an IP address, IP address information can help to identify which computers or other devices were used to access the online account.

26. In some cases, subscribers will communicate directly with a service provider about issues relating to the account, such as technical problems, billing inquiries, or complaints from or about other users. Service providers typically retain records about such communications, including records of contacts between the user and the provider's support services, as well records of any actions taken by the provider or user as a result of the communications.

27. In my training and experience, evidence of who was using an online account may be found in address books, contact or buddy lists, emails in the account, and pictures and files, whether stored as attachments or in the suite of the service provider's online applications. Therefore, the computers of the Service Providers are likely to contain stored electronic communications (including retrieved and un-retrieved email for their subscribers) and information concerning subscribers and their use of the

provider's services, such as account access information, email transaction information, documents, pictures, and account application information.

INFORMATION TO BE SEARCHED AND THINGS TO BE SEIZED

28. Your Affiant anticipates executing this warrant under the Electronic Communications Privacy Act, in particular 18 U.S.C. §§ 2703(a), 2703(b)(1)(A) and 2703(c)(1)(A), by using the warrant to require Google to disclose to the government copies of the records and other information (including the content of communications) particularly described in Section I of Attachment "B." Upon receipt of the information described in Section I of Attachment "B," government-authorized persons will review that information to locate the items described in Section II of Attachment "B."

CONCLUSION

29. Based on the forgoing, I request that the Court issue the proposed search warrant. This Court has jurisdiction to issue the requested warrant because it is "a court of competent jurisdiction" as defined by 18 U.S.C. § 2711. 18 U.S.C. §§ 2703(a), (b)(1)(A) & (c)(1)(A). Specifically, the Court is "a district court of the United States . . . that – has jurisdiction over the offense being investigated." 18 U.S.C. § 2711(3)(A)(i). Pursuant to 18 U.S.C. § 2703(g), the presence of a law enforcement officer is not required for the service or execution of this warrant.

REQUEST FOR SEALING

30. I further request that the Court order that all papers in support of this application, including the affidavit and search warrant, be sealed until further order of the Court. These documents discuss an ongoing criminal investigation that is neither public nor known to all of the targets of the investigation. Accordingly, there is good

cause to seal these documents because their premature disclosure may seriously jeopardize that investigation.

Respectfully Submitted,

Ryan S. Burke, Special Agent
Federal Bureau of Investigation

SWORN TO AND SUBSCRIBED
before me this 10th day of October 2017.

UNITED STATES MAGISTRATE JUDGE

ATTACHMENT "A"

ONLINE ACCOUNT TO BE SEARCHED

1. This warrant applies to information associated with the Google email account centralpark4804@gmail.com (the "Target Account") from its inception to present, which is stored at premises owned, maintained, controlled, or operated by Google, Inc., headquartered at 1600 Amphitheatre Way, Mountain View, California, 94043.

ATTACHMENT "B"
Particular Things to be Seized

I. **Information to be disclosed by the Service Provider**

To the extent that the information described in Attachment A is within the possession, custody, or control of Google, including any Emails, records, files, logs, or information that have been deleted but are still available to Service Provider, or have been preserved pursuant to a request made under 18 U.S.C. § 2703(f), Service Provider is required to disclose the following information to the government for each account or identifier listed in Attachment A from account inception to present:

a. The contents of all emails associated with the account, including copies of emails sent to and from the account, draft emails, the source and destination addresses associated with each email, the date and time at which each email was sent, and the size and length of each email;

b. All records or other information regarding the identification of the account, to include full name, physical address, telephone numbers and other identifiers, records of session times and durations, the date on which the account was created, the length of service, the types of service utilized, the IP address used to register the account, log-in IP addresses associated with session times and dates, account status, alternative email addresses provided during registration, methods of connecting, log files, and means and source of payment (including any credit or bank account number);

c. All records or other information stored in the Online Accounts, including address books, contact and buddy lists, calendar data, pictures, applications, documents, and other files;

d. All records pertaining to communications between Service Provider and any person regarding the account, including contacts with support services and records of actions taken.

e. All third-party application data and content associated with the Target Account through any Android operating system and/or any Google-related facility.

II. Information to be seized by the United States

After reviewing all information described in Section I, the United States will seize evidence of violations of Title 18, United States Code Sections 32(a) (Destruction/Damage of Aircraft or Aircraft Facilities); 37(a)(2) (Violence at International Airport); and 922(a)(3); 5 (Unlawful Interstate Transport/Delivery of Firearms by Non Federal Firearms Licensee) (the "Subject Offenses") that occur in the form of the following, from account inception to present:

a. Communications, transactions and records that may establish ownership and control (or the degree thereof) of the Target Account, including address books, contact or buddy lists, bills, invoices, receipts, registration records, bills, correspondence, notes, records, memoranda, telephone/address books, photographs, video recordings, audio recordings, lists of names, records of payment for access to newsgroups or other online subscription services, and attachments to said communications, transactions and records.

b. Communications, transactions and records to/from persons who may be co-conspirators of the Subject Offenses, or which may identify co-conspirators.

c. Communications, transactions and records which may show motivation to commit the Subject Offenses.

d. Communications, transactions and records that relate to the Subject Offenses.

e. The terms "communications," "transactions", "records," "documents," "programs," or "materials" include all information recorded in any form, visual or aural, and by any means, whether in handmade form (including, but not limited to, writings, drawings, paintings), photographic form (including, but not limited to, pictures or videos), or electrical, electronic or magnetic form, as well as digital data files. These terms also include any applications (i.e. software programs). These terms expressly include, among other things, Emails, instant messages, chat logs, correspondence attached as to Emails (or drafts), calendar entries, buddy lists.

ATTACHMENT "C"

PROTOCOL FOR SEARCHING THE ELECTRONIC DATA SEIZED PURSUANT TO THIS SEARCH WARRANT

1. In executing this warrant, the government must make reasonable efforts to use methods and procedures that will locate and expose in the electronic data produced in response to this search warrant ("the Search Warrant Data") those categories of data, files, documents, or other electronically stored information that are identified with particularity in the warrant, while minimizing exposure or examination of irrelevant, privileged, or confidential files to the extent reasonably practicable.

2. When the Search Warrant Data is received, the government will make a duplicate copy of the Search Warrant Data ("the Search Warrant Data Copy"). The original version of the Search Warrant Data will be sealed and preserved for purposes of: later judicial review or order to return or dispose of the Search Warrant Data; production to the defense in any criminal case if authorized by statute, rule, or the Constitution; for purposes of showing the chain of custody of the Search Warrant Data and the Search Warrant Data Copy; or for any other lawful purpose. The original of the Search Warrant Data will not be searched or examined except to ensure that it has been fully and completely replicated in the Search Warrant Data Copy.

3. The investigating agents will then search the entirety of the Search Warrant Data Copy using any and all methods and procedures deemed appropriate by the United States designed to identify the information listed as Information to be Seized in Attachment B, Section II. The United States may copy, extract or otherwise segregate information or data listed as Information to be Seized in Attachment B, Section II. Information or data so copied, extracted or otherwise segregated will no longer be subject to any handling restrictions that might be set out in this protocol beyond those required by binding law. To the extent evidence of crimes not within the scope of this warrant appear in plain view during this review, a supplemental or "piggyback" warrant will be applied for in order to further search that document, data, or other item.

4. Once the Search Warrant Data Copy has been thoroughly and completely examined for any document, data, or other items identified in Attachment B, Section II as Information to be Seized, the Search Warrant Data Copy will be sealed and not subject to any further search or examination unless authorized by another search warrant or other appropriate court order. The Search Warrant Data Copy will be held and preserved for the same purposes identified above in Paragraph 2.

5. The search procedures utilized for this review are at the sole discretion of the investigating and prosecuting authorities, and may include the following techniques (the following is a non-exclusive list, as other search procedures may be used):

a. examination of all of the data contained in the Search Warrant Data to view the data and determine whether that data falls within the items to be seized as set forth herein;

b. searching for and attempting to recover from the Search Warrant Data any deleted, hidden, or encrypted data to determine whether that data falls within the list of items to be seized as set forth herein (any data that is encrypted and unreadable will not be returned unless law enforcement personnel have determined that the data is not (1) an instrumentality of the offenses, (2) a fruit of the criminal activity, (3) contraband, (4) otherwise unlawfully possessed, or (5) evidence of the offenses specified above);

c. surveying various file directories and the individual files they contain;

d. opening files in order to determine their contents;

e. using hash values to narrow the scope of what may be found. Hash values are under- inclusive, but are still a helpful tool;

f. scanning storage areas;

g. performing keyword searches through all electronic storage areas to determine whether occurrences of language contained in such storage areas exist that are likely to appear in the evidence described in Attachment A; and/or

h. performing any other data analysis technique that may be necessary to locate and retrieve the evidence described in Attachment B, Section II.

Return and Review Procedures

6. Rule 41 of the Federal Rules of Criminal Procedure provides, in relevant part:

(e) Issuing the Warrant.

(2) Contents of the Warrant.

(A) Warrant to Search for and Seize a Person or Property. Except for a tracking-device warrant, the warrant must identify the person or property to be searched, identify any person or property to be seized, and designate the magistrate judge to whom it must be returned. The warrant must command the officer to:

(i) execute the warrant within a specified time no longer than 14 days;

(B) Warrant Seeking Electronically Stored Information. A warrant under Rule 41(e)(2)(A) may authorize the seizure of electronic storage media or the seizure or copying of electronically stored information. Unless otherwise specified, the warrant authorizes a later review of the media or information consistent with the warrant. The time for executing the warrant in Rule 41(e)(2)(A) and (f)(1)(A) refers to the seizure or on-site copying of the media or information, and not to any later off-site copying or review.

(f) Executing and Returning the Warrant.

(1) Warrant to Search for and Seize a Person or Property.

(B) Inventory. An officer present during the execution of the warrant must prepare and verify an inventory of any property seized. . . . In a case involving the seizure of electronic storage media or the seizure or copying of electronically stored information, the inventory may be limited to describing the physical storage media that were seized or copied. The officer may retain a copy of the electronically stored information that was seized or copied.

7. Pursuant to this Rule, the government understands and will act in accordance with the following:

a. Pursuant to Rule 41(e)(2)(A)(iii), within fourteen (14) days of the execution of the warrant, an agent is required to file an inventory return with the Court, that is, to file an itemized list of the property seized. Execution of the warrant begins when the United States serves the warrant on the named custodian; execution is complete when the custodian provides all Search Warrant Data to the United States. Within fourteen (14) days of completion of the execution of the warrant, the inventory will be filed.

b. Pursuant to Rule 41(e)(2)(B), Rule 41(e)(2)(A) governs the time within which the electronically stored information must be seized after the issuance of the warrant and copied after the execution of the warrant, not the "later review of the media or information" seized, or the later off-site digital copying of that media.

c. Under Rule 41(f)(1)(B), the inventory return that is to be filed with the court may be limited to a description of the "physical storage media" into which the Search Warrant Data that was seized was placed, not an itemization of the information or data stored on the "physical storage media" into which the Search Warrant Data was placed;

d. Under Rule 41(f)(1)(B), the government may retain a copy of that information for purposes of the investigation. The government proposes that the original storage media on which the Search Warrant Data was placed plus a full image copy of the seized Search Warrant Data be retained by the government.

e. If the person from whom any Search Warrant Data was seized requests the return of any information in the Search Warrant Data that is not set forth in Attachment B, Section II, that information will be copied onto appropriate media and returned to the person from whom the information was seized.

STEVEN W. MYHRE
Acting United States Attorney
District of Nevada
Cristina D. Silva
Patrick Burns
Assistant United States Attorneys
501 Las Vegas Blvd. South, Ste. 1100
Las Vegas, Nevada 89101
Telephone: (702) 388-6336
Fax (702) 388-6698
CSilva@usa.doj.gov
john.p.burns@usdoj.gov

Representing the United States of America

UNITED STATES DISTRICT COURT
DISTRICT OF NEVADA
-oOo-

IN THE MATTER OF THE SEARCH OF:

THE PREMISES KNOWN AS:
1372 BABBLING BROOK COURT,
MESQUITE, COUNTY OF CLARK,
STATE OF NEVADA.

Magistrate No. 17-mj-973-NJK

AFFIDAVIT IN SUPPORT OF
SEARCH WARRANT

(Under Seal)

STATE OF NEVADA   )
) ss:
COUNTY OF CLARK   )

AFFIDAVIT IN SUPPORT OF SEARCH WARRANT

1. I, Christopher W. McPeak, Special Agent, Federal Bureau of Investigation (FBI), having been duly sworn, hereby depose and say:

2. Your Affiant is a Special Agent with the FBI currently assigned to the Las Vegas, Nevada Division and has been so employed for over eight years. Prior to this he was employed for over five years as a Deputy Sheriff and Detective with the Orange County, Florida Sheriff's Office. As an FBI Agent, your Affiant is assigned to the FBI's Las Vegas Safe Streets Task Force (LVSSTF) and is responsible for investigating a variety of violent crimes, to include bank

robbery, kidnapping, extortion, robbery, carjackings, assaults and murders of federal officers, racketeering related violent offenses, as well as long-term investigations into the activities and operations of career criminals, criminal enterprises, drug trafficking organizations, and violent street gangs. Your Affiant has experience in conducting criminal investigations, including the investigation of criminal groups and conspiracies as well as the collection of evidence and the identification and use of witnesses.

3. The facts in this affidavit are derived from your Affiant's personal observations, his training and experience, and information obtained from other agents, detectives, and witnesses. This affidavit is intended to show merely that there is sufficient probable cause for the requested warrant and does not set forth all of the Affiant's knowledge about this matter.

PREMISES TO BE SEARCHED

4. The proposed search warrant seeks authorization to search the premises identified as 1372 Babbling Brook Court, Mesquite, Clark County, Nevada (hereinafter referred to as the "subject premises"), more fully described in Attachment "A" (attached hereto and incorporated herein by reference).

REQUEST FOR SEARCH WARRANT

5. Based on your Affiant's training and experience and the facts as set forth in this affidavit, there is probable cause to believe that violations of, *inter alia*:

   a. Destruction/Damage of Aircraft or Aircraft Facilities - 18 U.S.C. § 32(a);

   b. Violence at an International Airport - 18 U.S.C. § 37(a)(2);

   c. Unlawful Interstate Transport/Delivery of Firearms by Non-Federal Firearms Licensee – 18 U.S.C. § 922(a)(3) and (5); and

   d. Aiding and Abetting – 18 U.S.C. § 2,

(hereinafter referred to as the "subject offenses") have been committed by Stephen Paddock and others yet unknown; and this affidavit is made in support of an application for a search warrant

AO 106 (Rev. 04/10) Application for a Search Warrant

UNITED STATES DISTRICT COURT
for the
District of Nevada

I hereby attest and certify on __10-3-17__
that the foregoing document is a full true and correct
copy of the original on file in my office, and in my legal
custody.

CAM FERENBACH
U.S. MAGISTRATE JUDGE
DISTRICT OF NEVADA

In the Matter of the Search of
(Briefly describe the property to be searched or identify the person by name and address)
INSTAGRAM ACCOUNTS STORED AT PREMISES CONTROLLED BY FACEBOOK CORPORATION: Mariloudanley A2

Case No. By 2:17-mj-00959-VCF
Deputy Secretary

APPLICATION FOR A SEARCH WARRANT

I, a federal law enforcement officer or an attorney for the government, request a search warrant and state under penalty of perjury that I have reason to believe that on the following person or property *(identify the person or describe the property to be searched and give its location)*:
INSTAGRAM ACCOUNTS STORED AT PREMISES CONTROLLED BY FACEBOOK CORPORATION: Mariloudanley A2

located in the _____DEA_____ District of _____, there is now concealed *(identify the person or describe the property to be seized)*:
INSTAGRAM ACCOUNTS STORED AT PREMISES CONTROLLED BY FACEBOOK CORPORATION: Mariloudanley A2

The basis for the search under Fed. R. Crim. P. 41(c) is *(check one or more)*:
- ☒ evidence of a crime;
- ☒ contraband, fruits of crime, or other items illegally possessed;
- ☒ property designed for use, intended for use, or used in committing a crime;
- ☒ a person to be arrested or a person who is unlawfully restrained.

The search is related to a violation of:

Code Section	Offense Description
Title 26, United States Code, Section 5841.	Violation of National Firearms Act

FILED 2017 OCT -3 PM 3:36 BY _____ U.S. MAGISTRATE JUDGE

The application is based on these facts:
I believe there is probable cause to believe that in the subject accounts listed in Attachments "A1", "A2", "A3", "A4", "A5" there is proof that constitutes evidence of the commission of criminal offense(s); contraband, the fruits of crime and things otherwise criminally possessed and been used as the means of committing criminal offense(s)

- ☐ Continued on the attached sheet.
- ☐ Delayed notice of ____ days (give exact ending date if more than 30 days: _____) is requested under 18 U.S.C. § 3103a, the basis of which is set forth on the attached sheet.

/S/
Applicant's signature

Printed name and title

Sworn to before me and signed in my presence.

Date: __10-3-17__

City and state: __Las Vegas, Nevada__

CAM FERENBACH
Judge's signature
CAM FERENBACH
U.S. MAGISTRATE JUDGE
Printed name and title

AO 93 (Rev. 11/13) Search and Seizure Warrant

UNITED STATES DISTRICT COURT
for the
District of Nevada

In the Matter of the Search of
(Briefly describe the property to be searched or identify the person by name and address)

Mariloudanley A2

Case No. 2:17-mj-00959-VCF

I hereby attest and certify on:
that the foregoing document is a full true and correct copy of the original on file in my office, and in my legal custody.

CAM FERENBACH
U.S. MAGISTRATE JUDGE
DISTRICT OF NEVADA

By _____ ☐ Deputy ☒ Secretary

SEARCH AND SEIZURE WARRANT

To: Any authorized law enforcement officer

An application by a federal law enforcement officer or an attorney for the government requests the search of the following person or property located in the _____ District of _____ Nevada
(identify the person or describe the property to be searched and give its location):

SEE ATTACHMENT A2

I find that the affidavit(s), or any recorded testimony, establish probable cause to search and seize the person or property described above, and that such search will reveal *(identify the person or describe the property to be seized):*

SEE ATTACHMENTS B and C

YOU ARE COMMANDED to execute this warrant on or before 10-12-17 *(not to exceed 14 days)*
☒ in the daytime 6:00 a.m. to 10:00 p.m.   ☐ at any time in the day or night because good cause has been established.

Unless delayed notice is authorized below, you must give a copy of the warrant and a receipt for the property taken to the person from whom, or from whose premises, the property was taken, or leave the copy and receipt at the place where the property was taken.

The officer executing this warrant, or an officer present during the execution of the warrant, must prepare an inventory as required by law and promptly return this warrant and inventory to   CAM FERENBACH
(United States Magistrate Judge)

☐ Pursuant to 18 U.S.C. § 3103a(b), I find that immediate notification may have an adverse result listed in 18 U.S.C. § 2705 (except for delay of trial), and authorize the officer executing this warrant to delay notice to the person who, or whose property, will be searched or seized *(check the appropriate box)*
☐ for ____ days *(not to exceed 30)*   ☐ until, the facts justifying, the later specific date of _____

Date and time issued: 10-3-17 4:04p

City and state: Las Vegas, Nevada

CAM FERENBACH
Judge's signature

CAM FERENBACH
U.S. MAGISTRATE JUDGE
Printed name and title

SEALED

Office of the United States Attorney
District of Nevada
501 Las Vegas Boulevard, Suite 1100
Las Vegas, Nevada 89101
(702) 388-6336

Attachment "A2"

Property to Be Searched

This warrant applies to information associated with the Instagram user IDs **mariloudanley**, that is stored at premises owned, maintained, controlled, or operated by Facebook, a company headquartered in Menlo Park, California for the time period beginning September 1, 2016 to present.

ATTACHMENT "B"

Particular Things to be Seized

I. **Information to be disclosed by Facebook**

To the extent that the information described in Attachment A is within the possession, custody, or control of Instagram LLC ("Instagram"), including any messages, records, files, logs, or information that have been deleted but are still available to Instagram, or have been preserved pursuant to a request made under 18 U.S.C. § 2703(f) on October 3, 2017. Facebook is required to disclose the following information to the government for each user IDs listed in Attachment A for the period of September 1, 2016 to present:

(a) All contact and personal identifying information, including: full name, user identification number, birth date, gender, contact e-mail addresses, Instagram passwords, Instagram security questions and answers, physical address (including city, state, and zip code), telephone numbers, screen names, websites, and other personal identifiers;

(b) All activity logs for the account and all other documents showing the user's posts and other Instagram activities;

(c) All photos and videos uploaded by that user ID and all photos and videos uploaded by any user that have that user tagged in them;

(d) All profile information; status updates; links to videos, photographs, bios, articles, and other items; Wall postings; friend lists, including the friends' Instagram user identification numbers; future and past event postings; comments; and tags;

(e) All other records of communications and messages made or received by the user, chat history, and pending "Friend" requests;

(f) All user content created, uploaded, or shared by the account, including any comments made by the account on photographs or other content;

(g) All IP logs, including all records of the IP addresses that logged into the account;

(h) All records of the account's usage of the "Like" feature, including all Instagram posts and content that the user has "liked";

(i) All location data associated with the account, including geotags;

(j) All data and information that has been deleted by the user;

(k) All past and present lists of friends created by the account;

(l) All records of Instagram searches performed by the account;

(m) The types of service utilized by the user;

(n) The length of service (including start date) and the means and source of any payments associated with the service (including any credit card or bank account number);

(o) All privacy settings and other account settings, including privacy settings for individual Instagram posts and activities, and all records showing which Instagram users have been blocked by the account;

(p) All records pertaining to communications between Instagram and any person regarding the user or the user's Instagram account, including contacts with support services and records of actions taken.

(q) All information regarding the particular device or devices used to login to or access the account, including all device identifier information or cookie information, including all information about the particular device or devices used to access the account and the date and time of those accesses;

II. Information to be seized by the government

All information described above in Section I that constitutes fruits, evidence, and instrumentalities of violations of:

Violation of National Firearms Act – Registration of Firearms, Title 26, United States Code, Section 5841.

involving STEPHEN PADDOCK and others yet unidentified, including, for each user ID identified on Attachment "A," information pertaining to the following matters:

(a) Evidence showing the possession, use, purchase, or sale of firearms, firearms accessories, ammunition, or explosives by Paddock, including through conspiring and cooperating to possess, use, purchase, or sell prohibited firearms, firearms accessories, ammunition, or explosives.

(b) Evidence indicating how and when the Instagram account was accessed or used, to determine the chronological and geographic context of account access, use, and events relating to the crime under investigation and to the Facebook account owner;

(c) Evidence indicating the Instagram account owner's state of mind as it relates to the crime under investigation;

(d) The identity of the person(s) who created or used the user ID, including records that help reveal the whereabouts of such person(s).

(e) The identity of the person(s) who communicated with the user ID about matters relating to the illegal possession, purchase, use, or sale of firearms, firearms accessories, ammunition, or explosives, including records that help reveal their whereabouts.

The Warrant expressly incorporates the Affidavit submitted in support of the Warrant, and separately sealed, as though set forth fully herein.

ATTACHMENT C

PROTOCOL FOR SEARCHING THE ELECTRONIC DATA SEIZED

PURSUANT TO THIS SEARCH WARRANT

1. In executing this warrant, the government must make reasonable efforts to use methods and procedures that will locate and expose in the electronic data produced in response to this search warrant ("the Search Warrant Data") those categories of data, files, documents, or other electronically stored information that are identified with particularity in the warrant, while minimizing exposure or examination of irrelevant, privileged, or confidential files to the extent reasonably practicable.

2. When the Search Warrant Data is received, the government will make a duplicate copy of the Search Warrant Data ("the Search Warrant Data Copy"). The original version of the Search Warrant Data will be sealed and preserved for purposes of: later judicial review or order to return or dispose of the Search Warrant Data; production to the defense in any criminal case if authorized by statute, rule, or the Constitution; for purposes of showing the chain of custody of the Search Warrant Data and the Search Warrant Data Copy; or for any other lawful purpose. The original of the Search Warrant Data will not be searched or examined except to ensure that it has been fully and completely replicated in the Search Warrant Data Copy.

3. The investigating agents will then search the entirety of the Search Warrant Data Copy using any and all methods and procedures deemed appropriate by the United States designed to identify the information listed as Information to be Seized in Attachment B, Section II. The United States may copy, extract or otherwise segregate information or data listed as Information to be Seized in Attachment B, Section II. Information or data so copied, extracted or otherwise segregated will no longer be subject to any handling restrictions that might be set out in this protocol beyond those required by binding law. To the extent evidence of crimes not within the scope of this warrant appear in plain view during this review, a supplemental or "piggyback" warrant will be applied for in order to further search that document, data, or other item.

4. The Government will have ninety (90) days from receipt of the data disclosed under Attachment B, Section I to complete its examination of the Search Warrant Data Copy. Once the Search Warrant Data Copy has been thoroughly and completely examined for any document, data, or other items identified in Attachment B, Section II as Information to be Seized, the Search Warrant Data Copy will be sealed and not subject to any further search or examination unless authorized by another search warrant or other appropriate court order. The Search Warrant Data Copy will be held and preserved for the same purposes identified above in Paragraph 2.

5. The search procedures utilized for this review are at the sole discretion of the investigating and prosecuting authorities, and may include the following techniques (the following is a non-exclusive list, as other search procedures may be used):

a. examination of all of the data contained in the Search Warrant Data to view the data and determine whether that data falls within the items to be seized as set forth herein;

b. searching for and attempting to recover from the Search Warrant Data any deleted, hidden, or encrypted data to determine whether that data falls within the list of items to be seized as set forth herein (any data that is encrypted and unreadable will not be returned unless law enforcement personnel have determined that the data is not (1) an instrumentality of the offenses, (2) a fruit of the criminal activity, (3) contraband, (4) otherwise unlawfully possessed, or (5) evidence of the offenses specified above);

c. surveying various file directories and the individual files they contain;

d. opening files in order to determine their contents;

e. using hash values to narrow the scope of what may be found. Hash values are under-inclusive, but are still a helpful tool;

f. scanning storage areas;

g. performing keyword searches through all electronic storage areas to determine whether occurrences of language contained in such storage areas exist that are likely to appear in the evidence described in Attachment A; and/or

h. performing any other data analysis technique that may be necessary to locate and retrieve the evidence described in Attachment B, Section II.

Return and Review Procedures

6. Rule 41 of the Federal Rules of Criminal Procedure provides, in relevant part:

(e) Issuing the Warrant.

(2) Contents of the Warrant.

(A) Warrant to Search for and Seize a Person or Property. Except for a tracking-device warrant, the warrant must identify the person or property to be searched, identify any person or property to be seized, and designate the magistrate judge to whom it must be returned. The warrant must command the officer to:

(i) execute the warrant within a specified time no longer than 14 days;

(B) Warrant Seeking Electronically Stored Information. A warrant under Rule 41(e)(2)(A) may authorize the seizure of electronic storage media or the seizure or copying of electronically stored information. Unless otherwise specified, the warrant authorizes a later review of the media or information consistent with the warrant. The time for executing the warrant in Rule 41(e)(2)(A) and

(f)(1)(A) refers to the seizure or on-site copying of the media or information, and not to any later off-site copying or review.

(f) Executing and Returning the Warrant.

(1) Warrant to Search for and Seize a Person or Property.

(B) Inventory. An officer present during the execution of the warrant must prepare and verify an inventory of any property seized. . . . In a case involving the seizure of electronic storage media or the seizure or copying of electronically stored information, the inventory may be limited to describing the physical storage media that were seized or copied. The officer may retain a copy of the electronically stored information that was seized or copied.

7. Pursuant to this Rule, the government understands and will act in accordance with the following:

a. Pursuant to Rule 41(e)(2)(A)(iii), within fourteen (14) days of the execution of the warrant, an agent is required to file an inventory return with the Court, that is, to file an itemized list of the property seized. Execution of the warrant begins when the United States serves the warrant on the named custodian; execution is complete when the custodian provides all Search Warrant Data to the United States. Within fourteen (14) days of completion of the execution of the warrant, the inventory will be filed.

b. Pursuant to Rule 41(e)(2)(B), Rule 41(e)(2)(A) governs the time within which the electronically stored information must be seized after the issuance of the warrant and copied after the execution of the warrant, not the "later review of the media or information" seized, or the later off-site digital copying of that media.

c. Under Rule 41(f)(1)(B), the inventory return that is to be filed with the court may be limited to a description of the "physical storage media" into which the Search Warrant Data that was seized was placed, not an itemization of the information or data stored on the "physical storage media" into which the Search Warrant Data was placed;

d. Under Rule 41(f)(1)(B), the government may retain a copy of that information for purposes of the investigation. The government proposes that the original storage media on which the Search Warrant Data was placed plus a full image copy of the seized Search Warrant Data be retained by the government.

e. If the person from whom any Search Warrant Data was seized requests the return of any information in the Search Warrant Data that is not set forth in Attachment B, Section II, that information will be copied onto appropriate media and returned to the person from whom the information was seized.

AO 106 (Rev. 04/10) Application for a Search Warrant

UNITED STATES DISTRICT COURT
for the
District of Nevada

I hereby attest and certify on 10-3-17 that the foregoing document is a full true and correct copy of the original on file in my office, and in my legal custody.

CAM FERENBACH
U.S. MAGISTRATE JUDGE
DISTRICT OF NEVADA

In the Matter of the Search of
(Briefly describe the property to be searched or identify the person by name and address)
INSTAGRAM ACCOUNTS STORED AT PREMISES CONTROLLED BY FACEBOOK CORPORATION: Mariloudanleyy A3

Case No. 2:17-mj-00960-VCF

By _____ Deputy / Secretary

APPLICATION FOR A SEARCH WARRANT

I, a federal law enforcement officer or an attorney for the government, request a search warrant and state under penalty of perjury that I have reason to believe that on the following person or property *(identify the person or describe the property to be searched and give its location)*:

INSTAGRAM ACCOUNTS STORED AT PREMISES CONTROLLED BY FACEBOOK CORPORATION: Mariloudanleyy A3

located in the _____ DEA _____ District of _____, there is now concealed *(identify the person or describe the property to be seized)*:

INSTAGRAM ACCOUNTS STORED AT PREMISES CONTROLLED BY FACEBOOK CORPORATION: Mariloudanleyy A3

The basis for the search under Fed. R. Crim. P. 41(c) is *(check one or more)*:
- ☑ evidence of a crime;
- ☑ contraband, fruits of crime, or other items illegally possessed;
- ☑ property designed for use, intended for use, or used in committing a crime;
- ☑ a person to be arrested or a person who is unlawfully restrained.

The search is related to a violation of:

Code Section	Offense Description
Title 26, United States Code, Section 5841.	Violation of National Firearms Act

The application is based on these facts:
I believe there is probable cause to believe that in the subject accounts listed in Attachments "A1", "A2", "A3", "A4", "A5" there is proof that constitutes evidence of the commission of criminal offense(s); contraband, the fruits of crime and things otherwise criminally possessed and been used as the means of committing criminal offense(s)

- ☐ Continued on the attached sheet.
- ☐ Delayed notice of _____ days (give exact ending date if more than 30 days: _____) is requested under 18 U.S.C. § 3103a, the basis of which is set forth on the attached sheet.

/s/
Applicant's signature

_____
Printed name and title

Sworn to before me and signed in my presence.

Date: 10-3-17

City and state: Las Vegas, Nevada

CAM FERENBACH
Judge's signature

CAM FERENBACH
U.S. MAGISTRATE JUDGE
Printed name and title

AO 93 (Rev. 11/13) Search and Seizure Warrant

UNITED STATES DISTRICT COURT
for the
District of Nevada

In the Matter of the Search of)
(Briefly describe the property to be searched)
or identify the person by name and address)) Case No. 2:17-mj-973-NJK
)
1372 BABBLING BROOK COURT,)
MESQUITE, COUNTY OF CLARK, STATE OF NEVADA.)
)

SEARCH AND SEIZURE WARRANT

To: Any authorized law enforcement officer

An application by a federal law enforcement officer or an attorney for the government requests the search of the following person or property located in the __ __ District of __ Nevada
(identify the person or describe the property to be searched and give its location):

SEE ATTACHMENT A

I find that the affidavit(s), or any recorded testimony, establish probable cause to search and seize the person or property described above, and that such search will reveal *(identify the person or describe the property to be seized)*:

SEE ATTACHMENTS B

YOU ARE COMMANDED to execute this warrant on or before October 21, 2017 *(not to exceed 14 days)*
☒ in the daytime 6:00 a.m. to 10:00 p.m. ☐ at any time in the day or night because good cause has been established.

Unless delayed notice is authorized below, you must give a copy of the warrant and a receipt for the property taken to the person from whom, or from whose premises, the property was taken, or leave the copy and receipt at the place where the property was taken.

The officer executing this warrant, or an officer present during the execution of the warrant, must prepare an inventory as required by law and promptly return this warrant and inventory to _Nancy J. Koppe_
 (United States Magistrate Judge)

☐ Pursuant to 18 U.S.C. § 3103a(b), I find that immediate notification may have an adverse result listed in 18 U.S.C. § 2705 (except for delay of trial), and authorize the officer executing this warrant to delay notice to the person who, or whose property, will be searched or seized *(check the appropriate box)*
☐ for __ days *(not to exceed 30)* ☐ until, the facts justifying, the later specific date of __

Date and time issued: 10/7/2017 6:45 p.m.

Judge's signature

City and state: Las Vegas, Nevada

Nancy J. Koppe, US Magistrate Judge
Printed name and title

Attachment "A"

Description of Property/Premise to be Searched

1372 Babbling Brook Court
Mesquite, Clark County, Nevada

The subject premises is described as a one story, single family residence of apparent stucco frame construction. The premises are situated in the northeast corner Babbling Brook Court, which is a cul-de-sac. The premises faces approximately southwest and is located approximately 100 feet from the intersection of Babbling Brook Court and Cool Springs Lane. The residence is painted tan and the house numbers "1372" are affixed to the exterior wall facing the street.

Attachment "B"

Particular Items to be Seized

a. a thorough, microscopic examination and documentation of the subject premises to discover trace evidence, including but not limited to: fingerprints, blood, hair, fibers and other bodily fluid samples;

b. firearms to include handguns, shotguns and rifles, spent casings or live ammunition for the same, firearm accessories such as magazines or cylinders, firearm cleaning materials, and paperwork associated with the ownership of firearms;

c. United States and foreign currency, precious metals, jewelry, property deeds and other negotiable financial instruments including: stocks, bonds, securities, cashier's checks, money drafts, and letters of credit;

d. books, records, receipts, notes, ledgers, personal checks and other papers relating to the transportation, ordering, and purchase of firearms, firearms accessories, ammunition, explosives or explosives precursor materials, or material relating to any ideological extremism;

e. books, records, invoices, receipts, records of real estate transactions, bank statements and related records, gambling receipts and records, passbooks, money drafts, letters of credit, money orders, bank drafts, and cashier checks, bank checks, safe deposit box keys, money wrappers, and other items evidencing the obtaining, secreting, transfer, and/or concealment and/or expenditure of money;

f. any and all financial, credit card and bank account information including but not limited to bills and payment records, including those relating to the purchase of firearms, firearms accessories, ammunition, explosives, explosives precursor materials, body armor, range finding devices, scopes and other optical devices, glass cutters, and gas masks;

g. any and all records relating to the medical or psychological/psychiatric treatment of Stephen Paddock or Marilou Danley;

h. all types of safes and the contents thereof, including but not limited to, wall safes, floor safes, freestanding safes, locked strong boxes, and locked containers;

i. photographs, including still photos, negatives, video tapes, films, undeveloped film and the contents therein, slides;

j. cellular telephones address and/or telephone books, digital pagers, address and/or telephone books, Rolodex indices, electronic organizers, and papers reflecting names, addresses, telephone numbers, pager numbers, fax numbers, e-mail addresses, Facebook account information and other contact information related to co-conspirators, financial institutions, and other individuals or businesses with whom a financial relationship exists;

k. papers, tickets, notes, receipts, and other items relating to domestic and international travel.

l. any and all electronic storage devices, including: computer hard drives and external memory devices such as floppy disks, "thumb drives" (USB electronic storage drives), and compact disk "CD" and/or "DVD" storage devices.[3]

m. records evidencing occupancy or ownership of the premises described above, including, but not limited to, utility and telephone bills, mail envelopes, or addressed correspondence;

n. records or other items which evidence ownership or use of computer equipment found in the target location, including, but not limited to, sales receipts, bills for Internet access, and handwritten notes;

o. any and all records pertaining to the rental of self-storage units and post office boxes;

p. chemicals and other compounds which may constitute explosives or explosive precursors; and

q. improvised, commercial or military grade explosive devices, detonators, initiators, any components thereof, or any other weapon of mass destruction.

---

[3] Electronic equipment shall be seized, but not searched. Supplemental search warrant will be requested prior to the searching of seized electronic items.

STEVEN W. MYHRE
Acting United States Attorney
NICHOLAS D. DICKINSON
Assistant United States Attorney
District of Nevada
Nevada Bar No. 12940
501 Las Vegas Boulevard South, Suite 1100
Las Vegas, Nevada 89101
PHONE: (702) 388-6336
NDickinson@usdoj.gov

Counsel for the United States

FILED
2017 OCT -3 PM 3:59
U.S. MAGISTRATE JUDGE
BY_____

UNITED STATES DISTRICT COURT
DISTRICT OF NEVADA
-oOo-

IN THE MATTER OF SEARCH OF INFORMATION ASSOCIATED WITH INSTAGRAM ACCOUNTS STORED AT PREMISES CONTROLLED BY FACEBOOK CORPORATION: **stephenpaddock47 A1**	Magistrate No. 2:17-mj-00958-VCF **AFFIDAVIT** **(Under Seal)**
IN THE MATTER OF SEARCH OF INFORMATION ASSOCIATED WITH INSTAGRAM ACCOUNTS STORED AT PREMISES CONTROLLED BY FACEBOOK CORPORATION: **Mariloudanley A2**	Magistrate No. 2:17-mj-00959-VCF **AFFIDAVIT** **(Under Seal)**
IN THE MATTER OF SEARCH OF INFORMATION ASSOCIATED WITH INSTAGRAM ACCOUNTS STORED AT PREMISES CONTROLLED BY FACEBOOK CORPORATION: **Mariloudanleyy A3**	Magistrate No. 2:17-mj-00960-VCF **AFFIDAVIT** **(Under Seal)**

IN THE MATTER OF SEARCH OF INFORMATION ASSOCIATED WITH INSTAGRAM ACCOUNTS STORED AT PREMISES CONTROLLED BY FACEBOOK CORPORATION: Mariloudanleypaddock A4	Magistrate No. 2:17-mj-00961-VCF **AFFIDAVIT** (Under Seal)
IN THE MATTER OF SEARCH OF INFORMATION ASSOCIATED WITH INSTAGRAM ACCOUNTS STORED AT PREMISES CONTROLLED BY FACEBOOK CORPORATION: marilou.danley A5	Magistrate No. 2:17-mj-00962-VCF **AFFIDAVIT** (Under Seal)

STATE OF NEVADA)
) ss:
COUNTY OF CLARK)

AFFIDAVIT IN SUPPORT OF AN APPLICATION FOR A SEARCH WARRANT

I, Heather D. Burton, Special Agent, Federal Bureau of Investigation (FBI), having been duly sworn, hereby depose and say:

INTRODUCTION AND AGENT BACKGROUND

1. Your Affiant is a Special Agent with the FBI currently assigned to the Las Vegas, Nevada Division. She has been so employed for over three years. Prior to this she, was employed for five years as a United States Probation Officer in Memphis, Tennessee. Your Affiant is currently assigned to FBI Las Vegas Squad 6. Previously, she was assigned to the Las Vegas Safe Streets Task Force (LVSSTF) and was responsible for investigating a variety of violent crimes, to include bank robbery, kidnapping, extortion, robbery, carjacking, assault and murder of Federal Officers, racketeering related violent offenses, as well as long-term investigations into the activities and operations of criminal enterprises, drug trafficking organizations, and violent street gangs. Your Affiant has experience in conducting criminal investigations, including the investigation of

criminal groups and conspiracies as well as the collection of evidence and the identification and use of witnesses.

2. Your Affiant makes this affidavit in support of an application for a search warrant for information associated with certain Instagram, LLC (hereinafter "Instagram") user IDs that are stored at premises owned, maintained, controlled, or operated by Facebook Inc. (hereinafter "Facebook"), a social networking company headquartered in Menlo Park, California. The information to be searched is described in the following paragraphs and in Attachment A1, A2, A3, A4, A5 and B. This affidavit is made in support of an application for a search warrant under 18 U.S.C. §§ 2703(a), 2703(b)(1)(A) and 2703(c)(1)(A) to require Facebook to disclose to the government records and other information in its possession, pertaining to the subscriber or customer associated with user IDs. It is submitted that the information sought through the issuance of the requested warrant constitutes evidence of the following offense: Violation of National Firearms Act – Registration of Firearms, Title 26, United States Code, Section 5841.

3. The items to be searched are the associated Instagram user ID names as follows:

stephenpaddock47

mariloudanley

mariloudanleyy

mariloudanleypaddock

marilou.danley

4. Because this affidavit is being submitted for the limited purpose of securing a search warrant, your Affiant has not included each and every fact known to her concerning this investigation. Your Affiant has set forth only those facts that are necessary to establish probable cause for the above listed offense. The information used to support this search warrant was derived from reports of information obtained from witnesses as well as investigation conducted by other

Agents and law enforcement officers related to the incident. This affidavit contains information necessary to support probable cause to believe that the criminal offenses described herein were committed by the defendant, STEPHEN PADDOCK (hereinafter "PADDOCK"), and others yet unidentified, and is not intended to include each and every fact and matter observed by your Affiant or known to the Government. Moreover, to the extent this affidavit contains statements by witnesses, those statements are set forth only in part in substance and are intended to accurately convey the information, but not to be verbatim recitations. All noted times are approximate.

JURISDICTION

5. This Court has jurisdiction to issue the requested warrant because it is "a court of competent jurisdiction" as defined by 18 U.S.C. § 2711 and 18 U.S.C. §§ 2703(a), (b)(1)(A), and (c)(1)(A). Specifically, the Court is a "district court of the United States (including a magistrate judge of such a court) that . . . has jurisdiction over the offense being investigated. . . ." 18 U.S.C. § 2711(3)(A)(i), which took place in Las Vegas, Nevada.

BACKGROUND CONCERNING INSTAGRAM

6. Instagram, which is owned by Facebook, operates a free-access social-networking website of the same name that can be accessed at http://www.instagram.com. Instagram allows its users to create their own profile pages, which can include a short biography, a photo of themselves, videos and other information. Users can access Instagram through its website or by using a special electronic application ("app") created by the company that allows users to access the service through a mobile device.

7. Instagram permits users to post photos and videos to their profiles on Instagram and otherwise share them with others on Instagram, as well as certain other social-media services, including Flickr, Facebook, and Twitter. When posting or sharing a photo or video on Instagram, a user can add a caption to it, can add various "tags" that can be used to search for the photo or video

(e.g., a user may add the tag #vw to a photo so that people interested in Volkswagen vehicles can search for and find the photo), can add location information, and can add other information, as well as apply a variety of "filters" or other visual effects that can be used to modify the look of the posted photos. In addition, Instagram allows users to make comments on posted photos or videos, including photos or video that the user posts or posted by other users of Instagram. Users can also "like" photos.

8. Upon creating an Instagram account, an Instagram user must create a unique Instagram username and an account password. This information is collected and maintained by Instagram.

9. Instagram asks users to provide basic identity and contact information upon registration and also allows users to provide additional identity information for their user profile. This information may include the user's full name, e-mail address(es), and phone number(s), as well as potentially other personal information provided directly by the user to Instagram. Once an account is created, users may also adjust various privacy and account settings for the account on Instagram. This information is collected and maintained by Instagram.

10. Instagram allows users to have "friends," which are other individuals with whom the user can share information without making the information public. Friends on Instagram may come from either contact lists maintained by the user, other third-party social media websites and information, or searches conducted by the user on Instagram profiles. This information is collected and maintained by Instagram.

11. Instagram also allows users to "follow" another user, which means that they receive updates about posts made by the other user. Users may also "unfollow" users, that is, stop following them or block them, which prevents the blocked user from following that user.

12. Instagram allows users to post and share various types of user content, including

photos, videos comments, and other materials. User content that is posted to Instagram or shared through Instagram is collected and maintained by Instagram.

13. Instagram users can exchange private messages on Instagram with other users. These messages, which are similar to email messages, are sent to the recipient's "Inbox" on Instagram, which also stores copies of messages sent by the recipient, as well as other information.

14. Users on Instagram may also search Instagram for other users or particular types of photos or other content.

15. For each user, Instagram also collects and retains information, called "log file" information, every time a user requests access to Instagram, whether through a web page or through an app. Among the log file information that Instagram's servers automatically record is the particular web requests, any Internet Protocol ("IP") address associated with the request, type of browser used, any referencing/exit web pages and associated URLs, pages viewed, dates and times of access, and other information.

16. Instagram also collects and maintains "cookies," which are small text files that are placed on a user's computer or mobile device and that allows Instagram to identify the browser or device's accesses to the service.

17. Instagram also collects information on the particular devices used to access Instagram. In particular, Instagram may record "device identifiers," which includes data files and other information that may identify the particular electronic device that was used to access Instagram.

18. Instagram also collects metadata associated with user content. For example, Instagram collects any "hashtags" associated with user content (i.e., keywords used), "geotags" that mark the location of a photo and which may include latitude and longitude information, comments on photos, and other information.

19. Instagram also may communicate with the user, by email or otherwise. Instagram collects and maintains copies of communications between Instagram and the user.

20. Based on the information above, the computers of Instagram are likely to contain all the material described above with respect to accounts with the above referenced user IDs, including **stephenpaddock47, mariloudanley, mariloudanleyy, mariloudanleypaddock, and marilou.danley,** including stored electronic communications and information concerning subscribers and their use of Instagram, such as account access information, which would include information such as the IP addresses and devices used to access the account, as well as other account information that might be used to identify the actual user or users of the accounts at particular times.

STATEMENT OF PROBABLE CAUSE

21. On the evening of Sunday, October 1, 2017, the Route 91 Harvest, a music festival, was in progress at 3901 South Las Vegas Boulevard, Las Vegas, Nevada 89119. At approximately 2208 hours, the Las Vegas Metropolitan Police Department (LVMPD) received calls reporting shots had been fired at the concert and multiple victims were struck. LVMPD determined the shots were coming from Rooms 134 and 135 on the 32nd floor of the Mandalay Bay Resort and Casino, 3950 South Las Vegas Boulevard, Las Vegas, Nevada 89119.

22. Officers made entry into the room and located an individual later identified as Stephen Paddock, DOB [redacted] address 1372 Babbling Brook Court, Mesquite, Nevada 89034. Paddock was deceased from an apparent self-inflicted gunshot wound.

23. Officers found multiple firearms and hundreds of rounds of ammunition in the room in close proximity to Paddock's body. Additionally, investigators located over a thousand rounds of ammunition and explosive material in a vehicle associated with Paddock. Further, multiple firearms and a large quantity of ammunition were located at Paddock's residence at 1372 Babbling Brook Court, Mesquite.

24. Paddock's Nevada driver's license was located in the Mandalay Bay hotel room with Paddock, and both hotel rooms were registered in his name. A player's club card in name of Marilou Danley was located in Paddock's room, and the card returned to the same Babbling Brook address in Mesquite.

25. While monitoring an identified Facebook accounts of Marilou Danley (facebook.com/marilou.danley) after the shooting, LVMPD investigators noted that the account settings and privacy settings were changed on October 2, 2017, at approximately 0030 hours. At approximately 0246 hours, the Facebook account was deleted. Investigators discovered the following additional Instagram accounts associated with Stephen Paddock and Marilou Paddock: **stephenpaddock47, mariloudanley, mariloudanleyy, mariloudanleypaddock,** and **marilou.danley**. On October 3, 2017, a preservation request for all content pertaining to the these Instagram was submitted to Facebook to maximize the chance that the contents of the account remain preserved.

26. Based on my training and experience, a person who possesses large amounts of firearms and ammunition obtains those items over a period of time. Thus, I am requesting that the search period be from September 1, 2016 to the present.

27. Based on these stated facts, it is your Affiant's opinion that there is probable cause to believe that the Instagram accounts with user IDs **stephenpaddock47, mariloudanley, mariloudanleyy, mariloudanleypaddock,** and **marilou.danley** contain evidence related to PADDOCK's possession of firearms in violation of Title 26, United States Code, Section 5841. Your Affiant also submits that a review of photos and other non-public content on the subject accounts will likely produce further evidence of prior and additional violations of the enumerated offenses. I swear, under penalty of perjury, that the foregoing is true and correct to the best of my knowledge and belief.

INFORMATION TO BE SEARCHED AND THINGS TO BE SEIZED

28. Your Affiant anticipates executing this warrant under the Electronic Communications Privacy Act, in particular 18 U.S.C. §§ 2703(a), 2703(b)(1)(A) and 2703(c)(1)(A), by using the warrant to require Facebook to disclose to the government copies of the records and other information (including the content of communications) particularly described in Section I of Attachment "B." Upon receipt of the information described in Section I of Attachment "B," government-authorized persons will review that information to locate the items described in Section II of Attachment "B."

CONCLUSION

29. Based on the information set forth herein, Your Affiant has probable cause to believe that in the subject accounts listed in Attachments "A1", "A2", "A3", "A4", "A5" there is proof that constitutes evidence of the commission of criminal offense(s); contraband, the fruits of crime and things otherwise criminally possessed; and property designed or intended for use or which is or has been used as the means of committing criminal offense(s). The evidence to be searched for and seized is set forth in Attachment "B", which is attached hereto and incorporated herein by reference.

30. Based on the forgoing, your Affiant requests that the Court issue the proposed search warrant.

31. Pursuant to 18 U.S.C. § 2703(g), the presence of a law enforcement officer is not required for the service or execution of this warrant.

REQUEST FOR SEALING

31. I further request that the Court order that all papers in support of this application, including the affidavit and search warrant, be sealed until further order of the Court. These documents discuss an ongoing criminal investigation that is neither public nor known to all of the

targets of the investigation. Accordingly, there is good cause to seal these documents because their premature disclosure may seriously jeopardize that investigation.

Respectfully Submitted,

/s/
Heather D. Burton, Special Agent
Federal Bureau of Investigation

SWORN TO AND SUBSCRIBED
before me this 3rd day of October, 2017.

CAM FERENBACH
UNITED STATES MAGISTRATE JUDGE

I hereby attest and certify on 10-3-17 that the foregoing document is a full true and correct copy of the original on file in my office, and in my legal custody.

CAM FERENBACH
U.S. MAGISTRATE JUDGE
DISTRICT OF NEVADA

By _____ Deputy Secretary

Attachment "A1"

Property to Be Searched

This warrant applies to information associated with the Instagram user IDs **stephenpaddock47**, that is stored at premises owned, maintained, controlled, or operated by Facebook, a company headquartered in Menlo Park, California for the time period beginning September 1, 2016 to present.

Attachment "A2"

Property to Be Searched

This warrant applies to information associated with the Instagram user IDs **mariloudanley**, that is stored at premises owned, maintained, controlled, or operated by Facebook, a company headquartered in Menlo Park, California for the time period beginning September 1, 2016 to present.

Attachment "A3"

Property to Be Searched

This warrant applies to information associated with the Instagram user IDs **mariloudanleyy**, that is stored at premises owned, maintained, controlled, or operated by Facebook, a company headquartered in Menlo Park, California for the time period beginning September 1, 2016 to present.

Attachment "A4"

Property to Be Searched

This warrant applies to information associated with the Instagram user IDs **mariloudanleypaddock,** that is stored at premises owned, maintained, controlled, or operated by Facebook, a company headquartered in Menlo Park, California for the time period beginning September 1, 2016 to present.

Attachment "A5"

Property to Be Searched

This warrant applies to information associated with the Instagram user IDs and **marilou.danley** that is stored at premises owned, maintained, controlled, or operated by Facebook, a company headquartered in Menlo Park, California for the time period beginning September 1, 2016 to present.

ATTACHMENT "B"

Particular Things to be Seized

I. **Information to be disclosed by Facebook**

To the extent that the information described in Attachment A is within the possession, custody, or control of Instagram LLC ("Instagram"), including any messages, records, files, logs, or information that have been deleted but are still available to Instagram, or have been preserved pursuant to a request made under 18 U.S.C. § 2703(f) on October 3, 2017. Facebook is required to disclose the following information to the government for each user IDs listed in Attachment A for the period of September 1, 2016 to present:

(a) All contact and personal identifying information, including: full name, user identification number, birth date, gender, contact e-mail addresses, Instagram passwords, Instagram security questions and answers, physical address (including city, state, and zip code), telephone numbers, screen names, websites, and other personal identifiers;

(b) All activity logs for the account and all other documents showing the user's posts and other Instagram activities;

(c) All photos and videos uploaded by that user ID and all photos and videos uploaded by any user that have that user tagged in them;

(d) All profile information; status updates; links to videos, photographs, bios, articles, and other items; Wall postings; friend lists, including the friends' Instagram user identification numbers; future and past event postings; comments; and tags;

(e) All other records of communications and messages made or received by the user, chat history, and pending "Friend" requests;

(f) All user content created, uploaded, or shared by the account, including any comments made by the account on photographs or other content;

(g) All IP logs, including all records of the IP addresses that logged into the account;

(h) All records of the account's usage of the "Like" feature, including all Instagram posts and content that the user has "liked";

(i) All location data associated with the account, including geotags;

(j) All data and information that has been deleted by the user;

(k) All past and present lists of friends created by the account;

(l) All records of Instagram searches performed by the account;

(m) The types of service utilized by the user;

(n) The length of service (including start date) and the means and source of any payments associated with the service (including any credit card or bank account number);

(o) All privacy settings and other account settings, including privacy settings for individual Instagram posts and activities, and all records showing which Instagram users have been blocked by the account;

(p) All records pertaining to communications between Instagram and any person regarding the user or the user's Instagram account, including contacts with support services and records of actions taken.

(q) All information regarding the particular device or devices used to login to or access the account, including all device identifier information or cookie information, including all information about the particular device or devices used to access the account and the date and time of those accesses;

II. Information to be seized by the government

All information described above in Section I that constitutes fruits, evidence, and instrumentalities of violations of:

Violation of National Firearms Act – Registration of Firearms, Title 26, United States Code, Section 5841.

involving STEPHEN PADDOCK and others yet unidentified, including, for each user ID identified on Attachment "A," information pertaining to the following matters:

(a) Evidence showing the possession, use, purchase, or sale of firearms, firearms accessories, ammunition, or explosives by Paddock, including through conspiring and cooperating to possess, use, purchase, or sell prohibited firearms, firearms accessories, ammunition, or explosives.

(b) Evidence indicating how and when the Instagram account was accessed or used, to determine the chronological and geographic context of account access, use, and events relating to the crime under investigation and to the Facebook account owner;

(c) Evidence indicating the Instagram account owner's state of mind as it relates to the crime under investigation;

(d) The identity of the person(s) who created or used the user ID, including records that help reveal the whereabouts of such person(s).

(e) The identity of the person(s) who communicated with the user ID about matters relating to the illegal possession, purchase, use, or sale of firearms, firearms accessories, ammunition, or explosives, including records that help reveal their whereabouts.

The Warrant expressly incorporates the Affidavit submitted in support of the Warrant, and separately sealed, as though set forth fully herein.

ATTACHMENT C

PROTOCOL FOR SEARCHING THE ELECTRONIC DATA SEIZED

PURSUANT TO THIS SEARCH WARRANT

1. In executing this warrant, the government must make reasonable efforts to use methods and procedures that will locate and expose in the electronic data produced in response to this search warrant ("the Search Warrant Data") those categories of data, files, documents, or other electronically stored information that are identified with particularity in the warrant, while minimizing exposure or examination of irrelevant, privileged, or confidential files to the extent reasonably practicable.

2. When the Search Warrant Data is received, the government will make a duplicate copy of the Search Warrant Data ("the Search Warrant Data Copy"). The original version of the Search Warrant Data will be sealed and preserved for purposes of: later judicial review or order to return or dispose of the Search Warrant Data; production to the defense in any criminal case if authorized by statute, rule, or the Constitution; for purposes of showing the chain of custody of the Search Warrant Data and the Search Warrant Data Copy; or for any other lawful purpose. The original of the Search Warrant Data will not be searched or examined except to ensure that it has been fully and completely replicated in the Search Warrant Data Copy.

3. The investigating agents will then search the entirety of the Search Warrant Data Copy using any and all methods and procedures deemed appropriate by the United States designed to identify the information listed as Information to be Seized in Attachment B, Section II. The United States may copy, extract or otherwise segregate information or data listed as Information to be Seized in Attachment B, Section II. Information or data so copied, extracted or otherwise segregated will no longer be subject to any handling restrictions that might be set out in this protocol beyond those required by binding law. To the extent evidence of crimes not within the scope of this warrant appear in plain view during this review, a supplemental or "piggyback" warrant will be applied for in order to further search that document, data, or other item.

4. The Government will have ninety (90) days from receipt of the data disclosed under Attachment B, Section I to complete its examination of the Search Warrant Data Copy. Once the Search Warrant Data Copy has been thoroughly and completely examined for any document, data, or other items identified in Attachment B, Section II as Information to be Seized, the Search Warrant Data Copy will be sealed and not subject to any further search or examination unless authorized by another search warrant or other appropriate court order. The Search Warrant Data Copy will be held and preserved for the same purposes identified above in Paragraph 2.

5. The search procedures utilized for this review are at the sole discretion of the investigating and prosecuting authorities, and may include the following techniques (the following is a non-exclusive list, as other search procedures may be used):

a. examination of all of the data contained in the Search Warrant Data to view the data and determine whether that data falls within the items to be seized as set forth herein;

b. searching for and attempting to recover from the Search Warrant Data any deleted, hidden, or encrypted data to determine whether that data falls within the list of items to be seized as set forth herein (any data that is encrypted and unreadable will not be returned unless law enforcement personnel have determined that the data is not (1) an instrumentality of the offenses, (2) a fruit of the criminal activity, (3) contraband, (4) otherwise unlawfully possessed, or (5) evidence of the offenses specified above);

c. surveying various file directories and the individual files they contain;

d. opening files in order to determine their contents;

e. using hash values to narrow the scope of what may be found. Hash values are under-inclusive, but are still a helpful tool;

f. scanning storage areas;

g. performing keyword searches through all electronic storage areas to determine whether occurrences of language contained in such storage areas exist that are likely to appear in the evidence described in Attachment A; and/or

h. performing any other data analysis technique that may be necessary to locate and retrieve the evidence described in Attachment B, Section II.

Return and Review Procedures

6. Rule 41 of the Federal Rules of Criminal Procedure provides, in relevant part:

(e) Issuing the Warrant.

(2) Contents of the Warrant.

(A) Warrant to Search for and Seize a Person or Property. Except for a tracking-device warrant, the warrant must identify the person or property to be searched, identify any person or property to be seized, and designate the magistrate judge to whom it must be returned. The warrant must command the officer to:

(i) execute the warrant within a specified time no longer than 14 days;

(B) Warrant Seeking Electronically Stored Information. A warrant under Rule 41(e)(2)(A) may authorize the seizure of electronic storage media or the seizure or copying of electronically stored information. Unless otherwise specified, the warrant authorizes a later review of the media or information consistent with the warrant. The time for executing the warrant in Rule 41(e)(2)(A) and

(f)(1)(A) refers to the seizure or on-site copying of the media or information, and not to any later off-site copying or review.

(f) Executing and Returning the Warrant.

(1) Warrant to Search for and Seize a Person or Property.

(B) Inventory. An officer present during the execution of the warrant must prepare and verify an inventory of any property seized. . . . In a case involving the seizure of electronic storage media or the seizure or copying of electronically stored information, the inventory may be limited to describing the physical storage media that were seized or copied. The officer may retain a copy of the electronically stored information that was seized or copied.

7. Pursuant to this Rule, the government understands and will act in accordance with the following:

a. Pursuant to Rule 41(e)(2)(A)(iii), within fourteen (14) days of the execution of the warrant, an agent is required to file an inventory return with the Court, that is, to file an itemized list of the property seized. Execution of the warrant begins when the United States serves the warrant on the named custodian; execution is complete when the custodian provides all Search Warrant Data to the United States. Within fourteen (14) days of completion of the execution of the warrant, the inventory will be filed.

b. Pursuant to Rule 41(e)(2)(B), Rule 41(e)(2)(A) governs the time within which the electronically stored information must be seized after the issuance of the warrant and copied after the execution of the warrant, not the "later review of the media or information" seized, or the later off-site digital copying of that media.

c. Under Rule 41(f)(1)(B), the inventory return that is to be filed with the court may be limited to a description of the "physical storage media" into which the Search Warrant Data that was seized was placed, not an itemization of the information or data stored on the "physical storage media" into which the Search Warrant Data was placed;

d. Under Rule 41(f)(1)(B), the government may retain a copy of that information for purposes of the investigation. The government proposes that the original storage media on which the Search Warrant Data was placed plus a full image copy of the seized Search Warrant Data be retained by the government.

e. If the person from whom any Search Warrant Data was seized requests the return of any information in the Search Warrant Data that is not set forth in Attachment B, Section II, that information will be copied onto appropriate media and returned to the person from whom the information was seized.

SEALED

Office of the United States Attorney
District of Nevada
501 Las Vegas Boulevard, Suite 1100
Las Vegas, Nevada 89101
(702) 388-6336

Attachment "A1"

Property to Be Searched

This warrant applies to information associated with the Instagram user IDs **stephenpaddock47,** that is stored at premises owned, maintained, controlled, or operated by Facebook, a company headquartered in Menlo Park, California for the time period beginning September 1, 2016 to present.

ATTACHMENT "B"

Particular Things to be Seized

I. **Information to be disclosed by Facebook**

To the extent that the information described in Attachment A is within the possession, custody, or control of Instagram LLC ("Instagram"), including any messages, records, files, logs, or information that have been deleted but are still available to Instagram, or have been preserved pursuant to a request made under 18 U.S.C. § 2703(f) on October 3, 2017. Facebook is required to disclose the following information to the government for each user IDs listed in Attachment A for the period of September 1, 2016 to present:

(a) All contact and personal identifying information, including: full name, user identification number, birth date, gender, contact e-mail addresses, Instagram passwords, Instagram security questions and answers, physical address (including city, state, and zip code), telephone numbers, screen names, websites, and other personal identifiers;

(b) All activity logs for the account and all other documents showing the user's posts and other Instagram activities;

(c) All photos and videos uploaded by that user ID and all photos and videos uploaded by any user that have that user tagged in them;

(d) All profile information; status updates; links to videos, photographs, bios, articles, and other items; Wall postings; friend lists, including the friends' Instagram user identification numbers; future and past event postings; comments; and tags;

(e) All other records of communications and messages made or received by the user, chat history, and pending "Friend" requests;

(f) All user content created, uploaded, or shared by the account, including any comments made by the account on photographs or other content;

(g) All IP logs, including all records of the IP addresses that logged into the account;

(h) All records of the account's usage of the "Like" feature, including all Instagram posts and content that the user has "liked";

(i) All location data associated with the account, including geotags;

(j) All data and information that has been deleted by the user;

(k) All past and present lists of friends created by the account;

(l) All records of Instagram searches performed by the account;

(m) The types of service utilized by the user;

(n) The length of service (including start date) and the means and source of any payments associated with the service (including any credit card or bank account number);

(o) All privacy settings and other account settings, including privacy settings for individual Instagram posts and activities, and all records showing which Instagram users have been blocked by the account;

(p) All records pertaining to communications between Instagram and any person regarding the user or the user's Instagram account, including contacts with support services and records of actions taken.

(q) All information regarding the particular device or devices used to login to or access the account, including all device identifier information or cookie information, including all information about the particular device or devices used to access the account and the date and time of those accesses;

II. Information to be seized by the government

All information described above in Section I that constitutes fruits, evidence, and instrumentalities of violations of:

Violation of National Firearms Act – Registration of Firearms, Title 26, United States Code, Section 5841.

involving STEPHEN PADDOCK and others yet unidentified, including, for each user ID identified on Attachment "A," information pertaining to the following matters:

(a) Evidence showing the possession, use, purchase, or sale of firearms, firearms accessories, ammunition, or explosives by Paddock, including through conspiring and cooperating to possess, use, purchase, or sell prohibited firearms, firearms accessories, ammunition, or explosives.

(b) Evidence indicating how and when the Instagram account was accessed or used, to determine the chronological and geographic context of account access, use, and events relating to the crime under investigation and to the Facebook account owner;

(c) Evidence indicating the Instagram account owner's state of mind as it relates to the crime under investigation;

(d) The identity of the person(s) who created or used the user ID, including records that help reveal the whereabouts of such person(s).

(e) The identity of the person(s) who communicated with the user ID about matters relating to the illegal possession, purchase, use, or sale of firearms, firearms accessories, ammunition, or explosives, including records that help reveal their whereabouts.

The Warrant expressly incorporates the Affidavit submitted in support of the Warrant, and separately sealed, as though set forth fully herein.

ATTACHMENT C

PROTOCOL FOR SEARCHING THE ELECTRONIC DATA SEIZED

PURSUANT TO THIS SEARCH WARRANT

1. In executing this warrant, the government must make reasonable efforts to use methods and procedures that will locate and expose in the electronic data produced in response to this search warrant ("the Search Warrant Data") those categories of data, files, documents, or other electronically stored information that are identified with particularity in the warrant, while minimizing exposure or examination of irrelevant, privileged, or confidential files to the extent reasonably practicable.

2. When the Search Warrant Data is received, the government will make a duplicate copy of the Search Warrant Data ("the Search Warrant Data Copy"). The original version of the Search Warrant Data will be sealed and preserved for purposes of: later judicial review or order to return or dispose of the Search Warrant Data; production to the defense in any criminal case if authorized by statute, rule, or the Constitution; for purposes of showing the chain of custody of the Search Warrant Data and the Search Warrant Data Copy; or for any other lawful purpose. The original of the Search Warrant Data will not be searched or examined except to ensure that it has been fully and completely replicated in the Search Warrant Data Copy.

3. The investigating agents will then search the entirety of the Search Warrant Data Copy using any and all methods and procedures deemed appropriate by the United States designed to identify the information listed as Information to be Seized in Attachment B, Section II. The United States may copy, extract or otherwise segregate information or data listed as Information to be Seized in Attachment B, Section II. Information or data so copied, extracted or otherwise segregated will no longer be subject to any handling restrictions that might be set out in this protocol beyond those required by binding law. To the extent evidence of crimes not within the scope of this warrant appear in plain view during this review, a supplemental or "piggyback" warrant will be applied for in order to further search that document, data, or other item.

4. The Government will have ninety (90) days from receipt of the data disclosed under Attachment B, Section I to complete its examination of the Search Warrant Data Copy. Once the Search Warrant Data Copy has been thoroughly and completely examined for any document, data, or other items identified in Attachment B, Section II as Information to be Seized, the Search Warrant Data Copy will be sealed and not subject to any further search or examination unless authorized by another search warrant or other appropriate court order. The Search Warrant Data Copy will be held and preserved for the same purposes identified above in Paragraph 2.

5. The search procedures utilized for this review are at the sole discretion of the investigating and prosecuting authorities, and may include the following techniques (the following is a non-exclusive list, as other search procedures may be used):

a. examination of all of the data contained in the Search Warrant Data to view the data and determine whether that data falls within the items to be seized as set forth herein;

b. searching for and attempting to recover from the Search Warrant Data any deleted, hidden, or encrypted data to determine whether that data falls within the list of items to be seized as set forth herein (any data that is encrypted and unreadable will not be returned unless law enforcement personnel have determined that the data is not (1) an instrumentality of the offenses, (2) a fruit of the criminal activity, (3) contraband, (4) otherwise unlawfully possessed, or (5) evidence of the offenses specified above);

c. surveying various file directories and the individual files they contain;

d. opening files in order to determine their contents;.

e. using hash values to narrow the scope of what may be found. Hash values are under-inclusive, but are still a helpful tool;

f. scanning storage areas;

g. performing keyword searches through all electronic storage areas to determine whether occurrences of language contained in such storage areas exist that are likely to appear in the evidence described in Attachment A; and/or

h. performing any other data analysis technique that may be necessary to locate and retrieve the evidence described in Attachment B, Section II.

Return and Review Procedures

6. Rule 41 of the Federal Rules of Criminal Procedure provides, in relevant part:

(e) Issuing the Warrant.

(2) Contents of the Warrant.

(A) Warrant to Search for and Seize a Person or Property. Except for a tracking-device warrant, the warrant must identify the person or property to be searched, identify any person or property to be seized, and designate the magistrate judge to whom it must be returned. The warrant must command the officer to:

(i) execute the warrant within a specified time no longer than 14 days;

(B) Warrant Seeking Electronically Stored Information. A warrant under Rule 41(e)(2)(A) may authorize the seizure of electronic storage media or the seizure or copying of electronically stored information. Unless otherwise specified, the warrant authorizes a later review of the media or information consistent with the warrant. The time for executing the warrant in Rule 41(e)(2)(A) and

(f)(1)(A) refers to the seizure or on-site copying of the media or information, and not to any later off-site copying or review.

(f) Executing and Returning the Warrant.

(1) Warrant to Search for and Seize a Person or Property.

(B) Inventory. An officer present during the execution of the warrant must prepare and verify an inventory of any property seized. . . . In a case involving the seizure of electronic storage media or the seizure or copying of electronically stored information, the inventory may be limited to describing the physical storage media that were seized or copied. The officer may retain a copy of the electronically stored information that was seized or copied.

7. Pursuant to this Rule, the government understands and will act in accordance with the following:

a. Pursuant to Rule 41(e)(2)(A)(iii), within fourteen (14) days of the execution of the warrant, an agent is required to file an inventory return with the Court, that is, to file an itemized list of the property seized. Execution of the warrant begins when the United States serves the warrant on the named custodian; execution is complete when the custodian provides all Search Warrant Data to the United States. Within fourteen (14) days of completion of the execution of the warrant, the inventory will be filed.

b. Pursuant to Rule 41(e)(2)(B), Rule 41(e)(2)(A) governs the time within which the electronically stored information must be seized after the issuance of the warrant and copied after the execution of the warrant, not the "later review of the media or information" seized, or the later off-site digital copying of that media.

c. Under Rule 41(f)(1)(B), the inventory return that is to be filed with the court may be limited to a description of the "physical storage media" into which the Search Warrant Data that was seized was placed, not an itemization of the information or data stored on the "physical storage media" into which the Search Warrant Data was placed;

d. Under Rule 41(f)(1)(B), the government may retain a copy of that information for purposes of the investigation. The government proposes that the original storage media on which the Search Warrant Data was placed plus a full image copy of the seized Search Warrant Data be retained by the government.

e. If the person from whom any Search Warrant Data was seized requests the return of any information in the Search Warrant Data that is not set forth in Attachment B, Section II, that information will be copied onto appropriate media and returned to the person from whom the information was seized.

to search the subject premises for evidence and instrumentalities of the subject offenses, more fully described in Attachment "B" (attached hereto and incorporated herein by reference).

BACKGROUND OF INVESTIGATION

6. On the evening of Sunday, October 1, 2017, Route 91 Harvest, a music festival, was in progress at 3901 South Las Vegas Boulevard, Las Vegas, Nevada. At approximately 10:08 p.m., the Las Vegas Metropolitan Police Department (LVMPD) received calls reporting shots had been fired at the concert and multiple victims were struck (the "attack"). LVMPD determined the shots were coming from Rooms 134 and 135 on the 32nd floor of the Mandalay Bay Resort and Casino, located due west of the festival grounds at 3950 South Las Vegas Boulevard, Las Vegas, Nevada. These rooms are an elevated position which overlooks the concert venue. Witness statements and video footage captured during the attack indicates that the weapons being used were firing in a fully-automatic fashion.

7. LVMPD officers ultimately made entry into the room and located an individual later identified as Stephen Paddock. Paddock was deceased from an apparent self-inflicted gunshot wound.

8. Paddock's Nevada driver's license was located in the Mandalay Bay hotel room with Paddock, and both hotel rooms were registered in his name. A player's club card in name of Marilou Danley was located in Paddock's room, and the card returned to the address located on Babbling Brook Court in Mesquite, Nevada. FBI Agents located Danley, who was traveling outside the United States at the time of the shooting. It was ultimately determined that Danley resided with Paddock at the Babbling Brook address.

9. On October 2, 2017, local search warrants were obtained and executed on Paddock's Mandalay Bay hotel rooms, Paddock's vehicle parked in the Mandalay Bay parking

garage, and two Nevada residences owed by Paddock: 1372 Babbling Brook Court[1], and 1735 Del Webb Parkway, Reno, Nevada. Pursuant to those searches, Officers and Agents found over 20 firearms, hundreds of rounds of unfired ammunition (much of it in preloaded high-capacity magazines), range finding devices, several suitcases (some partially full of pre-loaded high capacity magazines) a set of body armor, an apparent homemade gas mask, and hundreds of spent cartridge cases in the Mandalay Bay hotel rooms, in close proximity to Paddock's body. Over a thousand rounds of rifle ammunition and a significant amount of explosive precursor material was found in Paddock's vehicle (specifically the binary explosive brand-named Tannerite). Additional explosive precursor material, approximately 18 firearms, and over 1,000 rounds of ammunition were located at the Mesquite residence. A large quantity of ammunition and multiple firearms were recovered from the Reno residence.

10. Immediately following the shooting, an extensive investigation was commenced which is currently being conducted jointly by LVMPD and the FBI, with the substantial support of numerous state, local and federal law enforcement agencies. As of this date, 58 people have been identified to have been killed in Paddock's attack and over 500 were reportedly injured. The preliminary reviews of the crime scenes in and around the Mandalay Bay led investigators to determine that in addition to firing upon the crowds at the festival grounds, Paddock also fired several high-caliber rifle shots at large fuel tanks within the property line of the McCarran International airport property. Multiple bullet impacts were located on the tank, which investigators believe was an attempt by Paddock to explode the tanks.

11. As the investigation progressed, investigators learned that Paddock planned the attack meticulously and took many methodical steps to avoid detection of his plot and to thwart the eventual law enforcement investigation that would follow. The steps included the apparent

---

[1] The search warrant for this location was approved by ▓▓▓▓▓▓▓▓▓▓▓▓▓▓▓▓▓▓. A copy of that search warrant is attached hereto as Exhibit 1.

destruction and/or concealment of digital storage media and the use of anonymously attributed communications devices. Based on your Affiant's training and experience, it is his belief that the methodical nature of the planning employed by Paddock, coupled with his efforts to undermine the preceding investigation, are factors indicative of a level of sophistication which is commonly found in mass casualty events such as this. However, your Affiant notes that this finding was not fully-developed in this case until several days into the investigation, after the subject premises had been searched in the hours immediately after the attack unfolded.

12. The investigation has also revealed that Paddock may have been treated for yet unidentified medical conditions, and that he spent significant time and expense prior to the attack purchasing and caching the weapons and other instrumentalities he used in the shooting. Some of these items included glass cutters, suitcases and a pre-paid cellular telephone. This cache included a substantial amount of ammunition, "Tannerite,"[2] glass cutters, numerous suitcases, and at least one identified pre-paid cellular telephone.

13. Investigators are currently conducting analysis of available financial records. To date, this analysis has revealed that Paddock made the purchases of items used in the attack throughout the last approximately 12 months. A large portion of the ammunition and firearms accessory purchases appear to have been made through Internet based retailers. Law enforcement continues to investigate the sourcing of purchases made by Paddock preceding the attack.

14. Subsequent to her identification as Paddock's companion and co-habitant at the subject premises, Marilou Danely returned to the United States and was thereafter voluntarily interviewed by law enforcement with her attorney present. During the interview, Danley corroborated much of what had been previously deduced by investigators, but she was adamant

---

[2] Tannerite is the brand name of a commercially available binary explosive commonly used as a reactive rifle target in shooting sports it can also be a precursor chemical for an improvised explosive devices.

that she had no prior inclination of Paddock intentions to conduct the attack. While investigators obtained a DNA buccal swab sample from Danley, she spontaneously stated that her fingerprints would likely be found on Paddock's ammunition because she occasionally participated in loading magazines. Danley has not been arrested and she has agreed to cooperate with investigators. Although, the investigation to date has not produced any conclusive evidence that Danley aided Paddock, had foreknowledge of his plans, or has been deceptive with law enforcement, this aspect of the investigation is still the subject of intensive review. Therefore, your Affiant asserts, for the purposes of this affidavit, that although there is currently no evidence to suggest criminal involvement by Danley, investigators are not yet prepared to rule this possibility out.

15. Investigators have reviewed the findings of the initial search of the subject premises and have determined that an additional, more exhaustive search is required. The proposed search would be focused on finding items of evidence or instrumentalities that may have been concealed inside or within the curtilage of the subject premises. In addition, the search will include a more thorough effort to identify any forensic trace evidence that may be located inside or within the curtilage of the subject premises.

PROBABLE CAUSE

16. Your Affiant believes that probable cause exists for this Court to authorize the proposed search, and that this probable cause is relatively unchanged from the probable cause that existed in the hour after the attack when the initial search was conducted. Additionally, information received from Danley during her interview and further investigation of the crime scene, as well as a fuller understanding of Paddock's mode of planning the attack, lead your Affiant to believe there is probable cause that additional evidence of the subject offenses may be located in the subject residence.

17. The primary identified resident of the subject premises, Stephen Paddock, is deceased and as such, no longer holds standing at 1372 Babbling Brook Court. Investigators are

currently unable to determine Danley's standing to provide consent to conduct this subsequent search. Therefore, although the FBI might already have all necessary authority to conduct the proposed search, your Affiant is seeking this search warrant out of an abundance of caution to be certain that any search conducted will comply with the Fourth Amendment and other applicable laws.

CONCLUSION

18. Based upon the aforementioned facts and circumstances, it is your Affiant's opinion that there is probable cause that the subject premises may contain evidence and instrumentalities concerning violations of the subject offenses herein. Your Affiant's training and experience provides the basis for his belief that a search of the subject premises will yield these items. As such, your Affiant seeks this Court's authorization to conduct a search of the subject premises as fully described in Attachment "A" for the items sought to be seized as described in Attachment "B."

Respectfully Submitted,

Christopher W. McPeak, Special Agent
Federal Bureau of Investigation

SWORN TO AND SUBSCRIBED
before me this 7th day of October, 2017.

HONORABLE NANCY J. KOPPE
UNITED STATES MAGISTRATE JUDGE

Attachment "A"

Description of Property/Premise to be Searched

1372 Babbling Brook Court
Mesquite, Clark County, Nevada

The subject premises is described as a one story, single family residence of apparent stucco frame construction. The premises are situated in the northeast corner Babbling Brook Court, which is a cul-de-sac. The premises faces approximately southwest and is located approximately 100 feet from the intersection of Babbling Brook Court and Cool Springs Lane. The residence is painted tan and the house numbers "1372" are affixed to the exterior wall facing the street.

Attachment "B"

Particular Items to be Seized

a. a thorough, microscopic examination and documentation of the subject premises to discover trace evidence, including but not limited to: fingerprints, blood, hair, fibers and other bodily fluid samples;

b. firearms to include handguns, shotguns and rifles, spent casings or live ammunition for the same, firearm accessories such as magazines or cylinders, firearm cleaning materials, and paperwork associated with the ownership of firearms;

c. United States and foreign currency, precious metals, jewelry, property deeds and other negotiable financial instruments including: stocks, bonds, securities, cashier's checks, money drafts, and letters of credit;

d. books, records, receipts, notes, ledgers, personal checks and other papers relating to the transportation, ordering, and purchase of firearms, firearms accessories, ammunition, explosives or explosives precursor materials, or material relating to any ideological extremism;

e. books, records, invoices, receipts, records of real estate transactions, bank statements and related records, gambling receipts and records, passbooks, money drafts, letters of credit, money orders, bank drafts, and cashier checks, bank checks, safe deposit box keys, money wrappers, and other items evidencing the obtaining, secreting, transfer, and/or concealment and /or expenditure of money;

f. any and all financial, credit card and bank account information including but not limited to bills and payment records, including those relating to the purchase of firearms, firearms accessories, ammunition, explosives, explosives precursor materials, body armor, range finding devices, scopes and other optical devices, glass cutters, and gas masks;

g. any and all records relating to the medical or psychological/psychiatric treatment of Stephen Paddock or Marilou Danley;

h. all types of safes and the contents thereof, including but not limited to, wall safes, floor safes, freestanding safes, locked strong boxes, and locked containers;

i. photographs, including still photos, negatives, video tapes, films, undeveloped film and the contents therein, slides;

j. cellular telephones address and/or telephone books, digital pagers, address and/or telephone books, Rolodex indices, electronic organizers, and papers reflecting names, addresses, telephone numbers, pager numbers, fax numbers, e-mail addresses, Facebook account information and other contact information related to co-conspirators, financial institutions, and other individuals or businesses with whom a financial relationship exists;

k. papers, tickets, notes, receipts, and other items relating to domestic and international travel.

l. any and all electronic storage devices, including: computer hard drives and external memory devices such as floppy disks, "thumb drives" (USB electronic storage drives), and compact disk "CD" and/or "DVD" storage devices.[3]

m. records evidencing occupancy or ownership of the premises described above, including, but not limited to, utility and telephone bills, mail envelopes, or addressed correspondence;

n. records or other items which evidence ownership or use of computer equipment found in the target location, including, but not limited to, sales receipts, bills for Internet access, and handwritten notes;

o. any and all records pertaining to the rental of self-storage units and post office boxes;

p. chemicals and other compounds which may constitute explosives or explosive precursors; and

q. improvised, commercial or military grade explosive devices, detonators, initiators, any components thereof, or any other weapon of mass destruction.

---

[3] Electronic equipment shall be seized, but not searched. Supplemental search warrant will be requested prior to the searching of seized electronic items.

EXHIBIT 1

AO 93 (Rev. 11/13) Search and Seizure Warrant

UNITED STATES DISTRICT COURT
for the
District of Nevada

In the Matter of the Search of
(Briefly describe the property to be searched or identify the person by name and address)

1372 BABBLING BROOK COURT,
MESQUITE, COUNTY OF CLARK, STATE OF NEVADA.

Case No. 2:17-mj-973-NJK

SEARCH AND SEIZURE WARRANT

To: Any authorized law enforcement officer

An application by a federal law enforcement officer or an attorney for the government requests the search of the following person or property located in the _____ District of _____ Nevada *(identify the person or describe the property to be searched and give its location)*:

SEE ATTACHMENT A

I find that the affidavit(s), or any recorded testimony, establish probable cause to search and seize the person or property described above, and that such search will reveal *(identify the person or describe the property to be seized)*:

SEE ATTACHMENTS B

YOU ARE COMMANDED to execute this warrant on or before October 21, 2017 *(not to exceed 14 days)*
☒ in the daytime 6:00 a.m. to 10:00 p.m.   ☐ at any time in the day or night because good cause has been established.

Unless delayed notice is authorized below, you must give a copy of the warrant and a receipt for the property taken to the person from whom, or from whose premises, the property was taken, or leave the copy and receipt at the place where the property was taken.

The officer executing this warrant, or an officer present during the execution of the warrant, must prepare an inventory as required by law and promptly return this warrant and inventory to _Nancy J. Koppe_
(United States Magistrate Judge)

☐ Pursuant to 18 U.S.C. § 3103a(b), I find that immediate notification may have an adverse result listed in 18 U.S.C. § 2705 (except for delay of trial), and authorize the officer executing this warrant to delay notice to the person who, or whose property, will be searched or seized *(check the appropriate box)*
☐ for ____ days *(not to exceed 30)*   ☐ until, the facts justifying, the later specific date of ____

Date and time issued: 10/7/2017 6:45 p.m.

_____
Judge's signature

City and state: Las Vegas, Nevada

Nancy J. Koppe, US Magistrate Judge
Printed name and title

Attachment "A"

Description of Property/Premise to be Searched

1372 Babbling Brook Court
Mesquite, Clark County, Nevada

The subject premises is described as a one story, single family residence of apparent stucco frame construction. The premises are situated in the northeast corner Babbling Brook Court, which is a cul-de-sac. The premises faces approximately southwest and is located approximately 100 feet from the intersection of Babbling Brook Court and Cool Springs Lane. The residence is painted tan and the house numbers "1372" are affixed to the exterior wall facing the street.

Attachment "B"

Particular Items to be Seized

a. a thorough, microscopic examination and documentation of the subject premises to discover trace evidence, including but not limited to: fingerprints, blood, hair, fibers and other bodily fluid samples;

b. firearms to include handguns, shotguns and rifles, spent casings or live ammunition for the same, firearm accessories such as magazines or cylinders, firearm cleaning materials, and paperwork associated with the ownership of firearms;

c. United States and foreign currency, precious metals, jewelry, property deeds and other negotiable financial instruments including: stocks, bonds, securities, cashier's checks, money drafts, and letters of credit;

d. books, records, receipts, notes, ledgers, personal checks and other papers relating to the transportation, ordering, and purchase of firearms, firearms accessories, ammunition, explosives or explosives precursor materials, or material relating to any ideological extremism;

e. books, records, invoices, receipts, records of real estate transactions, bank statements and related records, gambling receipts and records, passbooks, money drafts, letters of credit, money orders, bank drafts, and cashier checks, bank checks, safe deposit box keys, money wrappers, and other items evidencing the obtaining, secreting, transfer, and/or concealment and /or expenditure of money;

f. any and all financial, credit card and bank account information including but not limited to bills and payment records, including those relating to the purchase of firearms, firearms accessories, ammunition, explosives, explosives precursor materials, body armor, range finding devices, scopes and other optical devices, glass cutters, and gas masks;

g. any and all records relating to the medical or psychological/psychiatric treatment of Stephen Paddock or Marilou Danley;

h. all types of safes and the contents thereof, including but not limited to, wall safes, floor safes, freestanding safes, locked strong boxes, and locked containers;

i. photographs, including still photos, negatives, video tapes, films, undeveloped film and the contents therein, slides;

j. cellular telephones address and/or telephone books, digital pagers, address and/or telephone books, Rolodex indices, electronic organizers, and papers reflecting names, addresses, telephone numbers, pager numbers, fax numbers, e-mail addresses, Facebook account information and other contact information related to co-conspirators, financial institutions, and other individuals or businesses with whom a financial relationship exists;

k. papers, tickets, notes, receipts, and other items relating to domestic and international travel.

l. any and all electronic storage devices, including: computer hard drives and external memory devices such as floppy disks, "thumb drives" (USB electronic storage drives), and compact disk "CD" and/or "DVD" storage devices.[3]

m. records evidencing occupancy or ownership of the premises described above, including, but not limited to, utility and telephone bills, mail envelopes, or addressed correspondence;

n. records or other items which evidence ownership or use of computer equipment found in the target location, including, but not limited to, sales receipts, bills for Internet access, and handwritten notes;

o. any and all records pertaining to the rental of self-storage units and post office boxes;

p. chemicals and other compounds which may constitute explosives or explosive precursors; and

q. improvised, commercial or military grade explosive devices, detonators, initiators, any components thereof, or any other weapon of mass destruction.

---

[3] Electronic equipment shall be seized, but not searched. Supplemental search warrant will be requested prior to the searching of seized electronic items.

AO 93 (Rev. 11/13) Search and Seizure Warrant

UNITED STATES DISTRICT COURT
for the
District of Nevada

In the Matter of the Search of)
(Briefly describe the property to be searched)
or identify the person by name and address))   Case No.   2:17-mj-**973**-NJK
)
1372 BABBLING BROOK COURT,)
MESQUITE, COUNTY OF CLARK, STATE OF NEVADA.)
)

SEARCH AND SEIZURE WARRANT

To: Any authorized law enforcement officer

An application by a federal law enforcement officer or an attorney for the government requests the search of the following person or property located in the _____ District of _____ Nevada
(identify the person or describe the property to be searched and give its location):

SEE ATTACHMENT A

I find that the affidavit(s), or any recorded testimony, establish probable cause to search and seize the person or property described above, and that such search will reveal *(identify the person or describe the property to be seized):*

SEE ATTACHMENTS B

YOU ARE COMMANDED to execute this warrant on or before October 21, 2017 *(not to exceed 14 days)*
☒ in the daytime 6:00 a.m. to 10:00 p.m.   ☐ at any time in the day or night because good cause has been established.

Unless delayed notice is authorized below, you must give a copy of the warrant and a receipt for the property taken to the person from whom, or from whose premises, the property was taken, or leave the copy and receipt at the place where the property was taken.

The officer executing this warrant, or an officer present during the execution of the warrant, must prepare an inventory as required by law and promptly return this warrant and inventory to _____
(United States Magistrate Judge)

☐ Pursuant to 18 U.S.C. § 3103a(b), I find that immediate notification may have an adverse result listed in 18 U.S.C. § 2705 (except for delay of trial), and authorize the officer executing this warrant to delay notice to the person who, or whose property, will be searched or seized *(check the appropriate box)*
☐ for _____ days *(not to exceed 30)*   ☐ until, the facts justifying, the later specific date of _____

Date and time issued: 10/7/2017 6:45 p.m.

_____
Judge's signature

City and state: Las Vegas, Nevada   Nancy J. Koppe, US Magistrate Judge
Printed name and title

Attachment "A"

Description of Property/Premise to be Searched

1372 Babbling Brook Court
Mesquite, Clark County, Nevada

The subject premises is described as a one story, single family residence of apparent stucco frame construction. The premises are situated in the northeast corner Babbling Brook Court, which is a cul-de-sac. The premises faces approximately southwest and is located approximately 100 feet from the intersection of Babbling Brook Court and Cool Springs Lane. The residence is painted tan and the house numbers "1372" are affixed to the exterior wall facing the street.

Attachment "B"

Particular Items to be Seized

a. a thorough, microscopic examination and documentation of the subject premises to discover trace evidence, including but not limited to: fingerprints, blood, hair, fibers and other bodily fluid samples;

b. firearms to include handguns, shotguns and rifles, spent casings or live ammunition for the same, firearm accessories such as magazines or cylinders, firearm cleaning materials, and paperwork associated with the ownership of firearms;

c. United States and foreign currency, precious metals, jewelry, property deeds and other negotiable financial instruments including: stocks, bonds, securities, cashier's checks, money drafts, and letters of credit;

d. books, records, receipts, notes, ledgers, personal checks and other papers relating to the transportation, ordering, and purchase of firearms, firearms accessories, ammunition, explosives or explosives precursor materials, or material relating to any ideological extremism;

e. books, records, invoices, receipts, records of real estate transactions, bank statements and related records, gambling receipts and records, passbooks, money drafts, letters of credit, money orders, bank drafts, and cashier checks, bank checks, safe deposit box keys, money wrappers, and other items evidencing the obtaining, secreting, transfer, and/or concealment and /or expenditure of money;

f. any and all financial, credit card and bank account information including but not limited to bills and payment records, including those relating to the purchase of firearms, firearms accessories, ammunition, explosives, explosives precursor materials, body armor, range finding devices, scopes and other optical devices, glass cutters, and gas masks;

g. any and all records relating to the medical or psychological/psychiatric treatment of Stephen Paddock or Marilou Danley;

h. all types of safes and the contents thereof, including but not limited to, wall safes, floor safes, freestanding safes, locked strong boxes, and locked containers;

i. photographs, including still photos, negatives, video tapes, films, undeveloped film and the contents therein, slides;

j. cellular telephones address and/or telephone books, digital pagers, address and/or telephone books, Rolodex indices, electronic organizers, and papers reflecting names, addresses, telephone numbers, pager numbers, fax numbers, e-mail addresses, Facebook account information and other contact information related to co-conspirators, financial institutions, and other individuals or businesses with whom a financial relationship exists;

k. papers, tickets, notes, receipts, and other items relating to domestic and international travel.

l. any and all electronic storage devices, including: computer hard drives and external memory devices such as floppy disks, "thumb drives" (USB electronic storage drives), and compact disk "CD" and/or "DVD" storage devices.[3]

m. records evidencing occupancy or ownership of the premises described above, including, but not limited to, utility and telephone bills, mail envelopes, or addressed correspondence;

n. records or other items which evidence ownership or use of computer equipment found in the target location, including, but not limited to, sales receipts, bills for Internet access, and handwritten notes;

o. any and all records pertaining to the rental of self-storage units and post office boxes;

p. chemicals and other compounds which may constitute explosives or explosive precursors; and

q. improvised, commercial or military grade explosive devices, detonators, initiators, any components thereof, or any other weapon of mass destruction.

---

[3] Electronic equipment shall be seized, but not searched. Supplemental search warrant will be requested prior to the searching of seized electronic items.

STEVEN W. MYHRE
Acting United States Attorney
District of Nevada
Cristina D. Silva
Patrick Burns
Assistant United States Attorneys
501 Las Vegas Blvd. South, Ste. 1100
Las Vegas, Nevada 89101
Telephone: (702) 388-6336
Fax (702) 388-6698
CSilva@usa.doj.gov
john.p.burns@usdoj.gov

Representing the United States of America

UNITED STATES DISTRICT COURT
DISTRICT OF NEVADA
-oOo-

IN THE MATTER OF THE SEARCH OF:

THE PREMISES KNOWN AS:
**1372 BABBLING BROOK COURT,
MESQUITE, COUNTY OF CLARK,
STATE OF NEVADA.**

Magistrate No. 17-mj-973-NJK

AFFIDAVIT IN SUPPORT OF
SEARCH WARRANT

(Under Seal)

STATE OF NEVADA   )
) ss:
COUNTY OF CLARK   )

AFFIDAVIT IN SUPPORT OF SEARCH WARRANT

1. I, Christopher W. McPeak, Special Agent, Federal Bureau of Investigation (FBI), having been duly sworn, hereby depose and say:

2. Your Affiant is a Special Agent with the FBI currently assigned to the Las Vegas, Nevada Division and has been so employed for over eight years. Prior to this he was employed for over five years as a Deputy Sheriff and Detective with the Orange County, Florida Sheriff's Office. As an FBI Agent, your Affiant is assigned to the FBI's Las Vegas Safe Streets Task Force (LVSSTF) and is responsible for investigating a variety of violent crimes, to include bank

robbery, kidnapping, extortion, robbery, carjackings, assaults and murders of federal officers, racketeering related violent offenses, as well as long-term investigations into the activities and operations of career criminals, criminal enterprises, drug trafficking organizations, and violent street gangs. Your Affiant has experience in conducting criminal investigations, including the investigation of criminal groups and conspiracies as well as the collection of evidence and the identification and use of witnesses.

3. The facts in this affidavit are derived from your Affiant's personal observations, his training and experience, and information obtained from other agents, detectives, and witnesses. This affidavit is intended to show merely that there is sufficient probable cause for the requested warrant and does not set forth all of the Affiant's knowledge about this matter.

PREMISES TO BE SEARCHED

4. The proposed search warrant seeks authorization to search the premises identified as 1372 Babbling Brook Court, Mesquite, Clark County, Nevada (hereinafter referred to as the "subject premises"), more fully described in Attachment "A" (attached hereto and incorporated herein by reference).

REQUEST FOR SEARCH WARRANT

5. Based on your Affiant's training and experience and the facts as set forth in this affidavit, there is probable cause to believe that violations of, *inter alia*:

    a. Destruction/Damage of Aircraft or Aircraft Facilities - 18 U.S.C. § 32(a);

    b. Violence at an International Airport - 18 U.S.C. § 37(a)(2);

    c. Unlawful Interstate Transport/Delivery of Firearms by Non-Federal Firearms Licensee – 18 U.S.C. § 922(a)(3) and (5); and

    d. Aiding and Abetting – 18 U.S.C. § 2,

(hereinafter referred to as the "subject offenses") have been committed by Stephen Paddock and others yet unknown; and this affidavit is made in support of an application for a search warrant

AO 106 (Rev. 04/10) Application for a Search Warrant

UNITED STATES DISTRICT COURT
for the
District of Nevada

In the Matter of the Search of
(Briefly describe the property to be searched or identify the person by name and address)

INSTAGRAM ACCOUNTS STORED AT PREMISES CONTROLLED BY FACEBOOK CORPORATION: Mariloudanley A2

Case No. 2:17-mj-00959-VCF

I hereby attest and certify on 10-3-17 that the foregoing document is a full true and correct copy of the original on file in my office, and in my legal custody.

CAM FERENBACH
U.S. MAGISTRATE JUDGE
DISTRICT OF NEVADA

By _____ Deputy Secretary

APPLICATION FOR A SEARCH WARRANT

I, a federal law enforcement officer or an attorney for the government, request a search warrant and state under penalty of perjury that I have reason to believe that on the following person or property *(identify the person or describe the property to be searched and give its location)*:

INSTAGRAM ACCOUNTS STORED AT PREMISES CONTROLLED BY FACEBOOK CORPORATION: Mariloudanley A2

located in the _____ DEA _____ District of _____, there is now concealed *(identify the person or describe the property to be seized)*:

INSTAGRAM ACCOUNTS STORED AT PREMISES CONTROLLED BY FACEBOOK CORPORATION: Mariloudanley A2

The basis for the search under Fed. R. Crim. P. 41(c) is *(check one or more)*:

- ☑ evidence of a crime;
- ☑ contraband, fruits of crime, or other items illegally possessed;
- ☑ property designed for use, intended for use, or used in committing a crime;
- ☑ a person to be arrested or a person who is unlawfully restrained.

The search is related to a violation of:

Code Section	Offense Description
Title 26, United States Code, Section 5841.	Violation of National Firearms Act

FILED 2017 OCT -3 PM 3:36 BY _____ U.S. MAGISTRATE JUDGE

The application is based on these facts:
I believe there is probable cause to believe that in the subject accounts listed in Attachments "A1", "A2", "A3", "A4", "A5" there is proof that constitutes evidence of the commission of criminal offense(s); contraband, the fruits of crime and things otherwise criminally possessed and been used as the means of committing criminal offense(s)

- ☐ Continued on the attached sheet.
- ☐ Delayed notice of ____ days (give exact ending date if more than 30 days: _____) is requested under 18 U.S.C. § 3103a, the basis of which is set forth on the attached sheet.

/s/
Applicant's signature

_____
Printed name and title

Sworn to before me and signed in my presence.

Date: 10-3-17

City and state: Las Vegas, Nevada

CAM FERENBACH
Judge's signature

CAM FERENBACH
U.S. MAGISTRATE JUDGE
Printed name and title

AO 93 (Rev. 11/13) Search and Seizure Warrant

UNITED STATES DISTRICT COURT
for the
District of Nevada

In the Matter of the Search of
(Briefly describe the property to be searched or identify the person by name and address)

Mariloudanley A2

Case No. 2:17-mj-00959-VCF

CAM FERENBACH
U.S. MAGISTRATE JUDGE
DISTRICT OF NEVADA

By _____ Deputy / Secretary

I hereby attest and certify on: 10-3-17
that the foregoing document is a full true and correct copy of the original on file in my office, and in my legal custody.

SEARCH AND SEIZURE WARRANT

To: Any authorized law enforcement officer

An application by a federal law enforcement officer or an attorney for the government requests the search of the following person or property located in the _____ District of Nevada
(identify the person or describe the property to be searched and give its location):

SEE ATTACHMENT A2

I find that the affidavit(s), or any recorded testimony, establish probable cause to search and seize the person or property described above, and that such search will reveal *(identify the person or describe the property to be seized):*

SEE ATTACHMENTS B and C

YOU ARE COMMANDED to execute this warrant on or before 10-12-17 *(not to exceed 14 days)*
☒ in the daytime 6:00 a.m. to 10:00 p.m. ☐ at any time in the day or night because good cause has been established.

Unless delayed notice is authorized below, you must give a copy of the warrant and a receipt for the property taken to the person from whom, or from whose premises, the property was taken, or leave the copy and receipt at the place where the property was taken.

The officer executing this warrant, or an officer present during the execution of the warrant, must prepare an inventory as required by law and promptly return this warrant and inventory to CAM FERENBACH .
(United States Magistrate Judge)

☐ Pursuant to 18 U.S.C. § 3103a(b), I find that immediate notification may have an adverse result listed in 18 U.S.C. § 2705 (except for delay of trial), and authorize the officer executing this warrant to delay notice to the person who, or whose property, will be searched or seized *(check the appropriate box)*
☐ for _____ days *(not to exceed 30)* ☐ until, the facts justifying, the later specific date of _____ .

Date and time issued: 10-3-17 4:04p

City and state: Las Vegas, Nevada

CAM FERENBACH
Judge's signature

CAM FERENBACH
U.S. MAGISTRATE JUDGE
Printed name and title

SEALED

Office of the United States Attorney
District of Nevada
501 Las Vegas Boulevard, Suite 1100
Las Vegas, Nevada 89101
(702) 388-6336

Attachment "A2"

Property to Be Searched

This warrant applies to information associated with the Instagram user IDs **mariloudanley**, that is stored at premises owned, maintained, controlled, or operated by Facebook, a company headquartered in Menlo Park, California for the time period beginning September 1, 2016 to present.

ATTACHMENT "B"

Particular Things to be Seized

I. **Information to be disclosed by Facebook**

To the extent that the information described in Attachment A is within the possession, custody, or control of Instagram LLC ("Instagram"), including any messages, records, files, logs, or information that have been deleted but are still available to Instagram, or have been preserved pursuant to a request made under 18 U.S.C. § 2703(f) on October 3, 2017. Facebook is required to disclose the following information to the government for each user IDs listed in Attachment A for the period of September 1, 2016 to present:

(a) All contact and personal identifying information, including: full name, user identification number, birth date, gender, contact e-mail addresses, Instagram passwords, Instagram security questions and answers, physical address (including city, state, and zip code), telephone numbers, screen names, websites, and other personal identifiers;

(b) All activity logs for the account and all other documents showing the user's posts and other Instagram activities;

(c) All photos and videos uploaded by that user ID and all photos and videos uploaded by any user that have that user tagged in them;

(d) All profile information; status updates; links to videos, photographs, bios, articles, and other items; Wall postings; friend lists, including the friends' Instagram user identification numbers; future and past event postings; comments; and tags;

(e) All other records of communications and messages made or received by the user, chat history, and pending "Friend" requests;

(f) All user content created, uploaded, or shared by the account, including any comments made by the account on photographs or other content;

(g) All IP logs, including all records of the IP addresses that logged into the account;

(h) All records of the account's usage of the "Like" feature, including all Instagram posts and content that the user has "liked";

(i) All location data associated with the account, including geotags;

(j) All data and information that has been deleted by the user;

(k) All past and present lists of friends created by the account;

(l) All records of Instagram searches performed by the account;

(m) The types of service utilized by the user;

(n) The length of service (including start date) and the means and source of any payments associated with the service (including any credit card or bank account number);

(o) All privacy settings and other account settings, including privacy settings for individual Instagram posts and activities, and all records showing which Instagram users have been blocked by the account;

(p) All records pertaining to communications between Instagram and any person regarding the user or the user's Instagram account, including contacts with support services and records of actions taken.

(q) All information regarding the particular device or devices used to login to or access the account, including all device identifier information or cookie information, including all information about the particular device or devices used to access the account and the date and time of those accesses;

II. Information to be seized by the government

All information described above in Section I that constitutes fruits, evidence, and instrumentalities of violations of:

Violation of National Firearms Act – Registration of Firearms, Title 26, United States Code, Section 5841.

involving STEPHEN PADDOCK and others yet unidentified, including, for each user ID identified on Attachment "A," information pertaining to the following matters:

(a) Evidence showing the possession, use, purchase, or sale of firearms, firearms accessories, ammunition, or explosives by Paddock, including through conspiring and cooperating to possess, use, purchase, or sell prohibited firearms, firearms accessories, ammunition, or explosives.

(b) Evidence indicating how and when the Instagram account was accessed or used, to determine the chronological and geographic context of account access, use, and events relating to the crime under investigation and to the Facebook account owner;

(c) Evidence indicating the Instagram account owner's state of mind as it relates to the crime under investigation;

(d) The identity of the person(s) who created or used the user ID, including records that help reveal the whereabouts of such person(s).

(e) The identity of the person(s) who communicated with the user ID about matters relating to the illegal possession, purchase, use, or sale of firearms, firearms accessories, ammunition, or explosives, including records that help reveal their whereabouts.

The Warrant expressly incorporates the Affidavit submitted in support of the Warrant, and separately sealed, as though set forth fully herein.

ATTACHMENT C

PROTOCOL FOR SEARCHING THE ELECTRONIC DATA SEIZED
PURSUANT TO THIS SEARCH WARRANT

1. In executing this warrant, the government must make reasonable efforts to use methods and procedures that will locate and expose in the electronic data produced in response to this search warrant ("the Search Warrant Data") those categories of data, files, documents, or other electronically stored information that are identified with particularity in the warrant, while minimizing exposure or examination of irrelevant, privileged, or confidential files to the extent reasonably practicable.

2. When the Search Warrant Data is received, the government will make a duplicate copy of the Search Warrant Data ("the Search Warrant Data Copy"). The original version of the Search Warrant Data will be sealed and preserved for purposes of: later judicial review or order to return or dispose of the Search Warrant Data; production to the defense in any criminal case if authorized by statute, rule, or the Constitution; for purposes of showing the chain of custody of the Search Warrant Data and the Search Warrant Data Copy; or for any other lawful purpose. The original of the Search Warrant Data will not be searched or examined except to ensure that it has been fully and completely replicated in the Search Warrant Data Copy.

3. The investigating agents will then search the entirety of the Search Warrant Data Copy using any and all methods and procedures deemed appropriate by the United States designed to identify the information listed as Information to be Seized in Attachment B, Section II. The United States may copy, extract or otherwise segregate information or data listed as Information to be Seized in Attachment B, Section II. Information or data so copied, extracted or otherwise segregated will no longer be subject to any handling restrictions that might be set out in this protocol beyond those required by binding law. To the extent evidence of crimes not within the scope of this warrant appear in plain view during this review, a supplemental or "piggyback" warrant will be applied for in order to further search that document, data, or other item.

4. The Government will have ninety (90) days from receipt of the data disclosed under Attachment B, Section I to complete its examination of the Search Warrant Data Copy. Once the Search Warrant Data Copy has been thoroughly and completely examined for any document, data, or other items identified in Attachment B, Section II as Information to be Seized, the Search Warrant Data Copy will be sealed and not subject to any further search or examination unless authorized by another search warrant or other appropriate court order. The Search Warrant Data Copy will be held and preserved for the same purposes identified above in Paragraph 2.

5. The search procedures utilized for this review are at the sole discretion of the investigating and prosecuting authorities, and may include the following techniques (the following is a non-exclusive list, as other search procedures may be used):

a. examination of all of the data contained in the Search Warrant Data to view the data and determine whether that data falls within the items to be seized as set forth herein;

b. searching for and attempting to recover from the Search Warrant Data any deleted, hidden, or encrypted data to determine whether that data falls within the list of items to be seized as set forth herein (any data that is encrypted and unreadable will not be returned unless law enforcement personnel have determined that the data is not (1) an instrumentality of the offenses, (2) a fruit of the criminal activity, (3) contraband, (4) otherwise unlawfully possessed, or (5) evidence of the offenses specified above);

c. surveying various file directories and the individual files they contain;

d. opening files in order to determine their contents;

e. using hash values to narrow the scope of what may be found. Hash values are under-inclusive, but are still a helpful tool;

f. scanning storage areas;

g. performing keyword searches through all electronic storage areas to determine whether occurrences of language contained in such storage areas exist that are likely to appear in the evidence described in Attachment A; and/or

h. performing any other data analysis technique that may be necessary to locate and retrieve the evidence described in Attachment B, Section II.

Return and Review Procedures

6. Rule 41 of the Federal Rules of Criminal Procedure provides, in relevant part:

(e) Issuing the Warrant.

(2) Contents of the Warrant.

(A) Warrant to Search for and Seize a Person or Property. Except for a tracking-device warrant, the warrant must identify the person or property to be searched, identify any person or property to be seized, and designate the magistrate judge to whom it must be returned. The warrant must command the officer to:

(i) execute the warrant within a specified time no longer than 14 days;

(B) Warrant Seeking Electronically Stored Information. A warrant under Rule 41(e)(2)(A) may authorize the seizure of electronic storage media or the seizure or copying of electronically stored information. Unless otherwise specified, the warrant authorizes a later review of the media or information consistent with the warrant. The time for executing the warrant in Rule 41(e)(2)(A) and

(f)(1)(A) refers to the seizure or on-site copying of the media or information, and not to any later off-site copying or review.

(f) Executing and Returning the Warrant.

(1) Warrant to Search for and Seize a Person or Property.

(B) Inventory. An officer present during the execution of the warrant must prepare and verify an inventory of any property seized. . . . In a case involving the seizure of electronic storage media or the seizure or copying of electronically stored information, the inventory may be limited to describing the physical storage media that were seized or copied. The officer may retain a copy of the electronically stored information that was seized or copied.

7. Pursuant to this Rule, the government understands and will act in accordance with the following:

a. Pursuant to Rule 41(e)(2)(A)(iii), within fourteen (14) days of the execution of the warrant, an agent is required to file an inventory return with the Court, that is, to file an itemized list of the property seized. Execution of the warrant begins when the United States serves the warrant on the named custodian; execution is complete when the custodian provides all Search Warrant Data to the United States. Within fourteen (14) days of completion of the execution of the warrant, the inventory will be filed.

b. Pursuant to Rule 41(e)(2)(B), Rule 41(e)(2)(A) governs the time within which the electronically stored information must be seized after the issuance of the warrant and copied after the execution of the warrant, not the "later review of the media or information" seized, or the later off-site digital copying of that media.

c. Under Rule 41(f)(1)(B), the inventory return that is to be filed with the court may be limited to a description of the "physical storage media" into which the Search Warrant Data that was seized was placed, not an itemization of the information or data stored on the "physical storage media" into which the Search Warrant Data was placed;

d. Under Rule 41(f)(1)(B), the government may retain a copy of that information for purposes of the investigation. The government proposes that the original storage media on which the Search Warrant Data was placed plus a full image copy of the seized Search Warrant Data be retained by the government.

e. If the person from whom any Search Warrant Data was seized requests the return of any information in the Search Warrant Data that is not set forth in Attachment B, Section II, that information will be copied onto appropriate media and returned to the person from whom the information was seized.

AO 106 (Rev. 04/10) Application for a Search Warrant

UNITED STATES DISTRICT COURT
for the
District of Nevada

I hereby attest and certify on 10-3-17 that the foregoing document is a full true and correct copy of the original on file in my office, and in my legal custody.

CAM FERENBACH
U.S. MAGISTRATE JUDGE
DISTRICT OF NEVADA

By_____ Deputy Secretary

In the Matter of the Search of
(Briefly describe the property to be searched or identify the person by name and address)

INSTAGRAM ACCOUNTS STORED AT PREMISES CONTROLLED BY FACEBOOK CORPORATION: Mariloudanleyy A3

Case No. 2:17-mj-00960-VCF

APPLICATION FOR A SEARCH WARRANT

I, a federal law enforcement officer or an attorney for the government, request a search warrant and state under penalty of perjury that I have reason to believe that on the following person or property *(identify the person or describe the property to be searched and give its location)*:

INSTAGRAM ACCOUNTS STORED AT PREMISES CONTROLLED BY FACEBOOK CORPORATION: Mariloudanleyy A3

located in the _____DEA_____ District of _____, there is now concealed *(identify the person or describe the property to be seized)*:

INSTAGRAM ACCOUNTS STORED AT PREMISES CONTROLLED BY FACEBOOK CORPORATION: Mariloudanleyy A3

The basis for the search under Fed. R. Crim. P. 41(c) is *(check one or more)*:
- ☑ evidence of a crime;
- ☑ contraband, fruits of crime, or other items illegally possessed;
- ☑ property designed for use, intended for use, or used in committing a crime;
- ☑ a person to be arrested or a person who is unlawfully restrained.

The search is related to a violation of:

Code Section	Offense Description
Title 26, United States Code, Section 5841.	Violation of National Firearms Act

The application is based on these facts:
I believe there is probable cause to believe that in the subject accounts listed in Attachments "A1", "A2", "A3", "A4", "A5" there is proof that constitutes evidence of the commission of criminal offense(s); contraband, the fruits of crime and things otherwise criminally possessed and been used as the means of committing criminal offense(s)

- ☐ Continued on the attached sheet.
- ☐ Delayed notice of _____ days (give exact ending date if more than 30 days: _____) is requested under 18 U.S.C. § 3103a, the basis of which is set forth on the attached sheet.

/s/
Applicant's signature

_____
Printed name and title

Sworn to before me and signed in my presence.

Date: 10-3-17

City and state: Las Vegas, Nevada

CAM FERENBACH
Judge's signature

CAM FERENBACH
U.S. MAGISTRATE JUDGE
Printed name and title

AO 93 (Rev. 11/13) Search and Seizure Warrant

UNITED STATES DISTRICT COURT
for the
District of Nevada

In the Matter of the Search of)
(Briefly describe the property to be searched)
or identify the person by name and address))   Case No. 2:17-mj-973-NJK
)
1372 BABBLING BROOK COURT,)
MESQUITE, COUNTY OF CLARK, STATE OF NEVADA.)
)

SEARCH AND SEIZURE WARRANT

To: Any authorized law enforcement officer

An application by a federal law enforcement officer or an attorney for the government requests the search of the following person or property located in the _____ District of _____ Nevada
(identify the person or describe the property to be searched and give its location):

SEE ATTACHMENT A

I find that the affidavit(s), or any recorded testimony, establish probable cause to search and seize the person or property described above, and that such search will reveal *(identify the person or describe the property to be seized)*:

SEE ATTACHMENTS B

YOU ARE COMMANDED to execute this warrant on or before October 21, 2017 *(not to exceed 14 days)*
☒ in the daytime 6:00 a.m. to 10:00 p.m. ☐ at any time in the day or night because good cause has been established.

Unless delayed notice is authorized below, you must give a copy of the warrant and a receipt for the property taken to the person from whom, or from whose premises, the property was taken, or leave the copy and receipt at the place where the property was taken.

The officer executing this warrant, or an officer present during the execution of the warrant, must prepare an inventory as required by law and promptly return this warrant and inventory to _Nancy J. Koppe_
(United States Magistrate Judge)

☐ Pursuant to 18 U.S.C. § 3103a(b), I find that immediate notification may have an adverse result listed in 18 U.S.C. § 2705 (except for delay of trial), and authorize the officer executing this warrant to delay notice to the person who, or whose property, will be searched or seized *(check the appropriate box)*
  ☐ for _____ days *(not to exceed 30)*   ☐ until, the facts justifying, the later specific date of _____

Date and time issued: 10/7/2017 6:45 p.m.

Judge's signature

City and state: Las Vegas, Nevada   Nancy J. Koppe, US Magistrate Judge
                                                          Printed name and title

Attachment "A"

Description of Property/Premise to be Searched

1372 Babbling Brook Court
Mesquite, Clark County, Nevada

The subject premises is described as a one story, single family residence of apparent stucco frame construction. The premises are situated in the northeast corner Babbling Brook Court, which is a cul-de-sac. The premises faces approximately southwest and is located approximately 100 feet from the intersection of Babbling Brook Court and Cool Springs Lane. The residence is painted tan and the house numbers "1372" are affixed to the exterior wall facing the street.

Attachment "B"

Particular Items to be Seized

a. a thorough, microscopic examination and documentation of the subject premises to discover trace evidence, including but not limited to: fingerprints, blood, hair, fibers and other bodily fluid samples;

b. firearms to include handguns, shotguns and rifles, spent casings or live ammunition for the same, firearm accessories such as magazines or cylinders, firearm cleaning materials, and paperwork associated with the ownership of firearms;

c. United States and foreign currency, precious metals, jewelry, property deeds and other negotiable financial instruments including: stocks, bonds, securities, cashier's checks, money drafts, and letters of credit;

d. books, records, receipts, notes, ledgers, personal checks and other papers relating to the transportation, ordering, and purchase of firearms, firearms accessories, ammunition, explosives or explosives precursor materials, or material relating to any ideological extremism;

e. books, records, invoices, receipts, records of real estate transactions, bank statements and related records, gambling receipts and records, passbooks, money drafts, letters of credit, money orders, bank drafts, and cashier checks, bank checks, safe deposit box keys, money wrappers, and other items evidencing the obtaining, secreting, transfer, and/or concealment and /or expenditure of money;

f. any and all financial, credit card and bank account information including but not limited to bills and payment records, including those relating to the purchase of firearms, firearms accessories, ammunition, explosives, explosives precursor materials, body armor, range finding devices, scopes and other optical devices, glass cutters, and gas masks;

g. any and all records relating to the medical or psychological/psychiatric treatment of Stephen Paddock or Marilou Danley;

h. all types of safes and the contents thereof, including but not limited to, wall safes, floor safes, freestanding safes, locked strong boxes, and locked containers;

i. photographs, including still photos, negatives, video tapes, films, undeveloped film and the contents therein, slides;

j. cellular telephones address and/or telephone books, digital pagers, address and/or telephone books, Rolodex indices, electronic organizers, and papers reflecting names, addresses, telephone numbers, pager numbers, fax numbers, e-mail addresses, Facebook account information and other contact information related to co-conspirators, financial institutions, and other individuals or businesses with whom a financial relationship exists;

1

k. papers, tickets, notes, receipts, and other items relating to domestic and international travel.

l. any and all electronic storage devices, including: computer hard drives and external memory devices such as floppy disks, "thumb drives" (USB electronic storage drives), and compact disk "CD" and/or "DVD" storage devices.[3]

m. records evidencing occupancy or ownership of the premises described above, including, but not limited to, utility and telephone bills, mail envelopes, or addressed correspondence;

n. records or other items which evidence ownership or use of computer equipment found in the target location, including, but not limited to, sales receipts, bills for Internet access, and handwritten notes;

o. any and all records pertaining to the rental of self-storage units and post office boxes;

p. chemicals and other compounds which may constitute explosives or explosive precursors; and

q. improvised, commercial or military grade explosive devices, detonators, initiators, any components thereof, or any other weapon of mass destruction.

---

[3] Electronic equipment shall be seized, but not searched. Supplemental search warrant will be requested prior to the searching of seized electronic items.

AO 93 (Rev. 11/13) Search and Seizure Warrant

UNITED STATES DISTRICT COURT
for the
District of Nevada

2017 OCT 13 PM 12:30
U.S. MAGISTRATE JUDGE
BY_____

In the Matter of the Search of)
(Briefly describe the property to be searched)
or identify the person by name and address)) Case No. 2:17-mj-01009-NJK
)
EMAIL ACCOUNT CENTRALPARK1@LIVE.COM THAT)
IS STORED AT A PREMISES CONTROLLED BY)
MICROSOFT. A1)

SEARCH AND SEIZURE WARRANT

To: Any authorized law enforcement officer

An application by a federal law enforcement officer or an attorney for the government requests the search of the following person or property located in the _____ District of _____ Nevada _____
(identify the person or describe the property to be searched and give its location):

SEE ATTACHMENT A1

I find that the affidavit(s), or any recorded testimony, establish probable cause to search and seize the person or property described above, and that such search will reveal *(identify the person or describe the property to be seized)*:

SEE ATTACHMENTS B and C

☑ **YOU ARE COMMANDED** to execute this warrant on or before October 27, 2017 *(not to exceed 14 days)*
☑ in the daytime 6:00 a.m. to 10:00 p.m.   ☐ at any time in the day or night because good cause has been established.

Unless delayed notice is authorized below, you must give a copy of the warrant and a receipt for the property taken to the person from whom, or from whose premises, the property was taken, or leave the copy and receipt at the place where the property was taken.

The officer executing this warrant, or an officer present during the execution of the warrant, must prepare an inventory as required by law and promptly return this warrant and inventory to _____ NANCY J. KOPPE _____.
(United States Magistrate Judge)

☐ Pursuant to 18 U.S.C. § 3103a(b), I find that immediate notification may have an adverse result listed in 18 U.S.C. § 2705 (except for delay of trial), and authorize the officer executing this warrant to delay notice to the person who, or whose property, will be searched or seized *(check the appropriate box)*
☐ for ____ days *(not to exceed 30)*   ☐ until, the facts justifying, the later specific date of _____.

Date and time issued: 10/13/17 12:30 p.m.

NANCY J. KOPPE
Judge's signature

City and state: Las Vegas, Nevada

UNITED STATES MAGISTRATE JUDGE
Printed name and title

ATTACHMENT "A-1"

ONLINE ACCOUNT TO BE SEARCHED

This warrant applies to information associated with the Microsoft email account centralpark1@live.com (the "Target Account 1") from inception to present, which is stored at premises owned, maintained, controlled, or operated by Microsoft Corporation, headquartered at 1 Microsoft Way, Redmond, Washington, 98052.

ATTACHMENT "B"
Particular Things to be Seized

I. **Information to be disclosed by the Service Provider**

To the extent that the information described in Attachments A1 and A2 is within the possession, custody, or control of Microsoft, including any Emails, records, files, logs, or information that have been deleted but are still available to Service Provider, or have been preserved pursuant to a request made under 18 U.S.C. § 2703(f), Service Provider is required to disclose the following information to the government for each account or identifier listed in Attachments A-1 and A-2 from account inception to present:

a. The contents of all communications, transactions, records, documents, programs, or materials stored in or associated with any OneDrive accounts associated with or assigned to Target Accounts 1 and 2.

b. The contents of all communications, transactions, records, documents, programs, or materials stored in or associated with any Office 360 accounts associated with or assigned to Target Accounts 1 and 2.

c. The contents of all communications, transactions, records, documents, programs, or materials stored in or associated with any Microsoft Family Safety accounts or services associated with or assigned to Target Accounts 1 and 2.

d. The contents of all communications, transactions, records, documents, programs, or materials stored in or associated with any Windows Live Writer accounts or services associated with or assigned to Target Accounts 1 and 2.

e. The contents of all communications, transactions, records, documents, programs, or materials stored in or associated with any Windows Live Mail accounts or services associated with or assigned to Target Accounts 1 and 2.

f. The contents of all communications, transactions, records, documents, programs, or materials stored in or associated with any Windows Photo Gallery accounts or services associated with or assigned to Target Accounts 1 and 2.

g. The contents of all communications, transactions, records, documents, programs, or materials stored in or associated with any Windows Live Messenger accounts or services associated with or assigned to Target Accounts 1 and 2.

II. Information to be seized by the United States

After reviewing all information described in Section I, the United States will seize evidence of violations of Title 18, United States Code Sections 32(a) (Destruction/Damage of Aircraft or Aircraft Facilities); 37(a)(2) (Violence at International Airport); and 922(a)(3); and 5 (Unlawful Interstate Transport/Delivery of Firearms by Non Federal Firearms Licensee); and 2 (Aiding and Abetting) (the "Subject Offenses") that occur in the form of the following, from account inception to present:

a. Communications, transactions and records that may establish ownership and control (or the degree thereof) of the Target Account, including address books, contact or buddy lists, bills, invoices, receipts, registration records, bills, correspondence, notes, records, memoranda, telephone/address books, photographs, video recordings, audio recordings, lists of names, records of payment for access to newsgroups or other online subscription services, and attachments to said communications, transactions and records.

b. Communications, transactions and records to/from persons who may be co-conspirators of the Subject Offenses, or which may identify co-conspirators.

c. Communications, transactions and records which may show motivation to commit the Subject Offenses.

d. Communications, transactions and records that relate to the Subject Offenses.

e. The terms "communications," "transactions", "records," "documents," "programs," or "materials" include all information recorded in any form, visual or aural, and by any means, whether in handmade form (including, but not limited to, writings, drawings, paintings), photographic form (including, but not limited to, pictures or videos), or electrical, electronic or magnetic form, as well as digital data files. These terms also include any applications (i.e. software programs). These terms expressly include, among other things, Emails, instant messages, chat logs, correspondence attached as to Emails (or drafts), calendar entries, buddy lists.

AO 93 (Rev. 11/13) Search and Seizure Warrant

UNITED STATES DISTRICT COURT
for the
District of Nevada

2017 OCT 13 PM 12: 30
U.S. MAGISTRATE JUDGE
BY_____

In the Matter of the Search of)
(Briefly describe the property to be searched)
or identify the person by name and address))
) Case No. 2:17-mj-01009-NJK
EMAIL ACCOUNT CENTRALPARK1@LIVE.COM THAT)
IS STORED AT A PREMISES CONTROLLED BY)
MICROSOFT. A1)

SEARCH AND SEIZURE WARRANT

To: Any authorized law enforcement officer

An application by a federal law enforcement officer or an attorney for the government requests the search of the following person or property located in the _____ District of _____Nevada_____
(identify the person or describe the property to be searched and give its location):

SEE ATTACHMENT A1

I find that the affidavit(s), or any recorded testimony, establish probable cause to search and seize the person or property described above, and that such search will reveal *(identify the person or describe the property to be seized):*

SEE ATTACHMENTS B and C

☑ **YOU ARE COMMANDED** to execute this warrant on or before October 27, 2017 *(not to exceed 14 days)*
☑ in the daytime 6:00 a.m. to 10:00 p.m.   ☐ at any time in the day or night because good cause has been established.

Unless delayed notice is authorized below, you must give a copy of the warrant and a receipt for the property taken to the person from whom, or from whose premises, the property was taken, or leave the copy and receipt at the place where the property was taken.

The officer executing this warrant, or an officer present during the execution of the warrant, must prepare an inventory as required by law and promptly return this warrant and inventory to _____NANCY J. KOPPE_____.
(United States Magistrate Judge)

☐ Pursuant to 18 U.S.C. § 3103a(b), I find that immediate notification may have an adverse result listed in 18 U.S.C. § 2705 (except for delay of trial), and authorize the officer executing this warrant to delay notice to the person who, or whose property, will be searched or seized *(check the appropriate box)*
☐ for _____ days *(not to exceed 30)* ☐ until, the facts justifying, the later specific date of _____

Date and time issued: 10/13/17 12:30 p.m.

NANCY J. KOPPE
Judge's signature

City and state: Las Vegas, Nevada

UNITED STATES MAGISTRATE JUDGE
Printed name and title

ATTACHMENT "A-1"

ONLINE ACCOUNT TO BE SEARCHED

This warrant applies to information associated with the Microsoft email account centralpark1@live.com (the "Target Account 1") from inception to present, which is stored at premises owned, maintained, controlled, or operated by Microsoft Corporation, headquartered at 1 Microsoft Way, Redmond, Washington, 98052.

ATTACHMENT "B"
Particular Things to be Seized

I. Information to be disclosed by the Service Provider

To the extent that the information described in Attachments A1 and A2 is within the possession, custody, or control of Microsoft, including any Emails, records, files, logs, or information that have been deleted but are still available to Service Provider, or have been preserved pursuant to a request made under 18 U.S.C. § 2703(f), Service Provider is required to disclose the following information to the government for each account or identifier listed in Attachments A-1 and A-2 from account inception to present:

a. The contents of all communications, transactions, records, documents, programs, or materials stored in or associated with any OneDrive accounts associated with or assigned to Target Accounts 1 and 2.

b. The contents of all communications, transactions, records, documents, programs, or materials stored in or associated with any Office 360 accounts associated with or assigned to Target Accounts 1 and 2.

c. The contents of all communications, transactions, records, documents, programs, or materials stored in or associated with any Microsoft Family Safety accounts or services associated with or assigned to Target Accounts 1 and 2.

d. The contents of all communications, transactions, records, documents, programs, or materials stored in or associated with any Windows Live Writer accounts or services associated with or assigned to Target Accounts 1 and 2.

e. The contents of all communications, transactions, records, documents, programs, or materials stored in or associated with any Windows Live Mail accounts or services associated with or assigned to Target Accounts 1 and 2.

f. The contents of all communications, transactions, records, documents, programs, or materials stored in or associated with any Windows Photo Gallery accounts or services associated with or assigned to Target Accounts 1 and 2.

g. The contents of all communications, transactions, records, documents, programs, or materials stored in or associated with any Windows Live Messenger accounts or services associated with or assigned to Target Accounts 1 and 2.

II. Information to be seized by the United States

After reviewing all information described in Section I, the United States will seize evidence of violations of Title 18, United States Code Sections 32(a) (Destruction/Damage of Aircraft or Aircraft Facilities); 37(a)(2) (Violence at International Airport); and 922(a)(3); and 5 (Unlawful Interstate Transport/Delivery of Firearms by Non Federal Firearms Licensee); and 2 (Aiding and Abetting) (the "Subject Offenses") that occur in the form of the following, from account inception to present:

a. Communications, transactions and records that may establish ownership and control (or the degree thereof) of the Target Account, including address books, contact or buddy lists, bills, invoices, receipts, registration records, bills, correspondence, notes, records, memoranda, telephone/address books, photographs, video recordings, audio recordings, lists of names, records of payment for access to newsgroups or other online subscription services, and attachments to said communications, transactions and records.

b. Communications, transactions and records to/from persons who may be co-conspirators of the Subject Offenses, or which may identify co-conspirators.

c. Communications, transactions and records which may show motivation to commit the Subject Offenses.

d. Communications, transactions and records that relate to the Subject Offenses.

e. The terms "communications," "transactions", "records," "documents," "programs," or "materials" include all information recorded in any form, visual or aural, and by any means, whether in handmade form (including, but not limited to, writings, drawings, paintings), photographic form (including, but not limited to, pictures or videos), or electrical, electronic or magnetic form, as well as digital data files. These terms also include any applications (i.e. software programs). These terms expressly include, among other things, Emails, instant messages, chat logs, correspondence attached as to Emails (or drafts), calendar entries, buddy lists.

STEVEN W. MYHRE
Acting United States Attorney
District of Nevada
CRISTINA D. SILVA
PATRICK BURNS
Assistant United States Attorneys
501 Las Vegas Blvd. South, Ste. 1100
Las Vegas, Nevada 89101
Telephone: (702) 388-6336
Fax (702) 388-6698
john.p.burns@usdoj.gov

Attorney for the United States of America

UNITED STATES DISTRICT COURT
DISTRICT OF NEVADA
-oOo-

IN THE MATTER OF THE SEARCH OF INFORMATION ASSOCIATED WITH EMAIL ACCOUNT CENTRALPARK1@LIVE.COM THAT IS STORED AT A PREMISES CONTROLLED BY MICROSOFT. A1	Magistrate No. 2:17-mj-01009-NJK AFFIDAVIT IN SUPPORT OF AN APPLICATION FOR SEARCH WARRANTS (Under Seal)
IN THE MATTER OF THE SEARCH OF INFORMATION ASSOCIATED WITH EMAIL ACCOUNT MARILOUROSES@LIVE.COM THAT IS STORED AT A PREMISES CONTROLLED BY MICROSOFT. A2	Magistrate No. AFFIDAVIT IN SUPPORT OF AN APPLICATION FOR SEARCH WARRANTS (Under Seal)

STATE OF NEVADA   )
) ss:
COUNTY OF CLARK   )

///

///

AFFIDAVIT IN SUPPORT OF AN
APPLICATION FOR SEARCH WARRANTS

I, Zachary C. Mckinney, Special Agent, Federal Bureau of Investigation (FBI), having been duly sworn, hereby depose and say:

INTRODUCTION AND AGENT BACKGROUND

1. Your Affiant makes this affidavit in support of an application for search warrants for information associated with email accounts centralpark1@live.com ("Target Account 1") and marilouroses@live.com ("Target Account 2"). Target Account 1 is an account associated with STEPHEN PADDOCK. Target Account 2 is an account associated with MARILOU DANLEY. The information associated with both accounts is stored at a premises owned, maintained, controlled, or operated by Microsoft Corporation ("Microsoft"), an American multinational technology company based in Redmond, Washington that specializes in Internet-related services and products along with the development and manufacturing of computer-related items. Those online services include, but are not limited to, email services, cloud computing, and many other services. The information to be searched is described in the following paragraphs and in Attachment "A" (attached hereto and incorporated herein by reference). This affidavit is made in support of an application for search warrants under 18 U.S.C. §§ 2703(a), 2703(b)(1)(A), and 2703(c)(1)(A) to require Microsoft to disclose to the government records and other information in its possession, pertaining to the subscriber or customer associated with the Target Accounts.

2. I am a Special Agent with the Federal Bureau of Investigation, currently assigned to Las Vegas, Nevada. I have been employed as a Special Agent of the FBI since

March of 2017. Over the course of my employment with the FBI, I have conducted surveillance, analyzed telephone records, interviewed witnesses, supervised activities of sources, executed search warrants, and executed arrest warrants. These investigative activities have been conducted in conjunction with a variety of investigations, to include those involving robbery, drug trafficking, human trafficking, criminal enterprises, and more. In addition to my practical experiences, I received five months of extensive law enforcement training at the FBI Academy. Previous to the FBI, I was employed as a human intelligence gatherer with the United States Army. I was trained extensively in interrogation, interview, and source handling techniques and best practices. I also received an MBA in International Business and worked with ExxonMobil as a financial manager.

3. I make this affidavit in support of an application for a search warrant for information associated with the Microsoft accounts associated with centralpark1@live.com" and "marilouroses@live.com," which is stored at a premises owned, maintained, controlled, or operated by Microsoft Corporation, headquartered at One Microsoft Way, Redmond, WA 98052-6399, hereinafter referred to as "premises," and further described in Attachments A-1 and A-2 hereto.

    a. Destruction/Damage of Aircraft or Aircraft Facilities - 18 U.S.C.A. § 32(a);

    b. Violence at International Airport - 18 U.S.C. § 37(a)(2); and

    c. Unlawful Interstate Transport/Delivery of Firearms by Non Federal Firearms Licensee – 18 U.S.C. §§ 922(a)(3) and (5);

    d. Aiding and Abetting – 18 U.S.C. § 2.

(hereafter, "Subject Offenses") have been committed by STEPHEN PADDOCK, MARILOU DANLEY, and others yet unknown. There is also probable cause to search the information described in Attachment "A" for evidence of these crimes and information which might reveal the identities of others involved in these crimes, as described in Attachment "B" (attached hereto and incorporated herein by reference).

PROBABLE CAUSE

4. On the evening of Sunday, October 1, 2017, Route 91 Harvest, a music festival, was in progress at 3901 South Las Vegas Boulevard, Las Vegas, Nevada. At approximately 10:08 p.m., the Las Vegas Metropolitan Police Department (LVMPD) received calls reporting shots had been fired at the concert and multiple victims were struck. LVMPD determined the shots were coming from Rooms 134 and 135 on the 32nd floor of the Mandalay Bay Resort and Casino, located due west of the festival rounds at 3950 South Las Vegas Boulevard, Las Vegas, Nevada. These rooms are an elevated position which overlooks the concert venue. Witness statements and video footage captured during the attack indicates that the weapons being used were firing in a fully-automatic fashion.

5. LVMPD officers ultimately made entry into the room and located an individual later identified as Stephen Paddock. Paddock was deceased from an apparent self-inflicted gunshot wound.

6. Paddock's Nevada driver's license was located in the Mandalay Bay hotel room with Paddock, and both hotel rooms were registered in his name. A player's club card in name of Marilou Danley was located in Paddock's room, and the card returned to the address located on Babbling Brook Street in Mesquite, Nevada. FBI Agents

located Danley, who was traveling outside the United States at the time of the shooting. It was ultimately determined that Danley resided with Paddock at the Babbling Brook address.

7. On October 2, 2017, search warrants were executed on Paddock's Mandalay Bay hotel rooms, Paddock's vehicle at Mandalay Bay, and two Nevada residences owed by Paddock: 1372 Babbling Brook Court in Mesquite, and 1735 Del Webb Parkway in Reno, Nevada. Officers and Agents found over 20 firearms, hundreds of rounds of ammunition, and hundreds of spent shell casings in the Mandalay Bay hotel rooms, in close proximity to Paddock's body. Over a thousand rounds of rifle ammunition and 100 pounds of explosive material was found in Paddock's vehicle. Additional explosive material, approximately 18 firearms, and over 1,000 rounds of ammunition was located at the Mesquite residence. A large quantity of ammunition and multiple firearms were recovered from the Reno residence.

8. As of this date, 58 people have been identified to have been killed in Paddock's attack and another 557 were reportedly injured. Additionally, investigators discovered that STEPHEN PADDOCK also utilized a firearm to shoot large fuel tanks on Las Vegas McCarran International Airport property. Multiple bullet holes were found on the tank, which investigators believe was an attempt by STEPHEN PADDOCK to cause the tanks to explode.

9. In an effort to determine whether or not STEPHEN PADDOCK was assisted and/or conspired with unknown individuals, investigators have attempted to identify all of STEPHEN PADDOCK's associated. It was quickly determined that a casino player's card in the name of MARILOU DANLEY was located in the room at the

time of the attack. She has been identified thus far as the most likely person who aided or abetted STEPHEN PADDOCK based on her informing law enforcement that her fingerprints would likely be found on the ammunition used during the attack. Subsequently, investigators worked to identify the communication facilities utilized by STEPHEN PADDOCK and MARILOU DANLEY.

10. Based on a review of STEPHEN PADDOCK's financial accounts, Target Account 1 was determined to belong to STEPHEN PADDOCK. On October 3, 2017, investigators requested an emergency disclosure of records from Microsoft related to Target Account 1 so it could be immediately searched for any evidence of additional co-conspirators. Unfortunately, the information was only requested for a six-month timeframe. Within the account, investigators identified Target Account 2 as one that belonged to MARILOU DANLEY, which was clear based on the communications between the two email accounts. In an interview, DANLEY stated that PADDOCK had access to one of her email accounts, which investigators believe to be Target Account 2.

11. On September 25, 2017, an email was exchanged between the Target Accounts which discussed a wire transfer of funds which was to be sent by STEPHEN PADDOCK to MARILOU DANLEY. It is unclear what the purpose of the wire transfer was, but MARILOU DANLEY is known to have been in the Philippines at the time.

12. Additionally, on July 6, 2017, Target Account 1 sent an email to centralpark4804@gmail.com which read, "try an ar before u buy. we have huge selection. located in the las vegas area." Later that day, an email was received back from centralpark4804@gmail.com to Target Account 1 that read, "we have a wide variety of optics and ammunition to try." And lastly, Target Account 1 later sent an email to

centralpark4804@gmail.com that read, "for a thrill try out bumpfire ar's with a 100 round magazine." Investigators believe these communications may have been related to the eventual attack that occurred at the Mandalay Bay in Las Vegas.

13. Your Affiant believes the requested search warrants will yield significant information from Microsoft such as STEPHEN PADDOCK's and MARILOU DANLEY's contact lists, email messages content, IP address usage, photographs, third-party applications associated with the account, and more, which may constitute evidence of the planning of the attack and potentially identify other participants in the attack. Ultimately, your Affiant strongly believes the requested information will lead investigators to determine the full scope of STEPHEN PADDOCK's plan and MARILOU DANLEY's possible involvement.

14. Investigators have previously sought and obtained a search warrant to examine the contents of both Target Accounts 1 and 2. After execution of that warrant, however, it became apparent and was confirmed with Microsoft that Microsoft was refusing to provide data related to/contained in the OneDrive online storage files for either account. Microsoft indicated to investigators that it did not believe such information was encompassed by the items to be produced that were specified in the original warrant. Investigators believe therefore that there is additional evidence Microsoft currently possesses that relates to the OneDrive online storage service, as well as potentially in a suite of other online services that Microsoft offers, including Office 365, Windows Live Mail, Windows Live Writer, Windows Photo Gallery, Windows Live Messenger, Microsoft Family Safety, and Microsoft Outlook Hotmail Connector. Thus,

your Affiant seeks more specific authorization to seize and search the OneDrive and other service data specified in Attachment B of the instant warrant application.

RELEVANT TECHNICAL TERMS

15. The following non-exhaustive list of definitions applies to this Affidavit and the Attachments to this Affidavit:

    a. The "Internet" is a worldwide network of computer systems operated by governmental entities, corporations, and universities. In order to access the Internet, an individual computer user must subscribe to an access provider, which operates a host computer system with direct access to the Internet. The World Wide Web is a functionality of the Internet which allows users of the Internet to share information.

    b. "Internet Service Providers" are companies that provide access to the Internet. ISPs can also provide other services for their customers including website hosting, email service, remote storage, and co-location of computers and other communications equipment. ISPs offer different ways to access the Internet including telephone-based (dial-up), broadband-based access via a digital subscriber line (DSL) or cable television, dedicated circuits, or satellite-based subscription. ISPs typically charge a fee based upon the type of connection and volume of data (bandwidth). Many ISPs assign each subscriber an account name, such as a user name, an email address, and an email mailbox, and the subscriber typically creates a password for his/her account.

    c. "ISP Records" are records maintained by ISPs pertaining to their subscribers (regardless of whether those subscribers are individuals or entities). These records may include account application information, subscriber and billing information, account access information (often in the form of log files), emails, information concerning

content uploaded and/or stored on the ISP's servers, and other information, which may be stored both in computer data format and in written or printed record format. ISPs reserve and/or maintain computer disk storage space on their computer system for their subscribers' use. This service by ISPs allows for both temporary and long-term storage of electronic communications and many other types of electronic data and files.

      d. "Online service providers" (also referred to here as "service providers") are companies that provide online services such as email, chat or instant messaging, word processing applications, spreadsheet applications, presentation applications similar to PowerPoint, online calendar, photo storage and remote storage services. Sometimes they also can provide web hosting, remote storage, and co-location of computers and other communications equipment. Typically, each service provider assigns each subscriber an account name, such as a user name or screen name and the subscriber typically creates a password for his/her account.

      e. "Computer," as used herein, is defined as "an electronic, magnetic, optical, electrochemical, or other high speed data processing device performing logical or storage functions, and includes any data storage facility or communications facility directly related to or operating in conjunction with such device."

      f. A "server" is a centralized computer that provides services for other computers connected to it via a network. The other computers attached to a server are sometimes called "clients." For example, in a large company, it is common for individual employees to have client computers at their desktops. When the employees access their email, or access files stored on the network itself, those files are pulled electronically from the server, where they are stored, and are sent to the client's computer via the

network. Notably, servers can be physically stored in any location: it is not uncommon for a network's server to be located hundreds (and even thousands) of miles away from the client computers.

   g. "Internet Protocol address," or "IP address," refers to a unique number used by a computer to access the Internet. IP addresses can be dynamic, meaning that the Internet Service Provider (ISP) assigns a different unique number to a computer every time it accesses the Internet. IP addresses might also be static, that is, an ISP assigns a user's computer a particular IP address which is used each time the computer accesses the Internet.

   h. The term "domain" refers to a word used as a name for computers, networks, services, etc. A domain name typically represents a website, a server computer that hosts that website, or even some computer (or other digital device) connected to the internet. Essentially, when a website (or a server computer that hosts that website) is connected to the internet, it is assigned an IP address. Because IP addresses are difficult for people to remember, domain names are instead used because they are easier to remember than IP addresses. Domain names are formed by the rules and procedures of the Domain Name System (DNS). A common top level domain under these rules is ".com" for commercial organizations, ".gov" for the United States government, and ".org" for organizations. For example, www.usdoj.gov is the domain name that identifies a server used by the U.S. Department of Justice, and which uses IP address of 149.101.46.71.

   i. "Web hosting services" maintain server computers connected to the Internet. Their customers use those computers to operate websites on the Internet. Customers of web hosting companies place files, software code, databases, and other data

on servers. To do this, customers typically connect from their own computers to the server computers across the Internet.

j. The term "WhoIs" lookup refers to a search of a publicly available online database that lists information provided when a domain is registered or when an IP address is assigned.

k. The terms "communications," "records," "documents," "programs," or "materials" include all information recorded in any form, visual or aural, and by any means, whether in handmade form (including, but not limited to, writings, drawings, paintings), photographic form (including, but not limited to, pictures or videos), or electrical, electronic or magnetic form, as well as digital data files. These terms also include any applications (i.e. software programs). These terms expressly include, among other things, emails, instant messages, chat logs, correspondence attached as to emails (or drafts), calendar entries, buddy lists.

l. "Chat" is usually a real time electronic communication between two or more individuals. Unlike email, which is frequently sent, then read and responded to minutes, hours, or even days later, chats frequently involve an immediate conversation between individuals, similar to a face-to-face conversation. Nearly all chat programs are capable of saving the chat transcript, to enable users to preserve a record of the conversation. By default, some chat programs have this capability enabled, while others do not. Many popular web-based email providers, like Microsoft and Microsoft, provide chat functionality as part of the online services they provide to account holders.

///

///

FACTS ABOUT EMAIL PROVIDERS

16. In my training, my experience and this investigation, I have learned that Microsoft (the Service Provider) is a company that provides free web-based Internet email access to the general public, and that stored electronic communications, including opened and unopened email for Microsoft subscribers may be located on the computers of Microsoft. I have also learned that Microsoft Inc. provides various on-line service messaging services to the general public. Instant Messaging ("IM") is a form of real-time direct text-based communication between two or more people using shared clients. The text is conveyed via devices connected over a network such as the Internet. In addition to text, Microsoft's software allows users with the most current updated versions to utilize its webcam service. This option enables users from distances all over the world to view others who have installed a webcam on their end. Thus, the Service Provider's servers will contain a wide variety of the subscriber's files, including emails, address books, contact or buddy lists, calendar data, pictures, chat logs, and other files.

17. To use these services, subscribers register for online accounts like the Target Accounts. During the registration process, service providers such as the ones here ask subscribers to provide basic personal information. This information can include the subscriber's full name, physical address, telephone numbers and other identifiers, alternative email addresses, and, for paying subscribers, means and source of payment (including any credit card or bank account number). Based on my training and my experience, I know that subscribers may insert false information to conceal their identity; even if this proves to be the case, however, I know that this information often provide clues to their identity, location or illicit activities.

18. In general, when a subscriber receives an email, it is typically stored in the subscriber's "mail box" on that service provider's servers until the subscriber deletes the Email. If the subscriber does not delete the message, the message (and any attachments) can remain on that service provider's servers indefinitely.

19. Similarly, when the subscriber sends an email, it is initiated at the subscriber's computer, transferred via the Internet to the service provider's servers, and then transmitted to its end destination. That service provider often saves a copy of the email sent. Unless the sender of the email specifically deletes the Email from the provider's server, the email can remain on the system indefinitely.

20. A sent or received email typically includes the content of the message, source and destination addresses, the date and time at which the email was sent, and the size and length of the email. If an email user writes a draft message but does not send it, that message may also be saved by that service provider, but may not include all of these categories of data.

21. Just as a computer on a desk can be used to store a wide variety of files, so can online accounts, such as the accounts subject to this application. First, subscribers can store many types of files as attachments to emails in online accounts. Second, because service providers provide the services listed above (e.g. word processing, spreadsheets, pictures), subscribers who use these services usually store documents on servers maintained and/or owned by service providers. Thus, these online accounts often contain documents such as pictures, audio or video recordings, logs, spreadsheets, applications and other files.

22. Reviewing files stored in online accounts raises many of the same difficulties as with reviewing files stored on a local computer. For example, based on my training, my experience and this investigation, I know that subscribers of these online services can conceal their activities by altering files before they upload them to the online service. Subscribers can change file names to more innocuous sounding names (e.g. renaming "FraudRecords.doc" to "ChristmasList.doc"), they can change file extensions to make one kind of file appear like a different type of file (e.g. changing the spreadsheet "StolenCreditProfiles.xls" to "FamilyPhoto.jpg" to appear to be a picture file, where the file extension ".xls" denotes an Excel spreadsheet file and ".jpg" a JPEG format image file), or they can change the times and dates a file was last accessed or modified by changing a computer's system time/date and then uploading that file to the Online Accounts. Thus, to detect any files that the subscriber may have concealed, agents will need to review all of the files in the Target Accounts; they will, however, only seize the items that the Court authorizes to be seized. Similarly, subscribers can conceal their activities by encrypting files. Thus, these files may need to be decrypted to detect whether it constitutes an Item to be Seized.

23. I also believe that people engaged in crimes such as the one described herein often use online accounts because they give people engaged in these crimes a way to easily communicate with other co-conspirators. Moreover, online accounts are easily concealed from law enforcement. Unlike physical documents, electronic documents can be stored in a physical place far away, where they are less likely to be discovered.

24. Service providers typically retain certain transactional information about the creation and use of each account on their systems. This information can include the

date on which the account was created, the length of service, records of log-in (i.e., session) times and durations, the types of service utilized, the status of the account (including whether the account is inactive or closed), the methods used to connect to the account (such as logging into the account via websites controlled by the Service Provider), and other log files that reflect usage of the account. In addition, service providers often have records of the Internet Protocol address ("IP address") used to register the account and the IP addresses associated with particular logins to the account. Because every device that connects to the Internet must use an IP address, IP address information can help to identify which computers or other devices were used to access the online account.

25. In some cases, subscribers will communicate directly with a service provider about issues relating to the account, such as technical problems, billing inquiries, or complaints from or about other users. Service providers typically retain records about such communications, including records of contacts between the user and the provider's support services, as well records of any actions taken by the provider or user as a result of the communications.

26. In my training and experience, evidence of who was using an online account may be found in address books, contact or buddy lists, emails in the account, and pictures and files, whether stored as attachments or in the suite of the service provider's online applications. Therefore, the computers of the Service Providers are likely to contain stored electronic communications (including retrieved and un-retrieved email for their subscribers) and information concerning subscribers and their use of the provider's

services, such as account access information, email transaction information, documents, pictures, and account application information.

27. Microsoft maintains and offers its users the use of OneDrive. OneDrive is a file-hosting service operated by Microsoft as part of its suite of online services. It allows users to store files as well as other personal data like Windows settings or BitLocker recovery keys in the cloud. Files can be synced to a PC and accessed from a web browser or a mobile device, as well as shared publicly or with specific people. OneDrive offers 5 gigabytes of storage space free of charge; additional storage can be added either separately or through subscriptions to other Microsoft services including Office 365 and Groove Music.

28. Microsoft offers additional services that may be accessed in relation to and share associated information with a user's email account, including: Office 365, Windows Live Mail, Windows Live Writer, Windows Photo Gallery, Windows Live Messenger, Microsoft Family Safety, and Microsoft Outlook Hotmail Connector.

INFORMATION TO BE SEARCHED AND THINGS TO BE SEIZED

29. Your Affiant anticipates executing these warrants under the Electronic Communications Privacy Act, in particular 18 U.S.C. §§ 2703(a), 2703(b)(1)(A) and 2703(c)(1)(A), by using the warrant to require Microsoft to disclose to the government copies of the records and other information (including the content of communications) particularly described in Section I of Attachment "B." Upon receipt of the information described in Section I of Attachment "B," government-authorized persons will review that information to locate the items described in Section II of Attachment "B."

CONCLUSION

30. Based on the forgoing, I request that the Court issue the proposed search warrant. This Court has jurisdiction to issue the requested warrant because it is "a court of competent jurisdiction" as defined by 18 U.S.C. § 2711. 18 U.S.C. §§ 2703(a), (b)(1)(A) & (c)(1)(A). Specifically, the Court is "a district court of the United States . . . that – has jurisdiction over the offense being investigated." 18 U.S.C. § 2711(3)(A)(i). Pursuant to 18 U.S.C. § 2703(g), the presence of a law enforcement officer is not required for the service or execution of this warrant.

REQUEST FOR SEALING

31. I further request that the Court order that all papers in support of this application, including the affidavit and search warrant, be sealed until further order of the Court. These documents discuss an ongoing criminal investigation that is neither public nor known to all of the targets of the investigation. Accordingly, there is good cause to seal these documents because their premature disclosure may seriously jeopardize that investigation.

Respectfully Submitted,

/s/
Zachary C. McKinney, Special Agent
Federal Bureau of Investigation

SWORN TO AND SUBSCRIBED
before me this 13th day of October 2017.

NANCY J. KOPPE
UNITED STATES MAGISTRATE JUDGE

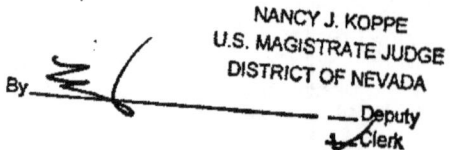

I hereby attest and certify on 10/13/17 that the foregoing document is a full true and correct copy of the original on file in my office, and in my legal custody.

NANCY J. KOPPE
U.S. MAGISTRATE JUDGE
DISTRICT OF NEVADA

By _____ Deputy Clerk

ATTACHMENT "A-1"

ONLINE ACCOUNT TO BE SEARCHED

This warrant applies to information associated with the Microsoft email account centralpark1@live.com (the "Target Account 1") from inception to present, which is stored at premises owned, maintained, controlled, or operated by Microsoft Corporation, headquartered at 1 Microsoft Way, Redmond, Washington, 98052.

ATTACHMENT "A-2"

ONLINE ACCOUNT TO BE SEARCHED

This warrant applies to information associated with the Microsoft email account marilouroses@live.com (the "Target Account 2") from inception to present, which is stored at premises owned, maintained, controlled, or operated by Microsoft Corporation, headquartered at 1 Microsoft Way, Redmond, Washington, 98052.

ATTACHMENT "B"
Particular Things to be Seized

I. **Information to be disclosed by the Service Provider**

To the extent that the information described in Attachments A1 and A2 is within the possession, custody, or control of Microsoft, including any Emails, records, files, logs, or information that have been deleted but are still available to Service Provider, or have been preserved pursuant to a request made under 18 U.S.C. § 2703(f), Service Provider is required to disclose the following information to the government for each account or identifier listed in Attachments A-1 and A-2 from account inception to present:

a. The contents of all communications, transactions, records, documents, programs, or materials stored in or associated with any OneDrive accounts associated with or assigned to Target Accounts 1 and 2.

b. The contents of all communications, transactions, records, documents, programs, or materials stored in or associated with any Office 360 accounts associated with or assigned to Target Accounts 1 and 2.

c. The contents of all communications, transactions, records, documents, programs, or materials stored in or associated with any Microsoft Family Safety accounts or services associated with or assigned to Target Accounts 1 and 2.

d. The contents of all communications, transactions, records, documents, programs, or materials stored in or associated with any Windows Live Writer accounts or services associated with or assigned to Target Accounts 1 and 2.

e. The contents of all communications, transactions, records, documents, programs, or materials stored in or associated with any Windows Live Mail accounts or services associated with or assigned to Target Accounts 1 and 2.

f. The contents of all communications, transactions, records, documents, programs, or materials stored in or associated with any Windows Photo Gallery accounts or services associated with or assigned to Target Accounts 1 and 2.

g. The contents of all communications, transactions, records, documents, programs, or materials stored in or associated with any Windows Live Messenger accounts or services associated with or assigned to Target Accounts 1 and 2.

II. **Information to be seized by the United States**

After reviewing all information described in Section I, the United States will seize evidence of violations of Title 18, United States Code Sections 32(a) (Destruction/Damage of Aircraft or Aircraft Facilities); 37(a)(2) (Violence at International Airport); and 922(a)(3); and 5 (Unlawful Interstate Transport/Delivery of Firearms by Non Federal Firearms Licensee); and 2 (Aiding and Abetting) (the "Subject Offenses") that occur in the form of the following, from account inception to present:

a. Communications, transactions and records that may establish ownership and control (or the degree thereof) of the Target Account, including address books, contact or buddy lists, bills, invoices, receipts, registration records, bills, correspondence, notes, records, memoranda, telephone/address books, photographs, video recordings, audio recordings, lists of names, records of payment for access to newsgroups or other online subscription services, and attachments to said communications, transactions and records.

b. Communications, transactions and records to/from persons who may be co-conspirators of the Subject Offenses, or which may identify co-conspirators.

c. Communications, transactions and records which may show motivation to commit the Subject Offenses.

d. Communications, transactions and records that relate to the Subject Offenses.

e. The terms "communications," "transactions", "records," "documents," "programs," or "materials" include all information recorded in any form, visual or aural, and by any means, whether in handmade form (including, but not limited to, writings, drawings, paintings), photographic form (including, but not limited to, pictures or videos), or electrical, electronic or magnetic form, as well as digital data files. These terms also include any applications (i.e. software programs). These terms expressly include, among other things, Emails, instant messages, chat logs, correspondence attached as to Emails (or drafts), calendar entries, buddy lists.

ATTACHMENT "C"

PROTOCOL FOR SEARCHING THE ELECTRONIC DATA SEIZED PURSUANT TO THIS SEARCH WARRANT

1. In executing this warrant, the government must make reasonable efforts to use methods and procedures that will locate and expose in the electronic data produced in response to this search warrant ("the Search Warrant Data") those categories of data, files, documents, or other electronically stored information that are identified with particularity in the warrant, while minimizing exposure or examination of irrelevant, privileged, or confidential files to the extent reasonably practicable.

2. When the Search Warrant Data is received, the government will make a duplicate copy of the Search Warrant Data ("the Search Warrant Data Copy"). The original version of the Search Warrant Data will be sealed and preserved for purposes of: later judicial review or order to return or dispose of the Search Warrant Data; production to the defense in any criminal case if authorized by statute, rule, or the Constitution; for purposes of showing the chain of custody of the Search Warrant Data and the Search Warrant Data Copy; or for any other lawful purpose. The original of the Search Warrant Data will not be searched or examined except to ensure that it has been fully and completely replicated in the Search Warrant Data Copy.

3. The investigating agents will then search the entirety of the Search Warrant Data Copy using any and all methods and procedures deemed appropriate by the United States designed to identify the information listed as Information to be Seized in Attachment B, Section II. The United States may copy, extract or otherwise segregate information or data listed as Information to be Seized in Attachment B, Section II. Information or data so copied, extracted or otherwise segregated will no longer be subject to any handling restrictions that might be set out in this protocol beyond those required by binding law. To the extent evidence of crimes not within the scope of this warrant appear in plain view during this review, a supplemental or "piggyback" warrant will be applied for in order to further search that document, data, or other item.

4. Once the Search Warrant Data Copy has been thoroughly and completely examined for any document, data, or other items identified in Attachment B, Section II as Information to be Seized, the Search Warrant Data Copy will be sealed and not subject to any further search or examination unless authorized by another search warrant or other appropriate court order. The Search Warrant Data Copy will be held and preserved for the same purposes identified above in Paragraph 2.

5. The search procedures utilized for this review are at the sole discretion of the investigating and prosecuting authorities, and may include the following techniques (the following is a non-exclusive list, as other search procedures may be used):

a. examination of all of the data contained in the Search Warrant Data to view the data and determine whether that data falls within the items to be seized as set forth herein;

b. searching for and attempting to recover from the Search Warrant Data any deleted, hidden, or encrypted data to determine whether that data falls within the list of items to be seized as set forth herein (any data that is encrypted and unreadable will not be returned unless law enforcement personnel have determined that the data is not (1) an instrumentality of the offenses, (2) a fruit of the criminal activity, (3) contraband, (4) otherwise unlawfully possessed, or (5) evidence of the offenses specified above);

c. surveying various file directories and the individual files they contain;

d. opening files in order to determine their contents;

e. using hash values to narrow the scope of what may be found. Hash values are under- inclusive, but are still a helpful tool;

f. scanning storage areas;

g. performing keyword searches through all electronic storage areas to determine whether occurrences of language contained in such storage areas exist that are likely to appear in the evidence described in Attachment A1 and A2; and/or

h. performing any other data analysis technique that may be necessary to locate and retrieve the evidence described in Attachment B, Section II.

Return and Review Procedures

6. Rule 41 of the Federal Rules of Criminal Procedure provides, in relevant part:

(e) Issuing the Warrant.

(2) Contents of the Warrant.

(A) Warrant to Search for and Seize a Person or Property. Except for a tracking-device warrant, the warrant must identify the person or property to be searched, identify any person or property to be seized, and designate the magistrate judge to whom it must be returned. The warrant must command the officer to:

(i) execute the warrant within a specified time no longer than 14 days;

(B) Warrant Seeking Electronically Stored Information. A warrant under Rule 41(e)(2)(A) may authorize the seizure of electronic storage media or the seizure or copying of electronically stored information. Unless otherwise specified, the warrant authorizes a later review of the media or information consistent with the warrant. The time for executing the warrant in Rule 41(e)(2)(A) and (f)(1)(A) refers to the seizure or on-site copying of the media or information, and not to any later off-site copying or review.

(f) Executing and Returning the Warrant.

(1) Warrant to Search for and Seize a Person or Property.

(B) Inventory. An officer present during the execution of the warrant must prepare and verify an inventory of any property seized. . . . In a case involving the seizure of electronic storage media or the seizure or copying of electronically stored information, the inventory may be limited to describing the physical storage media that were seized or copied. The officer may retain a copy of the electronically stored information that was seized or copied.

7. Pursuant to this Rule, the government understands and will act in accordance with the following:

a. Pursuant to Rule 41(e)(2)(A)(iii), within fourteen (14) days of the execution of the warrant, an agent is required to file an inventory return with the Court, that is, to file an itemized list of the property seized. Execution of the warrant begins when the United States serves the warrant on the named custodian; execution is complete when the custodian provides all Search Warrant Data to the United States. Within fourteen (14) days of completion of the execution of the warrant, the inventory will be filed.

b. Pursuant to Rule 41(e)(2)(B), Rule 41(e)(2)(A) governs the time within which the electronically stored information must be seized after the issuance of the warrant and copied after the execution of the warrant, not the "later review of the media or information" seized, or the later off-site digital copying of that media.

c. Under Rule 41(f)(1)(B), the inventory return that is to be filed with the court may be limited to a description of the "physical storage media" into which the Search Warrant Data that was seized was placed, not an itemization of the information or data stored on the "physical storage media" into which the Search Warrant Data was placed;

d. Under Rule 41(f)(1)(B), the government may retain a copy of that information for purposes of the investigation. The government proposes that the original storage media on which the Search Warrant Data was placed plus a full image copy of the seized Search Warrant Data be retained by the government.

e. If the person from whom any Search Warrant Data was seized requests the return of any information in the Search Warrant Data that is not set forth in Attachment B, Section II, that information will be copied onto appropriate media and returned to the person from whom the information was seized.

STEVEN W. MYHRE
Acting United States Attorney
District of Nevada
CRISTINA D. SILVA
PATRICK BURNS
Assistant United States Attorneys
501 Las Vegas Blvd. South, Ste. 1100
Las Vegas, Nevada 89101
Telephone: (702) 388-6336
Fax (702) 388-6698
john.p.burns@usdoj.gov

Attorney for the United States of America

UNITED STATES DISTRICT COURT
DISTRICT OF NEVADA
-oOo-

IN THE MATTER OF THE SEARCH OF INFORMATION ASSOCIATED WITH EMAIL ACCOUNT CENTRALPARK1@LIVE.COM THAT IS STORED AT A PREMISES CONTROLLED BY MICROSOFT. A1	Magistrate No. AFFIDAVIT IN SUPPORT OF AN APPLICATION FOR SEARCH WARRANTS (Under Seal)
IN THE MATTER OF THE SEARCH OF INFORMATION ASSOCIATED WITH EMAIL ACCOUNT MARILOUROSES@LIVE.COM THAT IS STORED AT A PREMISES CONTROLLED BY MICROSOFT. A2	Magistrate No. 2:17-mj-01010-NJK AFFIDAVIT IN SUPPORT OF AN APPLICATION FOR SEARCH WARRANTS (Under Seal)

STATE OF NEVADA   )
) ss:
COUNTY OF CLARK   )

///

///

AFFIDAVIT IN SUPPORT OF AN APPLICATION FOR SEARCH WARRANTS

I, Zachary C. Mckinney, Special Agent, Federal Bureau of Investigation (FBI), having been duly sworn, hereby depose and say:

INTRODUCTION AND AGENT BACKGROUND

1. Your Affiant makes this affidavit in support of an application for search warrants for information associated with email accounts centralpark1@live.com ("Target Account 1") and marilouroses@live.com ("Target Account 2"). Target Account 1 is an account associated with STEPHEN PADDOCK. Target Account 2 is an account associated with MARILOU DANLEY. The information associated with both accounts is stored at a premises owned, maintained, controlled, or operated by Microsoft Corporation ("Microsoft"), an American multinational technology company based in Redmond, Washington that specializes in Internet-related services and products along with the development and manufacturing of computer-related items. Those online services include, but are not limited to, email services, cloud computing, and many other services. The information to be searched is described in the following paragraphs and in Attachment "A" (attached hereto and incorporated herein by reference). This affidavit is made in support of an application for search warrants under 18 U.S.C. §§ 2703(a), 2703(b)(1)(A), and 2703(c)(1)(A) to require Microsoft to disclose to the government records and other information in its possession, pertaining to the subscriber or customer associated with the Target Accounts.

2. I am a Special Agent with the Federal Bureau of Investigation, currently assigned to Las Vegas, Nevada. I have been employed as a Special Agent of the FBI since

March of 2017. Over the course of my employment with the FBI, I have conducted surveillance, analyzed telephone records, interviewed witnesses, supervised activities of sources, executed search warrants, and executed arrest warrants. These investigative activities have been conducted in conjunction with a variety of investigations, to include those involving robbery, drug trafficking, human trafficking, criminal enterprises, and more. In addition to my practical experiences, I received five months of extensive law enforcement training at the FBI Academy. Previous to the FBI, I was employed as a human intelligence gatherer with the United States Army. I was trained extensively in interrogation, interview, and source handling techniques and best practices. I also received an MBA in International Business and worked with ExxonMobil as a financial manager.

3. I make this affidavit in support of an application for a search warrant for information associated with the Microsoft accounts associated with centralpark1@live.com" and "marilouroses@live.com," which is stored at a premises owned, maintained, controlled, or operated by Microsoft Corporation, headquartered at One Microsoft Way, Redmond, WA 98052-6399, hereinafter referred to as "premises," and further described in Attachments A-1 and A-2 hereto.

    a. Destruction/Damage of Aircraft or Aircraft Facilities - 18 U.S.C.A. § 32(a);

    b. Violence at International Airport - 18 U.S.C. § 37(a)(2); and

    c. Unlawful Interstate Transport/Delivery of Firearms by Non Federal Firearms Licensee – 18 U.S.C. §§ 922(a)(3) and (5);

    d. Aiding and Abetting – 18 U.S.C. § 2.

(hereafter, "Subject Offenses") have been committed by STEPHEN PADDOCK, MARILOU DANLEY, and others yet unknown. There is also probable cause to search the information described in Attachment "A" for evidence of these crimes and information which might reveal the identities of others involved in these crimes, as described in Attachment "B" (attached hereto and incorporated herein by reference).

PROBABLE CAUSE

4. On the evening of Sunday, October 1, 2017, Route 91 Harvest, a music festival, was in progress at 3901 South Las Vegas Boulevard, Las Vegas, Nevada. At approximately 10:08 p.m., the Las Vegas Metropolitan Police Department (LVMPD) received calls reporting shots had been fired at the concert and multiple victims were struck. LVMPD determined the shots were coming from Rooms 134 and 135 on the 32nd floor of the Mandalay Bay Resort and Casino, located due west of the festival rounds at 3950 South Las Vegas Boulevard, Las Vegas, Nevada. These rooms are an elevated position which overlooks the concert venue. Witness statements and video footage captured during the attack indicates that the weapons being used were firing in a fully-automatic fashion.

5. LVMPD officers ultimately made entry into the room and located an individual later identified as Stephen Paddock. Paddock was deceased from an apparent self-inflicted gunshot wound.

6. Paddock's Nevada driver's license was located in the Mandalay Bay hotel room with Paddock, and both hotel rooms were registered in his name. A player's club card in name of Marilou Danley was located in Paddock's room, and the card returned to the address located on Babbling Brook Street in Mesquite, Nevada. FBI Agents

located Danley, who was traveling outside the United States at the time of the shooting. It was ultimately determined that Danley resided with Paddock at the Babbling Brook address.

7. On October 2, 2017, search warrants were executed on Paddock's Mandalay Bay hotel rooms, Paddock's vehicle at Mandalay Bay, and two Nevada residences owed by Paddock: 1372 Babbling Brook Court in Mesquite, and 1735 Del Webb Parkway in Reno, Nevada. Officers and Agents found over 20 firearms, hundreds of rounds of ammunition, and hundreds of spent shell casings in the Mandalay Bay hotel rooms, in close proximity to Paddock's body. Over a thousand rounds of rifle ammunition and 100 pounds of explosive material was found in Paddock's vehicle. Additional explosive material, approximately 18 firearms, and over 1,000 rounds of ammunition was located at the Mesquite residence. A large quantity of ammunition and multiple firearms were recovered from the Reno residence.

8. As of this date, 58 people have been identified to have been killed in Paddock's attack and another 557 were reportedly injured. Additionally, investigators discovered that STEPHEN PADDOCK also utilized a firearm to shoot large fuel tanks on Las Vegas McCarran International Airport property. Multiple bullet holes were found on the tank, which investigators believe was an attempt by STEPHEN PADDOCK to cause the tanks to explode.

9. In an effort to determine whether or not STEPHEN PADDOCK was assisted and/or conspired with unknown individuals, investigators have attempted to identify all of STEPHEN PADDOCK's associated. It was quickly determined that a casino player's card in the name of MARILOU DANLEY was located in the room at the

time of the attack. She has been identified thus far as the most likely person who aided or abetted STEPHEN PADDOCK based on her informing law enforcement that her fingerprints would likely be found on the ammunition used during the attack. Subsequently, investigators worked to identify the communication facilities utilized by STEPHEN PADDOCK and MARILOU DANLEY.

10. Based on a review of STEPHEN PADDOCK's financial accounts, Target Account 1 was determined to belong to STEPHEN PADDOCK. On October 3, 2017, investigators requested an emergency disclosure of records from Microsoft related to Target Account 1 so it could be immediately searched for any evidence of additional co-conspirators. Unfortunately, the information was only requested for a six-month timeframe. Within the account, investigators identified Target Account 2 as one that belonged to MARILOU DANLEY, which was clear based on the communications between the two email accounts. In an interview, DANLEY stated that PADDOCK had access to one of her email accounts, which investigators believe to be Target Account 2.

11. On September 25, 2017, an email was exchanged between the Target Accounts which discussed a wire transfer of funds which was to be sent by STEPHEN PADDOCK to MARILOU DANLEY. It is unclear what the purpose of the wire transfer was, but MARILOU DANLEY is known to have been in the Philippines at the time.

12. Additionally, on July 6, 2017, Target Account 1 sent an email to centralpark4804@gmail.com which read, "try an ar before u buy. we have huge selection. located in the las vegas area." Later that day, an email was received back from centralpark4804@gmail.com to Target Account 1 that read, "we have a wide variety of optics and ammunition to try." And lastly, Target Account 1 later sent an email to

centralpark4804@gmail.com that read, "for a thrill try out bumpfire ar's with a 100 round magazine." Investigators believe these communications may have been related to the eventual attack that occurred at the Mandalay Bay in Las Vegas.

13. Your Affiant believes the requested search warrants will yield significant information from Microsoft such as STEPHEN PADDOCK's and MARILOU DANLEY's contact lists, email messages content, IP address usage, photographs, third-party applications associated with the account, and more, which may constitute evidence of the planning of the attack and potentially identify other participants in the attack. Ultimately, your Affiant strongly believes the requested information will lead investigators to determine the full scope of STEPHEN PADDOCK's plan and MARILOU DANLEY's possible involvement.

14. Investigators have previously sought and obtained a search warrant to examine the contents of both Target Accounts 1 and 2. After execution of that warrant, however, it became apparent and was confirmed with Microsoft that Microsoft was refusing to provide data related to/contained in the OneDrive online storage files for either account. Microsoft indicated to investigators that it did not believe such information was encompassed by the items to be produced that were specified in the original warrant. Investigators believe therefore that there is additional evidence Microsoft currently possesses that relates to the OneDrive online storage service, as well as potentially in a suite of other online services that Microsoft offers, including Office 365, Windows Live Mail, Windows Live Writer, Windows Photo Gallery, Windows Live Messenger, Microsoft Family Safety, and Microsoft Outlook Hotmail Connector. Thus,

your Affiant seeks more specific authorization to seize and search the OneDrive and other service data specified in Attachment B of the instant warrant application.

RELEVANT TECHNICAL TERMS

15. The following non-exhaustive list of definitions applies to this Affidavit and the Attachments to this Affidavit:

a. The "Internet" is a worldwide network of computer systems operated by governmental entities, corporations, and universities. In order to access the Internet, an individual computer user must subscribe to an access provider, which operates a host computer system with direct access to the Internet. The World Wide Web is a functionality of the Internet which allows users of the Internet to share information.

b. "Internet Service Providers" are companies that provide access to the Internet. ISPs can also provide other services for their customers including website hosting, email service, remote storage, and co-location of computers and other communications equipment. ISPs offer different ways to access the Internet including telephone-based (dial-up), broadband-based access via a digital subscriber line (DSL) or cable television, dedicated circuits, or satellite-based subscription. ISPs typically charge a fee based upon the type of connection and volume of data (bandwidth). Many ISPs assign each subscriber an account name, such as a user name, an email address, and an email mailbox, and the subscriber typically creates a password for his/her account.

c. "ISP Records" are records maintained by ISPs pertaining to their subscribers (regardless of whether those subscribers are individuals or entities). These records may include account application information, subscriber and billing information, account access information (often in the form of log files), emails, information concerning

content uploaded and/or stored on the ISP's servers, and other information, which may be stored both in computer data format and in written or printed record format. ISPs reserve and/or maintain computer disk storage space on their computer system for their subscribers' use. This service by ISPs allows for both temporary and long-term storage of electronic communications and many other types of electronic data and files.

        d. "Online service providers" (also referred to here as "service providers") are companies that provide online services such as email, chat or instant messaging, word processing applications, spreadsheet applications, presentation applications similar to PowerPoint, online calendar, photo storage and remote storage services. Sometimes they also can provide web hosting, remote storage, and co-location of computers and other communications equipment. Typically, each service provider assigns each subscriber an account name, such as a user name or screen name and the subscriber typically creates a password for his/her account.

        e. "Computer," as used herein, is defined as "an electronic, magnetic, optical, electrochemical, or other high speed data processing device performing logical or storage functions, and includes any data storage facility or communications facility directly related to or operating in conjunction with such device."

        f. A "server" is a centralized computer that provides services for other computers connected to it via a network. The other computers attached to a server are sometimes called "clients." For example, in a large company, it is common for individual employees to have client computers at their desktops. When the employees access their email, or access files stored on the network itself, those files are pulled electronically from the server, where they are stored, and are sent to the client's computer via the

network. Notably, servers can be physically stored in any location: it is not uncommon for a network's server to be located hundreds (and even thousands) of miles away from the client computers.

g. "Internet Protocol address," or "IP address," refers to a unique number used by a computer to access the Internet. IP addresses can be dynamic, meaning that the Internet Service Provider (ISP) assigns a different unique number to a computer every time it accesses the Internet. IP addresses might also be static, that is, an ISP assigns a user's computer a particular IP address which is used each time the computer accesses the Internet.

h. The term "domain" refers to a word used as a name for computers, networks, services, etc. A domain name typically represents a website, a server computer that hosts that website, or even some computer (or other digital device) connected to the internet. Essentially, when a website (or a server computer that hosts that website) is connected to the internet, it is assigned an IP address. Because IP addresses are difficult for people to remember, domain names are instead used because they are easier to remember than IP addresses. Domain names are formed by the rules and procedures of the Domain Name System (DNS). A common top level domain under these rules is ".com" for commercial organizations, ".gov" for the United States government, and ".org" for organizations. For example, www.usdoj.gov is the domain name that identifies a server used by the U.S. Department of Justice, and which uses IP address of 149.101.46.71.

i. "Web hosting services" maintain server computers connected to the Internet. Their customers use those computers to operate websites on the Internet. Customers of web hosting companies place files, software code, databases, and other data

on servers. To do this, customers typically connect from their own computers to the server computers across the Internet.

   j. The term "WhoIs" lookup refers to a search of a publicly available online database that lists information provided when a domain is registered or when an IP address is assigned.

   k. The terms "communications," "records," "documents," "programs," or "materials" include all information recorded in any form, visual or aural, and by any means, whether in handmade form (including, but not limited to, writings, drawings, paintings), photographic form (including, but not limited to, pictures or videos), or electrical, electronic or magnetic form, as well as digital data files. These terms also include any applications (i.e. software programs). These terms expressly include, among other things, emails, instant messages, chat logs, correspondence attached as to emails (or drafts), calendar entries, buddy lists.

   l. "Chat" is usually a real time electronic communication between two or more individuals. Unlike email, which is frequently sent, then read and responded to minutes, hours, or even days later, chats frequently involve an immediate conversation between individuals, similar to a face-to-face conversation. Nearly all chat programs are capable of saving the chat transcript, to enable users to preserve a record of the conversation. By default, some chat programs have this capability enabled, while others do not. Many popular web-based email providers, like Microsoft and Microsoft, provide chat functionality as part of the online services they provide to account holders.

///

///

FACTS ABOUT EMAIL PROVIDERS

16. In my training, my experience and this investigation, I have learned that Microsoft (the Service Provider) is a company that provides free web-based Internet email access to the general public, and that stored electronic communications, including opened and unopened email for Microsoft subscribers may be located on the computers of Microsoft. I have also learned that Microsoft Inc. provides various on-line service messaging services to the general public. Instant Messaging ("IM") is a form of real-time direct text-based communication between two or more people using shared clients. The text is conveyed via devices connected over a network such as the Internet. In addition to text, Microsoft's software allows users with the most current updated versions to utilize its webcam service. This option enables users from distances all over the world to view others who have installed a webcam on their end. Thus, the Service Provider's servers will contain a wide variety of the subscriber's files, including emails, address books, contact or buddy lists, calendar data, pictures, chat logs, and other files.

17. To use these services, subscribers register for online accounts like the Target Accounts. During the registration process, service providers such as the ones here ask subscribers to provide basic personal information. This information can include the subscriber's full name, physical address, telephone numbers and other identifiers, alternative email addresses, and, for paying subscribers, means and source of payment (including any credit card or bank account number). Based on my training and my experience, I know that subscribers may insert false information to conceal their identity; even if this proves to be the case, however, I know that this information often provide clues to their identity, location or illicit activities.

18. In general, when a subscriber receives an email, it is typically stored in the subscriber's "mail box" on that service provider's servers until the subscriber deletes the Email. If the subscriber does not delete the message, the message (and any attachments) can remain on that service provider's servers indefinitely.

19. Similarly, when the subscriber sends an email, it is initiated at the subscriber's computer, transferred via the Internet to the service provider's servers, and then transmitted to its end destination. That service provider often saves a copy of the email sent. Unless the sender of the email specifically deletes the Email from the provider's server, the email can remain on the system indefinitely.

20. A sent or received email typically includes the content of the message, source and destination addresses, the date and time at which the email was sent, and the size and length of the email. If an email user writes a draft message but does not send it, that message may also be saved by that service provider, but may not include all of these categories of data.

21. Just as a computer on a desk can be used to store a wide variety of files, so can online accounts, such as the accounts subject to this application. First, subscribers can store many types of files as attachments to emails in online accounts. Second, because service providers provide the services listed above (e.g. word processing, spreadsheets, pictures), subscribers who use these services usually store documents on servers maintained and/or owned by service providers. Thus, these online accounts often contain documents such as pictures, audio or video recordings, logs, spreadsheets, applications and other files.

22. Reviewing files stored in online accounts raises many of the same difficulties as with reviewing files stored on a local computer. For example, based on my training, my experience and this investigation, I know that subscribers of these online services can conceal their activities by altering files before they upload them to the online service. Subscribers can change file names to more innocuous sounding names (e.g. renaming "FraudRecords.doc" to "ChristmasList.doc"), they can change file extensions to make one kind of file appear like a different type of file (e.g. changing the spreadsheet "StolenCreditProfiles.xls" to "FamilyPhoto.jpg" to appear to be a picture file, where the file extension ".xls" denotes an Excel spreadsheet file and ".jpg" a JPEG format image file), or they can change the times and dates a file was last accessed or modified by changing a computer's system time/date and then uploading that file to the Online Accounts. Thus, to detect any files that the subscriber may have concealed, agents will need to review all of the files in the Target Accounts; they will, however, only seize the items that the Court authorizes to be seized. Similarly, subscribers can conceal their activities by encrypting files. Thus, these files may need to be decrypted to detect whether it constitutes an Item to be Seized.

23. I also believe that people engaged in crimes such as the one described herein often use online accounts because they give people engaged in these crimes a way to easily communicate with other co-conspirators. Moreover, online accounts are easily concealed from law enforcement. Unlike physical documents, electronic documents can be stored in a physical place far away, where they are less likely to be discovered.

24. Service providers typically retain certain transactional information about the creation and use of each account on their systems. This information can include the

date on which the account was created, the length of service, records of log-in (i.e., session) times and durations, the types of service utilized, the status of the account (including whether the account is inactive or closed), the methods used to connect to the account (such as logging into the account via websites controlled by the Service Provider), and other log files that reflect usage of the account. In addition, service providers often have records of the Internet Protocol address ("IP address") used to register the account and the IP addresses associated with particular logins to the account. Because every device that connects to the Internet must use an IP address, IP address information can help to identify which computers or other devices were used to access the online account.

25. In some cases, subscribers will communicate directly with a service provider about issues relating to the account, such as technical problems, billing inquiries, or complaints from or about other users. Service providers typically retain records about such communications, including records of contacts between the user and the provider's support services, as well records of any actions taken by the provider or user as a result of the communications.

26. In my training and experience, evidence of who was using an online account may be found in address books, contact or buddy lists, emails in the account, and pictures and files, whether stored as attachments or in the suite of the service provider's online applications. Therefore, the computers of the Service Providers are likely to contain stored electronic communications (including retrieved and un-retrieved email for their subscribers) and information concerning subscribers and their use of the provider's

services, such as account access information, email transaction information, documents, pictures, and account application information.

27. Microsoft maintains and offers its users the use of OneDrive. OneDrive is a file-hosting service operated by Microsoft as part of its suite of online services. It allows users to store files as well as other personal data like Windows settings or BitLocker recovery keys in the cloud. Files can be synced to a PC and accessed from a web browser or a mobile device, as well as shared publicly or with specific people. OneDrive offers 5 gigabytes of storage space free of charge; additional storage can be added either separately or through subscriptions to other Microsoft services including Office 365 and Groove Music.

28. Microsoft offers additional services that may be accessed in relation to and share associated information with a user's email account, including: Office 365, Windows Live Mail, Windows Live Writer, Windows Photo Gallery, Windows Live Messenger, Microsoft Family Safety, and Microsoft Outlook Hotmail Connector.

INFORMATION TO BE SEARCHED AND THINGS TO BE SEIZED

29. Your Affiant anticipates executing these warrants under the Electronic Communications Privacy Act, in particular 18 U.S.C. §§ 2703(a), 2703(b)(1)(A) and 2703(c)(1)(A), by using the warrant to require Microsoft to disclose to the government copies of the records and other information (including the content of communications) particularly described in Section I of Attachment "B." Upon receipt of the information described in Section I of Attachment "B," government-authorized persons will review that information to locate the items described in Section II of Attachment "B."

CONCLUSION

30. Based on the forgoing, I request that the Court issue the proposed search warrant. This Court has jurisdiction to issue the requested warrant because it is "a court of competent jurisdiction" as defined by 18 U.S.C. § 2711. 18 U.S.C. §§ 2703(a), (b)(1)(A) & (c)(1)(A). Specifically, the Court is "a district court of the United States . . . that – has jurisdiction over the offense being investigated." 18 U.S.C. § 2711(3)(A)(i). Pursuant to 18 U.S.C. § 2703(g), the presence of a law enforcement officer is not required for the service or execution of this warrant.

REQUEST FOR SEALING

31. I further request that the Court order that all papers in support of this application, including the affidavit and search warrant, be sealed until further order of the Court. These documents discuss an ongoing criminal investigation that is neither public nor known to all of the targets of the investigation. Accordingly, there is good cause to seal these documents because their premature disclosure may seriously jeopardize that investigation.

Respectfully Submitted,

/s/

Zachary C. McKinney, Special Agent
Federal Bureau of Investigation

SWORN TO AND SUBSCRIBED
before me this 13 day of October 2017.

_____
NANCY J. KOPPE
UNITED STATES MAGISTRATE JUDGE

I hereby attest and certify on 10/13/17 that the foregoing document is a full true and correct copy of the original on file in my office, and in my legal custody.

NANCY J. KOPPE
U.S. MAGISTRATE JUDGE
DISTRICT OF NEVADA

By_____ Deputy Clerk

ATTACHMENT "A-1"

ONLINE ACCOUNT TO BE SEARCHED

This warrant applies to information associated with the Microsoft email account centralpark1@live.com (the "Target Account 1") from inception to present, which is stored at premises owned, maintained, controlled, or operated by Microsoft Corporation, headquartered at 1 Microsoft Way, Redmond, Washington, 98052.

ATTACHMENT "A-2"

ONLINE ACCOUNT TO BE SEARCHED

This warrant applies to information associated with the Microsoft email account marilouroses@live.com (the "Target Account 2") from inception to present, which is stored at premises owned, maintained, controlled, or operated by Microsoft Corporation, headquartered at 1 Microsoft Way, Redmond, Washington, 98052.

ATTACHMENT "B"
Particular Things to be Seized

I. Information to be disclosed by the Service Provider

To the extent that the information described in Attachments A1 and A2 is within the possession, custody, or control of Microsoft, including any Emails, records, files, logs, or information that have been deleted but are still available to Service Provider, or have been preserved pursuant to a request made under 18 U.S.C. § 2703(f), Service Provider is required to disclose the following information to the government for each account or identifier listed in Attachments A-1 and A-2 from account inception to present:

a. The contents of all communications, transactions, records, documents, programs, or materials stored in or associated with any OneDrive accounts associated with or assigned to Target Accounts 1 and 2.

b. The contents of all communications, transactions, records, documents, programs, or materials stored in or associated with any Office 360 accounts associated with or assigned to Target Accounts 1 and 2.

c. The contents of all communications, transactions, records, documents, programs, or materials stored in or associated with any Microsoft Family Safety accounts or services associated with or assigned to Target Accounts 1 and 2.

d. The contents of all communications, transactions, records, documents, programs, or materials stored in or associated with any Windows Live Writer accounts or services associated with or assigned to Target Accounts 1 and 2.

e. The contents of all communications, transactions, records, documents, programs, or materials stored in or associated with any Windows Live Mail accounts or services associated with or assigned to Target Accounts 1 and 2.

f. The contents of all communications, transactions, records, documents, programs, or materials stored in or associated with any Windows Photo Gallery accounts or services associated with or assigned to Target Accounts 1 and 2.

g. The contents of all communications, transactions, records, documents, programs, or materials stored in or associated with any Windows Live Messenger accounts or services associated with or assigned to Target Accounts 1 and 2.

II. Information to be seized by the United States

After reviewing all information described in Section I, the United States will seize evidence of violations of Title 18, United States Code Sections 32(a) (Destruction/Damage of Aircraft or Aircraft Facilities); 37(a)(2) (Violence at International Airport); and 922(a)(3); and 5 (Unlawful Interstate Transport/Delivery of Firearms by Non Federal Firearms Licensee); and 2 (Aiding and Abetting) (the "Subject Offenses") that occur in the form of the following, from account inception to present:

a. Communications, transactions and records that may establish ownership and control (or the degree thereof) of the Target Account, including address books, contact or buddy lists, bills, invoices, receipts, registration records, bills, correspondence, notes, records, memoranda, telephone/address books, photographs, video recordings, audio recordings, lists of names, records of payment for access to newsgroups or other online subscription services, and attachments to said communications, transactions and records.

b. Communications, transactions and records to/from persons who may be co-conspirators of the Subject Offenses, or which may identify co-conspirators.

c. Communications, transactions and records which may show motivation to commit the Subject Offenses.

d. Communications, transactions and records that relate to the Subject Offenses.

e. The terms "communications," "transactions", "records," "documents," "programs," or "materials" include all information recorded in any form, visual or aural, and by any means, whether in handmade form (including, but not limited to, writings, drawings, paintings), photographic form (including, but not limited to, pictures or videos), or electrical, electronic or magnetic form, as well as digital data files. These terms also include any applications (i.e. software programs). These terms expressly include, among other things, Emails, instant messages, chat logs, correspondence attached as to Emails (or drafts), calendar entries, buddy lists.

ATTACHMENT "C"

PROTOCOL FOR SEARCHING THE ELECTRONIC DATA SEIZED PURSUANT TO THIS SEARCH WARRANT

1. In executing this warrant, the government must make reasonable efforts to use methods and procedures that will locate and expose in the electronic data produced in response to this search warrant ("the Search Warrant Data") those categories of data, files, documents, or other electronically stored information that are identified with particularity in the warrant, while minimizing exposure or examination of irrelevant, privileged, or confidential files to the extent reasonably practicable.

2. When the Search Warrant Data is received, the government will make a duplicate copy of the Search Warrant Data ("the Search Warrant Data Copy"). The original version of the Search Warrant Data will be sealed and preserved for purposes of: later judicial review or order to return or dispose of the Search Warrant Data; production to the defense in any criminal case if authorized by statute, rule, or the Constitution; for purposes of showing the chain of custody of the Search Warrant Data and the Search Warrant Data Copy; or for any other lawful purpose. The original of the Search Warrant Data will not be searched or examined except to ensure that it has been fully and completely replicated in the Search Warrant Data Copy.

3. The investigating agents will then search the entirety of the Search Warrant Data Copy using any and all methods and procedures deemed appropriate by the United States designed to identify the information listed as Information to be Seized in Attachment B, Section II. The United States may copy, extract or otherwise segregate information or data listed as Information to be Seized in Attachment B, Section II. Information or data so copied, extracted or otherwise segregated will no longer be subject to any handling restrictions that might be set out in this protocol beyond those required by binding law. To the extent evidence of crimes not within the scope of this warrant appear in plain view during this review, a supplemental or "piggyback" warrant will be applied for in order to further search that document, data, or other item.

4. Once the Search Warrant Data Copy has been thoroughly and completely examined for any document, data, or other items identified in Attachment B, Section II as Information to be Seized, the Search Warrant Data Copy will be sealed and not subject to any further search or examination unless authorized by another search warrant or other appropriate court order. The Search Warrant Data Copy will be held and preserved for the same purposes identified above in Paragraph 2.

5. The search procedures utilized for this review are at the sole discretion of the investigating and prosecuting authorities, and may include the following techniques (the following is a non-exclusive list, as other search procedures may be used):

   a. examination of all of the data contained in the Search Warrant Data to view the data and determine whether that data falls within the items to be seized as set forth herein;

   b. searching for and attempting to recover from the Search Warrant Data any deleted, hidden, or encrypted data to determine whether that data falls within the list of items to be seized as set forth herein (any data that is encrypted and unreadable will not be returned unless law enforcement personnel have determined that the data is not (1) an instrumentality of the offenses, (2) a fruit of the criminal activity, (3) contraband, (4) otherwise unlawfully possessed, or (5) evidence of the offenses specified above);

   c. surveying various file directories and the individual files they contain;

   d. opening files in order to determine their contents;

   e. using hash values to narrow the scope of what may be found. Hash values are under- inclusive, but are still a helpful tool;

   f. scanning storage areas;

   g. performing keyword searches through all electronic storage areas to determine whether occurrences of language contained in such storage areas exist that are likely to appear in the evidence described in Attachment A1 and A2; and/or

   h. performing any other data analysis technique that may be necessary to locate and retrieve the evidence described in Attachment B, Section II.

Return and Review Procedures

6. Rule 41 of the Federal Rules of Criminal Procedure provides, in relevant part:

(e) Issuing the Warrant.

(2) Contents of the Warrant.

(A) Warrant to Search for and Seize a Person or Property. Except for a tracking-device warrant, the warrant must identify the person or property to be searched, identify any person or property to be seized, and designate the magistrate judge to whom it must be returned. The warrant must command the officer to:

(i) execute the warrant within a specified time no longer than 14 days;

(B) Warrant Seeking Electronically Stored Information. A warrant under Rule 41(e)(2)(A) may authorize the seizure of electronic storage media or the seizure or copying of electronically stored information. Unless otherwise specified, the warrant authorizes a later review of the media or information consistent with the warrant. The time for executing the warrant in Rule 41(e)(2)(A) and (f)(1)(A) refers to the seizure or on-site copying of the media or information, and not to any later off-site copying or review.

(f) Executing and Returning the Warrant.

(1) Warrant to Search for and Seize a Person or Property.

(B) Inventory. An officer present during the execution of the warrant must prepare and verify an inventory of any property seized. . . . In a case involving the seizure of electronic storage media or the seizure or copying of electronically stored information, the inventory may be limited to describing the physical storage media that were seized or copied. The officer may retain a copy of the electronically stored information that was seized or copied.

7. Pursuant to this Rule, the government understands and will act in accordance with the following:

a. Pursuant to Rule 41(e)(2)(A)(iii), within fourteen (14) days of the execution of the warrant, an agent is required to file an inventory return with the Court, that is, to file an itemized list of the property seized. Execution of the warrant begins when the United States serves the warrant on the named custodian; execution is complete when the custodian provides all Search Warrant Data to the United States. Within fourteen (14) days of completion of the execution of the warrant, the inventory will be filed.

b. Pursuant to Rule 41(e)(2)(B), Rule 41(e)(2)(A) governs the time within which the electronically stored information must be seized after the issuance of the warrant and copied after the execution of the warrant, not the "later review of the media or information" seized, or the later off-site digital copying of that media.

c. Under Rule 41(f)(1)(B), the inventory return that is to be filed with the court may be limited to a description of the "physical storage media" into which the Search Warrant Data that was seized was placed, not an itemization of the information or data stored on the "physical storage media" into which the Search Warrant Data was placed;

d. Under Rule 41(f)(1)(B), the government may retain a copy of that information for purposes of the investigation. The government proposes that the original storage media on which the Search Warrant Data was placed plus a full image copy of the seized Search Warrant Data be retained by the government.

e. If the person from whom any Search Warrant Data was seized requests the return of any information in the Search Warrant Data that is not set forth in Attachment B, Section II, that information will be copied onto appropriate media and returned to the person from whom the information was seized.

AO 93 (Rev. 11/13) Search and Seizure Warrant

UNITED STATES DISTRICT COURT
for the
District of Nevada

In the Matter of the Search of
(Briefly describe the property to be searched or identify the person by name and address)

ACCOUNT(S) ASSOCIATED WITH THE CELLULAR DEVICE BEARING IMEI 990006880858377 STORED AT A PREMISES CONTROLLED BY GOOGLE

Case No. 2:17-mj- 971-NJK

SEARCH AND SEIZURE WARRANT

To: Any authorized law enforcement officer

An application by a federal law enforcement officer or an attorney for the government requests the search of the following person or property located in the _____ District of ___Nevada___
(identify the person or describe the property to be searched and give its location):

SEE ATTACHMENT A

I find that the affidavit(s), or any recorded testimony, establish probable cause to search and seize the person or property described above, and that such search will reveal *(identify the person or describe the property to be seized):*

SEE ATTACHMENTS B and C

YOU ARE COMMANDED to execute this warrant on or before ___October 20, 2017___ *(not to exceed 14 days)*
☒ in the daytime 6:00 a.m. to 10:00 p.m. ☐ at any time in the day or night because good cause has been established.

Unless delayed notice is authorized below, you must give a copy of the warrant and a receipt for the property taken to the person from whom, or from whose premises, the property was taken, or leave the copy and receipt at the place where the property was taken.

The officer executing this warrant, or an officer present during the execution of the warrant, must prepare an inventory as required by law and promptly return this warrant and inventory to ___Nancy J. Koppe___.
(United States Magistrate Judge)

☐ Pursuant to 18 U.S.C. § 3103a(b), I find that immediate notification may have an adverse result listed in 18 U.S.C. § 2705 (except for delay of trial), and authorize the officer executing this warrant to delay notice to the person who, or whose property, will be searched or seized *(check the appropriate box)*
☐ for ___ days *(not to exceed 30)* ☐ until, the facts justifying, the later specific date of _____.

Date and time issued: 10/6/2017 8:45 pm

Judge's signature

City and state: Las Vegas, Nevada

Nancy J. Koppe, US Magistrate Judge
Printed name and title

ATTACHMENT "A"

ONLINE ACCOUNT TO BE SEARCHED

1. This warrant applies to information related to the Google account associated with the cellular device bearing IMEI 990006880858377 (the "Target Account") from its inception to present, which is stored at premises owned, maintained, controlled, or operated by Google, Inc., headquartered at 1600 Amphitheatre Way, Mountain View, California, 94043.

ATTACHMENT "B"
Particular Things to be Seized

I. **Information to be disclosed by the Service Provider**

To the extent that the information described in Attachment A is within the possession, custody, or control of Google, including any Emails, records, files, logs, or information that have been deleted but are still available to Service Provider, or have been preserved pursuant to a request made under 18 U.S.C. § 2703(f), Service Provider is required to disclose the following information to the government for each account or identifier listed in Attachment A from account inception to present:

a. The contents of all messages and emails associated with the account, including copies of messages and emails sent to and from the account, draft messages/emails, the source and destination addresses associated with each message/email, the date and time at which each message/email was sent, and the size and length of each message/email;

b. All records or other information regarding the identification of the account, to include full name, physical address, telephone numbers and other identifiers, records of session times and durations, the date on which the account was created, the length of service, the types of service utilized, the IP address used to register the account, log-in IP addresses associated with session times and dates, account status, alternative email addresses provided during registration, methods of connecting, log files, and means and source of payment (including any credit or bank account number);

c. All records or other information stored in the Online Accounts, including address books, contact and buddy lists, calendar data, pictures, applications, documents, and other files;

d. All records pertaining to communications between Service Provider and any person regarding the account, including contacts with support services and records of actions taken.

e. All data and contents related to the following Google Services associated with the Target Account: Android; Gmail; Google Calendar; Google Docs; Google Drive; Google Talk; Multilogin; Web History; YouTube; and all other applications.

f. All information and content associated with any third-party application associated with the Target Account and the dates when the applications were installed;

g. Based on an analysis of cookies assigned to computers and devices that accessed the Target Account, identify all other Google accounts that have been accessed from any computers and devices that have logged into the Target Account.

II. **Information to be seized by the United States**

After reviewing all information described in Section I, the United States will seize evidence of violations of Title 18, United States Code Sections 32(a) (Destruction/Damage of Aircraft or Aircraft Facilities); 37(a)(2) (Violence at International Airport); and 922(a)(3); 5 (Unlawful Interstate Transport/Delivery of Firearms by Non Federal Firearms Licensee) (the "Subject Offenses") that occur in the form of the following, from account inception to present:

a. Communications, transactions and records that may establish ownership and control (or the degree thereof) of the Target Account, including address books, contact or buddy lists, bills, invoices, receipts, registration records, bills, correspondence, notes, records, memoranda, telephone/address books, photographs, video recordings, audio recordings, lists of names, records of payment for access to newsgroups or other online subscription services, and attachments to said communications, transactions and records.

b. Communications, transactions and records to/from persons who may be co-conspirators of the Subject Offenses, or which may identify co-conspirators.

c. Communications, transactions and records which may show motivation to commit the Subject Offenses.

d. Communications, transactions and records that relate to the Subject Offenses.

e. The terms "communications," "transactions", "records," "documents," "programs," or "materials" include all information recorded in any form, visual or aural, and by any means, whether in handmade form (including, but not limited to, writings, drawings, paintings), photographic form (including, but not limited to, pictures or videos), or electrical, electronic or magnetic form, as well as digital data files. These terms also include any applications (i.e. software programs). These terms expressly include, among other things, Emails, instant messages, chat logs, correspondence attached as to Emails (or drafts), calendar entries, buddy lists.

ATTACHMENT "C"

PROTOCOL FOR SEARCHING THE ELECTRONIC DATA SEIZED PURSUANT TO THIS SEARCH WARRANT

1. In executing this warrant, the government must make reasonable efforts to use methods and procedures that will locate and expose in the electronic data produced in response to this search warrant ("the Search Warrant Data") those categories of data, files, documents, or other electronically stored information that are identified with particularity in the warrant, while minimizing exposure or examination of irrelevant, privileged, or confidential files to the extent reasonably practicable.

2. When the Search Warrant Data is received, the government will make a duplicate copy of the Search Warrant Data ("the Search Warrant Data Copy"). The original version of the Search Warrant Data will be sealed and preserved for purposes of: later judicial review or order to return or dispose of the Search Warrant Data; production to the defense in any criminal case if authorized by statute, rule, or the Constitution; for purposes of showing the chain of custody of the Search Warrant Data and the Search Warrant Data Copy; or for any other lawful purpose. The original of the Search Warrant Data will not be searched or examined except to ensure that it has been fully and completely replicated in the Search Warrant Data Copy.

3. The investigating agents will then search the entirety of the Search Warrant Data Copy using any and all methods and procedures deemed appropriate by the United States designed to identify the information listed as Information to be Seized in Attachment B, Section II. The United States may copy, extract or otherwise segregate information or data listed as Information to be Seized in Attachment B, Section II. Information or data so copied, extracted or otherwise segregated will no longer be subject to any handling restrictions that might be set out in this protocol beyond those required by binding law. To the extent evidence of crimes not within the scope of this warrant appear in plain view during this review, a supplemental or "piggyback" warrant will be applied for in order to further search that document, data, or other item.

4. Once the Search Warrant Data Copy has been thoroughly and completely examined for any document, data, or other items identified in Attachment B, Section II as Information to be Seized, the Search Warrant Data Copy will be sealed and not subject to any further search or examination unless authorized by another search warrant or other appropriate court order. The Search Warrant Data Copy will be held and preserved for the same purposes identified above in Paragraph 2.

5. The search procedures utilized for this review are at the sole discretion of the investigating and prosecuting authorities, and may include the following techniques (the following is a non-exclusive list, as other search procedures may be used):

    a.   examination of all of the data contained in the Search Warrant Data to view the data and determine whether that data falls within the items to be seized as set forth herein;

    b.   searching for and attempting to recover from the Search Warrant Data any deleted, hidden, or encrypted data to determine whether that data falls within the list of items to be seized as set forth herein (any data that is encrypted and unreadable will not be returned unless law enforcement personnel have determined that the data is not (1) an instrumentality of the offenses, (2) a fruit of the criminal activity, (3) contraband, (4) otherwise unlawfully possessed, or (5) evidence of the offenses specified above);

    c.   surveying various file directories and the individual files they contain;

    d.   opening files in order to determine their contents;

    e.   using hash values to narrow the scope of what may be found. Hash values are under-inclusive, but are still a helpful tool;

    f.   scanning storage areas;

    g.   performing keyword searches through all electronic storage areas to determine whether occurrences of language contained in such storage areas exist that are likely to appear in the evidence described in Attachment A; and/or

    h.   performing any other data analysis technique that may be necessary to locate and retrieve the evidence described in Attachment B, Section II.

Return and Review Procedures

6. Rule 41 of the Federal Rules of Criminal Procedure provides, in relevant part:

(e) Issuing the Warrant.

(2) Contents of the Warrant.

(A) Warrant to Search for and Seize a Person or Property. Except for a tracking-device warrant, the warrant must identify the person or property to be searched, identify any person or property to be seized, and designate the magistrate judge to whom it must be returned. The warrant must command the officer to:

(i) execute the warrant within a specified time no longer than 14 days;

(B) Warrant Seeking Electronically Stored Information. A warrant under Rule 41(e)(2)(A) may authorize the seizure of electronic storage media or the seizure or copying of electronically stored information. Unless otherwise specified, the warrant authorizes a later review of the media or information consistent with the warrant. The time for executing the warrant in Rule 41(e)(2)(A) and (f)(1)(A) refers to the seizure or on-site copying of the media or information, and not to any later off-site copying or review.

(f) Executing and Returning the Warrant.

(1) Warrant to Search for and Seize a Person or Property.

(B) Inventory. An officer present during the execution of the warrant must prepare and verify an inventory of any property seized. . . . In a case involving the seizure of electronic storage media or the seizure or copying of electronically stored information, the inventory may be limited to describing the physical storage media that were seized or copied. The officer may retain a copy of the electronically stored information that was seized or copied.

7. Pursuant to this Rule, the government understands and will act in accordance with the following:

a. Pursuant to Rule 41(e)(2)(A)(iii), within fourteen (14) days of the execution of the warrant, an agent is required to file an inventory return with the Court, that is, to file an itemized list of the property seized. Execution of the warrant begins when the United States serves the warrant on the named custodian; execution is complete when the custodian provides all Search Warrant Data to the United States. Within fourteen (14) days of completion of the execution of the warrant, the inventory will be filed.

b. Pursuant to Rule 41(e)(2)(B), Rule 41(e)(2)(A) governs the time within which the electronically stored information must be seized after the issuance of the warrant and copied after the execution of the warrant, not the "later review of the media or information" seized, or the later off-site digital copying of that media.

c. Under Rule 41(f)(1)(B), the inventory return that is to be filed with the court may be limited to a description of the "physical storage media" into which the Search Warrant Data that was seized was placed, not an itemization of the information or data stored on the "physical storage media" into which the Search Warrant Data was placed;

d. Under Rule 41(f)(1)(B), the government may retain a copy of that information for purposes of the investigation. The government proposes that the original storage media on which the Search Warrant Data was placed plus a full image copy of the seized Search Warrant Data be retained by the government.

e. If the person from whom any Search Warrant Data was seized requests the return of any information in the Search Warrant Data that is not set forth in Attachment B, Section II, that information will be copied onto appropriate media and returned to the person from whom the information was seized.

STEVEN W. MYHRE
Acting United States Attorney
District of Nevada
CRISTINA D. SILVA
PATRICK BURNS
Assistant United States Attorneys
501 Las Vegas Blvd. South, Ste. 1100
Las Vegas, Nevada 89101
Telephone: (702) 388-6336
Fax (702) 388-6698
john.p.burns@usdoj.gov

Attorney for the United States of America

UNITED STATES DISTRICT COURT
DISTRICT OF NEVADA
-oOo-

IN THE MATTER OF THE SEARCH OF INFORMATION RELATED TO THE ACCOUNT(S) ASSOCIATED WITH THE CELLULAR DEVICE BEARING IMEI 990006880858377 THAT IS STORED AT A PREMISES CONTROLLED BY GOOGLE.	Magistrate No. 17-mj-971-NJK **AFFIDAVIT IN SUPPORT OF AN APPLICATION FOR A SEARCH WARRANT** (Under Seal)

STATE OF NEVADA)
) ss:
COUNTY OF CLARK)

AFFIDAVIT IN SUPPORT OF AN APPLICATION FOR A SEARCH WARRANT

I, Ryan S. Burke, Special Agent, Federal Bureau of Investigation (FBI), having been duly sworn, hereby depose and say:

INTRODUCTION AND AGENT BACKGROUND

1. Your Affiant makes this affidavit in support of an application for a search warrant for information related to the Google account(s) associated with the cellular device bearing IMEI 990006880858377 ["Target Account(s)"], which are associated with

STEPHEN PADDOCK. This information is stored at a premises owned, maintained, controlled, or operated by Google, Inc. ("Google"), an American multinational technology based in Mountain View, California that specializes in Internet-related services and products. Those services include, but are not limited to, online advertising technologies, a search engine, email services, cloud computing, and many other services. The information to be searched is described in the following paragraphs and in Attachment "A" (attached hereto and incorporated herein by reference). This affidavit is made in support of an application for a search warrant under 18 U.S.C. §§ 2703(a), 2703(b)(1)(A), and 2703(c)(1)(A) to require Google to disclose to the government records and other information in its possession, pertaining to the subscriber or customer associated with the Target Account.

2. I am an "investigative or law enforcement officer of the United States" within the meaning of Title 18, United States Code, Section 2510(7), that is, an officer of the United States who is empowered by law to conduct investigations of, and to make arrests for, offenses enumerated in Title 18, United States Code, Section 2516.

3. I have been employed as a Special Agent of the FBI for approximately five years, which began at the FBI Academy in October 2012. Upon completion of the academy, I was transferred to the Las Vegas Division's white collar crime squad and then the human trafficking squad. Since October 2015, I have been assigned to the Las Vegas Division's violent crime/gang squad. Additionally, I have been a certified member of the FBI's Cellular Analysis Survey Team since August 2015 due to my expertise in the field of historical cell site analysis.

4. During my tenure with the FBI, I have conducted surveillance, analyzed telephone records, interviewed witnesses, supervised activities of sources, executed search warrants, executed arrest warrants, and participated in court-authorized interceptions of wire and electronic communications. These investigative activities have been conducted in conjunction with a variety of investigations, to include those involving robbery, drug trafficking, kidnapping, murder, criminal enterprises, and more. In addition to my practical experiences, I received five months of extensive law enforcement training at the FBI Academy.

5. The facts in this affidavit are derived from your Affiant's personal observations, his training and experience, and information obtained from other agents, detectives, and witnesses. This affidavit is intended to show merely that there is sufficient probable cause for the requested warrant and does not set forth all of the Affiant's knowledge about this matter.

6. Based on your Affiant's training and experience and the facts as set forth in this affidavit, there is probable cause to believe that violations of:

    a. Destruction/Damage of Aircraft or Aircraft Facilities - 18 U.S.C.A. § 32(a);

    b. Violence at International Airport - 18 U.S.C. § 37(a)(2); and

    c. Unlawful Interstate Transport/Delivery of Firearms by Non Federal Firearms Licensee – 18 U.S.C. §§ 922(a)(3) and (5);

(hereafter, "Subject Offenses") have been committed by STEPHEN PADDOCK and others yet unknown. There is also probable cause to search the information described in Attachment "A" for evidence of these crimes and information which might reveal the

identities of others involved in these crimes, as described in Attachment "B" (attached hereto and incorporated herein by reference).

PROBABLE CAUSE

7. On the evening of Sunday, October 1, 2017, Route 91 Harvest, a music festival, was in progress at 3901 South Las Vegas Boulevard, Las Vegas, Nevada. At approximately 10:08 p.m., the Las Vegas Metropolitan Police Department (LVMPD) received calls reporting shots had been fired at the concert and multiple victims were struck. LVMPD determined the shots were coming from Rooms 134 and 135 on the 32nd floor of the Mandalay Bay Resort and Casino, located due west of the festival rounds at 3950 South Las Vegas Boulevard, Las Vegas, Nevada. These rooms are an elevated position which overlooks the concert venue. Witness statements and video footage captured during the attack indicates that the weapons being used were firing in a fully-automatic fashion.

8. LVMPD officers ultimately made entry into the room and located an individual later identified as Stephen Paddock. Paddock was deceased from an apparent self-inflicted gunshot wound.

9. Paddock's Nevada driver's license was located in the Mandalay Bay hotel room with Paddock, and both hotel rooms were registered in his name. A player's club card in name of Marilou Danley was located in Paddock's room, and the card returned to the address located on Babbling Brook Street in Mesquite, Nevada. FBI Agents located Danley, who was traveling outside the United States at the time of the shooting. It was ultimately determined that Danley resided with Paddock at the Babbling Brook address.

10. On October 2, 2017, search warrants were executed on Paddock's Mandalay Bay hotel rooms, Paddock's vehicle at Mandalay Bay, and two Nevada residences owed by Paddock: 1372 Babbling Brook Court in Mesquite, and 1735 Del Webb Parkway in Reno, Nevada. Officers and Agents found over 20 firearms, hundreds of rounds of ammunition, and hundreds of spent shell casings in the Mandalay Bay hotel rooms, in close proximity to Paddock's body. Over a thousand rounds of rifle ammunition and 100 pounds of explosive material was found in Paddock's vehicle. Additional explosive material, approximately 18 firearms, and over 1,000 rounds of ammunition was located at the Mesquite residence. A large quantity of ammunition and multiple firearms were recovered from the Reno residence.

11. As of this date, 58 people have been identified to have been killed in Paddock's attack and another 557 were reportedly injured. Additionally, investigators discovered that STEPHEN PADDOCK also utilized a firearm to shoot large fuel tanks on Las Vegas McCarran International Airport property. Multiple bullet holes were found on the tank, which investigators believe was an attempt by STEPHEN PADDOCK to cause the tanks to explode.

12. During the execution of the search warrant at the Mandalay Bay hotel room where the attack occurred, three cellular phones were seized. All of the phones are believed to have belonged to STEPHEN PADDOCK. Two of those phones were unlocked and able to be forensically examined. Neither phone contained significant information that allowed investigators to determine the full scope of STEPHEN PADDOCK's planning and preparation for the attack. The other phone, however, a ZTE Model Z837VL bearing IMEI 990006880858377, was locked and investigators do not believe it

can be forensically examined. Investigators believe the only way to gain access to the content of the locked ZTE phone will be through the authorization to demand information associated with the Target Account from Google, the company which owns the operating system software installed on the phone.

13. Your Affiant knows through training and experience that criminals typically make effort to secure and keep hidden information that may incriminate themselves or others. Due to the fact that two of the cellular phones were unlocked and the cellular phone associated with the Target Account was locked, your Affiant believes if there were any information related to a potential conspiracy it would be found within the Target Account.

14. Your Affiant believes the requested search warrant will yield significant information from Google such as STEPHEN PADDOCK's contact list, email message content, IP address usage, photographs, third-party applications, and more, which may constitute evidence of his planning of the attack and potentially identify other participants in the attack. Ultimately, your Affiant strongly believes the requested information will lead investigators to determine the full scope of STEPHEN PADDOCK's plan.

RELEVANT TECHNICAL TERMS

15. The following non-exhaustive list of definitions applies to this Affidavit and the Attachments to this Affidavit:

   a. The "Internet" is a worldwide network of computer systems operated by governmental entities, corporations, and universities. In order to access the Internet, an individual computer user must subscribe to an access provider, which operates a host computer system with direct access to the Internet. The World Wide Web is a functionality of the Internet which allows users of the Internet to share information.

  b. "Internet Service Providers" are companies that provide access to the Internet. ISPs can also provide other services for their customers including website hosting, email service, remote storage, and co-location of computers and other communications equipment. ISPs offer different ways to access the Internet including telephone-based (dial-up), broadband-based access via a digital subscriber line (DSL) or cable television, dedicated circuits, or satellite-based subscription. ISPs typically charge a fee based upon the type of connection and volume of data (bandwidth). Many ISPs assign each subscriber an account name, such as a user name, an email address, and an email mailbox, and the subscriber typically creates a password for his/her account.

  c. "ISP Records" are records maintained by ISPs pertaining to their subscribers (regardless of whether those subscribers are individuals or entities). These records may include account application information, subscriber and billing information, account access information (often in the form of log files), emails, information concerning content uploaded and/or stored on the ISP's servers, and other information, which may be stored both in computer data format and in written or printed record format. ISPs reserve and/or maintain computer disk storage space on their computer system for their subscribers' use. This service by ISPs allows for both temporary and long-term storage of electronic communications and many other types of electronic data and files.

  d. "Online service providers" (also referred to here as "service providers") are companies that provide online services such as email, chat or instant messaging, word processing applications, spreadsheet applications, presentation applications similar to PowerPoint, online calendar, photo storage and remote storage services. Sometimes they also can provide web hosting, remote storage, and co-location of computers and other communications equipment. Typically, each service provider assigns each subscriber an account name, such as a user name or screen name and the subscriber typically creates a password for his/her account.

    e.   "Computer," as used herein, is defined as "an electronic, magnetic, optical, electrochemical, or other high speed data processing device performing logical or storage functions, and includes any data storage facility or communications facility directly related to or operating in conjunction with such device."

    f.   A "server" is a centralized computer that provides services for other computers connected to it via a network. The other computers attached to a server are sometimes called "clients." For example, in a large company, it is common for individual employees to have client computers at their desktops. When the employees access their email, or access files stored on the network itself, those files are pulled electronically from the server, where they are stored, and are sent to the client's computer via the network. Notably, servers can be physically stored in any location: it is not uncommon for a network's server to be located hundreds (and even thousands) of miles away from the client computers.

    g.   "Internet Protocol address," or "IP address," refers to a unique number used by a computer to access the Internet. IP addresses can be dynamic, meaning that the Internet Service Provider (ISP) assigns a different unique number to a computer every time it accesses the Internet. IP addresses might also be static, that

is, an ISP assigns a user's computer a particular IP address which is used each time the computer accesses the Internet.

      h.   The term "domain" refers to a word used as a name for computers, networks, services, etc. A domain name typically represents a website, a server computer that hosts that website, or even some computer (or other digital device) connected to the internet. Essentially, when a website (or a server computer that hosts that website) is connected to the internet, it is assigned an IP address. Because IP addresses are difficult for people to remember, domain names are instead used because they are easier to remember than IP addresses. Domain names are formed by the rules and procedures of the Domain Name System (DNS). A common top level domain under these rules is ".com" for commercial organizations, ".gov" for the United States government, and ".org" for organizations. For example, www.usdoj.gov is the domain name that identifies a server used by the U.S. Department of Justice, and which uses IP address of 149.101.46.71.

      i.   "Web hosting services" maintain server computers connected to the Internet. Their customers use those computers to operate websites on the Internet. Customers of web hosting companies place files, software code, databases, and other data on servers. To do this, customers typically connect from their own computers to the server computers across the Internet.

      j.   The term "WhoIs" lookup refers to a search of a publicly available online database that lists information provided when a domain is registered or when an IP address is assigned.

      k.   The terms "communications," "records," "documents," "programs," or "materials" include all information recorded in any form, visual or aural, and by any

means, whether in handmade form (including, but not limited to, writings, drawings, paintings), photographic form (including, but not limited to, pictures or videos), or electrical, electronic or magnetic form, as well as digital data files. These terms also include any applications (i.e. software programs). These terms expressly include, among other things, emails, instant messages, chat logs, correspondence attached as to emails (or drafts), calendar entries, buddy lists.

l. "Chat" is usually a real time electronic communication between two or more individuals. Unlike email, which is frequently sent, then read and responded to minutes, hours, or even days later, chats frequently involve an immediate conversation between individuals, similar to a face-to-face conversation. Nearly all chat programs are capable of saving the chat transcript, to enable users to preserve a record of the conversation. By default, some chat programs have this capability enabled, while others do not. Many popular web-based email providers, like Google and Google, provide chat functionality as part of the online services they provide to account holders.

m. "Apps or Applications" are third-party programs that may be installed through the Android operating system, which is owned by Google, for use on a cellular device.

FACTS ABOUT GOOGLE

16. In my training, my experience and this investigation, I have learned that Google owns and operates Android OS, which is an operating system found on many cellular devices to include the device associated with the Target Account. Through this operating system, users can install applications with a variety of functionalities, such as

various social media websites, mapping software, banking portals, etc. Records of the applications installed on a specific device are maintained by Google.

17. In my training and experience, evidence of which applications were utilized by a specific device can be useful in identifying additional communication facilities, content of communications, financial account information, information related to whom the user associates with, and more. Oftentimes, an individual utilizing a Google account has the option to store certain information located on the device to a cloud, which Google also retains. All of this information can help investigators locate evidence of various criminal activity associated with the user.

INFORMATION TO BE SEARCHED AND THINGS TO BE SEIZED

18. Your Affiant anticipates executing this warrant under the Electronic Communications Privacy Act, in particular 18 U.S.C. §§ 2703(a), 2703(b)(1)(A) and 2703(c)(1)(A), by using the warrant to require Google to disclose to the government copies of the records and other information (including the content of communications) particularly described in Section I of Attachment "B." Upon receipt of the information described in Section I of Attachment "B," government-authorized persons will review that information to locate the items described in Section II of Attachment "B."

CONCLUSION

19. Based on the forgoing, I request that the Court issue the proposed search warrant. This Court has jurisdiction to issue the requested warrant because it is "a court of competent jurisdiction" as defined by 18 U.S.C. § 2711. 18 U.S.C. §§ 2703(a), (b)(1)(A) & (c)(1)(A). Specifically, the Court is "a district court of the United States . . . that – has jurisdiction over the offense being investigated." 18 U.S.C. § 2711(3)(A)(i). Pursuant to

18 U.S.C. § 2703(g), the presence of a law enforcement officer is not required for the service or execution of this warrant.

REQUEST FOR SEALING

20. I further request that the Court order that all papers in support of this application, including the affidavit and search warrant, be sealed until further order of the Court. These documents discuss an ongoing criminal investigation that is neither public nor known to all of the targets of the investigation. Accordingly, there is good cause to seal these documents because their premature disclosure may seriously jeopardize that investigation.

Respectfully Submitted,

Ryan S. Burke, Special Agent
Federal Bureau of Investigation

SWORN TO AND SUBSCRIBED
before me this __ day of October 2017.

UNITED STATES MAGISTRATE JUDGE

ATTACHMENT "A"

ONLINE ACCOUNT TO BE SEARCHED

1. This warrant applies to information related to the Google account associated with the cellular device bearing IMEI 990006880858377 (the "Target Account") from its inception to present, which is stored at premises owned, maintained, controlled, or operated by Google, Inc., headquartered at 1600 Amphitheatre Way, Mountain View, California, 94043.

ATTACHMENT "B"
Particular Things to be Seized

I. **Information to be disclosed by the Service Provider**

To the extent that the information described in Attachment A is within the possession, custody, or control of Google, including any Emails, records, files, logs, or information that have been deleted but are still available to Service Provider, or have been preserved pursuant to a request made under 18 U.S.C. § 2703(f), Service Provider is required to disclose the following information to the government for each account or identifier listed in Attachment A from account inception to present:

a. The contents of all messages and emails associated with the account, including copies of messages and emails sent to and from the account, draft messages/emails, the source and destination addresses associated with each message/email, the date and time at which each message/email was sent, and the size and length of each message/email;

b. All records or other information regarding the identification of the account, to include full name, physical address, telephone numbers and other identifiers, records of session times and durations, the date on which the account was created, the length of service, the types of service utilized, the IP address used to register the account, log-in IP addresses associated with session times and dates, account status, alternative email addresses provided during registration, methods of connecting, log files, and means and source of payment (including any credit or bank account number);

c. All records or other information stored in the Online Accounts, including address books, contact and buddy lists, calendar data, pictures, applications, documents, and other files;

d. All records pertaining to communications between Service Provider and any person regarding the account, including contacts with support services and records of actions taken.

e. All data and contents related to the following Google Services associated with the Target Account: Android; Gmail; Google Calendar; Google Docs; Google Drive; Google Talk; Multilogin; Web History; YouTube; and all other applications.

f. All information and content associated with any third-party application associated with the Target Account and the dates when the applications were installed;

g. Based on an analysis of cookies assigned to computers and devices that accessed the Target Account, identify all other Google accounts that have been accessed from any computers and devices that have logged into the Target Account.

II. Information to be seized by the United States

After reviewing all information described in Section I, the United States will seize evidence of violations of Title 18, United States Code Sections 32(a) (Destruction/Damage of Aircraft or Aircraft Facilities); 37(a)(2) (Violence at International Airport); and 922(a)(3); 5 (Unlawful Interstate Transport/Delivery of Firearms by Non Federal Firearms Licensee) (the "Subject Offenses") that occur in the form of the following, from account inception to present:

a. Communications, transactions and records that may establish ownership and control (or the degree thereof) of the Target Account, including address books, contact or buddy lists, bills, invoices, receipts, registration records, bills, correspondence, notes, records, memoranda, telephone/address books, photographs, video recordings, audio recordings, lists of names, records of payment for access to newsgroups or other online subscription services, and attachments to said communications, transactions and records.

b. Communications, transactions and records to/from persons who may be co-conspirators of the Subject Offenses, or which may identify co-conspirators.

c. Communications, transactions and records which may show motivation to commit the Subject Offenses.

d. Communications, transactions and records that relate to the Subject Offenses.

e. The terms "communications," "transactions", "records," "documents," "programs," or "materials" include all information recorded in any form, visual or aural, and by any means, whether in handmade form (including, but not limited to, writings, drawings, paintings), photographic form (including, but not limited to, pictures or videos), or electrical, electronic or magnetic form, as well as digital data files. These terms also include any applications (i.e. software programs). These terms expressly include, among other things, Emails, instant messages, chat logs, correspondence attached as to Emails (or drafts), calendar entries, buddy lists.

ATTACHMENT "C"

PROTOCOL FOR SEARCHING THE ELECTRONIC DATA SEIZED PURSUANT TO THIS SEARCH WARRANT

1. In executing this warrant, the government must make reasonable efforts to use methods and procedures that will locate and expose in the electronic data produced in response to this search warrant ("the Search Warrant Data") those categories of data, files, documents, or other electronically stored information that are identified with particularity in the warrant, while minimizing exposure or examination of irrelevant, privileged, or confidential files to the extent reasonably practicable.

2. When the Search Warrant Data is received, the government will make a duplicate copy of the Search Warrant Data ("the Search Warrant Data Copy"). The original version of the Search Warrant Data will be sealed and preserved for purposes of: later judicial review or order to return or dispose of the Search Warrant Data; production to the defense in any criminal case if authorized by statute, rule, or the Constitution; for purposes of showing the chain of custody of the Search Warrant Data and the Search Warrant Data Copy; or for any other lawful purpose. The original of the Search Warrant Data will not be searched or examined except to ensure that it has been fully and completely replicated in the Search Warrant Data Copy.

3. The investigating agents will then search the entirety of the Search Warrant Data Copy using any and all methods and procedures deemed appropriate by the United States designed to identify the information listed as Information to be Seized in Attachment B, Section II. The United States may copy, extract or otherwise segregate information or data listed as Information to be Seized in Attachment B, Section II. Information or data so copied, extracted or otherwise segregated will no longer be subject to any handling restrictions that might be set out in this protocol beyond those required by binding law. To the extent evidence of crimes not within the scope of this warrant appear in plain view during this review, a supplemental or "piggyback" warrant will be applied for in order to further search that document, data, or other item.

4. Once the Search Warrant Data Copy has been thoroughly and completely examined for any document, data, or other items identified in Attachment B, Section II as Information to be Seized, the Search Warrant Data Copy will be sealed and not subject to any further search or examination unless authorized by another search warrant or other appropriate court order. The Search Warrant Data Copy will be held and preserved for the same purposes identified above in Paragraph 2.

5. The search procedures utilized for this review are at the sole discretion of the investigating and prosecuting authorities, and may include the following techniques (the following is a non-exclusive list, as other search procedures may be used):

    a. examination of all of the data contained in the Search Warrant Data to view the data and determine whether that data falls within the items to be seized as set forth herein;

    b. searching for and attempting to recover from the Search Warrant Data any deleted, hidden, or encrypted data to determine whether that data falls within the list of items to be seized as set forth herein (any data that is encrypted and unreadable will not be returned unless law enforcement personnel have determined that the data is not (1) an instrumentality of the offenses, (2) a fruit of the criminal activity, (3) contraband, (4) otherwise unlawfully possessed, or (5) evidence of the offenses specified above);

    c. surveying various file directories and the individual files they contain;

    d. opening files in order to determine their contents;

    e. using hash values to narrow the scope of what may be found. Hash values are under-inclusive, but are still a helpful tool;

    f. scanning storage areas;

    g. performing keyword searches through all electronic storage areas to determine whether occurrences of language contained in such storage areas exist that are likely to appear in the evidence described in Attachment A; and/or

    h. performing any other data analysis technique that may be necessary to locate and retrieve the evidence described in Attachment B, Section II.

Return and Review Procedures

6. Rule 41 of the Federal Rules of Criminal Procedure provides, in relevant part:

(e) Issuing the Warrant.

(2) Contents of the Warrant.

(A) Warrant to Search for and Seize a Person or Property. Except for a tracking-device warrant, the warrant must identify the person or property to be searched, identify any person or property to be seized, and designate the magistrate judge to whom it must be returned. The warrant must command the officer to:

(i) execute the warrant within a specified time no longer than 14 days;

(B) Warrant Seeking Electronically Stored Information. A warrant under Rule 41(e)(2)(A) may authorize the seizure of electronic storage media or the seizure or copying of electronically stored information. Unless otherwise specified, the warrant authorizes a later review of the media or information consistent with the warrant. The time for executing the warrant in Rule 41(e)(2)(A) and (f)(1)(A) refers to the seizure or on-site copying of the media or information, and not to any later off-site copying or review.

(f) Executing and Returning the Warrant.

(1) Warrant to Search for and Seize a Person or Property.

(B) Inventory. An officer present during the execution of the warrant must prepare and verify an inventory of any property seized. . . . In a case involving the seizure of electronic storage media or the seizure or copying of electronically stored information, the inventory may be limited to describing the physical storage media that were seized or copied. The officer may retain a copy of the electronically stored information that was seized or copied.

7. Pursuant to this Rule, the government understands and will act in accordance with the following:

a. Pursuant to Rule 41(e)(2)(A)(iii), within fourteen (14) days of the execution of the warrant, an agent is required to file an inventory return with the Court, that is, to file an itemized list of the property seized. Execution of the warrant begins when the United States serves the warrant on the named custodian; execution is complete when the custodian provides all Search Warrant Data to the United States. Within fourteen (14) days of completion of the execution of the warrant, the inventory will be filed.

b. Pursuant to Rule 41(e)(2)(B), Rule 41(e)(2)(A) governs the time within which the electronically stored information must be seized after the issuance of the warrant and copied after the execution of the warrant, not the "later review of the media or information" seized, or the later off-site digital copying of that media.

c. Under Rule 41(f)(1)(B), the inventory return that is to be filed with the court may be limited to a description of the "physical storage media" into which the Search Warrant Data that was seized was placed, not an itemization of the information or data stored on the "physical storage media" into which the Search Warrant Data was placed;

d. Under Rule 41(f)(1)(B), the government may retain a copy of that information for purposes of the investigation. The government proposes that the original storage media on which the Search Warrant Data was placed plus a full image copy of the seized Search Warrant Data be retained by the government.

e. If the person from whom any Search Warrant Data was seized requests the return of any information in the Search Warrant Data that is not set forth in Attachment B, Section II, that information will be copied onto appropriate media and returned to the person from whom the information was seized.

AO 93 (Rev. 11/13) Search and Seizure Warrant

UNITED STATES DISTRICT COURT
for the
District of Nevada

In the Matter of the Search of)
(Briefly describe the property to be searched)
or identify the person by name and address))
) Case No. 2:17-mj-972-NJK
AMAZON ACCOUNT LINKED TO)
CENTRA! PARK1@LIVE.COM THAT IS STORED AT A)
PREMISES CONTROLLED BY AMAZON, INC.)

SEARCH AND SEIZURE WARRANT

To: Any authorized law enforcement officer

An application by a federal law enforcement officer or an attorney for the government requests the search of the following person or property located in the _____ District of _____ Nevada
(identify the person or describe the property to be searched and give its location):

SEE ATTACHMENT A

I find that the affidavit(s), or any recorded testimony, establish probable cause to search and seize the person or property described above, and that such search will reveal *(identify the person or describe the property to be seized)*:

SEE ATTACHMENTS B and C

YOU ARE COMMANDED to execute this warrant on or before October 20, 2017 *(not to exceed 14 days)*
☒ in the daytime 6:00 a.m. to 10:00 p.m.   ☐ at any time in the day or night because good cause has been established.

Unless delayed notice is authorized below, you must give a copy of the warrant and a receipt for the property taken to the person from whom, or from whose premises, the property was taken, or leave the copy and receipt at the place where the property was taken.

The officer executing this warrant, or an officer present during the execution of the warrant, must prepare an inventory as required by law and promptly return this warrant and inventory to ___Nancy J. Koppe___
(United States Magistrate Judge)

☐ Pursuant to 18 U.S.C. § 3103a(b), I find that immediate notification may have an adverse result listed in 18 U.S.C. § 2705 (except for delay of trial), and authorize the officer executing this warrant to delay notice to the person who, or whose property, will be searched or seized *(check the appropriate box)*
☐ for _____ days *(not to exceed 30)*   ☐ until, the facts justifying, the later specific date of _____.

Date and time issued: 10/6/2017 9:00 pm

_____
Judge's signature

City and state: Las Vegas, Nevada   Nancy J. Koppe, US Magistrate Judge
                                          Printed name and title

ATTACHMENT "A"

ONLINE ACCOUNT TO BE SEARCHED

1. This warrant applies to information related to the Amazon.com account associated with centralpark1@live.com (the "Target Amazon Account") from its inception to present, which is stored at premises owned, maintained, controlled, or operated by Amazon.com, Inc., headquartered at 300 Deschutes Way SW, Suite 304, Tumwater, WA 98501.

ATTACHMENT "B"
Particular Things to be Seized

I. **Information to be disclosed by the Service Provider**

To the extent that the information described in Attachment A is within the possession, custody, or control of Amazon.com, including any Emails, records, files, logs, or information that have been deleted but are still available to Service Provider, or have been preserved pursuant to a request made under 18 U.S.C. § 2703(f), Service Provider is required to disclose the following information to the government for each account or identifier listed in Attachment A from account inception to present:

a. All names, addresses, email addresses, shipping addresses, and billing information associated with the Target Amazon Account;
b. Date of account creation;
c. All purchase history;
d. Service usage information;
e. All Internet Protocol Address logs and information;
f. All messages and/or communications exchanged with Amazon.com representative;
g. Any and all information, files, and data in possession of Amazon.com and/or any other entities controlled or operation by Amazon.com, Inc. related to the Target Amazon Account.

II. **Information to be seized by the United States**

After reviewing all information described in Section I, the United States will seize evidence of violations of Title 18, United States Code Sections 32(a) (Destruction/Damage of Aircraft or Aircraft Facilities); 37(a)(2) (Violence at International Airport); and 922(a)(3); 5 (Unlawful Interstate Transport/Delivery of Firearms by Non Federal Firearms Licensee) (the "Subject Offenses") that occur in the form of the following, from account inception to present:

a. Communications, transactions and records that may establish ownership and control (or the degree thereof) of the Target Account, including address books, contact or buddy lists, bills, invoices, receipts, registration records, bills, correspondence, notes, records, memoranda, telephone/address books, photographs, video recordings, audio recordings, lists of names, records of

payment for access to newsgroups or other online subscription services, and attachments to said communications, transactions and records.

b. Communications, transactions and records to/from persons who may be co-conspirators of the Subject Offenses, or which may identify co-conspirators.

c. Communications, transactions and records which may show motivation to commit the Subject Offenses.

d. Communications, transactions and records that relate to the Subject Offenses.

e. Information related to wire transfers and/or the movement, possession, or storage of currency and valuable items.

ATTACHMENT "C"

PROTOCOL FOR SEARCHING THE ELECTRONIC DATA SEIZED PURSUANT TO THIS SEARCH WARRANT

1. In executing this warrant, the government must make reasonable efforts to use methods and procedures that will locate and expose in the electronic data produced in response to this search warrant ("the Search Warrant Data") those categories of data, files, documents, or other electronically stored information that are identified with particularity in the warrant, while minimizing exposure or examination of irrelevant, privileged, or confidential files to the extent reasonably practicable.

2. When the Search Warrant Data is received, the government will make a duplicate copy of the Search Warrant Data ("the Search Warrant Data Copy"). The original version of the Search Warrant Data will be sealed and preserved for purposes of: later judicial review or order to return or dispose of the Search Warrant Data; production to the defense in any criminal case if authorized by statute, rule, or the Constitution; for purposes of showing the chain of custody of the Search Warrant Data and the Search Warrant Data Copy; or for any other lawful purpose. The original of the Search Warrant Data will not be searched or examined except to ensure that it has been fully and completely replicated in the Search Warrant Data Copy.

3. The investigating agents will then search the entirety of the Search Warrant Data Copy using any and all methods and procedures deemed appropriate by the United States designed to identify the information listed as Information to be Seized in Attachment B, Section II. The United States may copy, extract or otherwise segregate information or data listed as Information to be Seized in Attachment B, Section II. Information or data so copied, extracted or otherwise segregated will no longer be subject to any handling restrictions that might be set out in this protocol beyond those required by binding law. To the extent evidence of crimes not within the scope of this warrant appear in plain view during this review, a supplemental or "piggyback" warrant will be applied for in order to further search that document, data, or other item.

4. Once the Search Warrant Data Copy has been thoroughly and completely examined for any document, data, or other items identified in Attachment B, Section II as Information to be Seized, the Search Warrant Data Copy will be sealed and not subject to any further search or examination unless authorized by another search warrant or other appropriate court order. The Search Warrant Data Copy will be held and preserved for the same purposes identified above in Paragraph 2.

5. The search procedures utilized for this review are at the sole discretion of the investigating and prosecuting authorities, and may include the following techniques (the following is a non-exclusive list, as other search procedures may be used):

a. examination of all of the data contained in the Search Warrant Data to view the data and determine whether that data falls within the items to be seized as set forth herein;

b. searching for and attempting to recover from the Search Warrant Data any deleted, hidden, or encrypted data to determine whether that data falls within the list of items to be seized as set forth herein (any data that is encrypted and unreadable will not be returned unless law enforcement personnel have determined that the data is not (1) an instrumentality of the offenses, (2) a fruit of the criminal activity, (3) contraband, (4) otherwise unlawfully possessed, or (5) evidence of the offenses specified above);

c. surveying various file directories and the individual files they contain;

d. opening files in order to determine their contents;

e. using hash values to narrow the scope of what may be found. Hash values are under- inclusive, but are still a helpful tool;

f. scanning storage areas;

g. performing keyword searches through all electronic storage areas to determine whether occurrences of language contained in such storage areas exist that are likely to appear in the evidence described in Attachment A; and/or

h. performing any other data analysis technique that may be necessary to locate and retrieve the evidence described in Attachment B, Section II.

Return and Review Procedures

6. Rule 41 of the Federal Rules of Criminal Procedure provides, in relevant part:

(e) Issuing the Warrant.

(2) Contents of the Warrant.

(A) Warrant to Search for and Seize a Person or Property. Except for a tracking-device warrant, the warrant must identify the person or property to be searched, identify any person or property to be seized, and designate the magistrate judge to whom it must be returned. The warrant must command the officer to:

(i) execute the warrant within a specified time no longer than 14 days;

(B) Warrant Seeking Electronically Stored Information. A warrant under Rule 41(e)(2)(A) may authorize the seizure of electronic storage media or the seizure or copying of electronically stored information. Unless otherwise specified, the warrant authorizes a later review of the media or information consistent with the warrant. The time for executing the warrant in Rule 41(e)(2)(A) and (f)(1)(A) refers to the seizure or on-site copying of the media or information, and not to any later off-site copying or review.

(f) Executing and Returning the Warrant.

(1) Warrant to Search for and Seize a Person or Property.

(B) Inventory. An officer present during the execution of the warrant must prepare and verify an inventory of any property seized. . . . In a case involving the seizure of electronic storage media or the seizure or copying of electronically stored information, the inventory may be limited to describing the physical storage media that were seized or copied. The officer may retain a copy of the electronically stored information that was seized or copied.

7. Pursuant to this Rule, the government understands and will act in accordance with the following:

a. Pursuant to Rule 41(e)(2)(A)(iii), within fourteen (14) days of the execution of the warrant, an agent is required to file an inventory return with the Court, that is, to file an itemized list of the property seized. Execution of the warrant begins when the United States serves the warrant on the named custodian; execution is complete when the custodian provides all Search Warrant Data to the United States. Within fourteen (14) days of completion of the execution of the warrant, the inventory will be filed.

b. Pursuant to Rule 41(e)(2)(B), Rule 41(e)(2)(A) governs the time within which the electronically stored information must be seized after the issuance of the warrant and copied after the execution of the warrant, not the "later review of the media or information" seized, or the later off-site digital copying of that media.

c. Under Rule 41(f)(1)(B), the inventory return that is to be filed with the court may be limited to a description of the "physical storage media" into which the Search Warrant Data that was seized was placed, not an itemization of the information or data stored on the "physical storage media" into which the Search Warrant Data was placed;

d. Under Rule 41(f)(1)(B), the government may retain a copy of that information for purposes of the investigation. The government proposes that the original storage media on which the Search Warrant Data was placed plus a full image copy of the seized Search Warrant Data be retained by the government.

e. If the person from whom any Search Warrant Data was seized requests the return of any information in the Search Warrant Data that is not set forth in Attachment B, Section II, that information will be copied onto appropriate media and returned to the person from whom the information was seized.

SEALED

Office of the United States Attorney
District of Nevada
501 Las Vegas Boulevard, Suite 1100
Las Vegas, Nevada 89101
(702) 388-6336

STEVEN W. MYHRE
Acting United States Attorney
District of Nevada
CRISTINA D. SILVA
PATRICK BURNS
Assistant United States Attorneys
501 Las Vegas Blvd. South, Ste. 1100
Las Vegas, Nevada 89101
Telephone: (702) 388-6336
Fax (702) 388-6698
john.p.burns@usdoj.gov

Attorney for the United States of America

UNITED STATES DISTRICT COURT
DISTRICT OF NEVADA
-oOo-

IN THE MATTER OF THE SEARCH OF INFORMATION RELATED TO THE AMAZON ACCOUNT LINKED TO CENTRALPARK1@LIVE.COM THAT IS STORED AT A PREMISES CONTROLLED BY AMAZON, INC.	Magistrate No. 17-mj-972-NJK **AFFIDAVIT IN SUPPORT OF AN APPLICATION FOR A SEARCH WARRANT** (Under Seal)

STATE OF NEVADA   )
) ss:
COUNTY OF CLARK   )

AFFIDAVIT IN SUPPORT OF AN APPLICATION FOR A SEARCH WARRANT

I, Ryan S. Burke, Special Agent, Federal Bureau of Investigation (FBI), having been duly sworn, hereby depose and say:

INTRODUCTION AND AGENT BACKGROUND

1. Your Affiant makes this affidavit in support of an application for a search warrant for information related to the Amazon account associated with email account centralpark1@live.com ("Target Amazon Account"). The Target Amazon Account is

associated with STEPHEN PADDOCK and the information is stored at a premises owned, maintained, controlled, or operated by Amazon.com, Inc. ("Amazon"), an American electronic commerce and cloud computing company based in Tumwater, Washington. More generally, Amazon is a website that allows account holders to browse for and purchase a variety of goods. Separately, Amazon offers and provides internet-based cloud services to various individuals/entities. The information to be searched is described in the following paragraphs and in Attachment "A" (attached hereto and incorporated herein by reference). This affidavit is made in support of an application for a search warrant under 18 U.S.C. §§ 2703(a), 2703(b)(1)(A), and 2703(c)(1)(A) to require Amazon to disclose to the government records and other information in its possession, pertaining to the subscriber or customer associated with the Target Amazon Account.

2. I am an "investigative or law enforcement officer of the United States" within the meaning of Title 18, United States Code, Section 2510(7), that is, an officer of the United States who is empowered by law to conduct investigations of, and to make arrests for, offenses enumerated in Title 18, United States Code, Section 2516.

3. I have been employed as a Special Agent of the FBI for approximately five years, which began at the FBI Academy in October 2012. Upon completion of the academy, I was transferred to the Las Vegas Division's white collar crime squad and then the human trafficking squad. Since October 2015, I have been assigned to the Las Vegas Division's violent crime/gang squad. Additionally, I have been a certified member of the FBI's Cellular Analysis Survey Team since August 2015 due to my expertise in the field of historical cell site analysis.

4. During my tenure with the FBI, I have conducted surveillance, analyzed telephone records, interviewed witnesses, supervised activities of sources, executed search warrants, executed arrest warrants, and participated in court-authorized interceptions of wire and electronic communications. These investigative activities have been conducted in conjunction with a variety of investigations, to include those involving robbery, drug trafficking, kidnapping, murder, criminal enterprises, and more. In addition to my practical experiences, I received five months of extensive law enforcement training at the FBI Academy.

5. The facts in this affidavit are derived from your Affiant's personal observations, his training and experience, and information obtained from other agents, detectives, and witnesses. This affidavit is intended to show merely that there is sufficient probable cause for the requested warrant and does not set forth all of the Affiant's knowledge about this matter.

6. Based on your Affiant's training and experience and the facts as set forth in this affidavit, there is probable cause to believe that violations of:

    a. Destruction/Damage of Aircraft or Aircraft Facilities - 18 U.S.C.A. § 32(a);

    b. Violence at International Airport - 18 U.S.C. § 37(a)(2); and

    c. Unlawful Interstate Transport/Delivery of Firearms by Non Federal Firearms Licensee – 18 USC 922(a)(3) and (5).

(hereafter, "Subject Offenses") have been committed by STEPHEN PADDOCK and others yet unknown. There is also probable cause to search the information described in Attachment "A" for evidence of these crimes and information which might reveal the

identities of others involved in these crimes, as described in Attachment "B" (attached hereto and incorporated herein by reference).

PROBABLE CAUSE

7. On the evening of Sunday, October 1, 2017, Route 91 Harvest, a music festival, was in progress at 3901 South Las Vegas Boulevard, Las Vegas, Nevada. At approximately 10:08 p.m., the Las Vegas Metropolitan Police Department (LVMPD) received calls reporting shots had been fired at the concert and multiple victims were struck. LVMPD determined the shots were coming from Rooms 134 and 135 on the 32nd floor of the Mandalay Bay Resort and Casino, located due west of the festival rounds at 3950 South Las Vegas Boulevard, Las Vegas, Nevada. These rooms are an elevated position which overlooks the concert venue. Witness statements and video footage captured during the attack indicates that the weapons being used were firing in a fully-automatic fashion.

8. LVMPD officers ultimately made entry into the room and located an individual later identified as STEPHEN PADDOCK. Paddock was deceased from an apparent self-inflicted gunshot wound.

9. Paddock's Nevada driver's license was located in the Mandalay Bay hotel room with Paddock, and both hotel rooms were registered in his name. A player's club card in name of Marilou Danley was located in Paddock's room, and the card returned to the address located on Babbling Brook Street in Mesquite, Nevada. FBI Agents located Danley, who was traveling outside the United States at the time of the shooting. It was ultimately determined that Danley resided with Paddock at the Babbling Brook address.

10. On October 2, 2017, search warrants were executed on Paddock's Mandalay Bay hotel rooms, Paddock's vehicle at Mandalay Bay, and two Nevada residences owned by Paddock: 1372 Babbling Brook Court in Mesquite, and 1735 Del Webb Parkway in Reno, Nevada. Officers and Agents found over 20 firearms, hundreds of rounds of ammunition, and hundreds of spent shell casings in the Mandalay Bay hotel rooms, in close proximity to Paddock's body. Over a thousand rounds of rifle ammunition and 100 pounds of explosive material were found in Paddock's vehicle. Additional explosive material, approximately 18 firearms, and over 1,000 rounds of ammunition were located at the Mesquite residence. A large quantity of ammunition and multiple firearms were recovered from the Reno residence.

11. As of this date, 58 people have been identified to have been killed in Paddock's attack and another 557 were reportedly injured. Additionally, investigators discovered that STEPHEN PADDOCK also utilized a firearm to shoot large fuel tanks on Las Vegas McCarran International Airport property. Multiple bullet holes were found on the tank, which investigators believe was an attempt by STEPHEN PADDOCK to cause the tanks to explode.

12. In an effort to determine whether or not STEPHEN PADDOCK was assisted and/or conspired with unknown individuals, investigators have attempted to identify all of STEPHEN PADDOCK's communication facilities. Based on a review of his financial accounts, email address centralpark1@live.com ("Email Account") was determined to belong to STEPHEN PADDOCK. On October 3, 2017, investigators requested an emergency disclosure of records from Microsoft related to the Email Account so it could be searched for any evidence of additional co-conspirators. Within

the Email Account, investigators identified the Target Amazon Account as one that required further investigation.

13. Numerous emails sent from Amazon to the Email Account were discovered in the Email Account which were addressed by Amazon to "Stephen" and listed STEPHEN PADDOCK's residence in Mesquite, Nevada as the shipping destination. For these reasons in conjunction with the Target Amazon Account being associated with the Email Account, investigators strongly believe the Target Amazon Account was controlled and operated by STEPHEN PADDOCK.

14. On September 7, 2017, the Email Account received an email relating to the Target Amazon Account's purchase of an EOTech 512.A65 Tactical Holographic firearm accessory. Within the email, which was addressed to STEPHEN PADDOCK, Amazon confirmed the firearm accessory would be delivered to STEPHEN PADDOCK's residence. Investigators believe this piece of equipment was utilized in the attack carried out by STEPHEN PADDOCK.

15. Your Affiant believes the requested search warrant will yield significant information from Amazon such as STEPHEN PADDOCK's search history, purchase history, IP addresses, shipping addresses, payment information, and more, which may constitute evidence of his planning of the attack and potentially identify other participants in the attack. Ultimately, your Affiant strongly believes the requested information will lead investigators to determine the full scope of STEPHEN PADDOCK's plan and/or conspiracy.

INFORMATION TO BE SEARCHED AND THINGS TO BE SEIZED

16. Your Affiant anticipates executing this warrant under the Electronic Communications Privacy Act, in particular 18 U.S.C. §§ 2703(a), 2703(b)(1)(A) and 2703(c)(1)(A), by using the warrant to require Amazon to disclose to the government copies of the records and other information (including the content of communications) particularly described in Section I of Attachment "B." Upon receipt of the information described in Section I of Attachment "B," government-authorized persons will review that information to locate the items described in Section II of Attachment "B."

CONCLUSION

17. Based on the forgoing, I request that the Court issue the proposed search warrant. This Court has jurisdiction to issue the requested warrant because it is "a court of competent jurisdiction" as defined by 18 U.S.C. § 2711. 18 U.S.C. §§ 2703(a), (b)(1)(A) & (c)(1)(A). Specifically, the Court is "a district court of the United States . . . that – has jurisdiction over the offense being investigated." 18 U.S.C. § 2711(3)(A)(i). Pursuant to 18 U.S.C. § 2703(g), the presence of a law enforcement officer is not required for the service or execution of this warrant.

REQUEST FOR SEALING

18. I further request that the Court order that all papers in support of this application, including the affidavit and search warrant, be sealed until further order of the Court. These documents discuss an ongoing criminal investigation that is neither public nor known to all of the targets of the investigation. Accordingly, there is good

///

cause to seal these documents because their premature disclosure may seriously jeopardize that investigation.

Respectfully Submitted,

_____
Ryan S. Burke, Special Agent
Federal Bureau of Investigation

SWORN TO AND SUBSCRIBED
before me this 6th day of October 2017.

_____
UNITED STATES MAGISTRATE JUDGE

ATTACHMENT "A"

ONLINE ACCOUNT TO BE SEARCHED

1. This warrant applies to information related to the Amazon.com account associated with centralpark1@live.com (the "Target Amazon Account") from its inception to present, which is stored at premises owned, maintained, controlled, or operated by Amazon.com, Inc., headquartered at 300 Deschutes Way SW, Suite 304, Tumwater, WA 98501.

ATTACHMENT "B"
Particular Things to be Seized

I. **Information to be disclosed by the Service Provider**

To the extent that the information described in Attachment A is within the possession, custody, or control of Amazon.com, including any Emails, records, files, logs, or information that have been deleted but are still available to Service Provider, or have been preserved pursuant to a request made under 18 U.S.C. § 2703(f), Service Provider is required to disclose the following information to the government for each account or identifier listed in Attachment A from account inception to present:

    a. All names, addresses, email addresses, shipping addresses, and billing information associated with the Target Amazon Account;
    b. Date of account creation;
    c. All purchase history;
    d. Service usage information;
    e. All Internet Protocol Address logs and information;
    f. All messages and/or communications exchanged with Amazon.com representative;
    g. Any and all information, files, and data in possession of Amazon.com and/or any other entities controlled or operation by Amazon.com, Inc. related to the Target Amazon Account.

II. **Information to be seized by the United States**

After reviewing all information described in Section I, the United States will seize evidence of violations of Title 18, United States Code Sections 32(a) (Destruction/Damage of Aircraft or Aircraft Facilities); 37(a)(2) (Violence at International Airport); and 922(a)(3); 5 (Unlawful Interstate Transport/Delivery of Firearms by Non Federal Firearms Licensee) (the "Subject Offenses") that occur in the form of the following, from account inception to present:

    a. Communications, transactions and records that may establish ownership and control (or the degree thereof) of the Target Account, including address books, contact or buddy lists, bills, invoices, receipts, registration records, bills, correspondence, notes, records, memoranda, telephone/address books, photographs, video recordings, audio recordings, lists of names, records of

payment for access to newsgroups or other online subscription services, and attachments to said communications, transactions and records.

b. Communications, transactions and records to/from persons who may be co-conspirators of the Subject Offenses, or which may identify co-conspirators.

c. Communications, transactions and records which may show motivation to commit the Subject Offenses.

d. Communications, transactions and records that relate to the Subject Offenses.

e. Information related to wire transfers and/or the movement, possession, or storage of currency and valuable items.

ATTACHMENT "C"

PROTOCOL FOR SEARCHING THE ELECTRONIC DATA SEIZED PURSUANT TO THIS SEARCH WARRANT

1. In executing this warrant, the government must make reasonable efforts to use methods and procedures that will locate and expose in the electronic data produced in response to this search warrant ("the Search Warrant Data") those categories of data, files, documents, or other electronically stored information that are identified with particularity in the warrant, while minimizing exposure or examination of irrelevant, privileged, or confidential files to the extent reasonably practicable.

2. When the Search Warrant Data is received, the government will make a duplicate copy of the Search Warrant Data ("the Search Warrant Data Copy"). The original version of the Search Warrant Data will be sealed and preserved for purposes of: later judicial review or order to return or dispose of the Search Warrant Data; production to the defense in any criminal case if authorized by statute, rule, or the Constitution; for purposes of showing the chain of custody of the Search Warrant Data and the Search Warrant Data Copy; or for any other lawful purpose. The original of the Search Warrant Data will not be searched or examined except to ensure that it has been fully and completely replicated in the Search Warrant Data Copy.

3. The investigating agents will then search the entirety of the Search Warrant Data Copy using any and all methods and procedures deemed appropriate by the United States designed to identify the information listed as Information to be Seized in Attachment B, Section II. The United States may copy, extract or otherwise segregate information or data listed as Information to be Seized in Attachment B, Section II. Information or data so copied, extracted or otherwise segregated will no longer be subject to any handling restrictions that might be set out in this protocol beyond those required by binding law. To the extent evidence of crimes not within the scope of this warrant appear in plain view during this review, a supplemental or "piggyback" warrant will be applied for in order to further search that document, data, or other item.

4. Once the Search Warrant Data Copy has been thoroughly and completely examined for any document, data, or other items identified in Attachment B, Section II as Information to be Seized, the Search Warrant Data Copy will be sealed and not subject to any further search or examination unless authorized by another search warrant or other appropriate court order. The Search Warrant Data Copy will be held and preserved for the same purposes identified above in Paragraph 2.

5. The search procedures utilized for this review are at the sole discretion of the investigating and prosecuting authorities, and may include the following techniques (the following is a non-exclusive list, as other search procedures may be used):

a. examination of all of the data contained in the Search Warrant Data to view the data and determine whether that data falls within the items to be seized as set forth herein;

b. searching for and attempting to recover from the Search Warrant Data any deleted, hidden, or encrypted data to determine whether that data falls within the list of items to be seized as set forth herein (any data that is encrypted and unreadable will not be returned unless law enforcement personnel have determined that the data is not (1) an instrumentality of the offenses, (2) a fruit of the criminal activity, (3) contraband, (4) otherwise unlawfully possessed, or (5) evidence of the offenses specified above);

c. surveying various file directories and the individual files they contain;

d. opening files in order to determine their contents;

e. using hash values to narrow the scope of what may be found. Hash values are under- inclusive, but are still a helpful tool;

f. scanning storage areas;

g. performing keyword searches through all electronic storage areas to determine whether occurrences of language contained in such storage areas exist that are likely to appear in the evidence described in Attachment A; and/or

h. performing any other data analysis technique that may be necessary to locate and retrieve the evidence described in Attachment B, Section II.

Return and Review Procedures

6. Rule 41 of the Federal Rules of Criminal Procedure provides, in relevant part:

(e) Issuing the Warrant.

(2) Contents of the Warrant.

(A) Warrant to Search for and Seize a Person or Property. Except for a tracking-device warrant, the warrant must identify the person or property to be searched, identify any person or property to be seized, and designate the magistrate judge to whom it must be returned. The warrant must command the officer to:

(i) execute the warrant within a specified time no longer than 14 days;

(B) Warrant Seeking Electronically Stored Information. A warrant under Rule 41(e)(2)(A) may authorize the seizure of electronic storage media or the seizure or copying of electronically stored information. Unless otherwise specified, the warrant authorizes a later review of the media or information consistent with the warrant. The time for executing the warrant in Rule 41(e)(2)(A) and (f)(1)(A) refers to the seizure or on-site copying of the media or information, and not to any later off-site copying or review.

(f) Executing and Returning the Warrant.

(1) Warrant to Search for and Seize a Person or Property.

(B) Inventory. An officer present during the execution of the warrant must prepare and verify an inventory of any property seized. . . . In a case involving the seizure of electronic storage media or the seizure or copying of electronically stored information, the inventory may be limited to describing the physical storage media that were seized or copied. The officer may retain a copy of the electronically stored information that was seized or copied.

7. Pursuant to this Rule, the government understands and will act in accordance with the following:

a. Pursuant to Rule 41(e)(2)(A)(iii), within fourteen (14) days of the execution of the warrant, an agent is required to file an inventory return with the Court, that is, to file an itemized list of the property seized. Execution of the warrant begins when the United States serves the warrant on the named custodian; execution is complete when the custodian provides all Search Warrant Data to the United States. Within fourteen (14) days of completion of the execution of the warrant, the inventory will be filed.

b. Pursuant to Rule 41(e)(2)(B), Rule 41(e)(2)(A) governs the time within which the electronically stored information must be seized after the issuance of the warrant and copied after the execution of the warrant, not the "later review of the media or information" seized, or the later off-site digital copying of that media.

c. Under Rule 41(f)(1)(B), the inventory return that is to be filed with the court may be limited to a description of the "physical storage media" into which the Search Warrant Data that was seized was placed, not an itemization of the information or data stored on the "physical storage media" into which the Search Warrant Data was placed;

d.   Under Rule 41(f)(1)(B), the government may retain a copy of that information for purposes of the investigation. The government proposes that the original storage media on which the Search Warrant Data was placed plus a full image copy of the seized Search Warrant Data be retained by the government.

e.   If the person from whom any Search Warrant Data was seized requests the return of any information in the Search Warrant Data that is not set forth in Attachment B, Section II, that information will be copied onto appropriate media and returned to the person from whom the information was seized.

AO 106 (Rev. 04/10) Application for a Search Warrant   10-3-17

UNITED STATES DISTRICT COURT
for the
District of Nevada

I hereby attest and certify on _____
that the foregoing document is a full true and correct
copy of the original on file in my office, and in my legal
custody.

CAM FERENBACH
U.S. MAGISTRATE JUDGE
DISTRICT OF NEVADA

By _____ Deputy Secretary

In the Matter of the Search of   )
(Briefly describe the property to be searched   )
or identify the person by name and address)   )   Case No.   2:17-mj-00958-VCF
)
INSTAGRAM ACCOUNTS STORED AT   )
PREMISES CONTROLLED BY   )
FACEBOOK CORPORATION: stephenpaddock47   A1   )

APPLICATION FOR A SEARCH WARRANT

I, a federal law enforcement officer or an attorney for the government, request a search warrant and state under penalty of perjury that I have reason to believe that on the following person or property *(identify the person or describe the property to be searched and give its location)*:
INSTAGRAM ACCOUNTS STORED AT PREMISES CONTROLLED BY FACEBOOK CORPORATION: stephenpaddock47   A1

located in the _____DEA_____ District of _____, there is now concealed *(identify the person or describe the property to be seized)*:
INSTAGRAM ACCOUNTS STORED AT PREMISES CONTROLLED BY FACEBOOK CORPORATION: stephenpaddock47   A1

The basis for the search under Fed. R. Crim. P. 41(c) is *(check one or more)*:
☒ evidence of a crime;
☒ contraband, fruits of crime, or other items illegally possessed;
☒ property designed for use, intended for use, or used in committing a crime;
☒ a person to be arrested or a person who is unlawfully restrained.

The search is related to a violation of:

Code Section	Offense Description
Title 26, United States Code, Section 5841.	Violation of National Firearms Act

FILED 2017 OCT -3 PM 3:34 BY _____ U.S. MAGISTRATE JUDGE

The application is based on these facts:
I believe there is probable cause to believe that in the subject accounts listed in Attachments "A1", "A2", "A3", "A4", "A5" there is proof that constitutes evidence of the commission of criminal offense(s); contraband, the fruits of crime and things otherwise criminally possessed and been used as the means of committing criminal offense(s)

☐ Continued on the attached sheet.
☐ Delayed notice of _____ days (give exact ending date if more than 30 days: _____) is requested under 18 U.S.C. § 3103a, the basis of which is set forth on the attached sheet.

_____
Applicant's signature

_____
Printed name and title

Sworn to before me and signed in my presence.

Date: 10-3-17

City and state: Las Vegas, Nevada

CAM FERENBACH

_____
Judge's signature
CAM FERENBACH
U.S. MAGISTRATE JUDGE
Printed name and title

AO 93 (Rev. 11/13) Search and Seizure Warrant

I hereby attest and certify on 10-3-17 that the foregoing document is a full true and correct copy of the original on file in my office, and in my legal custody.

CAM FERENBACH
U.S. MAGISTRATE JUDGE
DISTRICT OF NEVADA

By _____ Deputy Secretary

UNITED STATES DISTRICT COURT
for the
District of Nevada

In the Matter of the Search of)
(Briefly describe the property to be searched)
or identify the person by name and address))   Case No. 2:17-mj-00958-VCF
)
stephenpaddock47 A1)
)
)

SEARCH AND SEIZURE WARRANT

To: Any authorized law enforcement officer

An application by a federal law enforcement officer or an attorney for the government requests the search of the following person or property located in the _____ District of _____ Nevada _____
(identify the person or describe the property to be searched and give its location):

SEE ATTACHMENT A1

I find that the affidavit(s), or any recorded testimony, establish probable cause to search and seize the person or property described above, and that such search will reveal *(identify the person or describe the property to be seized):*

SEE ATTACHMENTS B and C

YOU ARE COMMANDED to execute this warrant on or before 10-12-17 *(not to exceed 14 days)*
☒ in the daytime 6:00 a.m. to 10:00 p.m.   ☐ at any time in the day or night because good cause has been established.

Unless delayed notice is authorized below, you must give a copy of the warrant and a receipt for the property taken to the person from whom, or from whose premises, the property was taken, or leave the copy and receipt at the place where the property was taken.

The officer executing this warrant, or an officer present during the execution of the warrant, must prepare an inventory as required by law and promptly return this warrant and inventory to   CAM FERENBACH   .
(United States Magistrate Judge)

☐ Pursuant to 18 U.S.C. § 3103a(b), I find that immediate notification may have an adverse result listed in 18 U.S.C. § 2705 (except for delay of trial), and authorize the officer executing this warrant to delay notice to the person who, or whose property, will be searched or seized *(check the appropriate box)*
☐ for ___ days *(not to exceed 30)*   ☐ until, the facts justifying, the later specific date of _____ .

Date and time issued: 10-3-17 4:03pm

City and state: Las Vegas, Nevada

CAM FERENBACH
Judge's signature

CAM FERENBACH
U.S. MAGISTRATE JUDGE
Printed name and title

STEVEN W. MYHRE
Acting United States Attorney
NICHOLAS D. DICKINSON
Assistant United States Attorney
District of Nevada
Nevada Bar No. 12940
501 Las Vegas Boulevard South, Suite 1100
Las Vegas, Nevada 89101
PHONE: (702) 388-6336
NDickinson@usdoj.gov

Counsel for the United States

FILED
2017 OCT -3 PM 3:59
U.S. MAGISTRATE JUDGE
BY_____

UNITED STATES DISTRICT COURT
DISTRICT OF NEVADA
-oOo-

IN THE MATTER OF SEARCH OF INFORMATION ASSOCIATED WITH INSTAGRAM ACCOUNTS STORED AT PREMISES CONTROLLED BY FACEBOOK CORPORATION: **stephenpaddock47 A1**	Magistrate No.	2:17-mj-00958-VCF **AFFIDAVIT** (Under Seal)
IN THE MATTER OF SEARCH OF INFORMATION ASSOCIATED WITH INSTAGRAM ACCOUNTS STORED AT PREMISES CONTROLLED BY FACEBOOK CORPORATION: **Mariloudanley A2**	Magistrate No.	2:17-mj-00959-VCF **AFFIDAVIT** (Under Seal)
IN THE MATTER OF SEARCH OF INFORMATION ASSOCIATED WITH INSTAGRAM ACCOUNTS STORED AT PREMISES CONTROLLED BY FACEBOOK CORPORATION: **Mariloudanleyy A3**	Magistrate No.	2:17-mj-00960-VCF **AFFIDAVIT** (Under Seal)

IN THE MATTER OF SEARCH OF INFORMATION ASSOCIATED WITH INSTAGRAM ACCOUNTS STORED AT PREMISES CONTROLLED BY FACEBOOK CORPORATION: Mariloudanleypaddock A4	Magistrate No. 2:17-mj-00961-VCF AFFIDAVIT (Under Seal)
IN THE MATTER OF SEARCH OF INFORMATION ASSOCIATED WITH INSTAGRAM ACCOUNTS STORED AT PREMISES CONTROLLED BY FACEBOOK CORPORATION: marilou.danley A5	Magistrate No. 2:17-mj-00962-VCF AFFIDAVIT (Under Seal)

STATE OF NEVADA)
) ss:
COUNTY OF CLARK)

AFFIDAVIT IN SUPPORT OF AN APPLICATION FOR A SEARCH WARRANT

I, Heather D. Burton, Special Agent, Federal Bureau of Investigation (FBI), having been duly sworn, hereby depose and say:

INTRODUCTION AND AGENT BACKGROUND

1. Your Affiant is a Special Agent with the FBI currently assigned to the Las Vegas, Nevada Division. She has been so employed for over three years. Prior to this she, was employed for five years as a United States Probation Officer in Memphis, Tennessee. Your Affiant is currently assigned to FBI Las Vegas Squad 6. Previously, she was assigned to the Las Vegas Safe Streets Task Force (LVSSTF) and was responsible for investigating a variety of violent crimes, to include bank robbery, kidnapping, extortion, robbery, carjacking, assault and murder of Federal Officers, racketeering related violent offenses, as well as long-term investigations into the activities and operations of criminal enterprises, drug trafficking organizations, and violent street gangs. Your Affiant has experience in conducting criminal investigations, including the investigation of

criminal groups and conspiracies as well as the collection of evidence and the identification and use of witnesses.

2. Your Affiant makes this affidavit in support of an application for a search warrant for information associated with certain Instagram, LLC (hereinafter "Instagram") user IDs that are stored at premises owned, maintained, controlled, or operated by Facebook Inc. (hereinafter "Facebook"), a social networking company headquartered in Menlo Park, California. The information to be searched is described in the following paragraphs and in Attachment A1, A2, A3, A4, A5 and B. This affidavit is made in support of an application for a search warrant under 18 U.S.C. §§ 2703(a), 2703(b)(1)(A) and 2703(c)(1)(A) to require Facebook to disclose to the government records and other information in its possession, pertaining to the subscriber or customer associated with user IDs. It is submitted that the information sought through the issuance of the requested warrant constitutes evidence of the following offense: Violation of National Firearms Act – Registration of Firearms, Title 26, United States Code, Section 5841.

3. The items to be searched are the associated Instagram user ID names as follows:

stephenpaddock47

mariloudanley

mariloudanleyy

mariloudanleypaddock

marilou.danley

4. Because this affidavit is being submitted for the limited purpose of securing a search warrant, your Affiant has not included each and every fact known to her concerning this investigation. Your Affiant has set forth only those facts that are necessary to establish probable cause for the above listed offense. The information used to support this search warrant was derived from reports of information obtained from witnesses as well as investigation conducted by other

Agents and law enforcement officers related to the incident. This affidavit contains information necessary to support probable cause to believe that the criminal offenses described herein were committed by the defendant, STEPHEN PADDOCK (hereinafter "PADDOCK"), and others yet unidentified, and is not intended to include each and every fact and matter observed by your Affiant or known to the Government. Moreover, to the extent this affidavit contains statements by witnesses, those statements are set forth only in part in substance and are intended to accurately convey the information, but not to be verbatim recitations. All noted times are approximate.

JURISDICTION

5. This Court has jurisdiction to issue the requested warrant because it is "a court of competent jurisdiction" as defined by 18 U.S.C. § 2711 and 18 U.S.C. §§ 2703(a), (b)(1)(A), and (c)(1)(A). Specifically, the Court is a "district court of the United States (including a magistrate judge of such a court) that ... has jurisdiction over the offense being investigated...." 18 U.S.C. § 2711(3)(A)(i), which took place in Las Vegas, Nevada.

BACKGROUND CONCERNING INSTAGRAM

6. Instagram, which is owned by Facebook, operates a free-access social-networking website of the same name that can be accessed at http://www.instagram.com. Instagram allows its users to create their own profile pages, which can include a short biography, a photo of themselves, videos and other information. Users can access Instagram through its website or by using a special electronic application ("app") created by the company that allows users to access the service through a mobile device.

7. Instagram permits users to post photos and videos to their profiles on Instagram and otherwise share them with others on Instagram, as well as certain other social-media services, including Flickr, Facebook, and Twitter. When posting or sharing a photo or video on Instagram, a user can add a caption to it, can add various "tags" that can be used to search for the photo or video

(e.g., a user may add the tag #vw to a photo so that people interested in Volkswagen vehicles can search for and find the photo), can add location information, and can add other information, as well as apply a variety of "filters" or other visual effects that can be used to modify the look of the posted photos. In addition, Instagram allows users to make comments on posted photos or videos, including photos or video that the user posts or posted by other users of Instagram. Users can also "like" photos.

8. Upon creating an Instagram account, an Instagram user must create a unique Instagram username and an account password. This information is collected and maintained by Instagram.

9. Instagram asks users to provide basic identity and contact information upon registration and also allows users to provide additional identity information for their user profile. This information may include the user's full name, e-mail address(es), and phone number(s), as well as potentially other personal information provided directly by the user to Instagram. Once an account is created, users may also adjust various privacy and account settings for the account on Instagram. This information is collected and maintained by Instagram.

10. Instagram allows users to have "friends," which are other individuals with whom the user can share information without making the information public. Friends on Instagram may come from either contact lists maintained by the user, other third-party social media websites and information, or searches conducted by the user on Instagram profiles. This information is collected and maintained by Instagram.

11. Instagram also allows users to "follow" another user, which means that they receive updates about posts made by the other user. Users may also "unfollow" users, that is, stop following them or block them, which prevents the blocked user from following that user.

12. Instagram allows users to post and share various types of user content, including

photos, videos comments, and other materials. User content that is posted to Instagram or shared through Instagram is collected and maintained by Instagram.

13. Instagram users can exchange private messages on Instagram with other users. These messages, which are similar to email messages, are sent to the recipient's "Inbox" on Instagram, which also stores copies of messages sent by the recipient, as well as other information.

14. Users on Instagram may also search Instagram for other users or particular types of photos or other content.

15. For each user, Instagram also collects and retains information, called "log file" information, every time a user requests access to Instagram, whether through a web page or through an app. Among the log file information that Instagram's servers automatically record is the particular web requests, any Internet Protocol ("IP") address associated with the request, type of browser used, any referencing/exit web pages and associated URLs, pages viewed, dates and times of access, and other information.

16. Instagram also collects and maintains "cookies," which are small text files that are placed on a user's computer or mobile device and that allows Instagram to identify the browser or device's accesses to the service.

17. Instagram also collects information on the particular devices used to access Instagram. In particular, Instagram may record "device identifiers," which includes data files and other information that may identify the particular electronic device that was used to access Instagram.

18. Instagram also collects metadata associated with user content. For example, Instagram collects any "hashtags" associated with user content (i.e., keywords used), "geotags" that mark the location of a photo and which may include latitude and longitude information, comments on photos, and other information.

19. Instagram also may communicate with the user, by email or otherwise. Instagram collects and maintains copies of communications between Instagram and the user.

20. Based on the information above, the computers of Instagram are likely to contain all the material described above with respect to accounts with the above referenced user IDs, including **stephenpaddock47, mariloudanley, mariloudanleyy, mariloudanleypaddock, and marilou.danley,** including stored electronic communications and information concerning subscribers and their use of Instagram, such as account access information, which would include information such as the IP addresses and devices used to access the account, as well as other account information that might be used to identify the actual user or users of the accounts at particular times.

STATEMENT OF PROBABLE CAUSE

21. On the evening of Sunday, October 1, 2017, the Route 91 Harvest, a music festival, was in progress at 3901 South Las Vegas Boulevard, Las Vegas, Nevada 89119. At approximately 2208 hours, the Las Vegas Metropolitan Police Department (LVMPD) received calls reporting shots had been fired at the concert and multiple victims were struck. LVMPD determined the shots were coming from Rooms 134 and 135 on the 32nd floor of the Mandalay Bay Resort and Casino, 3950 South Las Vegas Boulevard, Las Vegas, Nevada 89119.

22. Officers made entry into the room and located an individual later identified as Stephen Paddock, DOB █████████ address 1372 Babbling Brook Court, Mesquite, Nevada 89034. Paddock was deceased from an apparent self-inflicted gunshot wound.

23. Officers found multiple firearms and hundreds of rounds of ammunition in the room in close proximity to Paddock's body. Additionally, investigators located over a thousand rounds of ammunition and explosive material in a vehicle associated with Paddock. Further, multiple firearms and a large quantity of ammunition were located at Paddock's residence at 1372 Babbling Brook Court, Mesquite.

24. Paddock's Nevada driver's license was located in the Mandalay Bay hotel room with Paddock, and both hotel rooms were registered in his name. A player's club card in name of Marilou Danley was located in Paddock's room, and the card returned to the same Babbling Brook address in Mesquite.

25. While monitoring an identified Facebook accounts of Marilou Danley (facebook.com/marilou.danley) after the shooting, LVMPD investigators noted that the account settings and privacy settings were changed on October 2, 2017, at approximately 0030 hours. At approximately 0246 hours, the Facebook account was deleted. Investigators discovered the following additional Instagram accounts associated with Stephen Paddock and Marilou Paddock: **stephenpaddock47, mariloudanley, mariloudanleyy, mariloudanleypaddock,** and **marilou.danley**. On October 3, 2017, a preservation request for all content pertaining to the these Instagram was submitted to Facebook to maximize the chance that the contents of the account remain preserved.

26. Based on my training and experience, a person who possesses large amounts of firearms and ammunition obtains those items over a period of time. Thus, I am requesting that the search period be from September 1, 2016 to the present.

27. Based on these stated facts, it is your Affiant's opinion that there is probable cause to believe that the Instagram accounts with user IDs **stephenpaddock47, mariloudanley, mariloudanleyy, mariloudanleypaddock,** and **marilou.danley** contain evidence related to PADDOCK's possession of firearms in violation of Title 26, United States Code, Section 5841. Your Affiant also submits that a review of photos and other non-public content on the subject accounts will likely produce further evidence of prior and additional violations of the enumerated offenses. I swear, under penalty of perjury, that the foregoing is true and correct to the best of my knowledge and belief.

INFORMATION TO BE SEARCHED AND THINGS TO BE SEIZED

28. Your Affiant anticipates executing this warrant under the Electronic Communications Privacy Act, in particular 18 U.S.C. §§ 2703(a), 2703(b)(1)(A) and 2703(c)(1)(A), by using the warrant to require Facebook to disclose to the government copies of the records and other information (including the content of communications) particularly described in Section I of Attachment "B." Upon receipt of the information described in Section I of Attachment "B," government-authorized persons will review that information to locate the items described in Section II of Attachment "B."

CONCLUSION

29. Based on the information set forth herein, Your Affiant has probable cause to believe that in the subject accounts listed in Attachments "A1", "A2", "A3", "A4", "A5" there is proof that constitutes evidence of the commission of criminal offense(s); contraband, the fruits of crime and things otherwise criminally possessed; and property designed or intended for use or which is or has been used as the means of committing criminal offense(s). The evidence to be searched for and seized is set forth in Attachment "B", which is attached hereto and incorporated herein by reference.

30. Based on the forgoing, your Affiant requests that the Court issue the proposed search warrant.

31. Pursuant to 18 U.S.C. § 2703(g), the presence of a law enforcement officer is not required for the service or execution of this warrant.

REQUEST FOR SEALING

31. I further request that the Court order that all papers in support of this application, including the affidavit and search warrant, be sealed until further order of the Court. These documents discuss an ongoing criminal investigation that is neither public nor known to all of the

targets of the investigation. Accordingly, there is good cause to seal these documents because their premature disclosure may seriously jeopardize that investigation.

Respectfully Submitted,

/S/
Heather D. Burton, Special Agent
Federal Bureau of Investigation

SWORN TO AND SUBSCRIBED
before me this 3rd day of October, 2017.

CAM FERENBACH
UNITED STATES MAGISTRATE JUDGE

I hereby attest and certify on 10-3-17 that the foregoing document is a full true and correct copy of the original on file in my office, and in my legal custody.

CAM FERENBACH
U.S. MAGISTRATE JUDGE
DISTRICT OF NEVADA

By _____ Deputy Secretary

Attachment "A1"

Property to Be Searched

This warrant applies to information associated with the Instagram user IDs **stephenpaddock47,** that is stored at premises owned, maintained, controlled, or operated by Facebook, a company headquartered in Menlo Park, California for the time period beginning September 1, 2016 to present.

Attachment "A2"

Property to Be Searched

This warrant applies to information associated with the Instagram user IDs **mariloudanley**, that is stored at premises owned, maintained, controlled, or operated by Facebook, a company headquartered in Menlo Park, California for the time period beginning September 1, 2016 to present.

Attachment "A3"

Property to Be Searched

This warrant applies to information associated with the Instagram user IDs **mariloudanleyy**, that is stored at premises owned, maintained, controlled, or operated by Facebook, a company headquartered in Menlo Park, California for the time period beginning September 1, 2016 to present.

STEVEN W. MYHRE
Acting United States Attorney
NICHOLAS D. DICKINSON
Assistant United States Attorney
District of Nevada
Nevada Bar No. 12940
501 Las Vegas Boulevard South, Suite 1100
Las Vegas, Nevada 89101
PHONE: (702) 388-6336
NDickinson@usdoj.gov

Counsel for the United States

FILED
2017 OCT -3 PM 3:59
U.S. MAGISTRATE JUDGE
BY_____

UNITED STATES DISTRICT COURT
DISTRICT OF NEVADA
-oOo-

IN THE MATTER OF SEARCH OF INFORMATION ASSOCIATED WITH INSTAGRAM ACCOUNTS STORED AT PREMISES CONTROLLED BY FACEBOOK CORPORATION: **stephenpaddock47 A1**	Magistrate No. 2:17-mj-00958-VCF **AFFIDAVIT** (Under Seal)
IN THE MATTER OF SEARCH OF INFORMATION ASSOCIATED WITH INSTAGRAM ACCOUNTS STORED AT PREMISES CONTROLLED BY FACEBOOK CORPORATION: **Mariloudanley A2**	Magistrate No. 2:17-mj-00959-VCF **AFFIDAVIT** (Under Seal)
IN THE MATTER OF SEARCH OF INFORMATION ASSOCIATED WITH INSTAGRAM ACCOUNTS STORED AT PREMISES CONTROLLED BY FACEBOOK CORPORATION: **Mariloudanleyy A3**	Magistrate No. 2:17-mj-00960-VCF **AFFIDAVIT** (Under Seal)

(e.g., a user may add the tag #vw to a photo so that people interested in Volkswagen vehicles can search for and find the photo), can add location information, and can add other information, as well as apply a variety of "filters" or other visual effects that can be used to modify the look of the posted photos. In addition, Instagram allows users to make comments on posted photos or videos, including photos or video that the user posts or posted by other users of Instagram. Users can also "like" photos.

8. Upon creating an Instagram account, an Instagram user must create a unique Instagram username and an account password. This information is collected and maintained by Instagram.

9. Instagram asks users to provide basic identity and contact information upon registration and also allows users to provide additional identity information for their user profile. This information may include the user's full name, e-mail address(es), and phone number(s), as well as potentially other personal information provided directly by the user to Instagram. Once an account is created, users may also adjust various privacy and account settings for the account on Instagram. This information is collected and maintained by Instagram.

10. Instagram allows users to have "friends," which are other individuals with whom the user can share information without making the information public. Friends on Instagram may come from either contact lists maintained by the user, other third-party social media websites and information, or searches conducted by the user on Instagram profiles. This information is collected and maintained by Instagram.

11. Instagram also allows users to "follow" another user, which means that they receive updates about posts made by the other user. Users may also "unfollow" users, that is, stop following them or block them, which prevents the blocked user from following that user.

12. Instagram allows users to post and share various types of user content, including

photos, videos comments, and other materials. User content that is posted to Instagram or shared through Instagram is collected and maintained by Instagram.

13. Instagram users can exchange private messages on Instagram with other users. These messages, which are similar to email messages, are sent to the recipient's "Inbox" on Instagram, which also stores copies of messages sent by the recipient, as well as other information.

14. Users on Instagram may also search Instagram for other users or particular types of photos or other content.

15. For each user, Instagram also collects and retains information, called "log file" information, every time a user requests access to Instagram, whether through a web page or through an app. Among the log file information that Instagram's servers automatically record is the particular web requests, any Internet Protocol ("IP") address associated with the request, type of browser used, any referencing/exit web pages and associated URLs, pages viewed, dates and times of access, and other information.

16. Instagram also collects and maintains "cookies," which are small text files that are placed on a user's computer or mobile device and that allows Instagram to identify the browser or device's accesses to the service.

17. Instagram also collects information on the particular devices used to access Instagram. In particular, Instagram may record "device identifiers," which includes data files and other information that may identify the particular electronic device that was used to access Instagram.

18. Instagram also collects metadata associated with user content. For example, Instagram collects any "hashtags" associated with user content (i.e., keywords used), "geotags" that mark the location of a photo and which may include latitude and longitude information, comments on photos, and other information.

19. Instagram also may communicate with the user, by email or otherwise. Instagram collects and maintains copies of communications between Instagram and the user.

20. Based on the information above, the computers of Instagram are likely to contain all the material described above with respect to accounts with the above referenced user IDs, including **stephenpaddock47, mariloudanley, mariloudanleyy, mariloudanleypaddock, and marilou.danley,** including stored electronic communications and information concerning subscribers and their use of Instagram, such as account access information, which would include information such as the IP addresses and devices used to access the account, as well as other account information that might be used to identify the actual user or users of the accounts at particular times.

STATEMENT OF PROBABLE CAUSE

21. On the evening of Sunday, October 1, 2017, the Route 91 Harvest, a music festival, was in progress at 3901 South Las Vegas Boulevard, Las Vegas, Nevada 89119. At approximately 2208 hours, the Las Vegas Metropolitan Police Department (LVMPD) received calls reporting shots had been fired at the concert and multiple victims were struck. LVMPD determined the shots were coming from Rooms 134 and 135 on the 32nd floor of the Mandalay Bay Resort and Casino, 3950 South Las Vegas Boulevard, Las Vegas, Nevada 89119.

22. Officers made entry into the room and located an individual later identified as Stephen Paddock, DOB ███████ address 1372 Babbling Brook Court, Mesquite, Nevada 89034. Paddock was deceased from an apparent self-inflicted gunshot wound.

23. Officers found multiple firearms and hundreds of rounds of ammunition in the room in close proximity to Paddock's body. Additionally, investigators located over a thousand rounds of ammunition and explosive material in a vehicle associated with Paddock. Further, multiple firearms and a large quantity of ammunition were located at Paddock's residence at 1372 Babbling Brook Court, Mesquite.

24. Paddock's Nevada driver's license was located in the Mandalay Bay hotel room with Paddock, and both hotel rooms were registered in his name. A player's club card in name of Marilou Danley was located in Paddock's room, and the card returned to the same Babbling Brook address in Mesquite.

25. While monitoring an identified Facebook accounts of Marilou Danley (facebook.com/marilou.danley) after the shooting, LVMPD investigators noted that the account settings and privacy settings were changed on October 2, 2017, at approximately 0030 hours. At approximately 0246 hours, the Facebook account was deleted. Investigators discovered the following additional Instagram accounts associated with Stephen Paddock and Marilou Paddock: **stephenpaddock47, mariloudanley, mariloudanleyy, mariloudanleypaddock,** and **marilou.danley**. On October 3, 2017, a preservation request for all content pertaining to the these Instagram was submitted to Facebook to maximize the chance that the contents of the account remain preserved.

26. Based on my training and experience, a person who possesses large amounts of firearms and ammunition obtains those items over a period of time. Thus, I am requesting that the search period be from September 1, 2016 to the present.

27. Based on these stated facts, it is your Affiant's opinion that there is probable cause to believe that the Instagram accounts with user IDs **stephenpaddock47, mariloudanley, mariloudanleyy, mariloudanleypaddock,** and **marilou.danley** contain evidence related to PADDOCK's possession of firearms in violation of Title 26, United States Code, Section 5841. Your Affiant also submits that a review of photos and other non-public content on the subject accounts will likely produce further evidence of prior and additional violations of the enumerated offenses. I swear, under penalty of perjury, that the foregoing is true and correct to the best of my knowledge and belief.

INFORMATION TO BE SEARCHED AND THINGS TO BE SEIZED

28. Your Affiant anticipates executing this warrant under the Electronic Communications Privacy Act, in particular 18 U.S.C. §§ 2703(a), 2703(b)(1)(A) and 2703(c)(1)(A), by using the warrant to require Facebook to disclose to the government copies of the records and other information (including the content of communications) particularly described in Section I of Attachment "B." Upon receipt of the information described in Section I of Attachment "B," government-authorized persons will review that information to locate the items described in Section II of Attachment "B."

CONCLUSION

29. Based on the information set forth herein, Your Affiant has probable cause to believe that in the subject accounts listed in Attachments "A1", "A2", "A3", "A4", "A5" there is proof that constitutes evidence of the commission of criminal offense(s); contraband, the fruits of crime and things otherwise criminally possessed; and property designed or intended for use or which is or has been used as the means of committing criminal offense(s). The evidence to be searched for and seized is set forth in Attachment "B", which is attached hereto and incorporated herein by reference.

30. Based on the forgoing, your Affiant requests that the Court issue the proposed search warrant.

31. Pursuant to 18 U.S.C. § 2703(g), the presence of a law enforcement officer is not required for the service or execution of this warrant.

REQUEST FOR SEALING

31. I further request that the Court order that all papers in support of this application, including the affidavit and search warrant, be sealed until further order of the Court. These documents discuss an ongoing criminal investigation that is neither public nor known to all of the

targets of the investigation. Accordingly, there is good cause to seal these documents because their premature disclosure may seriously jeopardize that investigation.

Respectfully Submitted,

/s/
Heather D. Burton, Special Agent
Federal Bureau of Investigation

SWORN TO AND SUBSCRIBED
before me this 3rd day of October, 2017.

CAM FERENBACH
UNITED STATES MAGISTRATE JUDGE

I hereby attest and certify on 10-3-17 that the foregoing document is a full true and correct copy of the original on file in my office, and in my legal custody.

CAM FERENBACH
U.S. MAGISTRATE JUDGE
DISTRICT OF NEVADA

By _____ Deputy Secretary

Attachment "A1"

Property to Be Searched

This warrant applies to information associated with the Instagram user IDs **stephenpaddock47,** that is stored at premises owned, maintained, controlled, or operated by Facebook, a company headquartered in Menlo Park, California for the time period beginning September 1, 2016 to present.

Attachment "A2"

Property to Be Searched

This warrant applies to information associated with the Instagram user IDs **mariloudanley**, that is stored at premises owned, maintained, controlled, or operated by Facebook, a company headquartered in Menlo Park, California for the time period beginning September 1, 2016 to present.

Attachment "A3"

Property to Be Searched

This warrant applies to information associated with the Instagram user IDs **mariloudanleyy**, that is stored at premises owned, maintained, controlled, or operated by Facebook, a company headquartered in Menlo Park, California for the time period beginning September 1, 2016 to present.

Attachment "A4"

Property to Be Searched

This warrant applies to information associated with the Instagram user IDs **mariloudanleypaddock,** that is stored at premises owned, maintained, controlled, or operated by Facebook, a company headquartered in Menlo Park, California for the time period beginning September 1, 2016 to present.

Attachment "A5"

Property to Be Searched

This warrant applies to information associated with the Instagram user IDs and **marilou.danley** that is stored at premises owned, maintained, controlled, or operated by Facebook, a company headquartered in Menlo Park, California for the time period beginning September 1, 2016 to present.

ATTACHMENT "B"

Particular Things to be Seized

I. **Information to be disclosed by Facebook**

To the extent that the information described in Attachment A is within the possession, custody, or control of Instagram LLC ("Instagram"), including any messages, records, files, logs, or information that have been deleted but are still available to Instagram, or have been preserved pursuant to a request made under 18 U.S.C. § 2703(f) on October 3, 2017. Facebook is required to disclose the following information to the government for each user IDs listed in Attachment A for the period of September 1, 2016 to present:

(a) All contact and personal identifying information, including: full name, user identification number, birth date, gender, contact e-mail addresses, Instagram passwords, Instagram security questions and answers, physical address (including city, state, and zip code), telephone numbers, screen names, websites, and other personal identifiers;

(b) All activity logs for the account and all other documents showing the user's posts and other Instagram activities;

(c) All photos and videos uploaded by that user ID and all photos and videos uploaded by any user that have that user tagged in them;

(d) All profile information; status updates; links to videos, photographs, bios, articles, and other items; Wall postings; friend lists, including the friends' Instagram user identification numbers; future and past event postings; comments; and tags;

(e) All other records of communications and messages made or received by the user, chat history, and pending "Friend" requests;

(f) All user content created, uploaded, or shared by the account, including any comments made by the account on photographs or other content;

(g) All IP logs, including all records of the IP addresses that logged into the account;

(h) All records of the account's usage of the "Like" feature, including all Instagram posts and content that the user has "liked";

(i) All location data associated with the account, including geotags;

(j) All data and information that has been deleted by the user;

(k) All past and present lists of friends created by the account;

(l) All records of Instagram searches performed by the account;

(m) The types of service utilized by the user;

(n) The length of service (including start date) and the means and source of any payments associated with the service (including any credit card or bank account number);

(o) All privacy settings and other account settings, including privacy settings for individual Instagram posts and activities, and all records showing which Instagram users have been blocked by the account;

(p) All records pertaining to communications between Instagram and any person regarding the user or the user's Instagram account, including contacts with support services and records of actions taken.

(q) All information regarding the particular device or devices used to login to or access the account, including all device identifier information or cookie information, including all information about the particular device or devices used to access the account and the date and time of those accesses;

ATTACHMENT C

PROTOCOL FOR SEARCHING THE ELECTRONIC DATA SEIZED

PURSUANT TO THIS SEARCH WARRANT

1. In executing this warrant, the government must make reasonable efforts to use methods and procedures that will locate and expose in the electronic data produced in response to this search warrant ("the Search Warrant Data") those categories of data, files, documents, or other electronically stored information that are identified with particularity in the warrant, while minimizing exposure or examination of irrelevant, privileged, or confidential files to the extent reasonably practicable.

2. When the Search Warrant Data is received, the government will make a duplicate copy of the Search Warrant Data ("the Search Warrant Data Copy"). The original version of the Search Warrant Data will be sealed and preserved for purposes of: later judicial review or order to return or dispose of the Search Warrant Data; production to the defense in any criminal case if authorized by statute, rule, or the Constitution; for purposes of showing the chain of custody of the Search Warrant Data and the Search Warrant Data Copy; or for any other lawful purpose. The original of the Search Warrant Data will not be searched or examined except to ensure that it has been fully and completely replicated in the Search Warrant Data Copy.

3. The investigating agents will then search the entirety of the Search Warrant Data Copy using any and all methods and procedures deemed appropriate by the United States designed to identify the information listed as Information to be Seized in Attachment B, Section II. The United States may copy, extract or otherwise segregate information or data listed as Information to be Seized in Attachment B, Section II. Information or data so copied, extracted or otherwise segregated will no longer be subject to any handling restrictions that might be set out in this protocol beyond those required by binding law. To the extent evidence of crimes not within the scope of this warrant appear in plain view during this review, a supplemental or "piggyback" warrant will be applied for in order to further search that document, data, or other item.

4. The Government will have ninety (90) days from receipt of the data disclosed under Attachment B, Section I to complete its examination of the Search Warrant Data Copy. Once the Search Warrant Data Copy has been thoroughly and completely examined for any document, data, or other items identified in Attachment B, Section II as Information to be Seized, the Search Warrant Data Copy will be sealed and not subject to any further search or examination unless authorized by another search warrant or other appropriate court order. The Search Warrant Data Copy will be held and preserved for the same purposes identified above in Paragraph 2.

5. The search procedures utilized for this review are at the sole discretion of the investigating and prosecuting authorities, and may include the following techniques (the following is a non-exclusive list, as other search procedures may be used):

a. examination of all of the data contained in the Search Warrant Data to view the data and determine whether that data falls within the items to be seized as set forth herein;

b. searching for and attempting to recover from the Search Warrant Data any deleted, hidden, or encrypted data to determine whether that data falls within the list of items to be seized as set forth herein (any data that is encrypted and unreadable will not be returned unless law enforcement personnel have determined that the data is not (1) an instrumentality of the offenses, (2) a fruit of the criminal activity, (3) contraband, (4) otherwise unlawfully possessed, or (5) evidence of the offenses specified above);

c. surveying various file directories and the individual files they contain;

d. opening files in order to determine their contents;

e. using hash values to narrow the scope of what may be found. Hash values are under-inclusive, but are still a helpful tool;

f. scanning storage areas;

g. performing keyword searches through all electronic storage areas to determine whether occurrences of language contained in such storage areas exist that are likely to appear in the evidence described in Attachment A; and/or

h. performing any other data analysis technique that may be necessary to locate and retrieve the evidence described in Attachment B, Section II.

Return and Review Procedures

6. Rule 41 of the Federal Rules of Criminal Procedure provides, in relevant part:

(e) Issuing the Warrant.

(2) Contents of the Warrant.

(A) Warrant to Search for and Seize a Person or Property. Except for a tracking-device warrant, the warrant must identify the person or property to be searched, identify any person or property to be seized, and designate the magistrate judge to whom it must be returned. The warrant must command the officer to:

(i) execute the warrant within a specified time no longer than 14 days;

(B) Warrant Seeking Electronically Stored Information. A warrant under Rule 41(e)(2)(A) may authorize the seizure of electronic storage media or the seizure or copying of electronically stored information. Unless otherwise specified, the warrant authorizes a later review of the media or information consistent with the warrant. The time for executing the warrant in Rule 41(e)(2)(A) and

(f)(1)(A) refers to the seizure or on-site copying of the media or information, and not to any later off-site copying or review.

(f) Executing and Returning the Warrant.

(1) Warrant to Search for and Seize a Person or Property.

(B) Inventory. An officer present during the execution of the warrant must prepare and verify an inventory of any property seized. . . . In a case involving the seizure of electronic storage media or the seizure or copying of electronically stored information, the inventory may be limited to describing the physical storage media that were seized or copied. The officer may retain a copy of the electronically stored information that was seized or copied.

7. Pursuant to this Rule, the government understands and will act in accordance with the following:

a. Pursuant to Rule 41(e)(2)(A)(iii), within fourteen (14) days of the execution of the warrant, an agent is required to file an inventory return with the Court, that is, to file an itemized list of the property seized. Execution of the warrant begins when the United States serves the warrant on the named custodian; execution is complete when the custodian provides all Search Warrant Data to the United States. Within fourteen (14) days of completion of the execution of the warrant, the inventory will be filed.

b. Pursuant to Rule 41(e)(2)(B), Rule 41(e)(2)(A) governs the time within which the electronically stored information must be seized after the issuance of the warrant and copied after the execution of the warrant, not the "later review of the media or information" seized, or the later off-site digital copying of that media.

c. Under Rule 41(f)(1)(B), the inventory return that is to be filed with the court may be limited to a description of the "physical storage media" into which the Search Warrant Data that was seized was placed, not an itemization of the information or data stored on the "physical storage media" into which the Search Warrant Data was placed;

d. Under Rule 41(f)(1)(B), the government may retain a copy of that information for purposes of the investigation. The government proposes that the original storage media on which the Search Warrant Data was placed plus a full image copy of the seized Search Warrant Data be retained by the government.

e. If the person from whom any Search Warrant Data was seized requests the return of any information in the Search Warrant Data that is not set forth in Attachment B, Section II, that information will be copied onto appropriate media and returned to the person from whom the information was seized.

SEALED

Office of the United States Attorney
District of Nevada
501 Las Vegas Boulevard, Suite 1100
Las Vegas, Nevada 89101
(702) 388-6336

Attachment "A1"

Property to Be Searched

This warrant applies to information associated with the Instagram user IDs **stephenpaddock47**, that is stored at premises owned, maintained, controlled, or operated by Facebook, a company headquartered in Menlo Park, California for the time period beginning September 1, 2016 to present.

ATTACHMENT "B"

Particular Things to be Seized

I. **Information to be disclosed by Facebook**

To the extent that the information described in Attachment A is within the possession, custody, or control of Instagram LLC ("Instagram"), including any messages, records, files, logs, or information that have been deleted but are still available to Instagram, or have been preserved pursuant to a request made under 18 U.S.C. § 2703(f) on October 3, 2017. Facebook is required to disclose the following information to the government for each user IDs listed in Attachment A for the period of September 1, 2016 to present:

(a) All contact and personal identifying information, including: full name, user identification number, birth date, gender, contact e-mail addresses, Instagram passwords, Instagram security questions and answers, physical address (including city, state, and zip code), telephone numbers, screen names, websites, and other personal identifiers;

(b) All activity logs for the account and all other documents showing the user's posts and other Instagram activities;

(c) All photos and videos uploaded by that user ID and all photos and videos uploaded by any user that have that user tagged in them;

(d) All profile information; status updates; links to videos, photographs, bios, articles, and other items; Wall postings; friend lists, including the friends' Instagram user identification numbers; future and past event postings; comments; and tags;

(e) All other records of communications and messages made or received by the user, chat history, and pending "Friend" requests;

(f) All user content created, uploaded, or shared by the account, including any comments made by the account on photographs or other content;

(g) All IP logs, including all records of the IP addresses that logged into the account;

(h) All records of the account's usage of the "Like" feature, including all Instagram posts and content that the user has "liked";

(i) All location data associated with the account, including geotags;

(j) All data and information that has been deleted by the user;

(k) All past and present lists of friends created by the account;

(l) All records of Instagram searches performed by the account;

(m) The types of service utilized by the user;

(n) The length of service (including start date) and the means and source of any payments associated with the service (including any credit card or bank account number);

(o) All privacy settings and other account settings, including privacy settings for individual Instagram posts and activities, and all records showing which Instagram users have been blocked by the account;

(p) All records pertaining to communications between Instagram and any person regarding the user or the user's Instagram account, including contacts with support services and records of actions taken.

(q) All information regarding the particular device or devices used to login to or access the account, including all device identifier information or cookie information, including all information about the particular device or devices used to access the account and the date and time of those accesses;

II.   Information to be seized by the government

All information described above in Section I that constitutes fruits, evidence, and instrumentalities of violations of:

> Violation of National Firearms Act – Registration of Firearms, Title 26, United States Code, Section 5841.

involving STEPHEN PADDOCK and others yet unidentified, including, for each user ID identified on Attachment "A," information pertaining to the following matters:

(a) Evidence showing the possession, use, purchase, or sale of firearms, firearms accessories, ammunition, or explosives by Paddock, including through conspiring and cooperating to possess, use, purchase, or sell prohibited firearms, firearms accessories, ammunition, or explosives.

(b) Evidence indicating how and when the Instagram account was accessed or used, to determine the chronological and geographic context of account access, use, and events relating to the crime under investigation and to the Facebook account owner;

(c) Evidence indicating the Instagram account owner's state of mind as it relates to the crime under investigation;

(d) The identity of the person(s) who created or used the user ID, including records that help reveal the whereabouts of such person(s).

(e) The identity of the person(s) who communicated with the user ID about matters relating to the illegal possession, purchase, use, or sale of firearms, firearms accessories, ammunition, or explosives, including records that help reveal their whereabouts.

The Warrant expressly incorporates the Affidavit submitted in support of the Warrant, and separately sealed, as though set forth fully herein.

ATTACHMENT C

PROTOCOL FOR SEARCHING THE ELECTRONIC DATA SEIZED

PURSUANT TO THIS SEARCH WARRANT

1. In executing this warrant, the government must make reasonable efforts to use methods and procedures that will locate and expose in the electronic data produced in response to this search warrant ("the Search Warrant Data") those categories of data, files, documents, or other electronically stored information that are identified with particularity in the warrant, while minimizing exposure or examination of irrelevant, privileged, or confidential files to the extent reasonably practicable.

2. When the Search Warrant Data is received, the government will make a duplicate copy of the Search Warrant Data ("the Search Warrant Data Copy"). The original version of the Search Warrant Data will be sealed and preserved for purposes of: later judicial review or order to return or dispose of the Search Warrant Data; production to the defense in any criminal case if authorized by statute, rule, or the Constitution; for purposes of showing the chain of custody of the Search Warrant Data and the Search Warrant Data Copy; or for any other lawful purpose. The original of the Search Warrant Data will not be searched or examined except to ensure that it has been fully and completely replicated in the Search Warrant Data Copy.

3. The investigating agents will then search the entirety of the Search Warrant Data Copy using any and all methods and procedures deemed appropriate by the United States designed to identify the information listed as Information to be Seized in Attachment B, Section II. The United States may copy, extract or otherwise segregate information or data listed as Information to be Seized in Attachment B, Section II. Information or data so copied, extracted or otherwise segregated will no longer be subject to any handling restrictions that might be set out in this protocol beyond those required by binding law. To the extent evidence of crimes not within the scope of this warrant appear in plain view during this review, a supplemental or "piggyback" warrant will be applied for in order to further search that document, data, or other item.

4. The Government will have ninety (90) days from receipt of the data disclosed under Attachment B, Section I to complete its examination of the Search Warrant Data Copy. Once the Search Warrant Data Copy has been thoroughly and completely examined for any document, data, or other items identified in Attachment B, Section II as Information to be Seized, the Search Warrant Data Copy will be sealed and not subject to any further search or examination unless authorized by another search warrant or other appropriate court order. The Search Warrant Data Copy will be held and preserved for the same purposes identified above in Paragraph 2.

5. The search procedures utilized for this review are at the sole discretion of the investigating and prosecuting authorities, and may include the following techniques (the following is a non-exclusive list, as other search procedures may be used):

a. examination of all of the data contained in the Search Warrant Data to view the data and determine whether that data falls within the items to be seized as set forth herein;

b. searching for and attempting to recover from the Search Warrant Data any deleted, hidden, or encrypted data to determine whether that data falls within the list of items to be seized as set forth herein (any data that is encrypted and unreadable will not be returned unless law enforcement personnel have determined that the data is not (1) an instrumentality of the offenses, (2) a fruit of the criminal activity, (3) contraband, (4) otherwise unlawfully possessed, or (5) evidence of the offenses specified above);

c. surveying various file directories and the individual files they contain;

d. opening files in order to determine their contents;.

e. using hash values to narrow the scope of what may be found. Hash values are under-inclusive, but are still a helpful tool;

f. scanning storage areas;

g. performing keyword searches through all electronic storage areas to determine whether occurrences of language contained in such storage areas exist that are likely to appear in the evidence described in Attachment A; and/or

h. performing any other data analysis technique that may be necessary to locate and retrieve the evidence described in Attachment B, Section II.

Return and Review Procedures

6. Rule 41 of the Federal Rules of Criminal Procedure provides, in relevant part:

(e) Issuing the Warrant.

(2) Contents of the Warrant.

(A) Warrant to Search for and Seize a Person or Property. Except for a tracking-device warrant, the warrant must identify the person or property to be searched, identify any person or property to be seized, and designate the magistrate judge to whom it must be returned. The warrant must command the officer to:

(i) execute the warrant within a specified time no longer than 14 days;

(B) Warrant Seeking Electronically Stored Information. A warrant under Rule 41(e)(2)(A) may authorize the seizure of electronic storage media or the seizure or copying of electronically stored information. Unless otherwise specified, the warrant authorizes a later review of the media or information consistent with the warrant. The time for executing the warrant in Rule 41(e)(2)(A) and

(f)(1)(A) refers to the seizure or on-site copying of the media or information, and not to any later off-site copying or review.

(f) Executing and Returning the Warrant.

(1) Warrant to Search for and Seize a Person or Property.

(B) Inventory. An officer present during the execution of the warrant must prepare and verify an inventory of any property seized. . . . In a case involving the seizure of electronic storage media or the seizure or copying of electronically stored information, the inventory may be limited to describing the physical storage media that were seized or copied. The officer may retain a copy of the electronically stored information that was seized or copied.

7. Pursuant to this Rule, the government understands and will act in accordance with the following:

a. Pursuant to Rule 41(e)(2)(A)(iii), within fourteen (14) days of the execution of the warrant, an agent is required to file an inventory return with the Court, that is, to file an itemized list of the property seized. Execution of the warrant begins when the United States serves the warrant on the named custodian; execution is complete when the custodian provides all Search Warrant Data to the United States. Within fourteen (14) days of completion of the execution of the warrant, the inventory will be filed.

b. Pursuant to Rule 41(e)(2)(B), Rule 41(e)(2)(A) governs the time within which the electronically stored information must be seized after the issuance of the warrant and copied after the execution of the warrant, not the "later review of the media or information" seized, or the later off-site digital copying of that media.

c. Under Rule 41(f)(1)(B), the inventory return that is to be filed with the court may be limited to a description of the "physical storage media" into which the Search Warrant Data that was seized was placed, not an itemization of the information or data stored on the "physical storage media" into which the Search Warrant Data was placed;

d. Under Rule 41(f)(1)(B), the government may retain a copy of that information for purposes of the investigation. The government proposes that the original storage media on which the Search Warrant Data was placed plus a full image copy of the seized Search Warrant Data be retained by the government.

e. If the person from whom any Search Warrant Data was seized requests the return of any information in the Search Warrant Data that is not set forth in Attachment B, Section II, that information will be copied onto appropriate media and returned to the person from whom the information was seized.

to search the subject premises for evidence and instrumentalities of the subject offenses, more fully described in Attachment "B" (attached hereto and incorporated herein by reference).

BACKGROUND OF INVESTIGATION

6. On the evening of Sunday, October 1, 2017, Route 91 Harvest, a music festival, was in progress at 3901 South Las Vegas Boulevard, Las Vegas, Nevada. At approximately 10:08 p.m., the Las Vegas Metropolitan Police Department (LVMPD) received calls reporting shots had been fired at the concert and multiple victims were struck (the "attack"). LVMPD determined the shots were coming from Rooms 134 and 135 on the 32nd floor of the Mandalay Bay Resort and Casino, located due west of the festival grounds at 3950 South Las Vegas Boulevard, Las Vegas, Nevada. These rooms are an elevated position which overlooks the concert venue. Witness statements and video footage captured during the attack indicates that the weapons being used were firing in a fully-automatic fashion.

7. LVMPD officers ultimately made entry into the room and located an individual later identified as Stephen Paddock. Paddock was deceased from an apparent self-inflicted gunshot wound.

8. Paddock's Nevada driver's license was located in the Mandalay Bay hotel room with Paddock, and both hotel rooms were registered in his name. A player's club card in name of Marilou Danley was located in Paddock's room, and the card returned to the address located on Babbling Brook Court in Mesquite, Nevada. FBI Agents located Danley, who was traveling outside the United States at the time of the shooting. It was ultimately determined that Danley resided with Paddock at the Babbling Brook address.

9. On October 2, 2017, local search warrants were obtained and executed on Paddock's Mandalay Bay hotel rooms, Paddock's vehicle parked in the Mandalay Bay parking

garage, and two Nevada residences owed by Paddock: 1372 Babbling Brook Court[1], and 1735 Del Webb Parkway, Reno, Nevada. Pursuant to those searches, Officers and Agents found over 20 firearms, hundreds of rounds of unfired ammunition (much of it in preloaded high-capacity magazines), range finding devices, several suitcases (some partially full of pre-loaded high capacity magazines) a set of body armor, an apparent homemade gas mask, and hundreds of spent cartridge cases in the Mandalay Bay hotel rooms, in close proximity to Paddock's body. Over a thousand rounds of rifle ammunition and a significant amount of explosive precursor material was found in Paddock's vehicle (specifically the binary explosive brand-named Tannerite). Additional explosive precursor material, approximately 18 firearms, and over 1,000 rounds of ammunition were located at the Mesquite residence. A large quantity of ammunition and multiple firearms were recovered from the Reno residence.

10. Immediately following the shooting, an extensive investigation was commenced which is currently being conducted jointly by LVMPD and the FBI, with the substantial support of numerous state, local and federal law enforcement agencies. As of this date, 58 people have been identified to have been killed in Paddock's attack and over 500 were reportedly injured. The preliminary reviews of the crime scenes in and around the Mandalay Bay led investigators to determine that in addition to firing upon the crowds at the festival grounds, Paddock also fired several high-caliber rifle shots at large fuel tanks within the property line of the McCarran International airport property. Multiple bullet impacts were located on the tank, which investigators believe was an attempt by Paddock to explode the tanks.

11. As the investigation progressed, investigators learned that Paddock planned the attack meticulously and took many methodical steps to avoid detection of his plot and to thwart the eventual law enforcement investigation that would follow. The steps included the apparent

---

[1] The search warrant for this location was approved by ▓▓▓▓▓▓▓▓▓▓▓▓▓▓▓▓▓▓▓▓▓▓▓▓. A copy of that search warrant is attached hereto as Exhibit 1.

destruction and/or concealment of digital storage media and the use of anonymously attributed communications devices. Based on your Affiant's training and experience, it is his belief that the methodical nature of the planning employed by Paddock, coupled with his efforts to undermine the preceding investigation, are factors indicative of a level of sophistication which is commonly found in mass casualty events such as this. However, your Affiant notes that this finding was not fully-developed in this case until several days into the investigation, after the subject premises had been searched in the hours immediately after the attack unfolded.

12. The investigation has also revealed that Paddock may have been treated for yet unidentified medical conditions, and that he spent significant time and expense prior to the attack purchasing and caching the weapons and other instrumentalities he used in the shooting. Some of these items included glass cutters, suitcases and a pre-paid cellular telephone. This cache included a substantial amount of ammunition, "Tannerite,"[2] glass cutters, numerous suitcases, and at least one identified pre-paid cellular telephone.

13. Investigators are currently conducting analysis of available financial records. To date, this analysis has revealed that Paddock made the purchases of items used in the attack throughout the last approximately 12 months. A large portion of the ammunition and firearms accessory purchases appear to have been made through Internet based retailers. Law enforcement continues to investigate the sourcing of purchases made by Paddock preceding the attack.

14. Subsequent to her identification as Paddock's companion and co-habitant at the subject premises, Marilou Danely returned to the United States and was thereafter voluntarily interviewed by law enforcement with her attorney present. During the interview, Danley corroborated much of what had been previously deduced by investigators, but she was adamant

---

[2] Tannerite is the brand name of a commercially available binary explosive commonly used as a reactive rifle target in shooting sports it can also be a precursor chemical for an improvised explosive devices.

that she had no prior inclination of Paddock intentions to conduct the attack. While investigators obtained a DNA buccal swab sample from Danley, she spontaneously stated that her fingerprints would likely be found on Paddock's ammunition because she occasionally participated in loading magazines. Danley has not been arrested and she has agreed to cooperate with investigators. Although, the investigation to date has not produced any conclusive evidence that Danley aided Paddock, had foreknowledge of his plans, or has been deceptive with law enforcement, this aspect of the investigation is still the subject of intensive review. Therefore, your Affiant asserts, for the purposes of this affidavit, that although there is currently no evidence to suggest criminal involvement by Danley, investigators are not yet prepared to rule this possibility out.

15. Investigators have reviewed the findings of the initial search of the subject premises and have determined that an additional, more exhaustive search is required. The proposed search would be focused on finding items of evidence or instrumentalities that may have been concealed inside or within the curtilage of the subject premises. In addition, the search will include a more thorough effort to identify any forensic trace evidence that may be located inside or within the curtilage of the subject premises.

PROBABLE CAUSE

16. Your Affiant believes that probable cause exists for this Court to authorize the proposed search, and that this probable cause is relatively unchanged from the probable cause that existed in the hour after the attack when the initial search was conducted. Additionally, information received from Danley during her interview and further investigation of the crime scene, as well as a fuller understanding of Paddock's mode of planning the attack, lead your Affiant to believe there is probable cause that additional evidence of the subject offenses may be located in the subject residence.

17. The primary identified resident of the subject premises, Stephen Paddock, is deceased and as such, no longer holds standing at 1372 Babbling Brook Court. Investigators are

currently unable to determine Danley's standing to provide consent to conduct this subsequent search. Therefore, although the FBI might already have all necessary authority to conduct the proposed search, your Affiant is seeking this search warrant out of an abundance of caution to be certain that any search conducted will comply with the Fourth Amendment and other applicable laws.

CONCLUSION

18. Based upon the aforementioned facts and circumstances, it is your Affiant's opinion that there is probable cause that the subject premises may contain evidence and instrumentalities concerning violations of the subject offenses herein. Your Affiant's training and experience provides the basis for his belief that a search of the subject premises will yield these items. As such, your Affiant seeks this Court's authorization to conduct a search of the subject premises as fully described in Attachment "A" for the items sought to be seized as described in Attachment "B."

Respectfully Submitted,

Christopher W. McPeak, Special Agent
Federal Bureau of Investigation

SWORN TO AND SUBSCRIBED
before me this 7th day of October, 2017.

HONORABLE NANCY J. KOPPE
UNITED STATES MAGISTRATE JUDGE

Attachment "A"

Description of Property/Premise to be Searched

1372 Babbling Brook Court
Mesquite, Clark County, Nevada

The subject premises is described as a one story, single family residence of apparent stucco frame construction. The premises are situated in the northeast corner Babbling Brook Court, which is a cul-de-sac. The premises faces approximately southwest and is located approximately 100 feet from the intersection of Babbling Brook Court and Cool Springs Lane. The residence is painted tan and the house numbers "1372" are affixed to the exterior wall facing the street.

Attachment "B"

Particular Items to be Seized

a. a thorough, microscopic examination and documentation of the subject premises to discover trace evidence, including but not limited to: fingerprints, blood, hair, fibers and other bodily fluid samples;

b. firearms to include handguns, shotguns and rifles, spent casings or live ammunition for the same, firearm accessories such as magazines or cylinders, firearm cleaning materials, and paperwork associated with the ownership of firearms;

c. United States and foreign currency, precious metals, jewelry, property deeds and other negotiable financial instruments including: stocks, bonds, securities, cashier's checks, money drafts, and letters of credit;

d. books, records, receipts, notes, ledgers, personal checks and other papers relating to the transportation, ordering, and purchase of firearms, firearms accessories, ammunition, explosives or explosives precursor materials, or material relating to any ideological extremism;

e. books, records, invoices, receipts, records of real estate transactions, bank statements and related records, gambling receipts and records, passbooks, money drafts, letters of credit, money orders, bank drafts, and cashier checks, bank checks, safe deposit box keys, money wrappers, and other items evidencing the obtaining, secreting, transfer, and/or concealment and /or expenditure of money;

f. any and all financial, credit card and bank account information including but not limited to bills and payment records, including those relating to the purchase of firearms, firearms accessories, ammunition, explosives, explosives precursor materials, body armor, range finding devices, scopes and other optical devices, glass cutters, and gas masks;

g. any and all records relating to the medical or psychological/psychiatric treatment of Stephen Paddock or Marilou Danley;

h. all types of safes and the contents thereof, including but not limited to, wall safes, floor safes, freestanding safes, locked strong boxes, and locked containers;

i. photographs, including still photos, negatives, video tapes, films, undeveloped film and the contents therein, slides;

j. cellular telephones address and/or telephone books, digital pagers, address and/or telephone books, Rolodex indices, electronic organizers, and papers reflecting names, addresses, telephone numbers, pager numbers, fax numbers, e-mail addresses, Facebook account information and other contact information related to co-conspirators, financial institutions, and other individuals or businesses with whom a financial relationship exists;

k. papers, tickets, notes, receipts, and other items relating to domestic and international travel.

l. any and all electronic storage devices, including: computer hard drives and external memory devices such as floppy disks, "thumb drives" (USB electronic storage drives), and compact disk "CD" and/or "DVD" storage devices.[3]

m. records evidencing occupancy or ownership of the premises described above, including, but not limited to, utility and telephone bills, mail envelopes, or addressed correspondence;

n. records or other items which evidence ownership or use of computer equipment found in the target location, including, but not limited to, sales receipts, bills for Internet access, and handwritten notes;

o. any and all records pertaining to the rental of self-storage units and post office boxes;

p. chemicals and other compounds which may constitute explosives or explosive precursors; and

q. improvised, commercial or military grade explosive devices, detonators, initiators, any components thereof, or any other weapon of mass destruction.

---

[3] Electronic equipment shall be seized, but not searched. Supplemental search warrant will be requested prior to the searching of seized electronic items.

EXHIBIT 1

SEALED

Office of the United States Attorney
District of Nevada
501 Las Vegas Boulevard, Suite 1100
Las Vegas, Nevada 89101
(702) 388-6336

AO 93 (Rev. 11/13) Search and Seizure Warrant

UNITED STATES DISTRICT COURT
for the
District of Nevada

In the Matter of the Search of)
(Briefly describe the property to be searched)
or identify the person by name and address))
)   Case No.   2:17-mj-473-NJK
1372 BABBLING BROOK COURT,)
MESQUITE, COUNTY OF CLARK, STATE OF NEVADA.)
)

SEARCH AND SEIZURE WARRANT

To: Any authorized law enforcement officer

An application by a federal law enforcement officer or an attorney for the government requests the search of the following person or property located in the _____ District of _____ Nevada *(identify the person or describe the property to be searched and give its location)*:

SEE ATTACHMENT A

I find that the affidavit(s), or any recorded testimony, establish probable cause to search and seize the person or property described above, and that such search will reveal *(identify the person or describe the property to be seized)*:

SEE ATTACHMENTS B

YOU ARE COMMANDED to execute this warrant on or before October 21, 2017 *(not to exceed 14 days)*
☒ in the daytime 6:00 a.m. to 10:00 p.m. ☐ at any time in the day or night because good cause has been established.

Unless delayed notice is authorized below, you must give a copy of the warrant and a receipt for the property taken to the person from whom, or from whose premises, the property was taken, or leave the copy and receipt at the place where the property was taken.

The officer executing this warrant, or an officer present during the execution of the warrant, must prepare an inventory as required by law and promptly return this warrant and inventory to _____
(United States Magistrate Judge)

☐ Pursuant to 18 U.S.C. § 3103a(b), I find that immediate notification may have an adverse result listed in 18 U.S.C. § 2705 (except for delay of trial), and authorize the officer executing this warrant to delay notice to the person who, or whose property, will be searched or seized *(check the appropriate box)*
☐ for _____ days *(not to exceed 30)* ☐ until, the facts justifying, the later specific date of _____

Date and time issued: 10/7/2017 6:45 pm

City and state: Las Vegas, Nevada

Judge's signature

Mary J. Koppe, US Magistrate Judge
Printed name and title

Attachment "A"

Description of Property/Premise to be Searched

1372 Babbling Brook Court
Mesquite, Clark County, Nevada

The subject premises is described as a one story, single family residence of apparent stucco frame construction. The premises are situated in the northeast corner Babbling Brook Court, which is a cul-de-sac. The premises faces approximately southwest and is located approximately 100 feet from the intersection of Babbling Brook Court and Cool Springs Lane. The residence is painted tan and the house numbers "1372" are affixed to the exterior wall facing the street.

Attachment "B"

Particular Items to be Seized

a. a thorough, microscopic examination and documentation of the subject premises to discover trace evidence, including but not limited to: fingerprints, blood, hair, fibers and other bodily fluid samples;

b. firearms to include handguns, shotguns and rifles, spent casings or live ammunition for the same, firearm accessories such as magazines or cylinders, firearm cleaning materials, and paperwork associated with the ownership of firearms;

c. United States and foreign currency, precious metals, jewelry, property deeds and other negotiable financial instruments including: stocks, bonds, securities, cashier's checks, money drafts, and letters of credit;

d. books, records, receipts, notes, ledgers, personal checks and other papers relating to the transportation, ordering, and purchase of firearms, firearms accessories, ammunition, explosives or explosives precursor materials, or material relating to any ideological extremism;

e. books, records, invoices, receipts, records of real estate transactions, bank statements and related records, gambling receipts and records, passbooks, money drafts, letters of credit, money orders, bank drafts, and cashier checks, bank checks, safe deposit box keys, money wrappers, and other items evidencing the obtaining, secreting, transfer, and/or concealment and /or expenditure of money;

f. any and all financial, credit card and bank account information including but not limited to bills and payment records, including those relating to the purchase of firearms, firearms accessories, ammunition, explosives, explosives precursor materials, body armor, range finding devices, scopes and other optical devices, glass cutters, and gas masks;

g. any and all records relating to the medical or psychological/psychiatric treatment of Stephen Paddock or Marilou Danley;

h. all types of safes and the contents thereof, including but not limited to, wall safes, floor safes, freestanding safes, locked strong boxes, and locked containers;

i. photographs, including still photos, negatives, video tapes, films, undeveloped film and the contents therein, slides;

j. cellular telephones address and/or telephone books, digital pagers, address and/or telephone books, Rolodex indices, electronic organizers, and papers reflecting names, addresses, telephone numbers, pager numbers, fax numbers, e-mail addresses, Facebook account information and other contact information related to co-conspirators, financial institutions, and other individuals or businesses with whom a financial relationship exists;

1

Attachment "A4"

Property to Be Searched

This warrant applies to information associated with the Instagram user IDs **mariloudanleypaddock**, that is stored at premises owned, maintained, controlled, or operated by Facebook, a company headquartered in Menlo Park, California for the time period beginning September 1, 2016 to present.

Attachment "A5"

Property to Be Searched

This warrant applies to information associated with the Instagram user IDs and **marilou.danley** that is stored at premises owned, maintained, controlled, or operated by Facebook, a company headquartered in Menlo Park, California for the time period beginning September 1, 2016 to present.

ATTACHMENT "B"

Particular Things to be Seized

I.   **Information to be disclosed by Facebook**

To the extent that the information described in Attachment A is within the possession, custody, or control of Instagram LLC ("Instagram"), including any messages, records, files, logs, or information that have been deleted but are still available to Instagram, or have been preserved pursuant to a request made under 18 U.S.C. § 2703(f) on October 3, 2017. Facebook is required to disclose the following information to the government for each user IDs listed in Attachment A for the period of September 1, 2016 to present:

(a) All contact and personal identifying information, including: full name, user identification number, birth date, gender, contact e-mail addresses, Instagram passwords, Instagram security questions and answers, physical address (including city, state, and zip code), telephone numbers, screen names, websites, and other personal identifiers;

(b) All activity logs for the account and all other documents showing the user's posts and other Instagram activities;

(c) All photos and videos uploaded by that user ID and all photos and videos uploaded by any user that have that user tagged in them;

(d) All profile information; status updates; links to videos, photographs, bios, articles, and other items; Wall postings; friend lists, including the friends' Instagram user identification numbers; future and past event postings; comments; and tags;

(e) All other records of communications and messages made or received by the user, chat history, and pending "Friend" requests;

(f) All user content created, uploaded, or shared by the account, including any comments made by the account on photographs or other content;

(g) All IP logs, including all records of the IP addresses that logged into the account;

(h) All records of the account's usage of the "Like" feature, including all Instagram posts and content that the user has "liked";

(i) All location data associated with the account, including geotags;

(j) All data and information that has been deleted by the user;

(k) All past and present lists of friends created by the account;

(l) All records of Instagram searches performed by the account;

(m) The types of service utilized by the user;

(n) The length of service (including start date) and the means and source of any payments associated with the service (including any credit card or bank account number);

(o) All privacy settings and other account settings, including privacy settings for individual Instagram posts and activities, and all records showing which Instagram users have been blocked by the account;

(p) All records pertaining to communications between Instagram and any person regarding the user or the user's Instagram account, including contacts with support services and records of actions taken.

(q) All information regarding the particular device or devices used to login to or access the account, including all device identifier information or cookie information, including all information about the particular device or devices used to access the account and the date and time of those accesses;

ATTACHMENT C

PROTOCOL FOR SEARCHING THE ELECTRONIC DATA SEIZED

PURSUANT TO THIS SEARCH WARRANT

1. In executing this warrant, the government must make reasonable efforts to use methods and procedures that will locate and expose in the electronic data produced in response to this search warrant ("the Search Warrant Data") those categories of data, files, documents, or other electronically stored information that are identified with particularity in the warrant, while minimizing exposure or examination of irrelevant, privileged, or confidential files to the extent reasonably practicable.

2. When the Search Warrant Data is received, the government will make a duplicate copy of the Search Warrant Data ("the Search Warrant Data Copy"). The original version of the Search Warrant Data will be sealed and preserved for purposes of: later judicial review or order to return or dispose of the Search Warrant Data; production to the defense in any criminal case if authorized by statute, rule, or the Constitution; for purposes of showing the chain of custody of the Search Warrant Data and the Search Warrant Data Copy; or for any other lawful purpose. The original of the Search Warrant Data will not be searched or examined except to ensure that it has been fully and completely replicated in the Search Warrant Data Copy.

3. The investigating agents will then search the entirety of the Search Warrant Data Copy using any and all methods and procedures deemed appropriate by the United States designed to identify the information listed as Information to be Seized in Attachment B, Section II. The United States may copy, extract or otherwise segregate information or data listed as Information to be Seized in Attachment B, Section II. Information or data so copied, extracted or otherwise segregated will no longer be subject to any handling restrictions that might be set out in this protocol beyond those required by binding law. To the extent evidence of crimes not within the scope of this warrant appear in plain view during this review, a supplemental or "piggyback" warrant will be applied for in order to further search that document, data, or other item.

4. The Government will have ninety (90) days from receipt of the data disclosed under Attachment B, Section I to complete its examination of the Search Warrant Data Copy. Once the Search Warrant Data Copy has been thoroughly and completely examined for any document, data, or other items identified in Attachment B, Section II as Information to be Seized, the Search Warrant Data Copy will be sealed and not subject to any further search or examination unless authorized by another search warrant or other appropriate court order. The Search Warrant Data Copy will be held and preserved for the same purposes identified above in Paragraph 2.

5. The search procedures utilized for this review are at the sole discretion of the investigating and prosecuting authorities, and may include the following techniques (the following is a non-exclusive list, as other search procedures may be used):

a. examination of all of the data contained in the Search Warrant Data to view the data and determine whether that data falls within the items to be seized as set forth herein;

b. searching for and attempting to recover from the Search Warrant Data any deleted, hidden, or encrypted data to determine whether that data falls within the list of items to be seized as set forth herein (any data that is encrypted and unreadable will not be returned unless law enforcement personnel have determined that the data is not (1) an instrumentality of the offenses, (2) a fruit of the criminal activity, (3) contraband, (4) otherwise unlawfully possessed, or (5) evidence of the offenses specified above);

c. surveying various file directories and the individual files they contain;

d. opening files in order to determine their contents;

e. using hash values to narrow the scope of what may be found. Hash values are under-inclusive, but are still a helpful tool;

f. scanning storage areas;

g. performing keyword searches through all electronic storage areas to determine whether occurrences of language contained in such storage areas exist that are likely to appear in the evidence described in Attachment A; and/or

h. performing any other data analysis technique that may be necessary to locate and retrieve the evidence described in Attachment B, Section II.

Return and Review Procedures

6. Rule 41 of the Federal Rules of Criminal Procedure provides, in relevant part:

(e) Issuing the Warrant.

(2) Contents of the Warrant.

(A) Warrant to Search for and Seize a Person or Property. Except for a tracking-device warrant, the warrant must identify the person or property to be searched, identify any person or property to be seized, and designate the magistrate judge to whom it must be returned. The warrant must command the officer to:

(i) execute the warrant within a specified time no longer than 14 days;

(B) Warrant Seeking Electronically Stored Information. A warrant under Rule 41(e)(2)(A) may authorize the seizure of electronic storage media or the seizure or copying of electronically stored information. Unless otherwise specified, the warrant authorizes a later review of the media or information consistent with the warrant. The time for executing the warrant in Rule 41(e)(2)(A) and

(f)(1)(A) refers to the seizure or on-site copying of the media or information, and not to any later off-site copying or review.

(f) Executing and Returning the Warrant.

(1) Warrant to Search for and Seize a Person or Property.

(B) Inventory. An officer present during the execution of the warrant must prepare and verify an inventory of any property seized. . . . In a case involving the seizure of electronic storage media or the seizure or copying of electronically stored information, the inventory may be limited to describing the physical storage media that were seized or copied. The officer may retain a copy of the electronically stored information that was seized or copied.

7. Pursuant to this Rule, the government understands and will act in accordance with the following:

a. Pursuant to Rule 41(e)(2)(A)(iii), within fourteen (14) days of the execution of the warrant, an agent is required to file an inventory return with the Court, that is, to file an itemized list of the property seized. Execution of the warrant begins when the United States serves the warrant on the named custodian; execution is complete when the custodian provides all Search Warrant Data to the United States. Within fourteen (14) days of completion of the execution of the warrant, the inventory will be filed.

b. Pursuant to Rule 41(e)(2)(B), Rule 41(e)(2)(A) governs the time within which the electronically stored information must be seized after the issuance of the warrant and copied after the execution of the warrant, not the "later review of the media or information" seized, or the later off-site digital copying of that media.

c. Under Rule 41(f)(1)(B), the inventory return that is to be filed with the court may be limited to a description of the "physical storage media" into which the Search Warrant Data that was seized was placed, not an itemization of the information or data stored on the "physical storage media" into which the Search Warrant Data was placed;

d. Under Rule 41(f)(1)(B), the government may retain a copy of that information for purposes of the investigation. The government proposes that the original storage media on which the Search Warrant Data was placed plus a full image copy of the seized Search Warrant Data be retained by the government.

e. If the person from whom any Search Warrant Data was seized requests the return of any information in the Search Warrant Data that is not set forth in Attachment B, Section II, that information will be copied onto appropriate media and returned to the person from whom the information was seized.

SEALED

Office of the United States Attorney
District of Nevada
501 Las Vegas Boulevard, Suite 1100
Las Vegas, Nevada 89101
(702) 388-6336

Attachment "A1"

Property to Be Searched

This warrant applies to information associated with the Instagram user IDs **stephenpaddock47**, that is stored at premises owned, maintained, controlled, or operated by Facebook, a company headquartered in Menlo Park, California for the time period beginning September 1, 2016 to present.

ATTACHMENT "B"

Particular Things to be Seized

I. Information to be disclosed by Facebook

To the extent that the information described in Attachment A is within the possession, custody, or control of Instagram LLC ("Instagram"), including any messages, records, files, logs, or information that have been deleted but are still available to Instagram, or have been preserved pursuant to a request made under 18 U.S.C. § 2703(f) on October 3, 2017. Facebook is required to disclose the following information to the government for each user IDs listed in Attachment A for the period of September 1, 2016 to present:

(a) All contact and personal identifying information, including: full name, user identification number, birth date, gender, contact e-mail addresses, Instagram passwords, Instagram security questions and answers, physical address (including city, state, and zip code), telephone numbers, screen names, websites, and other personal identifiers;

(b) All activity logs for the account and all other documents showing the user's posts and other Instagram activities;

(c) All photos and videos uploaded by that user ID and all photos and videos uploaded by any user that have that user tagged in them;

(d) All profile information; status updates; links to videos, photographs, bios, articles, and other items; Wall postings; friend lists, including the friends' Instagram user identification numbers; future and past event postings; comments; and tags;

(e) All other records of communications and messages made or received by the user, chat history, and pending "Friend" requests;

(f) All user content created, uploaded, or shared by the account, including any comments made by the account on photographs or other content;

(g) All IP logs, including all records of the IP addresses that logged into the account;

(h) All records of the account's usage of the "Like" feature, including all Instagram posts and content that the user has "liked";

(i) All location data associated with the account, including geotags;

(j) All data and information that has been deleted by the user;

(k) All past and present lists of friends created by the account;

(l) All records of Instagram searches performed by the account;

(m) The types of service utilized by the user;

(n) The length of service (including start date) and the means and source of any payments associated with the service (including any credit card or bank account number);

(o) All privacy settings and other account settings, including privacy settings for individual Instagram posts and activities, and all records showing which Instagram users have been blocked by the account;

(p) All records pertaining to communications between Instagram and any person regarding the user or the user's Instagram account, including contacts with support services and records of actions taken.

(q) All information regarding the particular device or devices used to login to or access the account, including all device identifier information or cookie information, including all information about the particular device or devices used to access the account and the date and time of those accesses;

II. Information to be seized by the government

All information described above in Section I that constitutes fruits, evidence, and instrumentalities of violations of:

Violation of National Firearms Act – Registration of Firearms, Title 26, United States Code, Section 5841.

involving STEPHEN PADDOCK and others yet unidentified, including, for each user ID identified on Attachment "A," information pertaining to the following matters:

(a) Evidence showing the possession, use, purchase, or sale of firearms, firearms accessories, ammunition, or explosives by Paddock, including through conspiring and cooperating to possess, use, purchase, or sell prohibited firearms, firearms accessories, ammunition, or explosives.

(b) Evidence indicating how and when the Instagram account was accessed or used, to determine the chronological and geographic context of account access, use, and events relating to the crime under investigation and to the Facebook account owner;

(c) Evidence indicating the Instagram account owner's state of mind as it relates to the crime under investigation;

(d) The identity of the person(s) who created or used the user ID, including records that help reveal the whereabouts of such person(s).

(e) The identity of the person(s) who communicated with the user ID about matters relating to the illegal possession, purchase, use, or sale of firearms, firearms accessories, ammunition, or explosives, including records that help reveal their whereabouts.

The Warrant expressly incorporates the Affidavit submitted in support of the Warrant, and separately sealed, as though set forth fully herein.

ATTACHMENT C

PROTOCOL FOR SEARCHING THE ELECTRONIC DATA SEIZED

PURSUANT TO THIS SEARCH WARRANT

1. In executing this warrant, the government must make reasonable efforts to use methods and procedures that will locate and expose in the electronic data produced in response to this search warrant ("the Search Warrant Data") those categories of data, files, documents, or other electronically stored information that are identified with particularity in the warrant, while minimizing exposure or examination of irrelevant, privileged, or confidential files to the extent reasonably practicable.

2. When the Search Warrant Data is received, the government will make a duplicate copy of the Search Warrant Data ("the Search Warrant Data Copy"). The original version of the Search Warrant Data will be sealed and preserved for purposes of: later judicial review or order to return or dispose of the Search Warrant Data; production to the defense in any criminal case if authorized by statute, rule, or the Constitution; for purposes of showing the chain of custody of the Search Warrant Data and the Search Warrant Data Copy; or for any other lawful purpose. The original of the Search Warrant Data will not be searched or examined except to ensure that it has been fully and completely replicated in the Search Warrant Data Copy.

3. The investigating agents will then search the entirety of the Search Warrant Data Copy using any and all methods and procedures deemed appropriate by the United States designed to identify the information listed as Information to be Seized in Attachment B, Section II. The United States may copy, extract or otherwise segregate information or data listed as Information to be Seized in Attachment B, Section II. Information or data so copied, extracted or otherwise segregated will no longer be subject to any handling restrictions that might be set out in this protocol beyond those required by binding law. To the extent evidence of crimes not within the scope of this warrant appear in plain view during this review, a supplemental or "piggyback" warrant will be applied for in order to further search that document, data, or other item.

4. The Government will have ninety (90) days from receipt of the data disclosed under Attachment B, Section I to complete its examination of the Search Warrant Data Copy. Once the Search Warrant Data Copy has been thoroughly and completely examined for any document, data, or other items identified in Attachment B, Section II as Information to be Seized, the Search Warrant Data Copy will be sealed and not subject to any further search or examination unless authorized by another search warrant or other appropriate court order. The Search Warrant Data Copy will be held and preserved for the same purposes identified above in Paragraph 2.

5. The search procedures utilized for this review are at the sole discretion of the investigating and prosecuting authorities, and may include the following techniques (the following is a non-exclusive list, as other search procedures may be used):

a. examination of all of the data contained in the Search Warrant Data to view the data and determine whether that data falls within the items to be seized as set forth herein;

b. searching for and attempting to recover from the Search Warrant Data any deleted, hidden, or encrypted data to determine whether that data falls within the list of items to be seized as set forth herein (any data that is encrypted and unreadable will not be returned unless law enforcement personnel have determined that the data is not (1) an instrumentality of the offenses, (2) a fruit of the criminal activity, (3) contraband, (4) otherwise unlawfully possessed, or (5) evidence of the offenses specified above);

c. surveying various file directories and the individual files they contain;

d. opening files in order to determine their contents;

e. using hash values to narrow the scope of what may be found. Hash values are under-inclusive, but are still a helpful tool;

f. scanning storage areas;

g. performing keyword searches through all electronic storage areas to determine whether occurrences of language contained in such storage areas exist that are likely to appear in the evidence described in Attachment A; and/or

h. performing any other data analysis technique that may be necessary to locate and retrieve the evidence described in Attachment B, Section II.

Return and Review Procedures

6. Rule 41 of the Federal Rules of Criminal Procedure provides, in relevant part:

(e) Issuing the Warrant.

(2) Contents of the Warrant.

(A) Warrant to Search for and Seize a Person or Property. Except for a tracking-device warrant, the warrant must identify the person or property to be searched, identify any person or property to be seized, and designate the magistrate judge to whom it must be returned. The warrant must command the officer to:

(i) execute the warrant within a specified time no longer than 14 days;

(B) Warrant Seeking Electronically Stored Information. A warrant under Rule 41(e)(2)(A) may authorize the seizure of electronic storage media or the seizure or copying of electronically stored information. Unless otherwise specified, the warrant authorizes a later review of the media or information consistent with the warrant. The time for executing the warrant in Rule 41(e)(2)(A) and

(f)(1)(A) refers to the seizure or on-site copying of the media or information, and not to any later off-site copying or review.

(f) Executing and Returning the Warrant.

(1) Warrant to Search for and Seize a Person or Property.

(B) Inventory. An officer present during the execution of the warrant must prepare and verify an inventory of any property seized. . . . In a case involving the seizure of electronic storage media or the seizure or copying of electronically stored information, the inventory may be limited to describing the physical storage media that were seized or copied. The officer may retain a copy of the electronically stored information that was seized or copied.

7. Pursuant to this Rule, the government understands and will act in accordance with the following:

a. Pursuant to Rule 41(e)(2)(A)(iii), within fourteen (14) days of the execution of the warrant, an agent is required to file an inventory return with the Court, that is, to file an itemized list of the property seized. Execution of the warrant begins when the United States serves the warrant on the named custodian; execution is complete when the custodian provides all Search Warrant Data to the United States. Within fourteen (14) days of completion of the execution of the warrant, the inventory will be filed.

b. Pursuant to Rule 41(e)(2)(B), Rule 41(e)(2)(A) governs the time within which the electronically stored information must be seized after the issuance of the warrant and copied after the execution of the warrant, not the "later review of the media or information" seized, or the later off-site digital copying of that media.

c. Under Rule 41(f)(1)(B), the inventory return that is to be filed with the court may be limited to a description of the "physical storage media" into which the Search Warrant Data that was seized was placed, not an itemization of the information or data stored on the "physical storage media" into which the Search Warrant Data was placed;

d. Under Rule 41(f)(1)(B), the government may retain a copy of that information for purposes of the investigation. The government proposes that the original storage media on which the Search Warrant Data was placed plus a full image copy of the seized Search Warrant Data be retained by the government.

e. If the person from whom any Search Warrant Data was seized requests the return of any information in the Search Warrant Data that is not set forth in Attachment B, Section II, that information will be copied onto appropriate media and returned to the person from whom the information was seized.

to search the subject premises for evidence and instrumentalities of the subject offenses, more fully described in Attachment "B" (attached hereto and incorporated herein by reference).

BACKGROUND OF INVESTIGATION

6. On the evening of Sunday, October 1, 2017, Route 91 Harvest, a music festival, was in progress at 3901 South Las Vegas Boulevard, Las Vegas, Nevada. At approximately 10:08 p.m., the Las Vegas Metropolitan Police Department (LVMPD) received calls reporting shots had been fired at the concert and multiple victims were struck (the "attack"). LVMPD determined the shots were coming from Rooms 134 and 135 on the 32nd floor of the Mandalay Bay Resort and Casino, located due west of the festival grounds at 3950 South Las Vegas Boulevard, Las Vegas, Nevada. These rooms are an elevated position which overlooks the concert venue. Witness statements and video footage captured during the attack indicates that the weapons being used were firing in a fully-automatic fashion.

7. LVMPD officers ultimately made entry into the room and located an individual later identified as Stephen Paddock. Paddock was deceased from an apparent self-inflicted gunshot wound.

8. Paddock's Nevada driver's license was located in the Mandalay Bay hotel room with Paddock, and both hotel rooms were registered in his name. A player's club card in name of Marilou Danley was located in Paddock's room, and the card returned to the address located on Babbling Brook Court in Mesquite, Nevada. FBI Agents located Danley, who was traveling outside the United States at the time of the shooting. It was ultimately determined that Danley resided with Paddock at the Babbling Brook address.

9. On October 2, 2017, local search warrants were obtained and executed on Paddock's Mandalay Bay hotel rooms, Paddock's vehicle parked in the Mandalay Bay parking

garage, and two Nevada residences owed by Paddock: 1372 Babbling Brook Court[1], and 1735 Del Webb Parkway, Reno, Nevada. Pursuant to those searches, Officers and Agents found over 20 firearms, hundreds of rounds of unfired ammunition (much of it in preloaded high-capacity magazines), range finding devices, several suitcases (some partially full of pre-loaded high capacity magazines) a set of body armor, an apparent homemade gas mask, and hundreds of spent cartridge cases in the Mandalay Bay hotel rooms, in close proximity to Paddock's body. Over a thousand rounds of rifle ammunition and a significant amount of explosive precursor material was found in Paddock's vehicle (specifically the binary explosive brand-named Tannerite). Additional explosive precursor material, approximately 18 firearms, and over 1,000 rounds of ammunition were located at the Mesquite residence. A large quantity of ammunition and multiple firearms were recovered from the Reno residence.

10. Immediately following the shooting, an extensive investigation was commenced which is currently being conducted jointly by LVMPD and the FBI, with the substantial support of numerous state, local and federal law enforcement agencies. As of this date, 58 people have been identified to have been killed in Paddock's attack and over 500 were reportedly injured. The preliminary reviews of the crime scenes in and around the Mandalay Bay led investigators to determine that in addition to firing upon the crowds at the festival grounds, Paddock also fired several high-caliber rifle shots at large fuel tanks within the property line of the McCarran International airport property. Multiple bullet impacts were located on the tank, which investigators believe was an attempt by Paddock to explode the tanks.

11. As the investigation progressed, investigators learned that Paddock planned the attack meticulously and took many methodical steps to avoid detection of his plot and to thwart the eventual law enforcement investigation that would follow. The steps included the apparent

---

[1] The search warrant for this location was approved by ▓▓▓▓▓▓▓▓▓▓▓▓▓▓▓▓. A copy of that search warrant is attached hereto as Exhibit 1.

destruction and/or concealment of digital storage media and the use of anonymously attributed communications devices. Based on your Affiant's training and experience, it is his belief that the methodical nature of the planning employed by Paddock, coupled with his efforts to undermine the preceding investigation, are factors indicative of a level of sophistication which is commonly found in mass casualty events such as this. However, your Affiant notes that this finding was not fully-developed in this case until several days into the investigation, after the subject premises had been searched in the hours immediately after the attack unfolded.

12. The investigation has also revealed that Paddock may have been treated for yet unidentified medical conditions, and that he spent significant time and expense prior to the attack purchasing and caching the weapons and other instrumentalities he used in the shooting. Some of these items included glass cutters, suitcases and a pre-paid cellular telephone. This cache included a substantial amount of ammunition, "Tannerite,"[2] glass cutters, numerous suitcases, and at least one identified pre-paid cellular telephone.

13. Investigators are currently conducting analysis of available financial records. To date, this analysis has revealed that Paddock made the purchases of items used in the attack throughout the last approximately 12 months. A large portion of the ammunition and firearms accessory purchases appear to have been made through Internet based retailers. Law enforcement continues to investigate the sourcing of purchases made by Paddock preceding the attack.

14. Subsequent to her identification as Paddock's companion and co-habitant at the subject premises, Marilou Danely returned to the United States and was thereafter voluntarily interviewed by law enforcement with her attorney present. During the interview, Danley corroborated much of what had been previously deduced by investigators, but she was adamant

---

[2] Tannerite is the brand name of a commercially available binary explosive commonly used as a reactive rifle target. in shooting sports it can also be a precursor chemical for an improvised explosive devices.

that she had no prior inclination of Paddock intentions to conduct the attack. While investigators obtained a DNA buccal swab sample from Danley, she spontaneously stated that her fingerprints would likely be found on Paddock's ammunition because she occasionally participated in loading magazines. Danley has not been arrested and she has agreed to cooperate with investigators. Although, the investigation to date has not produced any conclusive evidence that Danley aided Paddock, had foreknowledge of his plans, or has been deceptive with law enforcement, this aspect of the investigation is still the subject of intensive review. Therefore, your Affiant asserts, for the purposes of this affidavit, that although there is currently no evidence to suggest criminal involvement by Danley, investigators are not yet prepared to rule this possibility out.

15. Investigators have reviewed the findings of the initial search of the subject premises and have determined that an additional, more exhaustive search is required. The proposed search would be focused on finding items of evidence or instrumentalities that may have been concealed inside or within the curtilage of the subject premises. In addition, the search will include a more thorough effort to identify any forensic trace evidence that may be located inside or within the curtilage of the subject premises.

PROBABLE CAUSE

16. Your Affiant believes that probable cause exists for this Court to authorize the proposed search, and that this probable cause is relatively unchanged from the probable cause that existed in the hour after the attack when the initial search was conducted. Additionally, information received from Danley during her interview and further investigation of the crime scene, as well as a fuller understanding of Paddock's mode of planning the attack, lead your Affiant to believe there is probable cause that additional evidence of the subject offenses may be located in the subject residence.

17. The primary identified resident of the subject premises, Stephen Paddock, is deceased and as such, no longer holds standing at 1372 Babbling Brook Court. Investigators are

currently unable to determine Danley's standing to provide consent to conduct this subsequent search. Therefore, although the FBI might already have all necessary authority to conduct the proposed search, your Affiant is seeking this search warrant out of an abundance of caution to be certain that any search conducted will comply with the Fourth Amendment and other applicable laws.

CONCLUSION

18. Based upon the aforementioned facts and circumstances, it is your Affiant's opinion that there is probable cause that the subject premises may contain evidence and instrumentalities concerning violations of the subject offenses herein. Your Affiant's training and experience provides the basis for his belief that a search of the subject premises will yield these items. As such, your Affiant seeks this Court's authorization to conduct a search of the subject premises as fully described in Attachment "A" for the items sought to be seized as described in Attachment "B."

Respectfully Submitted,

Christopher W. McPeak, Special Agent
Federal Bureau of Investigation

SWORN TO AND SUBSCRIBED
before me this 7th day of October, 2017.

HONORABLE NANCY J. KOPPE
UNITED STATES MAGISTRATE JUDGE

Attachment "A"

Description of Property/Premise to be Searched

1372 Babbling Brook Court
Mesquite, Clark County, Nevada

The subject premises is described as a one story, single family residence of apparent stucco frame construction. The premises are situated in the northeast corner Babbling Brook Court, which is a cul-de-sac. The premises faces approximately southwest and is located approximately 100 feet from the intersection of Babbling Brook Court and Cool Springs Lane. The residence is painted tan and the house numbers "1372" are affixed to the exterior wall facing the street.

Attachment "B"

Particular Items to be Seized

a. a thorough, microscopic examination and documentation of the subject premises to discover trace evidence, including but not limited to: fingerprints, blood, hair, fibers and other bodily fluid samples;

b. firearms to include handguns, shotguns and rifles, spent casings or live ammunition for the same, firearm accessories such as magazines or cylinders, firearm cleaning materials, and paperwork associated with the ownership of firearms;

c. United States and foreign currency, precious metals, jewelry, property deeds and other negotiable financial instruments including: stocks, bonds, securities, cashier's checks, money drafts, and letters of credit;

d. books, records, receipts, notes, ledgers, personal checks and other papers relating to the transportation, ordering, and purchase of firearms, firearms accessories, ammunition, explosives or explosives precursor materials, or material relating to any ideological extremism;

e. books, records, invoices, receipts, records of real estate transactions, bank statements and related records, gambling receipts and records, passbooks, money drafts, letters of credit, money orders, bank drafts, and cashier checks, bank checks, safe deposit box keys, money wrappers, and other items evidencing the obtaining, secreting, transfer, and/or concealment and /or expenditure of money;

f. any and all financial, credit card and bank account information including but not limited to bills and payment records, including those relating to the purchase of firearms, firearms accessories, ammunition, explosives, explosives precursor materials, body armor, range finding devices, scopes and other optical devices, glass cutters, and gas masks;

g. any and all records relating to the medical or psychological/psychiatric treatment of Stephen Paddock or Marilou Danley;

h. all types of safes and the contents thereof, including but not limited to, wall safes, floor safes, freestanding safes, locked strong boxes, and locked containers;

i. photographs, including still photos, negatives, video tapes, films, undeveloped film and the contents therein, slides;

j. cellular telephones address and/or telephone books, digital pagers, address and/or telephone books, Rolodex indices, electronic organizers, and papers reflecting names, addresses, telephone numbers, pager numbers, fax numbers, e-mail addresses, Facebook account information and other contact information related to co-conspirators, financial institutions, and other individuals or businesses with whom a financial relationship exists;

k. papers, tickets, notes, receipts, and other items relating to domestic and international travel.

l. any and all electronic storage devices, including: computer hard drives and external memory devices such as floppy disks, "thumb drives" (USB electronic storage drives), and compact disk "CD" and/or "DVD" storage devices.[3]

m. records evidencing occupancy or ownership of the premises described above, including, but not limited to, utility and telephone bills, mail envelopes, or addressed correspondence;

n. records or other items which evidence ownership or use of computer equipment found in the target location, including, but not limited to, sales receipts, bills for Internet access, and handwritten notes;

o. any and all records pertaining to the rental of self-storage units and post office boxes;

p. chemicals and other compounds which may constitute explosives or explosive precursors; and

q. improvised, commercial or military grade explosive devices, detonators, initiators, any components thereof, or any other weapon of mass destruction.

---

[3] Electronic equipment shall be seized, but not searched. Supplemental search warrant will be requested prior to the searching of seized electronic items.

EXHIBIT 1

SEALED

Office of the United States Attorney
District of Nevada
501 Las Vegas Boulevard, Suite 1100
Las Vegas, Nevada 89101
(702) 388-6336

AO 93 (Rev 11/13) Search and Seizure Warrant

UNITED STATES DISTRICT COURT
for the
District of Nevada

In the Matter of the Search of
(Briefly describe the property to be searched or identify the person by name and address)

1372 BABBLING BROOK COURT,
MESQUITE, COUNTY OF CLARK, STATE OF NEVADA.

Case No. 2:17-mj-973-NJK

SEARCH AND SEIZURE WARRANT

To: Any authorized law enforcement officer

An application by a federal law enforcement officer or an attorney for the government requests the search of the following person or property located in the District of Nevada
(identify the person or describe the property to be searched and give its location):

SEE ATTACHMENT A

I find that the affidavit(s), or any recorded testimony, establish probable cause to search and seize the person or property described above, and that such search will reveal *(identify the person or describe the property to be seized):*

SEE ATTACHMENTS B

YOU ARE COMMANDED to execute this warrant on or before October 21, 2017 *(not to exceed 14 days)*
☒ in the daytime 6:00 a.m. to 10:00 p.m.   ☐ at any time in the day or night because good cause has been established.

Unless delayed notice is authorized below, you must give a copy of the warrant and a receipt for the property taken to the person from whom, or from whose premises, the property was taken, or leave the copy and receipt at the place where the property was taken.

The officer executing this warrant, or an officer present during the execution of the warrant, must prepare an inventory as required by law and promptly return this warrant and inventory to _____
(United States Magistrate Judge)

☐ Pursuant to 18 U.S.C. § 3103a(b), I find that immediate notification may have an adverse result listed in 18 U.S.C. § 2705 (except for delay of trial), and authorize the officer executing this warrant to delay notice to the person who, or whose property, will be searched or seized *(check the appropriate box)*
☐ for _____ days *(not to exceed 30)*   ☐ until, the facts justifying, the later specific date of _____

Date and time issued: 10/7/2017 6:45 p.m.

_____
Judge's signature

City and state: Las Vegas, Nevada   Nancy J. Koppe, US Magistrate Judge
Printed name and title

Attachment "A"

Description of Property/Premise to be Searched

1372 Babbling Brook Court
Mesquite, Clark County, Nevada

The subject premises is described as a one story, single family residence of apparent stucco frame construction. The premises are situated in the northeast corner Babbling Brook Court, which is a cul-de-sac. The premises faces approximately southwest and is located approximately 100 feet from the intersection of Babbling Brook Court and Cool Springs Lane. The residence is painted tan and the house numbers "1372" are affixed to the exterior wall facing the street.

Attachment "B"

Particular Items to be Seized

a. a thorough, microscopic examination and documentation of the subject premises to discover trace evidence, including but not limited to: fingerprints, blood, hair, fibers and other bodily fluid samples;

b. firearms to include handguns, shotguns and rifles, spent casings or live ammunition for the same, firearm accessories such as magazines or cylinders, firearm cleaning materials, and paperwork associated with the ownership of firearms;

c. United States and foreign currency, precious metals, jewelry, property deeds and other negotiable financial instruments including: stocks, bonds, securities, cashier's checks, money drafts, and letters of credit;

d. books, records, receipts, notes, ledgers, personal checks and other papers relating to the transportation, ordering, and purchase of firearms, firearms accessories, ammunition, explosives or explosives precursor materials, or material relating to any ideological extremism;

e. books, records, invoices, receipts, records of real estate transactions, bank statements and related records, gambling receipts and records, passbooks, money drafts, letters of credit, money orders, bank drafts, and cashier checks, bank checks, safe deposit box keys, money wrappers, and other items evidencing the obtaining, secreting, transfer, and/or concealment and/or expenditure of money;

f. any and all financial, credit card and bank account information including but not limited to bills and payment records, including those relating to the purchase of firearms, firearms accessories, ammunition, explosives, explosives precursor materials, body armor, range finding devices, scopes and other optical devices, glass cutters, and gas masks;

g. any and all records relating to the medical or psychological/psychiatric treatment of Stephen Paddock or Marilou Danley;

h. all types of safes and the contents thereof, including but not limited to, wall safes, floor safes, freestanding safes, locked strong boxes, and locked containers;

i. photographs, including still photos, negatives, video tapes, films, undeveloped film and the contents therein, slides;

j. cellular telephones address and/or telephone books, digital pagers, address and/or telephone books, Rolodex indices, electronic organizers, and papers reflecting names, addresses, telephone numbers, pager numbers, fax numbers, e-mail addresses, Facebook account information and other contact information related to co-conspirators, financial institutions, and other individuals or businesses with whom a financial relationship exists;

1

SEALED

Office of the United States Attorney
District of Nevada
501 Las Vegas Boulevard, Suite 1100
Las Vegas, Nevada 89101
(702) 388-6336

AO 93 (Rev. 11/13) Search and Seizure Warrant

UNITED STATES DISTRICT COURT
for the
District of Nevada

FILED 2017 OCT 13 PM 12:30
U.S. MAGISTRATE JUDGE
BY_____

In the Matter of the Search of
(Briefly describe the property to be searched or identify the person by name and address)

EMAIL ACCOUNT CENTRALPARK1@LIVE.COM THAT IS STORED AT A PREMISES CONTROLLED BY MICROSOFT. A1

Case No. 2:17-mj-01009-NJK

SEARCH AND SEIZURE WARRANT

To: Any authorized law enforcement officer

An application by a federal law enforcement officer or an attorney for the government requests the search of the following person or property located in the _____ District of _____ Nevada
(identify the person or describe the property to be searched and give its location):

SEE ATTACHMENT A1

I find that the affidavit(s), or any recorded testimony, establish probable cause to search and seize the person or property described above, and that such search will reveal *(identify the person or describe the property to be seized):*

SEE ATTACHMENTS B and C

YOU ARE COMMANDED to execute this warrant on or before October 27, 2017 *(not to exceed 14 days)*
☑ in the daytime 6:00 a.m. to 10:00 p.m.   ☐ at any time in the day or night because good cause has been established.

Unless delayed notice is authorized below, you must give a copy of the warrant and a receipt for the property taken to the person from whom, or from whose premises, the property was taken, or leave the copy and receipt at the place where the property was taken.

The officer executing this warrant, or an officer present during the execution of the warrant, must prepare an inventory as required by law and promptly return this warrant and inventory to _____ NANCY J. KOPPE _____
(United States Magistrate Judge)

☐ Pursuant to 18 U.S.C. § 3103a(b), I find that immediate notification may have an adverse result listed in 18 U.S.C. § 2705 (except for delay of trial), and authorize the officer executing this warrant to delay notice to the person who, or whose property, will be searched or seized *(check the appropriate box)*
☐ for ___ days *(not to exceed 30)* ☐ until, the facts justifying, the later specific date of _____

Date and time issued: 10/13/17 12:30 p.m.

NANCY J. KOPPE
Judge's signature
UNITED STATES MAGISTRATE JUDGE
Printed name and title

City and state: Las Vegas, Nevada

ATTACHMENT "A-1"

ONLINE ACCOUNT TO BE SEARCHED

This warrant applies to information associated with the Microsoft email account centralpark1@live.com (the "Target Account 1") from inception to present, which is stored at premises owned, maintained, controlled, or operated by Microsoft Corporation, headquartered at 1 Microsoft Way, Redmond, Washington, 98052.

ATTACHMENT "B"
Particular Things to be Seized

I. **Information to be disclosed by the Service Provider**

To the extent that the information described in Attachments A1 and A2 is within the possession, custody, or control of Microsoft, including any Emails, records, files, logs, or information that have been deleted but are still available to Service Provider, or have been preserved pursuant to a request made under 18 U.S.C. § 2703(f), Service Provider is required to disclose the following information to the government for each account or identifier listed in Attachments A-1 and A-2 from account inception to present:

a. The contents of all communications, transactions, records, documents, programs, or materials stored in or associated with any OneDrive accounts associated with or assigned to Target Accounts 1 and 2.

b. The contents of all communications, transactions, records, documents, programs, or materials stored in or associated with any Office 360 accounts associated with or assigned to Target Accounts 1 and 2.

c. The contents of all communications, transactions, records, documents, programs, or materials stored in or associated with any Microsoft Family Safety accounts or services associated with or assigned to Target Accounts 1 and 2.

d. The contents of all communications, transactions, records, documents, programs, or materials stored in or associated with any Windows Live Writer accounts or services associated with or assigned to Target Accounts 1 and 2.

e. The contents of all communications, transactions, records, documents, programs, or materials stored in or associated with any Windows Live Mail accounts or services associated with or assigned to Target Accounts 1 and 2.

f. The contents of all communications, transactions, records, documents, programs, or materials stored in or associated with any Windows Photo Gallery accounts or services associated with or assigned to Target Accounts 1 and 2.

g. The contents of all communications, transactions, records, documents, programs, or materials stored in or associated with any Windows Live Messenger accounts or services associated with or assigned to Target Accounts 1 and 2.

II. **Information to be seized by the United States**

After reviewing all information described in Section I, the United States will seize evidence of violations of Title 18, United States Code Sections 32(a) (Destruction/Damage of Aircraft or Aircraft Facilities); 37(a)(2) (Violence at International Airport); and 922(a)(3); and 5 (Unlawful Interstate Transport/Delivery of Firearms by Non Federal Firearms Licensee); and 2 (Aiding and Abetting) (the "Subject Offenses") that occur in the form of the following, from account inception to present:

a. Communications, transactions and records that may establish ownership and control (or the degree thereof) of the Target Account, including address books, contact or buddy lists, bills, invoices, receipts, registration records, bills, correspondence, notes, records, memoranda, telephone/address books, photographs, video recordings, audio recordings, lists of names, records of payment for access to newsgroups or other online subscription services, and attachments to said communications, transactions and records.

b. Communications, transactions and records to/from persons who may be co-conspirators of the Subject Offenses, or which may identify co-conspirators.

c. Communications, transactions and records which may show motivation to commit the Subject Offenses.

d. Communications, transactions and records that relate to the Subject Offenses.

e. The terms "communications," "transactions", "records," "documents," "programs," or "materials" include all information recorded in any form, visual or aural, and by any means, whether in handmade form (including, but not limited to, writings, drawings, paintings), photographic form (including, but not limited to, pictures or videos), or electrical, electronic or magnetic form, as well as digital data files. These terms also include any applications (i.e. software programs). These terms expressly include, among other things, Emails, instant messages, chat logs, correspondence attached as to Emails (or drafts), calendar entries, buddy lists.

ATTACHMENT "C"

PROTOCOL FOR SEARCHING THE ELECTRONIC DATA SEIZED PURSUANT TO THIS SEARCH WARRANT

1. In executing this warrant, the government must make reasonable efforts to use methods and procedures that will locate and expose in the electronic data produced in response to this search warrant ("the Search Warrant Data") those categories of data, files, documents, or other electronically stored information that are identified with particularity in the warrant, while minimizing exposure or examination of irrelevant, privileged, or confidential files to the extent reasonably practicable.

2. When the Search Warrant Data is received, the government will make a duplicate copy of the Search Warrant Data ("the Search Warrant Data Copy"). The original version of the Search Warrant Data will be sealed and preserved for purposes of: later judicial review or order to return or dispose of the Search Warrant Data; production to the defense in any criminal case if authorized by statute, rule, or the Constitution; for purposes of showing the chain of custody of the Search Warrant Data and the Search Warrant Data Copy; or for any other lawful purpose. The original of the Search Warrant Data will not be searched or examined except to ensure that it has been fully and completely replicated in the Search Warrant Data Copy.

3. The investigating agents will then search the entirety of the Search Warrant Data Copy using any and all methods and procedures deemed appropriate by the United States designed to identify the information listed as Information to be Seized in Attachment B, Section II. The United States may copy, extract or otherwise segregate information or data listed as Information to be Seized in Attachment B, Section II. Information or data so copied, extracted or otherwise segregated will no longer be subject to any handling restrictions that might be set out in this protocol beyond those required by binding law. To the extent evidence of crimes not within the scope of this warrant appear in plain view during this review, a supplemental or "piggyback" warrant will be applied for in order to further search that document, data, or other item.

4. Once the Search Warrant Data Copy has been thoroughly and completely examined for any document, data, or other items identified in Attachment B, Section II as Information to be Seized, the Search Warrant Data Copy will be sealed and not subject to any further search or examination unless authorized by another search warrant or other appropriate court order. The Search Warrant Data Copy will be held and preserved for the same purposes identified above in Paragraph 2.

5. The search procedures utilized for this review are at the sole discretion of the investigating and prosecuting authorities, and may include the following techniques (the following is a non-exclusive list, as other search procedures may be used):

    a. examination of all of the data contained in the Search Warrant Data to view the data and determine whether that data falls within the items to be seized as set forth herein;

    b. searching for and attempting to recover from the Search Warrant Data any deleted, hidden, or encrypted data to determine whether that data falls within the list of items to be seized as set forth herein (any data that is encrypted and unreadable will not be returned unless law enforcement personnel have determined that the data is not (1) an instrumentality of the offenses, (2) a fruit of the criminal activity, (3) contraband, (4) otherwise unlawfully possessed, or (5) evidence of the offenses specified above);

    c. surveying various file directories and the individual files they contain;

    d. opening files in order to determine their contents;

    e. using hash values to narrow the scope of what may be found. Hash values are under- inclusive, but are still a helpful tool;

    f. scanning storage areas;

    g. performing keyword searches through all electronic storage areas to determine whether occurrences of language contained in such storage areas exist that are likely to appear in the evidence described in Attachment A1 and A2; and/or

    h. performing any other data analysis technique that may be necessary to locate and retrieve the evidence described in Attachment B, Section II.

Return and Review Procedures

6. Rule 41 of the Federal Rules of Criminal Procedure provides, in relevant part:

(e) Issuing the Warrant.

(2) Contents of the Warrant.

(A) Warrant to Search for and Seize a Person or Property. Except for a tracking-device warrant, the warrant must identify the person or property to be searched, identify any person or property to be seized, and designate the magistrate judge to whom it must be returned. The warrant must command the officer to:

(i) execute the warrant within a specified time no longer than 14 days;

(B) Warrant Seeking Electronically Stored Information. A warrant under Rule 41(e)(2)(A) may authorize the seizure of electronic storage media or the seizure or copying of electronically stored information. Unless otherwise specified, the warrant authorizes a later review of the media or information consistent with the warrant. The time for executing the warrant in Rule 41(e)(2)(A) and (f)(1)(A) refers to the seizure or on-site copying of the media or information, and not to any later off-site copying or review.

(f) Executing and Returning the Warrant.

(1) Warrant to Search for and Seize a Person or Property.

(B) Inventory. An officer present during the execution of the warrant must prepare and verify an inventory of any property seized. . . . In a case involving the seizure of electronic storage media or the seizure or copying of electronically stored information, the inventory may be limited to describing the physical storage media that were seized or copied. The officer may retain a copy of the electronically stored information that was seized or copied.

7. Pursuant to this Rule, the government understands and will act in accordance with the following:

a. Pursuant to Rule 41(e)(2)(A)(iii), within fourteen (14) days of the execution of the warrant, an agent is required to file an inventory return with the Court, that is, to file an itemized list of the property seized. Execution of the warrant begins when the United States serves the warrant on the named custodian; execution is complete when the custodian provides all Search Warrant Data to the United States. Within fourteen (14) days of completion of the execution of the warrant, the inventory will be filed.

b. Pursuant to Rule 41(e)(2)(B), Rule 41(e)(2)(A) governs the time within which the electronically stored information must be seized after the issuance of the warrant and copied after the execution of the warrant, not the "later review of the media or information" seized, or the later off-site digital copying of that media.

c. Under Rule 41(f)(1)(B), the inventory return that is to be filed with the court may be limited to a description of the "physical storage media" into which the Search Warrant Data that was seized was placed, not an itemization of the information or data stored on the "physical storage media" into which the Search Warrant Data was placed;

d. Under Rule 41(f)(1)(B), the government may retain a copy of that information for purposes of the investigation. The government proposes that the original storage media on which the Search Warrant Data was placed plus a full image copy of the seized Search Warrant Data be retained by the government.

e. If the person from whom any Search Warrant Data was seized requests the return of any information in the Search Warrant Data that is not set forth in Attachment B, Section II, that information will be copied onto appropriate media and returned to the person from whom the information was seized.

SEALED

In Re: Sealed Warrants
(Case No. 2:17-cv-02775-JAD-PAL)

Office of the United States Attorney
District of Nevada
501 Las Vegas Boulevard South,
Suite 1100
Las Vegas, Nevada 89101
(702) 388-6336

FILED

2017 OCT 13 PH 12:30

U.S. MAGISTRATE JUDGE

BY_____

SEALED

Office of the United States Attorney
District of Nevada
501 Las Vegas Boulevard, Suite 1100
Las Vegas, Nevada 89101
(702) 388-6336

SEALED

Office of the United States Attorney
District of Nevada
501 Las Vegas Boulevard, Suite 1100
Las Vegas, Nevada 89101
(702) 388-6336

AO 93 (Rev. 11/13) Search and Seizure Warrant

UNITED STATES DISTRICT COURT
for the
District of Nevada

2017 OCT 13 PM 12: 30

U.S. MAGISTRATE JUDGE
BY_____

In the Matter of the Search of)
(Briefly describe the property to be searched)
or identify the person by name and address))
) Case No. 2:17-mj-01009-NJK
EMAIL ACCOUNT CENTRALPARK1@LIVE.COM THAT)
IS STORED AT A PREMISES CONTROLLED BY)
MICROSOFT. A1)

SEARCH AND SEIZURE WARRANT

To: Any authorized law enforcement officer

An application by a federal law enforcement officer or an attorney for the government requests the search of the following person or property located in the _____ District of _____Nevada_____
(identify the person or describe the property to be searched and give its location):

SEE ATTACHMENT A1

I find that the affidavit(s), or any recorded testimony, establish probable cause to search and seize the person or property described above, and that such search will reveal *(identify the person or describe the property to be seized):*

SEE ATTACHMENTS B and C

YOU ARE COMMANDED to execute this warrant on or before October 27, 2017 *(not to exceed 14 days)*
☑ in the daytime 6:00 a.m. to 10:00 p.m.   ☐ at any time in the day or night because good cause has been established.

Unless delayed notice is authorized below, you must give a copy of the warrant and a receipt for the property taken to the person from whom, or from whose premises, the property was taken, or leave the copy and receipt at the place where the property was taken.

The officer executing this warrant, or an officer present during the execution of the warrant, must prepare an inventory as required by law and promptly return this warrant and inventory to _____NANCY J. KOPPE_____
(United States Magistrate Judge)

☐ Pursuant to 18 U.S.C. § 3103a(b), I find that immediate notification may have an adverse result listed in 18 U.S.C. § 2705 (except for delay of trial), and authorize the officer executing this warrant to delay notice to the person who, or whose property, will be searched or seized *(check the appropriate box)*
☐ for ___ days *(not to exceed 30)*   ☐ until, the facts justifying, the later specific date of _____

Date and time issued: 10/13/17 12:30 p.m.

NANCY J. KOPPE
Judge's signature

City and state: Las Vegas, Nevada

UNITED STATES MAGISTRATE JUDGE
Printed name and title

ATTACHMENT "A-1"

ONLINE ACCOUNT TO BE SEARCHED

This warrant applies to information associated with the Microsoft email account centralpark1@live.com (the "Target Account 1") from inception to present, which is stored at premises owned, maintained, controlled, or operated by Microsoft Corporation, headquartered at 1 Microsoft Way, Redmond, Washington, 98052.

ATTACHMENT "B"
Particular Things to be Seized

I. **Information to be disclosed by the Service Provider**

To the extent that the information described in Attachments A1 and A2 is within the possession, custody, or control of Microsoft, including any Emails, records, files, logs, or information that have been deleted but are still available to Service Provider, or have been preserved pursuant to a request made under 18 U.S.C. § 2703(f), Service Provider is required to disclose the following information to the government for each account or identifier listed in Attachments A-1 and A-2 from account inception to present:

a. The contents of all communications, transactions, records, documents, programs, or materials stored in or associated with any OneDrive accounts associated with or assigned to Target Accounts 1 and 2.

b. The contents of all communications, transactions, records, documents, programs, or materials stored in or associated with any Office 360 accounts associated with or assigned to Target Accounts 1 and 2.

c. The contents of all communications, transactions, records, documents, programs, or materials stored in or associated with any Microsoft Family Safety accounts or services associated with or assigned to Target Accounts 1 and 2.

d. The contents of all communications, transactions, records, documents, programs, or materials stored in or associated with any Windows Live Writer accounts or services associated with or assigned to Target Accounts 1 and 2.

e. The contents of all communications, transactions, records, documents, programs, or materials stored in or associated with any Windows Live Mail accounts or services associated with or assigned to Target Accounts 1 and 2.

f. The contents of all communications, transactions, records, documents, programs, or materials stored in or associated with any Windows Photo Gallery accounts or services associated with or assigned to Target Accounts 1 and 2.

g. The contents of all communications, transactions, records, documents, programs, or materials stored in or associated with any Windows Live Messenger accounts or services associated with or assigned to Target Accounts 1 and 2.

II. Information to be seized by the United States

After reviewing all information described in Section I, the United States will seize evidence of violations of Title 18, United States Code Sections 32(a) (Destruction/Damage of Aircraft or Aircraft Facilities); 37(a)(2) (Violence at International Airport); and 922(a)(3); and 5 (Unlawful Interstate Transport/Delivery of Firearms by Non Federal Firearms Licensee); and 2 (Aiding and Abetting) (the "Subject Offenses") that occur in the form of the following, from account inception to present:

a. Communications, transactions and records that may establish ownership and control (or the degree thereof) of the Target Account, including address books, contact or buddy lists, bills, invoices, receipts, registration records, bills, correspondence, notes, records, memoranda, telephone/address books, photographs, video recordings, audio recordings, lists of names, records of payment for access to newsgroups or other online subscription services, and attachments to said communications, transactions and records.

b. Communications, transactions and records to/from persons who may be co-conspirators of the Subject Offenses, or which may identify co-conspirators.

c. Communications, transactions and records which may show motivation to commit the Subject Offenses.

d. Communications, transactions and records that relate to the Subject Offenses.

e. The terms "communications," "transactions", "records," "documents," "programs," or "materials" include all information recorded in any form, visual or aural, and by any means, whether in handmade form (including, but not limited to, writings, drawings, paintings), photographic form (including, but not limited to, pictures or videos), or electrical, electronic or magnetic form, as well as digital data files. These terms also include any applications (i.e. software programs). These terms expressly include, among other things, Emails, instant messages, chat logs, correspondence attached as to Emails (or drafts), calendar entries, buddy lists.

ATTACHMENT "C"

PROTOCOL FOR SEARCHING THE ELECTRONIC DATA SEIZED PURSUANT TO THIS SEARCH WARRANT

1. In executing this warrant, the government must make reasonable efforts to use methods and procedures that will locate and expose in the electronic data produced in response to this search warrant ("the Search Warrant Data") those categories of data, files, documents, or other electronically stored information that are identified with particularity in the warrant, while minimizing exposure or examination of irrelevant, privileged, or confidential files to the extent reasonably practicable.

2. When the Search Warrant Data is received, the government will make a duplicate copy of the Search Warrant Data ("the Search Warrant Data Copy"). The original version of the Search Warrant Data will be sealed and preserved for purposes of: later judicial review or order to return or dispose of the Search Warrant Data; production to the defense in any criminal case if authorized by statute, rule, or the Constitution; for purposes of showing the chain of custody of the Search Warrant Data and the Search Warrant Data Copy; or for any other lawful purpose. The original of the Search Warrant Data will not be searched or examined except to ensure that it has been fully and completely replicated in the Search Warrant Data Copy.

3. The investigating agents will then search the entirety of the Search Warrant Data Copy using any and all methods and procedures deemed appropriate by the United States designed to identify the information listed as Information to be Seized in Attachment B, Section II. The United States may copy, extract or otherwise segregate information or data listed as Information to be Seized in Attachment B, Section II. Information or data so copied, extracted or otherwise segregated will no longer be subject to any handling restrictions that might be set out in this protocol beyond those required by binding law. To the extent evidence of crimes not within the scope of this warrant appear in plain view during this review, a supplemental or "piggyback" warrant will be applied for in order to further search that document, data, or other item.

4. Once the Search Warrant Data Copy has been thoroughly and completely examined for any document, data, or other items identified in Attachment B, Section II as Information to be Seized, the Search Warrant Data Copy will be sealed and not subject to any further search or examination unless authorized by another search warrant or other appropriate court order. The Search Warrant Data Copy will be held and preserved for the same purposes identified above in Paragraph 2.

5. The search procedures utilized for this review are at the sole discretion of the investigating and prosecuting authorities, and may include the following techniques (the following is a non-exclusive list, as other search procedures may be used):

a. examination of all of the data contained in the Search Warrant Data to view the data and determine whether that data falls within the items to be seized as set forth herein;

b. searching for and attempting to recover from the Search Warrant Data any deleted, hidden, or encrypted data to determine whether that data falls within the list of items to be seized as set forth herein (any data that is encrypted and unreadable will not be returned unless law enforcement personnel have determined that the data is not (1) an instrumentality of the offenses, (2) a fruit of the criminal activity, (3) contraband, (4) otherwise unlawfully possessed, or (5) evidence of the offenses specified above);

c. surveying various file directories and the individual files they contain;

d. opening files in order to determine their contents;

e. using hash values to narrow the scope of what may be found. Hash values are under- inclusive, but are still a helpful tool;

f. scanning storage areas;

g. performing keyword searches through all electronic storage areas to determine whether occurrences of language contained in such storage areas exist that are likely to appear in the evidence described in Attachment A1 and A2; and/or

h. performing any other data analysis technique that may be necessary to locate and retrieve the evidence described in Attachment B, Section II.

Return and Review Procedures

6. Rule 41 of the Federal Rules of Criminal Procedure provides, in relevant part:

(e) Issuing the Warrant.

(2) Contents of the Warrant.

(A) Warrant to Search for and Seize a Person or Property. Except for a tracking-device warrant, the warrant must identify the person or property to be searched, identify any person or property to be seized, and designate the magistrate judge to whom it must be returned. The warrant must command the officer to:

(i) execute the warrant within a specified time no longer than 14 days;

(B) Warrant Seeking Electronically Stored Information. A warrant under Rule 41(e)(2)(A) may authorize the seizure of electronic storage media or the seizure or copying of electronically stored information. Unless otherwise specified, the warrant authorizes a later review of the media or information consistent with the warrant. The time for executing the warrant in Rule 41(e)(2)(A) and (f)(1)(A) refers to the seizure or on-site copying of the media or information, and not to any later off-site copying or review.

(f) Executing and Returning the Warrant.

(1) Warrant to Search for and Seize a Person or Property.

(B) Inventory. An officer present during the execution of the warrant must prepare and verify an inventory of any property seized. . . . In a case involving the seizure of electronic storage media or the seizure or copying of electronically stored information, the inventory may be limited to describing the physical storage media that were seized or copied. The officer may retain a copy of the electronically stored information that was seized or copied.

7. Pursuant to this Rule, the government understands and will act in accordance with the following:

a. Pursuant to Rule 41(e)(2)(A)(iii), within fourteen (14) days of the execution of the warrant, an agent is required to file an inventory return with the Court, that is, to file an itemized list of the property seized. Execution of the warrant begins when the United States serves the warrant on the named custodian; execution is complete when the custodian provides all Search Warrant Data to the United States. Within fourteen (14) days of completion of the execution of the warrant, the inventory will be filed.

b. Pursuant to Rule 41(e)(2)(B), Rule 41(e)(2)(A) governs the time within which the electronically stored information must be seized after the issuance of the warrant and copied after the execution of the warrant, not the "later review of the media or information" seized, or the later off-site digital copying of that media.

c. Under Rule 41(f)(1)(B), the inventory return that is to be filed with the court may be limited to a description of the "physical storage media" into which the Search Warrant Data that was seized was placed, not an itemization of the information or data stored on the "physical storage media" into which the Search Warrant Data was placed;

d. Under Rule 41(f)(1)(B), the government may retain a copy of that information for purposes of the investigation. The government proposes that the original storage media on which the Search Warrant Data was placed plus a full image copy of the seized Search Warrant Data be retained by the government.

e. If the person from whom any Search Warrant Data was seized requests the return of any information in the Search Warrant Data that is not set forth in Attachment B, Section II, that information will be copied onto appropriate media and returned to the person from whom the information was seized.

SEALED

In Re: Sealed Warrants
(Case No. 2:17-cv-02775-JAD-PAL)

Office of the United States Attorney
District of Nevada
501 Las Vegas Boulevard South,
Suite 1100
Las Vegas, Nevada 89101
(702) 388-6336

FILED

2017 OCT 13 PM 12:30

U.S. MAGISTRATE JUDGE

BY_____

SEALED

Office of the United States Attorney
District of Nevada
501 Las Vegas Boulevard, Suite 1100
Las Vegas, Nevada 89101
(702) 388-6336

www.ingramcontent.com/pod-product-compliance
Lightning Source LLC
Chambersburg PA
CBHW060256240426
43661CB00060B/2809